A History of the
Guyanese Working People, 1881-1905

Johns Hopkins Studies in Atlantic History and Culture
Richard Price and Franklin W. Knight, general editors

By the Same Author

West Africa and the Atlantic Slave Trade (1969)
A History of the Upper Guinea Coast, 1545-1800 (1970)
How Europe Underdeveloped Africa (1972)

WALTER RODNEY

A History of the Guyanese Working People, 1881-1905

THE JOHNS HOPKINS UNIVERSITY PRESS

Baltimore and London

This book has been brought to publication
with the generous assistance of
the Andrew W. Mellon Foundation

The Johns Hopkins University Press, Baltimore, Maryland 21218
The Johns Hopkins Press Ltd., London

Library of Congress Cataloging in Publication Data

Rodney, Walter.
A history of the Guyanese working people, 1881-1905.

(Johns Hopkins studies in Atlantic history and culture)
Bibliography: pp. 263-72
Includes index.
1. Labor and laboring classes—Guyana—History.
2. Plantations—Guyana—History.
3. Elite (Social sciences)—Guyana—History.
I. Title.   II. Series.
HD8330.3.R62   305.5'6   81-4149
ISBN 0-8018-2428-1   AACR2
ISBN 0-8018-2447-8 (pbk.)

For Pauline Rodney
and the working people of Guyana

CONTENTS

List of Illustrations

Plates

Contents

Maps

Figures

EDITORS' NOTE

Walter Rodney was born in Guyana in 1942. He read history at the University of the West Indies at Mona, Jamaica, which was then an external College of London University. At the School of Oriental and African Studies he pursued the study of African history, earning his doctorate in 1966, thereby becoming the first West Indian to earn a higher degree in the field. In 1970, his revised dissertation was published by Oxford University Press as *A History of the Upper Guinea Coast, 1545-1800*.

During Rodney's formative years, important changes were taking place in the Caribbean, in Africa, and in international politics. The collapse of the West Indies Federation in May 1963 (a federation which he strongly advocated as a university student), the emergence of new political states in Africa and the English Antilles during the 1950s and the 1960s, and the impact of these new states in such international organizations as the United Nations and the Organization of American States deeply affected him throughout his life. Rodney's writings and teaching reflected his profound intellectual sensibility to the politics and peoples of Africa and the Caribbean.

Rodney was an eloquent speaker and brilliant writer. After teaching for some time in Tanzania, he accepted a position as a lecturer in African history at the University of the West Indies. His attempts to understand the political and social problems of independent Jamaica led to the publication *Groundings with My Brothers* (1971). Apparently displeased, the Jamaican government declared Rodney *persona non grata* while he was on a speaking engagement in Canada and denied him a re-entry permit to the island. Rodney then returned to teach in Tanzania and wrote *How Europe Underdeveloped Africa* (1972). In 1974, the University of Guyana invited him to return as their professor in African history. Rodney returned to Guyana. Despite the revocation of his job offer, he remained in his native land conducting research on the history of the Guyanese people, writing and lecturing locally as well as abroad. Inevitably he entered politics. It was a difficult and dangerous existence, but he persevered, eventually organizing the Working People's Alliance, a combination of parties opposed to the government of Guyana.

Only months before violent death terminated his young, active, and brilliant career, Rodney submitted the manuscript for this book to Johns Hopkins Studies in Atlantic History and Culture. He later revised it from jail, while awaiting trial on charges of arson. During these final weeks, he asked his friend George Lamming, the distinguished Barbadian writer, to provide a substantive introduction to the book. Indeed, under difficult circumstances, Lamming has cooperated on this project with special sensitivity and has produced an illuminating essay of lasting significance.

After Rodney's death, the series editors assumed the task of seeing the book through publication. Franklin W. Knight accepted responsibility for the mechanical duties and technical decisions that would normally have been handled at this stage by the author, attempting to remain faithful to what he understood to be the author's intent. We trust that Walter Rodney's *A History of the Guyanese Working People, 1881-1905*, in its published form, will serve his memory well, and are confident that it will be recognized as an outstanding contribution to the historiography of Guyana, the Caribbean, and the immigrant peoples of the New World.

FRANKLIN W. KNIGHT
RICHARD PRICE

ACKNOWLEDGMENTS

Elsa Goveia, for all she contributed to my growth as a historian over twenty years; Pat, Shaka, Kanini, Asha, Uncle Henry, and other members of my family, for their active support of my commitment to research and writing; a number of Guyanese who cannot now be named because they are employed by the Burnham state, for their help in research, typing, and photographs; Bonita Bone Harris and Roberta, for their help in research and typing; Karen de Souza, for her help in proofreading; Colin Carto (Abyssinian), for map work; Brian Rodway, for restoring old photographs; Andaiye, for research and local editing; and Eusi Kwayana, for example.

W.R.

FOREWORD

On the evening of June 23, 1980, Walter Rodney was buried, at the age of thirty-eight. It was a people's funeral. Earlier in the day, thousands of Guyanese had walked over a distance of twelve miles behind the murdered body of this young historian. He was not the first victim of political murder in Guyana, but the radical nature of his commitment as a teacher and activist, the startling promise that his life symbolized, made of his death something of a novel tragedy.

Directive had gone out to government employees that they should avoid this occasion; yet no one could recall, in the entire history of the country, so large and faithful a gathering assembled to reflect on the horror that had been inflicted on the nation. For Guyana had become a land of horrors. Democracy was no longer on trial here. The question was whether it would survive this official crucifixion.

The Caribbean has been deprived of a great creative mind; but Walter Rodney had achieved at an early age, the special distinction of being a permanent part of a unique tradition of intellectual leadership among Africans and people of African descent in the Americas. He belongs to the same order of importance as Marcus Garvey and W.E.B. Dubois, George Padmore and C.L.R. James. Products of various doctrines of imperialism, they had initiated through the work, as writers and orators of distinction, a profound reversal of values. It is not possible to have a comprehensive view of all the ramifications of Africa's encounter with Europe without reference to these men.

Walter Rodney consolidated and extended that work. His scholarship was sure, but it was also a committed and partisan scholarship. He believed that history was a way of ordering knowledge which could become as active part of the consciousness of an uncertified mass of ordinary people and which could be used by all as an instrument of social change. He taught from that assumption. He wrote out of that conviction. And it seemed to have been the informing influence on his relations with the organized working people of Guyana.

Rodney begins this enquiry some two centuries after the introduction of slave labor and about fifty years after the formal emancipation. It is an indication of his sense of priorities, his critical realism as a historian, that he should deliberately focus our interest on the peculiar character of the landscape. It is not just a casual reminder that this coastal strip of Guyana was hazardous terrain. It is the emphatic and persuasive way he situates men and women in nature. He can be at once elaborate and precise in defining the categories of capital and labor; but first he plunges us into the sodden realities of mud and feces, the menace of flood either from the sea or from overwhelming torrents of rain.

Unlike many a Caribbean island, Guyana did not offer itself easily for human settlement. There was no instant welcome. Every triumph of cultivation was subdued by the constant fear that overnight the ocean would advance and swallow up the achievement. The morning would awaken men to the smell of animal corpses. For days there would follow the spectacle of a rotting goat or sheep or cow, a decomposition of carcasses stuck or afloat across the hidden landscape. Workers quenched their thirst from the same mud water. Fever struck; gastroenteritis prevailed. They waded through a catalogue of pestilence. Transport was impossible. Work had to stop. It was a daily battle for survival. Sometimes they recovered just in time to lament the arrival of fierce and prolonged drought. One tries hard to imagine the fate of children, and it may not be surprising that there is little mention of them here. Meanwhile, the planters fretted over the disintegration of roads, the inconvenience of sick workers. The harshness of their rule reflected the panic and impatience they felt at the loss of capital.

Dutch agricultural engineering had devised a way of reclaiming the land, and African labor found in the concept of the polder a means of digging and draining while setting up a structure of dams that would offer some defense against the sea and other threats of flood. It was a stupendous effort by labor to make the land suitable for cultivation of sugar cane, and the maintenance of the polder would be a continuing anxiety. Reflecting the scale of labor involved in the original construction of waterways,

> the Venn Commission of 1948 estimated that each square mile of cane cultivation involved the provision of 49 miles of drainage canals and ditches, and 16 miles of higher level of waterways used for transformation and irrigation. The commissioners noted that the construction of these waterways must have entailed the moving of at least one hundred million tons of soil.

The point Rodney wants to be remembered is the means whereby such labor was undertaken.

> This meant that slaves moved 100 million tons of heavy water-logged clay with shovel in hand, while enduring conditions of perpetual mud and water. . . . Working people continued making a tremendous contribution to the *humanization* of the Guyanese coastal landscape.

It is the operative word, humanization, that confirms his real intention. Such an emphasis leads to an overwhelming conclusion. The history of humanizing this landscape is primarily the history of those hands. Retelling this history was the task Rodney had set for himself over two volumes, the first of which must now be the last. It was the task of excavating and reaffirming that particular history.

Caribbean scholars have, on the whole, concentrated on the intricate arguments and provisions made by those who ruled the land, those whose concept of social responsibility was confined to their exercise of power and to the protection of their interests as a dominant ruling group. This is an important contribution, but Rodney was engaged in illuminating our understanding from a different perspective. Working people of African and Indian ancestry in Guyana have had a history of active struggle, which it has been our habit to omit or underestimate in political discourse about the past.

If they often met with failure against the combined power of planters and the imperial parliament that sponsored their oppression, it remains true that every struggle planted a seed of creative disruption and aided the process that released new social forces in the continuing drama between capital and labor. Moreover, it is in the course of that struggle that we can discover the origins and growth of the middle and professional classes. And it is their failure to grasp the meaning and possibilities of this connection that still makes them so vulnerable to continuing external influence.

But is is also in that dramatic encounter with nature that Rodney offers us a view of certain tendencies that help to define the mind of the ruling group. Neither planters nor parliament could legislate the contingencies of nature; rich and poor alike were condemned to live in a state of emergency. The politics of survival were argued in the language of dams, dikes, canals, drainage, and irrigation. Flood and drought were alternating names for the same demon, which could visit dispossession and even total disaster on the unfortunate. But a common defense against natural disaster was often undermined by rival capitalist interests.

When Rodney begins this enquiry, in 1881, the legislature was the exclusive forum of the white planter class. Justice in the swamps was ordained by the rule of skin. This abnormality would further complicate what started as a history of contradictions. Work makes possible a process of production, and the planters perceived this to be true. But work is also the essential base on which people struggle to create a design for social living. Planters could not perceive this to be true without contradicting their original reason for being there. The workers' achievement of humanizing the landscape and creating a design for social living had to be interpreted and dealt with as a threat to the foundations of the planter enterprise. Planters were therefore unanimous in their recognition of labor as a potential enemy. But such agreement could not always survive the conflict within their own ranks. And so in Guyana in the last decades of the nineteenth century, this social defect of the planter class would be brutally exposed by the challenge of nature.

It was certainly in everyone's interest to provide a common defense against the sea; flood water did not discriminate among its victims. When the dams burst, and the dikes gave way, and the canals were drowned, the subsequent damage could be seen as a collective disaster. But there was no binding concept of community to meet a challenge of such scale. The villagers, enduring at their subsistence level, were without any resources of wealth. They didn't qualify for credit, and loans for the purpose of sea defense would only be granted if there were an absolute certainty these would be recovered. Any obligation of a collective character had, therefore, to be met by the planter class, the only body of men whose personal fortunes and political authority could guarantee some measure of protection against the possibility of destruction. But even when individual fortunes were at stake, many of them worried over the apparent conflict of development costs and returns on capital. It seemed unsound business to tie up capital in costs of protecting their property over a period that might prove such protection to be unprofitable.

In spite of the impartial fury of the elements, many would calculate their first priority according to the advantage of the individual estate. They were profoundly resistant to any experiment in social collaboration. It is as though the principle of material self-interest feels itself betrayed by such forms of human partnership.

If this point is emphasized, it is simply to invite the imagination to grasp how utterly naked and defenseless poor villagers were in this sordid conflict of planter self-interests. Engineers might argue until the sky came down, yet many a planter found it difficult to grasp why the impoverished village could not possibly be asked to meet the cost of their own defense against the sea.

But it was, perhaps, inconceivable that a sense of communal responsibility could develop in this planter type, since Guyana was perceived as just one corner in a wider imperial playground for private speculation. The international character of the capitalist experiment encouraged the imaginative and energetic to shift scene whenever fortunes waned and disenchantment set in. So Quintin Hogg, a wealthy planter with large holdings in Guyana and the Caribbean, could tell the West India Royal Commission of 1897:

> I myself have just gone in for a block of land in the Malaya peninsula for putting in coffee, exactly the coffee I should put in Demerara. I pay for my labour there 4 pence or 5 pence per day. Why should I go and put coffee in Demerara? My machinery will not serve me, and I should have to pay double and treble for my labour to what I have to pay in the East.

Sugar or coffee, it made no difference what the crop was. Malaya workers or Guyana workers, it made no difference which hands made possible the process of production that would satisfy Hogg's expanding self-interest.

There is abundant evidence that this imperial approach to the Caribbean has not changed substantially. The region is still defined, in some areas, as a blue chip investment. A new breed of speculators arrive from Europe and

North America with the assurance that labor is cheap and that the work force can be made stable with the promise of becoming modern consumers. The earliest signs of serious revolt within the working class persuade them that it is time to depart. And they shift, Hogg-fashion, to more accommodating regions.

It is the history of this class, emerging from the ordeal of free labor, that enables us to see how external factors worked to impose very definite limitations on the initiative of the Guyanese people; how the scale and special character of the landscape, grander and more varied than the islands, encouraged the imagination to vary its response to other possibilities of survival than the dominant activity of the sugar plantation. But it was the politics of sugar that determined the frontiers of struggle.

The African work force was hardly emancipated from slavery when they recognized that free labor had provided them with a new mode of organized resistance. Rodney records 1841 as the year in which the Guyanese workers successfully organized the first strike in the history of the working class in that country. They had initiated a pattern of resistance that would take different forms.

Later, men would organize themselves into mobile task gangs, visiting different plantations and checking out the conditions of work before committing themselves to any agreement with an employer. It was an exercise of freedom that threatened the planters' monopoly of control over the conduct of the existing labor force. And since sugar cane was the kind of crop that had to be gotten from the field to the factory within a very short time, excessive delay could mean ruination. Planter and worker understood this urgency. Workers would, therefore, effectively time the withdrawal of their labor when it would be most needed.

It is Rodney's contention that the ex-slaves became plantation workers immediately after slavery was abolished and proceeded to think and act very much as modern proletarians would. We cannot grasp the cultural history of the Guyanese people without investigating further the mode of thought and struggle that resulted from this conscious resistance of workers to the exploitative rule of the planter class. Each struggle would alert the planters to the need for a new strategy of control, and each strategy served to introduce a new stage of conflict between the work force and the planter class. More crucial to our understanding of this history is the nature of the conflict that would arise within the ranks of the workers themselves.

In their attempt to curb the bargaining power of free labor, the planters used their political authority to provide them with alternative supplies of labor. This was the decisive role that Indian indentured labor would play and that would make for a wholly new development in the cultural history of the region. There was no objective need for new laborers, but the planter class felt it an absolute necessity to control the threat always present in the exercise of free labor.

Indentured labor was bound labor. It was deprived of all mobility and v'as therefore condemned to provide that reliability of service a crop like sugar demanded. The planter class, with the full permission of the metropolitan power, had given itself the legal right to deploy this labor as it pleased. As Rodney emphasizes here, with great relevance to many a contemporary situation, what the ruling class could not acquire by the normal play of the market forces had now been appropriated through legal sanctions. Indentured Indian labor was enslaved by the tyranny of the law that decided their relations to the land where they walked, and worked, and slept.

The state in a capitalist society is never an impartial agent mediating the conflicts that arise between contending classes. It is, in open or devious ways, always an instrument of the existing ruling group.

The presence of this indentured labor had a direct and immediate effect on the bargaining power of the free labor force. Time and again the planter class would, without apology or misgiving, affirm this point. Sandbach Parker observed, "so long as an estate has a large Coolie gang, Creoles must give way in prices asked or see the work done by indentured labourers—and this is a strong reason why the number of Coolies on estates must not be reduced . . . ."

The Royal Commission of 1897 confirmed this evidence of the real motive behind this strategy for an alternative labor supply.

QUESTION: What is your opinion with regard to increasing the supply of coolies when there is in the colony at present time an excess of labour?
ANSWER: The supply of labour has no bearing on the sugar industry; the origin of immigration hinges on this point. You may have work for a black man or a coloured man, and they will not do it. In planting cane, if you leave certain agricultural work over, your crop is ruined. Therefore it is absolutely necessary that you should have bound labor that you can command. There are certain kinds of work which absolutely must be done at certain time—such as replanting in rainy weather—and for this an indentured gang is absolutely necessary.

Here we can perceive the origins of what would later be known as the racial conflict in Guyana. This has become a normal way of responding to all forms of crisis in that country. And some scholars are even disappointed when they investigate situations that do not provide them with the evidence of social disruption they had anticipated.

But Rodney rivets our attention on the nature of the labor experience that Indians shared with the Africans who had come before. There can be no question that Indian workers were now condemned to a history of humiliation almost indistinguishable from the memories of African slavery. The rigidity of the labor laws made every hint of recalcitrance an occasion for criminal conviction. Doctors and magistrates became instruments of the planters' will. Since pain was invisible, the Indian worker often had to argue his illness before doctors who were paid not to believe what they had heard. Indian women were made a new target of sexual assault by the lawless, white over-seers.

But there is an aspect of this persecution that demands close attention, for it refutes the rumor of docility that influenced relations between Indian and African workers. Arrests, however frequent, never persuaded the Indian workers to cease resistance. There were thirty-one strikes in 1886, fifteen in 1887, and forty-two in 1888. This is not the conduct of a docile labor force. The contradiction was too obvious to go unnoticed, and one white overseer, W. Alleyne Ireland, was persuaded to emphasize it in recording his experience of Indian labor in Guyana.

As to immigrants submitting like blind men to their employers as willing-ly as one would desire, the annual reports of the Immigration Agent General show contrary evidence. Between 1874 and 1895, 65,084 indentured im-migrants were convicted of breaches of the labor contract.

But there also appeared among the Indian indentured labor force highly politicized elements who could analyze and articulate the nature of the enterprise that had brought them from their homes. Bechu, a Bengali, in-stinctively drew comparisons with the African predicament and showed how well he understood the system that he had been forced to serve.

> My countrymen like myself, have had the misfortune to come to Demerara, the political system of which colony has very appropriately been divined and defined by Mr. Trollope under a happy inspiration as "a despotism tempered by sugar." To these twin forces, the Immigration System is as sacred as the old system of slavery in former days, and for one in my humble position to have ventured to touch it with profane hands or to have dared to unveil it is considered on this side of the Atlantic to be a capital and inexpiable offence.

Peter Ruhomon, representing a later generation of Creole Indian, repeated Bechu's comparison with slavery, and went on to name the system that organized their lives.

> No trick of sophistry or twist of logic can ever avail to defend the system of semi-slavery paraded under the guise of indentured immigration, under which Indians were brought to the Colony to labour on the sugar planta-tions, in the interests of a powerful and privileged body of capitalists.

Nevertheless, the emotive language of race and race conflict has dominated our mode of perceiving the relations of the Guyanese working class to the politics of national liberation. Over the last three decades, as the struggle for workers' democracy has intensified, politicians of all races have found it convenient to use this mode of perception in explaining their failure to mobilize the total Guyanese work force. The difference of cultural legacies between African and Indian workers has made little contribution to the experience of conflict, but it is clear that race was effectively adopted both by planters of the nineteenth century and contemporary leaders as an effective strategy of control in their bid for the allegiance of the Guyanese working class.

It was Walter Rodney's tireless opposition to this betrayal of a people that finally cost him his life. He sought with colleagues of his own generation to cut through this miasma of race which had been nurtured with such mischievous care and which served to obscure that fundamental unity of interests that might otherwise have advanced African and Indian labor in a decisive struggle to control their common destiny.

Admirers of Rodney's earlier work *Groundings with My Brothers* must come to realize that the great emphasis he placed on the moral necessity of Black Power—the ancestral dignity that African peoples must rediscover and keep alive—was only part of a larger assignment in his intellectual life. It was no part of his intention to promote a racial sectarian attitude in our approach to the problems of human society, and especially in the concrete circumstances of Caribbean society. He takes great pains, therefore, to make us open and generous before the predicament of Indians, to make us register and internalize the fact of their suffering and the very great contribution they have made in the struggle for the creative survival of the Guyanese people. An authentic history of the Guyanese working people is equally their history.

This perception of the Indian as alien *and other*, a problem to be contained after the departure of the imperial power, has been a major part of the thought and feeling of the majority of Afro-Guyanese and a stubborn conviction among the black middle layers of Guyanese society. Indian power in politics and business has been regarded as an example of an Indian strategy for conquest. And this accusation persists even though, in the fashionable arithmetic of democracy, their numerical superiority might have justified such an ambition for supreme political power.

It is, of course, a dangerous fallacy to calculate human response on the basic of percentages. A specific group comprises ten percent of the population and is therefore confined to a comparable share of responsibility and reward. We know there is no such thing as ten percent of a person.

Every implication of this work serves as a corrective to this mode of thought. Rodney marshals an abundance of documentary evidence to demonstrate how ex-indentured Indians, like the ex-slaves who acquired land, were the beginning of new social groups, responding to new forms of economic activity. And whenever accumulation occurred, social stratification would emerge. It makes for great distortion, therefore, when we speak of Indians as a monolithic group, identifying the interests of the poor agricultural sugar worker with those of a large rice farmer.

It is one of the most instructive aspects of this book that we are allowed to see how the original force of estate labor, supplied by both groups, would acquire new levels of social function and open out into the emergence of new and distinct class formations.

The Afro-Guyanese, who had had a longer association with the culture of the dominant European group, now made a huge investment of talent in education. The school became the most accessible means of rescuing their offspring from the enslavement of estate labor. The history of the Afro-Guyanese middle class is the history of the school. Many a black lawyer would have started his career as a primary school headmaster, a position of great status and importance to a mass of unlettered and aspiring ex-slaves.

But what began as a necessary strategy of self-emancipation would become, in our time, a major obstacle to national liberation. For the mystique of the educated one has proved to be a mystifying influence on the Guyanese and West Indian masses throughout the process of decolonization. It has been one of the permanent features of the imperial experiment. Education was a means of escape from the realities of labor, a continuing flight from the foundations of society. To grow up was to grow away. Cultural imperialism is not an empty or evasive phrase. It is the process and effect of a tutelage that has clung to the ex-colonial like his skin.

It is the supreme distinction of Walter Rodney that he had initiated in his personal and professional life a decisive break with the tradition he had been trained to serve. And throughout this work, the reader is made to feel that his academic authority is always fused and humanized by a sense of personal involvement with the matters in hand. He lived to survive the distortions of his training and the crippling ambivalence of his class.

He worked on the assumption that men deserved to be liberated from those hostile forms of ownership that are based exclusively on the principle of material self-interest that negate the fundamental purpose of work. At the deepest levels of a man's being it cannot make sense that he should voluntarily labor for those whose style of thinking declares them to be his enemies and whose triumph in the management of human affairs remains a persistent threat to the dignity of his person. This book is further confirmation of that thesis. It was the last contribution Rodney would make during his life to our understanding of the history of labor in the transformation of his country and to our perception of the role of class in the continuing struggle for social justice.

January 28, 1981   GEORGE LAMMING

A History of the
Guyanese Working People, 1881-1905

CHAPTER 1

Internal and External Constraints on the Development of the Working People

> The canal flowed with calm,
> Telling nothing of what it knew
> Of the rainstorms and high winds,
> And the droughts of years gone by,
> Of the stench of dead cows
> And the thunder of purple clouds.
> *Edgar Mittelholzer*

Physical Environment and Class Interests

Judged by the area of concentrated settlement and cultivation, the colony of British Guiana was no less insular than the societies of the West Indies, with which it had so much in common. The census of 1881 enumerated a total of 252,186 persons. It merely touched a few settlements on the island rivers; and because of this limitation, the figure of 7,708 Amerindians was probably an understatement.[1] Nevertheless, it remains true that the vast majority of inhabitants at that time were a product of migration and transplant over the previous two centuries and that they were confined to the coastal strip. Generations of blacks working under white masters had markedly transformed this coastal habitat. James Rodway, the most authoritative of the country's pioneer historians, quickly focused on their environmental transformation in introducing his *History of British Guiana* in 1891. Rodway noted that "every acre at present in cultivation has been the scene of a struggle with the sea in front and the flood behind. As a result of this arduous labour during two centuries, a narrow strip of land along the coast has been rescued from the mangrove swamp and kept under cultivation by an elaborate system of dams and dykes."[2]

The "narrow strip of land" lies within a coastal plain that covers an area of 1,750 square miles out of Guyana's surface area of 83,000 square miles. The maximum width of the coastal plain is about forty miles on the Corentyne to the east but it practically ends on the Essequibo coast. Most of the coastal plain comprises clays at sea level or as low as six feet below sea level. Water-logged conditions are the understandable consequence of constant flooding from the sea and from the heavy rainfall, which averages about 90 inches per annum on the coast and the near interior. Apart from a few natural sand ridges at seven to ten feet above sea level, all areas of the coast that came under permanent cultivation had first to be drained and protected from further inundation.[3]

The first indigenous Guyanese, in the persons of the Amerindians, displayed a preference for inland locations, where shifting agriculture was heavily supplemented by fishing and hunting. The upstream position of the early Dutch trading posts was mainly meant to faciliate exchange with the Amerindians, and Dutch agriculture was initially carried on within a belt that lay between approximately thirty to one hundred miles upriver. However, the significant trend of the second half of the eighteenth century was that of coastal reclamation and settlement.

Problems of sea defense and land reclamation had been effectively tackled in the Low Countries during the first millennium A.D., and particularly from the eleventh century onward. The people of the Low Countries gave to the world the concept of a *polder*, referring to a piece of usable land created by digging and then draining a water-covered area. The Dutch population constantly improved their techniques in this aspect of agricultural engineering, and Dutch experience was transferred to the Guianas when it became necessary to carve out individual but contiguous plantations on the coastal plain. Each plantation required a front dam along the sea front, or "façade," together with a back dam of corresponding length and two connecting sideline dams, to complete the rectangular polder. The dams were meant to keep out the salt water at all times, while the fresh water from the swampy rear had to be let in and out in a calculated manner. An elaborate system of canals served to provide drainage, irrigation, and transportation—the volume of water in an estate's canals being regulated by a large *koker*, ór sluice, in the front dam and a smaller back-dam koker.

An enduring Dutch and European contribution to the technology of Guyanese coastal agriculture is undeniable. Yet one must guard against the mystification implicit in the assertion that it was the Europeans who built the dams and dug the canals.[4] In their own homelands, Dutch peasants and workers provided the labor to construct the polders. The Dutch in the Guiana colonies were capitalist entrepreneurs; they were few in number; and they merely supervised the labor of Africans subjected to slavery. The Venn Sugar Commission of 1948 estimated that each square mile of cane cultivation involved the provision of forty-nine miles of drainage canals and ditches and sixteen miles of the higher level of waterways used for transportation and irrigation. The Commissioners noted that the original construc-

Shovelmen digging canal

tion of these waterways must have entailed the moving of at least 100 million tons of soil.[5] This meant that slaves moved 100 million tons of heavy, water-logged clay with shovel in hand, while enduring conditions of perpetual mud and water.

Working people continued to make a tremendous contribution to the humanization of the Guyanese coastal environment. However, they were generally forced to react to circumstances, being in no position to control the available technology or to initiate environmental intervention. The planter class, even in its moments of greatest weakness, was solidly entrenched within the colonial political system, which was itself one of the most powerful of the constraints on the lives of Guianese working people. Of course, there were many important respects in which the coastal environment played a determining role in limiting the activities of *all* sections of the population. It is certainly impossible to provide an intelligible narrative or analysis with-out an understanding of the peculiarities of the narrow strip of empoldered coastland to which the majority of the people were confined.

As soon as slavery ended, planters in British Guiana established work schedules to be fulfilled before the laborer was paid for his nine-hour work-ing day. At the top of these schedules were listed two tasks: (1) digging canals 12 feet by 5 feet, and throwing the ground on both sides—600 cubic feet in nine hours; and (2) throwing back 6-foot parapets from the above—72 feet in nine hours.[6]

When Indian indentured laborers were added to the Guianese population in the post-Emancipation period, they too had to face up to the steady work diet of mud and water in the maintenance of dams and the cleaning of trenches. For a long while, Africans remained the specialist shovelmen, but a report on the digging of a new canal back of Plantation Annandale in 1885 drew attention to the unusual fact that the task was accomplished by Indian immigrants.[7]

The need to ensure good drainage of empoldered land, along with the complementary problem of irrigation, constantly preoccupied the planters. The cycle of flood and drought constituted a recurrent theme, partly because of variations in the annual rainfall. A year averaging less than 70 inches was usually reported as a drought. In 1883, the annual rainfall amounted to 62.94 inches—the lowest since 1873—and it was drier still in 1885. There was also the likelihood that certain parts of the coast would be more deprived than others. The Corentyne usually received the lightest rainfall, but even by their standards, the year 1899 was said at the time to have been the worst drought in living memory.[8] At the other extreme, one notes the massive rainfall of 135.24 inches in 1893, which was more than sufficient to give rise to floods.

However, flood and drought did not await wet and dry years respectively; rather, they jostled each other within each year. Monthly distribution was the important variable. The records of the Georgetown Botanical Gardens give the average rainfall per month for the years 1881-1905.

Month	Inches	Month	Inches	Month	Inches
January	9.35	May	11.05	September	3.10
February	6.52	June	12.42	October	2.10
March	6.90	July	10.63	November	5.11
April	7.30	August	5.75	December	12.53

The figures readily identify a short rainy season in December and January and a long rainy season from May through July. Irrespective of the total annual rainfall, there was always the risk of flooding when precipitation was heavy in a given short period. Thus the rainfall was considered moderate in 1881, but rains in December and the following January caused extensive flooding. Some 15 inches of rain fell within a 36-hour period during the first week of January 1882. The pattern in 1887 was rather different, there being a sustained heavy rainy season extending from December 1886 through to March 1887. Older residents claimed that the resultant floods were the worst the territory had experienced in forty years.[9] Yet during this and other wet years, it was possible to read reports of drought in subsequent months. (See table A1 for evidences of this pattern of flood followed by drought.) Sometimes the eventual runoff of the water after several distressing weeks was succeeded by drought. The coastlands lacked adequate fresh water conservation and other means of providing for irrigation and potable water supplies. This was particularly true of the months of September to November, following the long rains. By November, the whole community was usually anxiously awaiting the next rainy season, and real crisis ensued if this failed to oblige.

For instance, the rains had not yet started on 6 December 1884, and the editor of the *Argosy* bewailed the fact that "a drought of three months duration in a country with no irrigation save what the rainfall supplies is nothing short of a calamity." Ironically, the year 1884 had opened with serious floods.

Flooding was as likely to come from the sea pouring through breaches in the sea dams as from direct inundation and the overflow of fresh water from behind the back dams. Drainage had to be conceptualized in conjunction with irrigation, and both were meaningless without sea defense. Many planters in the nineteenth century seemingly lived in fear that for each one of them the day might dawn when their puny efforts to keep out the sea might come to nought. When an estate was said to have "gone under," this was more than a merely figurative expression, because it was usually the invading sea that completed the demise of a failing estate. Maps of the Demerara estuary in the eighteenth century indicate the existence of estates that were subsequently swallowed by the sea. An estate fought the sea at a line of defense constituted by the front dam. If it proved economically or technically impossible to continue repairing a front dam in a given location, then the estate "retired" that dam many roods inland and renewed the struggle after conceding many valuable acres of its frontlands.

The sea could put to rout not only small private planters, but also large proprietors and capitalist companies. The affairs of Quintin Hogg offer an excellent case in point. By the mid 1870s, Quintin Hogg was the leading partner in the firm of Curtis, Campbell, and Hogg. He also made independent purchases of several estates and was accounted the leading British capitalist with West Indian interests. A number of Quintin Hogg's estates were in the immediate vicinity of Georgetown—Plantation Bel Air being the most important. He estimated that his expenditure on the sea defenses of Bel Air exceeded £80,000, or $384,000, over the period between June 1873 and December 1879.[10] Bel Air was a flourishing concern so long as its sea defenses could be kept in good order. In 1882, it produced what was regarded as an enormous crop of 6,000 hogsheads of sugar.[11] (One hogshead = 18 cwt. or 2,000 lbs.) However, the action of the sea was remorseless in eroding or sweeping away the man-made dikes needed to protect Bel Air, particularly in February 1886 when the spring tides were unusually high. Bel Air was abandoned as a sugar plantation shortly afterwards. A similar situation developed with respect to the Colonial Company and its Windsor Forest plantation on the West Coast Demerara. Between January 1874 and January 1879, the sea defenses of Windsor Forest required an outlay of $49,200. This plantation survived for many more years, but when it eventually went under in 1909, it was owing to a renewal of the sea-defense problem in a form too acute for the budget of the Colonial Company, in spite of its major holdings in British Guiana and Trinidad.[12]

Without exception, all classes and races resident on the Guyana coastlands of necessity evinced a keen interest in sea defense and related matters. (See table A2.) The planter class had the largest economic stake as proprietors of approximately 142,000 acres of polder in 1880, divided among 113 sugar estates. It was also the class that was able to bring the force of law and the state treasury into a resolution of issues. Consequently, the expressed preoccupation with sea defense and environmental conditions came most often from the planters. This should not obscure the fact that the state of the sea defenses affected the work and likelihood of free African and Indian wage earners, of Indian indentured laborers, and of peasant farmers of varied ancestry. Indeed, they were affected more acutely than those whites who owned and supervised plantation production.

Building and maintaining a polder was always a costly enterprise. In 1886, one of the best informed planters published itemized calculations on the basic cost of empoldering a plantation having a façade of 100 roods and side line dams extending to a depth of 750 roods. (One Rhineland rood = 12.32 ft.)[13]

100 roods front dam	$ 800
Drainage and shipping sluice	1,500
750 roods side line and middle walk	4,450
100 roods back dam	800
Back dam koker	250
Total	$7,800

The sum of $7,800, or £1,628, was a considerable one in the last quarter of the nineteenth century, especially since it represented investment preliminary to any agricultural pursuit, and it was exclusive of other charges on the land such as those for the maintenance of roads and bridges. The unit 100 x 750 roods was the norm for the distribution of coastal lands in Demerara from the mid-eighteenth century. This meant an estate of approximately 265 acres. By 1881 many plantations had absorbed the façade of three or four of the original grants, and the proprietors had already exercised their option of acquiring successive second and third depths of 750 roods each.

It was required that a banked "company canal" be cut between alternate estates to allow access to the second and third depths. Company canals were expensive to maintain, and the same applied in greater measure to the special canals constructed in the Dutch period to open up large acreages of agricultural land at some distance from the foreshore—notably the three "Canals Pelder" in Demerara and the Grand Canal on the East Bank Berbice. The planting community could not afford to keep these strategic canals in good repair. Wealthy landowners barely managed to improve their own drainage, irrigation, and sea defenses; while poorer proprietors often sold out or abandoned cultivation because of expenses under these heads. It is therefore not

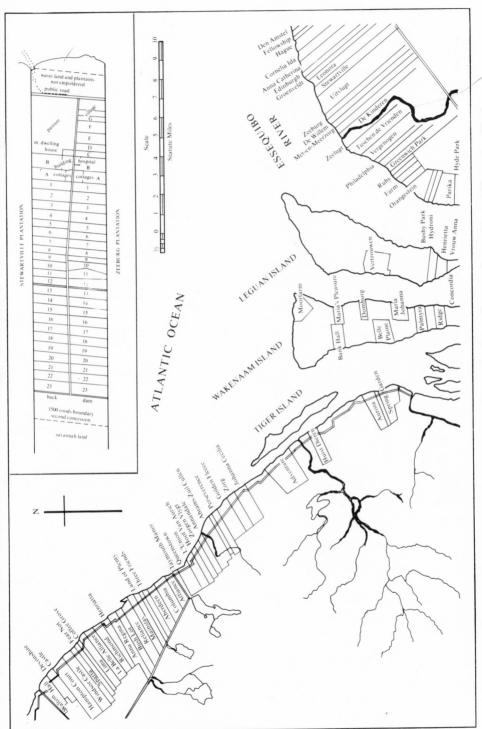

British Guiana Coastal Estates, c. 1880: West Essequibo River Estuary. Inset: Plan of Plantation Uitvlugt

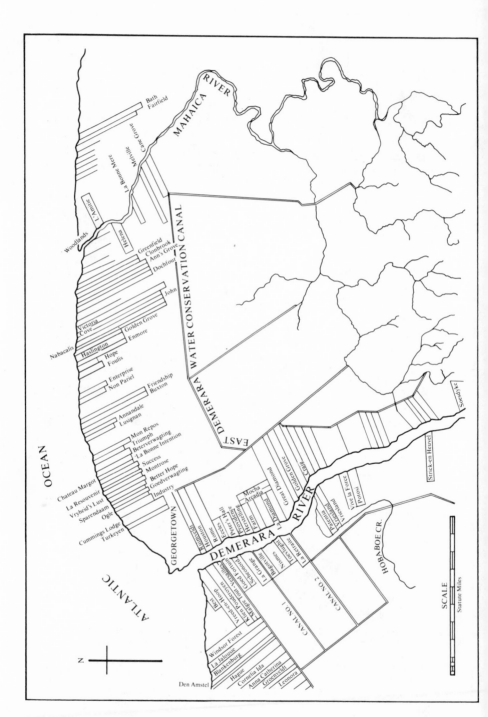

SCALE

Statute Miles

8

in the least surprising that these problems overwhelmed the common people who were organized into villages, and who inherited the responsibility of polder maintenance from the former estate owners of their localities.

In the Caribbean islands, the decisive transition from small-scale to large-scale farming was effected when sugar was introduced to replace cotton as the main staple. In Guiana, the coastal environment, and consequently the heavy cost of polder agriculture, further decreased the prospects for economic success on the part of smaller capitalists and peasants. Cotton and coffee estates were usually smaller than those devoted to sugar, which became generalized during the second quarter of the nineteenth century. The upkeep of dams and canals had to be met irrespective of the crop cultivated, and only sugar made enough profits and received enough subventions to overcome all hurdles. Peasant production of plantains and "ground provisions" became significant from the 1840s, so that by the decade of the 1880s peasant farmers had had considerable exposure to the expense and worry incurred on account of sea defense, drainage, and irrigation. As compared with the larger and more profitable plantations, each village fell constantly short of the requirements of proper polder development. A difference of six inches in the height of a dam could determine whether or not it stood firm, just as the cleaning of trenches and canals could go a long way toward averting flooding. The village authorities were aware of these facts, but they simply could not afford to pay the bill. For instance, few villages could emulate plantations that bought steam-driven drainage pumps or "drainage engines" at a cost of approximately $30,000 in the 1870s. Most villages had to wait on low tide before they could open their main sea kokers (ten hours each day, in two shifts) and hope that the outflow would be adequate. The three villages of Plaisance, Beterverwagting, and Buxton-Friendship, which installed drainage engines, found them an intolerable burden. The capital debt was crushing. Funds were not available to keep the pumps in good repair, and as their condition deteriorated, they consumed ever increasing quantities of expensive imported coal. As a result, when the floods came and the drainage engines were most needed, they remained inactive through malfunction or lack of coal.

The enormous influence of flood and drought was brought to bear on several facets of the lives of working people. They were unemployed in periods that were extremely dry because estates had to cut back on their allocations of task work. Any drought in November-December and a drop in the level of water in the canals meant that punts could not operate to carry canes from the fields to the factories; cane cutting and grinding therefore ceased. When the rains were excessive the ultimate result was the same—namely, an increase in seasonal unemployment. In times of drought planters fumed and fretted, while workers had little to drink or even eat. The incidence of gastroenteric disease shot up, and such water as was available was

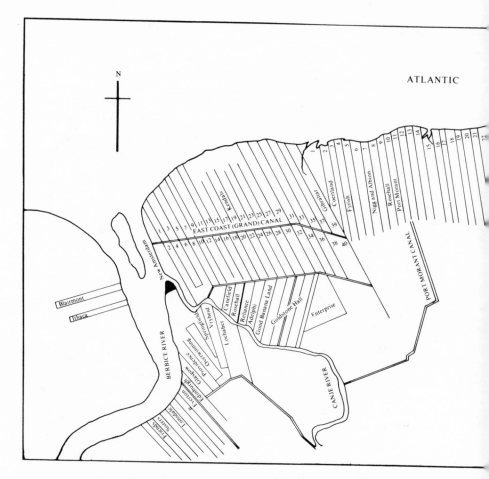

British Guiana Coastal Estates, c. 1880: East of Berbice River

imbibed along with the mud of the trenches. Floods took an even greater toll on health, on livestock, on crops, on the roads and dams, and on the capacity of the villagers to pay rates and retain possession of their houses and provision lots.

Sophia Ross, of Hopetown village, was charged, convicted, and fined four dollars for trespassing on Plantation Bath in November 1884. She had gone there to get water from an estate trench to satisfy her thirst. The alternative would have been to travel miles "aback," as most villagers on the West Coast Berbice were then doing, to obtain a little brackish discolored water.[14] This seemingly petty conviction highlights the toil and trauma involved in so basic an operation as securing supplies of drinking water. During floods the available water was polluted. A correspondent of the *Chronicle*

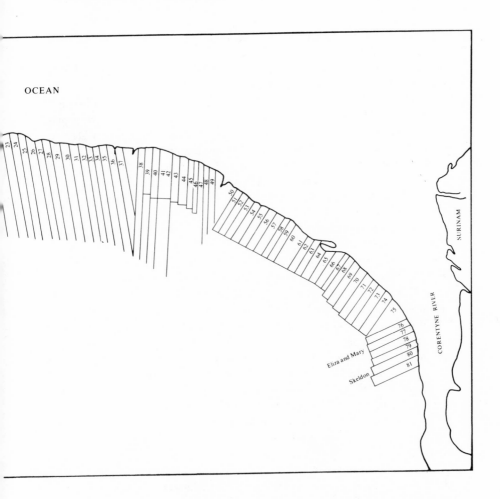

wrote feelingly from Buxton in January 1902 to describe the "feculent matter floating about and around dwelling houses, low houses [having] floors
soaking in the water."[15] Observers conveyed an impression of a total assault
on the faculties of sight and smell—by the decomposing cattle carcasses at
Mahaica-Mahaicony after a drought, by the floating bloated livestock when
the Essequibo Coast was inundated, or by the sickening stench arising from a
stagnant mass of semisalt water and rotting fish to windward, after Gibraltar-
Fyrish on the Corentyne had been under water for two weeks.

Some living conditions on the Guiana coastlands were shared by all classes,
and they were beyond the immediate control of any persons in the society at
the time. There was certainly a great deal of ignorance concerning many
aspects of the coastal environment, and to that extent, it was impossible to

plan improvements. People knew that some parts of the coastline were subject to erosion while others were being built up, and that over a period of years, the same stretch on which the tides had been depositing sediment became in turn a section exposed to erosion, or "wash," as it was termed locally. However, sufficient scientific observation and measurement had not yet been made by the late nineteenth century with respect to the tidal patterns in British Guiana. The processes of accretion and erosion then seemed almost capricious; and in October 1882 the legislature conceded that "great uncertainty exists as to the currents and position of the set of the wash along the foreshore of the colony, thereby causing great uncertainty as to the causes which lead to banks forming at certain points and washing away at others."[16]

In 1879, the assistance of the Colonial Office was sought in procuring the services of a qualified and experienced hydraulic engineer. The appointee, Hora Siccama, had had experience in Holland and the Dutch East Indies. At the magnificent salary of nearly $30,000 per year, Siccama was one of the first of the highly paid foreign technicians to advise the government of British Guiana. His reports on aspects of sea defense, drainage, irrigation, and harbor development might well have formed the basis for a sustained scientific assault on these problems, but there was no continuity in research, or agreement on implementation after his departure in May 1882.[17] For example, some planters favored fascine dikes, others relied on the increasing use of piled granite boulders, and still others were partisans of groin construction. Subsequent reports in the present century pointed out that the numerous experiments on sea defense were either theoretically unsound or poorly applied, the valuable sugar estates on the East and West Coasts of Demerara being particularly guilty of many costly errors.[18]

During polder construction, some creeks were blocked or "stopped off," thereby reducing the effectiveness of natural drainage. The company canals upon which the Dutch insisted also acted as safety valves to the back dams when the small creeks were cut off by empoldering. Advantage was taken of the force of water in the company canal to keep the drainage channel clear of silt. The Canals Polder and the Grand Canal were laid out so as to make the best use of the scour of the rivers and creeks, and there were others which utilized the tidal flow of the Mahaica and Mahaicony rivers. However, the reduction of natural drainage outlets had proceeded considerably by the latter part of the nineteenth century, while the çanals which might have compensated for this loss were in a poor state. Each engineering intervention had it own hazards. There were times when sea dams were improved and drainage suffered. Alternatively, when irrigation conservancies were built, the discharge of their overflow contributed to flooding.[19] These were issues which had to await technical enlightenment at a later date.

While ignorance prevailed, plantation and village were equally exposed to natural hazards. The poverty of the villagers then led to their drainage being poorer, their irrigation problems more acute, and their dams being in a state of perpetual disrepair. While Quintin Hogg was battling the sea on the lower East Coast Demerara in the 1870s, the villagers of Buxton were doing likewise with incomparably smaller resources. The villages of Den Amstel and Fellowship on the West Coast Demerara were adversely affected by the same "wash" which caused the Colonial Company to consider abandoning the existing outer dam of Plantation Windsor Forest in 1880. Generally speaking, the historical record is limited to references to the state of the villages in mere footnotes to the discussion of the fate of the planters. Thus, crisis at Plantation Better Hope would be the occasion for revealing the threat to sea defenses at neighboring Plaisance Village, while imminent inundation by the sea at Plantation Clonbrook gave mention to the plight of the villagers of Ann's Grove. The extent and the reality of suffering was surely greater as far as the common people were concerned, since the villagers were not simply the victims of "natural" environmental forces and limited technology. Rather, as workers and peasants, they were doubly disadvantaged by the social and political inequality of the colonial capitalist system.

Capitalist competition and self-interest caused polder husbandry to be approached as a private rather than a public venture. When an estate retired its sea dam, this measure of self-defense placed tremendous pressure on the adjacent properties, whose sideline dams became exposed to the action of the tides. Debates in the legislature in January 1883 revealed that nearly every estate had at one time or another unilaterally retired its sea dam. This could be interpreted as a strategy for diverting attacks of the sea from a given estate to its neighbors. An ordinance of 1873 had sought to compel proprietors to seek the permission of the legislature in order to change the alignment of any front dam. Apparently, this was often circumvented by throwing up a new dam within any outer dam beset by erosion—the outer dam being left to be washed away. In any event, petitions to retire dams led to conflicts within the body of planter legislators who, in this context, were defending the interests of individual estates rather than the well-being of the planter class as a whole.[20]

Many far-sighted planters appreciated that polder maintenance should be dealt with collectively. The wealthy firms represented by the West India Committee were among the first to demand concerted action under government supervision. They recommended the appointment of Hora Siccama; they pressed for agreement on large-scale schemes for water supplies on the East Coast and West Coast Demerara; and they supported the Sea Defense Ordinance of 1883 which empowered the Colonial Civil Engineer to make regulations to protect the foreshore and to order estate proprietors to execute certain sea defense works. Nevertheless, colonywide or even regional schemes for irrigation, sea defense, and drainage made very little progress during the period under review, because planters could not arrive at a consensus to take action. The Colonial Civil Engineer reported in April 1893 that the regional Sea Defence Boards set up by the Sea Defence Ordinances had failed, owing to the impossibility of getting proprietors of estates to agree.[21] Many years later (in December 1914), W. Middleton Campbell wrote the Colonial Office on the subject of irrigation and observed with evident frustration that "the whole system of water has been under discussion to my knowledge for thirty-five years, and there are so many 'cooks' that the 'broth' has always been spoiled."[22] Campbell, who was then head of Curtis Campbell & Company, was correct, since it was in 1878 that attention was first focused on the need for a reliable water supply in East Demerara. What is of critical importance is that the disagreements on these issues were not merely based on conflicting technical appraisals of what was to be done, but also resulted from the promotion of divergent capitalist interests.

After the West India Committee had secured Siccama's appointment, he made firm recommendations on the question of an East Demerara water supply. Yet this was the same unresolved matter to which Middleton Campbell was to refer more than thirty years later. One principal reason for the continued disagreement was the unwillingness of the planters on the East Bank Demerara to sanction any proposals that linked their water supply with that of the city of Georgetown, or that seemed to place upon them developmental costs that would tie up a proportion of their capital over a long period. Attempts to have a coastwide program of sea defense were firmly opposed by some proprietors who calculated that their estates might be better off avoiding any share of the financial burden. For instance, estates that had façades along the river spent less on their front dams than those exposed to the sea. Plantation Diamond on the East Bank Demerara was by far the most valuable and profitable estate owned by Sandbach Parker, and this company spearheaded the opposition to a collective approach to sea defense during the 1890s.[23] Besides, planters with sea dams often lost their anxiety over sea defense when their own foreshore was being built up by deposits, and either the courida or mangrove was helping stabilization. Thus, in 1895, the owner of Plantation Hope at Mahaica confidently asserted that there had been no dangerous "wash" affecting his dams since about 1868, and he was most lukewarm about the prospect of government going to the aid of other private capitalists who had the mischance to be then experiencing erosion. Had this proprietor known that erosion and accretion tended to reverse themselves over a thirty-year cycle, he might have been less sanguine about the changes of Plantation Hope continuing to manage its own sea defense expenditure. As it was, in the year 1898, the estate had little other than its name to offer protection against the "wash." This was the kind of calculation and miscalculation that individual capitalists frequently made.[24]

In spite of disagreements, the planter class established two water conservancies that were to prove long-lasting. The first was the disputed East Demerara or Lamaha Water Conservancy, which was extended and remodeled under Siccama, while the Boerasirie Conservancy came into operation in West Demerara in 1884-85. These schemes were primarily for irrigation, but they improved the entire water system of the estates they served.

Political decision making within British Guiana was centered in the legislature. There were the planters shaped policy and authorized the finances that made policy implementation possible. The only potential countervailing force in the local context was the governor, who in theory had as one of his functions supervision over the well-being of the mass of the population. However, even when the governor of the day was not closely allied with the planters, this did not alter the fact that working people could gain political expression in the legislature only as supplicants. Besides, planters also controlled the many other sectors of the state that impinged directly or indirectly on the use of physical resources: notably, the various statutory boards that regulated sanitation, drainage, roads, and so on. It was all but impossible for peasants and workers to circumvent the entrenched constitutional power of the plantation owners.

The legislature was an arena in which planters were free to disagree among themselves over the approach to maintaining proper polder conditions in Guiana. But when the planter-dominated legislature did arrive at decisions which approximated to the interests of the planter class as a whole, they seldom extended any consideration to the villagers and small proprietors who faced the same difficulties. With monotonous regularity, the annual reports of the inspector of villages related instances of poor drainage leading to flooding of provision grounds, severe economic reverses, and nonpayment of village rates. These seemingly had little impact on official consciousness, and even direct petitions by destitute villagers received no sympathy. Governor Irving, who assumed duties in May 1882, displayed unusual concern and judgment in dealing with environmental problems. He was the first governor to successfully urge the legislature to vote funds for village drainage and sanitation, and in so doing he remarked that

> the root of the matter is the maintenance of the Polder without which agricultural industry in British Guiana is no more possible than it would be in England without rainfall. The legislature has hitherto refused to recognise any distinction between a polder owned by one planter and yielding several thousand tons of sugar and one occupied by a negro population of several thousand yielding crops of plantains and ground provisions. The present vote marks a new departure in the administration

of the country—I regard it as a recognition of the fact that the Colony is something more than a collection of sugar estates.[25]

As it turned out, improvements initiated by Governor Irving proved marginal and short-lived. Throughout the period under discussion, villagers suffered from "natural" disasters, not merely because of the technological inadequacy of the society, but because the planter class discriminated against working people in the allocation of resources for polder protection.

It was common practice for planters and their official allies to scoff at the villagers and to interpret their troubles as deriving from their own inherent inadequacies. Large proprietors, in their private capacity and as the controllers of state power, had innumerable opportunities for adding to the burdens of peasants and laborers, while maintaining a tone of moral condemnation.[26] Only the cultivation of sugar cane was considered industrious by the planters, while peasant production of provisions was said to have been a waste of time and resources. This attitude strongly influenced planter decisions on most of the questions connected with sea defense, drainage, and irrigation.

In March 1883, the residents of Potosi, West Bank Demerara, asked the legislature for a loan of $800 to rebuild their dams. Their petition explained that the children of one Molyneaux had inherited the estate in a very dilapidated condition in 1872. They threw up back dams, cleaned the trenches, cultivated part of the land, and rented the remaining portion. The returns on their labor were reasonable until the dams gave way during the floods of 1879-80. The small request for $800—to be repaid over five years—was opposed by William Russell, the leading planter of the day and one who was perfectly aware of the high costs of polder maintenance. Speaking on behalf of large landed capital, Russell claimed that laziness ruled supreme throughout the area of the Canals Polder where peasants had taken over from former coffee planters after withdrawing from sugar estates in West Demerara. Russell argued that if and when the government helped to make up the dams, the farmers would grow nothing other than plantains and ground provisions. Therefore, he resolved, "he would set his face and record his vote against such experiments."[27]

The legislature rejected both the Potosi petition and another request from William Correia, who was the small capitalist owner at nearby Patentia and Sisters' Village. It was no secret that the poor state of Canal No. 1 and Canal No. 2 exposed West Demerara to floods of ruinous dimensions. Similarly, the Grand Canal in East Berbice had fallen into a state of total disrepair and there was no remedy when the Canje creek overflowed. In March 1884, a petition from Courtland-Fyrish on the Corentyne urged that the Grand Canal be dug out and that compensation be paid the villagers for losses in recent floods. The planter assembly did no more than promise to investigate.[28]

If the villagers could not obtain small loans and relief funds to cope with sea defense and drainage, then their position was doubly jeopardized. Even the largest of the capitalists needed government credit. Quintin Hogg asked for a loan of $144,000 to help with the Bel Air sea dams in 1879, citing as a precedent a loan given to the Colonial Company to assist with sea defenses on the West Coast Demerara. The administration responded favorably to Hogg's argument that securing Bel Air's front dam was in the public interest, especially since it helped to defend Georgetown.[29] The argument was valid, but by the same reasoning all sea and river dams were part of the national sea defense system, and their maintenance was to a greater or lesser extent in the public interest. The Sea Defence Ordinance of 1883 represented only a partial acceptance of the principle that sea defense transcended private proprietary interests. At this point, and for many years afterward, it remained easier for the bigger capitalists to make use of avenues of credit opened up by the government. All loans for drainage, irrigation, and defense were regarded as strictly recoverable. A peasantry living close to subsistence was not a good financial risk; and the members of the legislature were constantly being reminded of the outstanding deficit on loans offered to villages for items such as drainage engines and new kokers. At a more fundamental level, the dismissal of village requests by a planter-dominated assembly was surely an expression of the class struggle between the planters and the villagized working people. The latter did not fail to perceive their problems in this light.

On 2 March 1882, a public meeting on flood crisis was held at Geneva school in Canal No. 1. It was attended by a large number of residents, including Indian peasants who had begun to acquire lots in the district after their indentureship. The chairman was one Mr. Harman of Vauxhall, whose introductory remarks were characterized by penetrating awareness of the class nature of government intervention (or nonintervention) in matters pertinent to the struggle within the coastal environment. William Russell had told the legislature that the Canals Polder should be drained and the cost met by the peasants of the district, rather than being a burden on the general taxpayers. Harman commented ironically, "How kind of Mr. Russell to protect the general taxpayers. How about the Best Groyne and the hundreds of thousands of dollars that had been fooled away behind the East Coast?"* "But," Harman continued, "that had been done for the rich sugar estate proprietors and that made all the difference." Harman, who was clearly an informed leader of the working people, also alluded to the fact that the bridges across the three Canals Polder were kept by those locally resident,

---

*Government expenditure on the East Best Groyne and the West Best Groyne totaled approximately $70,500 between 1875 and 1879, according to the annual administrative returns. The second part of the reference concerns the East Demerara water supply schemes.

while the West Bank Mahaica Creek Canal drained sugar estates, and government quietly shifted the cost of the bridge on to the shoulders of the general taxpayers.[30]

With the government failing to display any real sympathy for the villagers, it was only to be expected that planters often took private action which proved prejudicial to small cultivators and house owners. A glaring issue of this kind was exposed when the legislature received a report on a dispute between the villagers at Sparendaam and the adjacent estate of Goedverwagting. This estate placed a stop-off in their common sideline dam in May 1885, cutting the village off from the main drainage outlet. The estate management justified their action on the grounds that they had put in a drainage engine to which the villagers had not contributed. However, the villagers had a right to the same drainage as the plantation of which their lots formed a part; and if the estate found it advantageous to switch to steam power in place of the gravitational drainage which was in use when the lots were sold, the change should not have entailed additional charge to the villagers. The matter was so straightforward that government officials should have acted on it immediately, instead of waiting for the villagers to petition the legislature and bear the expense and suffering until the issue was finally reserved in March 1887.[31]

It is rare to find instances such as the above when the interests of an estate were subordinated, albeit belatedly, to those of any given body of the working people, as far as the vital aspects of polder management were concerned. On the contrary, it became an article of faith among many villagers that estates consciously and selectively released impounded water on to village lands at many intervals over the course of our history. The planters countered by saying that persons often resorted to the criminal act of cutting estate dams. Thus, in June 1882, it was alleged that villagers had cut the sideline dam at Plantation Providence (East Bank Demerara) at great cost to the estate.[32] This specific charge may or may not have been justified, but it would be correct to acknowledge that this was a technique available to, and used by, some sections of the population who were oppressed by the planter class. The use of fire against growing crops had been common throughout the plantation zone of the Americas since slavery, and the use of the flood was a peculiarity appropriate to the coastlands of British Guiana.

Sea defense, drainage, and irrigation were problems demanding the scientific intervention of civil engineers. They were also being tackled within a specific set of class relations. The hands that dug the canals and the feet that trod the dams were taking an active part in the class struggle which would eventually mold the Guyanese people.

International Capitalist Forces

Beyond the polder and the shores of British Guiana, there were further constraints imposed upon working-class action by the colonial status of the society. In this connection, one is concerned not so much with the deliberate political decisions taken by the colonizing power, but rather with the forces arising from the Caribbean involvement in the genesis of Euro-American capitalism. After slavery, Caribbean economies lost their preeminence in the process of capital accumulation, but dependent integration into the world capitalist system remained a significant feature. The periods of prosperity and depression, as reflected in the "business cycles" of the metropolitan capitalist countries, provided some of the circumstances which shaped the lives of Guianese—irrespective of whether or not persons were aware of this external environment.

An international depression prevailed between 1873 and 1879. Engels identified this slump as the sixth since the phenomenon manifested itself in 1825; and he noted that capitalist production was thrown out of gear about once every ten years, when markets became glutted and commerce came to a standstill.[33] The Marxist insight that there would be a continuation of the cycle of boom and slump proved itself fully in subsequent decades, as the capitalist system expanded its industrialized operations. The depression of 1873-79 was followed by others in 1882-86, 1890-96, 1901-2 (Europe), and 1903-4 (America); and their impact extended outwards from the capitalist epicenters to zones of production such as the Caribbean.[34]

Generally speaking, the rhythms of the business cycle were superimposed upon the colonial economies by way of price mechanisms. The onset of economic depression was usually felt somewhat later in British Guiana than in Europe, and correspondingly, recovery was manifested after it had already made its appearance in the principal capitalist economies. Thus, the results of the depression of the 1870s were still being felt in 1880; the boom in Europe of 1880-82 touched the colony briefly in 1882-83; the depression of the 1880s in British Guiana lasted from 1884 to 1888; while that of the late 1890s barely paused before it was part of another slump in the first years of this century. Moreover, the period from 1873 to 1896 was characterized by a deep structural crisis in the development of modern capitalism. Apart from short-term fluctuations, prices of industrial and agricultural goods moved consistently downwards, and were actually lower at the end of the nineteenth century than they were at mid-century.[35] The dependent economy of British Guiana suffered severely from the overall fall in prices for at least two reasons. Firstly, there was a steeper fall in the prices of the colony's staple exports than there was in the prices of the principal imports, and secondly, the colony was unable to enact legislative and fiscal measures to defend its productive forces—as was done by the capitalist states themselves.

British Guiana's initiation into the world economy was effected primarily by means of the production and export of cane sugar. The fate of its inhabitants was heavily influenced not only by the general movements of commodity prices but by the specific market performance of the varieties of cane sugar which originated in the colony. Good weather, proper polder maintenance, and high yields did not guarantee the highest financial returns on each sugar harvest; and it was not surprising that most discussions of government expenditure were premised upon international sugar prices. For instance, in 1879, planters vigorously opposed the project for extending the East Coast Demerara railway across the West Coast Berbice. Their argument was that "great depression exists in the mercantile and proprietary bodies, in consequence of the unusually low price ruling for their staple articles of export, such as sugar, rum, molasses and hardwood in the (British) home market."[36] Contemporaries were again speaking of commercial disaster in 1884, owing to the astonishingly low price to which sugar fell. It had stood at an average of $107.26 per ton in 1883, while by the end of 1884 it was no more than $69.84 per ton. Worse was to follow in 1886 and in the 1890s. (See Table A3.) If one follows the record of the West Indian planters and their moaning over hard times from the 1840s onwards, there might be a tendency to be dismissive of their cry in 1896 that things were worse than they had ever been before, but sugar did reach an unparalleled low of $46.08 per ton at that point. No marked or sustained price rise was noticeable until 1903-4, because it was then that the rival European beet sugar ceased to be heavily subsidized.

A great deal has been written on the subject of beet sugar bounties by the planters themselves, by the West India Royal Commission of 1897, and by subsequent historians.[37] In reviewing their own lengthy involvement in the sugar industry, the spokesmen of Booker Brothers, McConnell and Company had this to say:

> From 1883 onwards the dumping of large quantities of State-subsidised European beet sugar markedly affected prices and led to a considerable reduction of colonial sugar production. In the year 1886 alone, Germany dumped 760,000 tons of beet sugar on the United Kingdom and the United States markets. It was a blow which the British Guiana sugar industry could not withstand.[38]

Bounties drastically lowered the price at which beet sugar entered export markets and therefore forced cane sugar prices down to a point where they were scarcely remunerative for many producers. Yet, in assessing the distress suffered by the West Indian sugar industry during the last two decades of the nineteenth century, too much weight has been given to the operation of bounties in isolation from other factors. Bounties were themselves an expression of competitive national capital in the context of cyclical crises in the capitalist economies. Poor harvests in some years and overproduction and glutted markets in other years threatened to destroy large areas of economic activity. Given the specter of unemployment and ruin for several social strata, European governments were galvanized into passing protective measures—export subsidies being among these.

Before 1850, less than 15 percent of the world's sugar supply came from beet. Thirty years later, the quantity produced surpassed that of sugar cane—with Germany as the major supplier, followed by France, Austria-Hungary, and Russia. This phenomenal expansion came largely because the new beet sugar industry was able to exploit its full growth potential by the application of scientific principles to crop selection, husbandry, and sugar extraction. Bounties not only helped in the capture of export markets but also stimulated efforts for higher yielding varieties and more intensive extraction of sugar. There were other benefits to agriculture in the form of crop rotation and the use of beet products as stockfeed, so that marginal lands were brought into cultivation. Each of the European countries involved tended to meet setbacks to their respective industries by increasing the subsidies—hence the promotion of "crisis exports," whereby export bounties ensured that beet sugar would enter foreign markets at slump prices which were lower than the cost of production. It was surely no coincidence that European governments placed great store on beet sugar bounties during the period constituting the long economic trough from 1873 onwards; while the fact that several governments used similar strategies led to sharper competition, more ingenious subsidies, greater beet sugar production, and still lower prices for all types of sugar in the markets of the United Kingdom and North America.

In contrast, the effect of bounties on the West Indies was to deepen the predicament caused by the depressions of the 1880s and 1890s, to reduce the proportion of West Indian sugar entering "traditional" markets and to decrease the area under production. In 1887, a well-informed article on the causes of the' commercial depression appeared in the *West Indian Quarterly* (published in British Guiana). The contributor was aware that there was a fall in the price of all commodities starting in 1874. He used 1867 as a base year to calculate a fall from 100 to 72 units by 1877. He noted further that by 1885, sugar had declined to 59 percent of the average price between 1867 and 1877; and that in 1886 the deterioration in West Indian sugar prices was again worse than for other commodities.[39] Studies of the cost of living in England confirm that sugar prices declined more appreciably and more consistently than the prices of other major commodities in the latter part of the nineteenth century.[40] Sugar from British Guiana fetched good prices by Caribbean standards, but the colony could not preserve its share of the British market, nor could it avoid a reduction in the acreage under cane over the period 1884-1904. (See Table A4.)

As a consequence of their dependency, the colonies of the West Indies were economically helpless in the face of capitalist crisis and were almost impotent to politically safeguard their own interests. The nature of the British economy was such that the ruling class aimed at the importation of cheap raw materials and food. The British government took no serious steps against continental beet sugar subsidies, since they contributed to making sugar the cheapest item in the consumer budget of the English population. The Board of Trade consistently maintained that the continuation of the bounties was an advantage to Britain, and the West Indian Royal Commission of 1897 calculated the monetary aspect of the advantage to be £2,000,000 ($9,600,000) per annum. Czarnikow, the largest sugar brokers in London, told the West Indian Commission that they scarcely handled cane sugar; while the records of the Liverpool refinery of Henry Tate reveal a dramatic decline in the percentage of cane sugar refined:[41]

	1877	1882	1889	1892	1897	1899
Cane	60.5%	50%	40%	21.2%	1.6%	0%
Beet	39.5	50	60	78.8	98.4	100

Admittedly, there were a few firms, such as Macfie of Liverpool, which utilized roughly equal proportions of cane sugar and beet sugar; while the Glebe Sugar Refining Company in Brecknock, and Crosfield of Liverpool, long maintained the reputation of confining their manufacture to cane sugar. However the sectors of the British sugar refining industry which expanded did so by adopting new technology for processing sugar from both beet and cane. Since the per capita consumption of sugar was constantly on the increase in Britain during the very years of distress for the British West Indian sugar industry, it meant that the region was not benefiting from the expansion of world trade in this commodity.

A number of sugar refiners lobbied forcefully against the continental beet bounties. They protested the fact that the bounties had stimulated the importation into Britain of *refined* beet and hence their share of the domestic market had not kept pace with the growth in consumption. Refiners also documented that the (profit) margin between raw and refined sugar had been reduced. But neither they nor the West Indian planters had what might today be termed the political "clout" to force the British capitalist state to favor and protect the West Indian sugar industry. Their influence was countered by the argument that cheap sugar promoted the development of the confectionery industry. The latter united their interest with that of the consumers and campaigned effectively with the slogan "a free breakfast table." When the refining and confectionery industries are jointly considered, it is obvious that there was an increase of productive capacity in the United

Kingdom. The waste and destruction of productive forces took place within colonial economies. Consequently, the adverse effects of beet sugar bounties did not constitute a major political liability in Britain.

The above considerations explain the futility of the chorus of complaints from the West Indies against depressed sugar prices and against beet competition in particular. Planters and the chamber of commerce in Georgetown added their petitions to those from the other British West Indian territories and from the West India Committee. They asked that Britain prevail on other European states to abolish bounties, or failing that, impose a countervailing duty. The international sugar conference in London in November-December 1887 was the closest that the West India lobby came to success. It was attended by delegates from Germany, Belgium, Austria-Hungary, Denmark, Spain, France, Italy, the Netherlands, Russia, and Sweden, while British officials supposedly represented the British sugar loaf industry as well as colonial producers. Agreement was actually reached to review and curtail sugar bounties, but the British Parliament refused to ratify the requisite treaty. The consumer interest and the welfare of the confectionery industry were held to be paramount.[42]

The Conference of the Confectioners' Association of the United Kingdom held at Nottingham early in 1900 set forth their position as follows: "The Confectionery Trade owes much of its development in recent years and its present condition of prosperity to the abundant supply of cheap sugar of regular quality from continental ports and deprecates any legislation for the abolition of bounties that would have the effect of curtailing such supplies."[43] By this time, however, the situation was changing somewhat—mainly because the continental powers were finding it difficult to bear the burden of ever increasing bounty subsidies. It was this latter factor, rather than West Indian lobbying, that was principally responsible for the Brussels Sugar Convention of 1902 and the easing of subsidized beet competition, beginning with the following year.

Meanwhile, estate proprietors were forced to search for means to cut production costs as far as possible so as to create a profit margin even at the lowest prices. Planters in the late nineteenth century built upon a tradition of experimentation and a willingness to adopt new techniques that dated from the early introduction of the vacuum pan in 1830. There was heavy investment in factory plant in 1870-72, when good sugar prices made capital and credit accessible and when the returns on capital were immediate and significant.[44] The next spurt in factory modernization came between 1880 and 1886. Proprietors used the surplus gained between 1880 and 1883 to continue technological renovation after the onset of depression, realizing that this was one of their main hopes of countering the international price fall. By 1886, the cost of production was down by approximately thirty-four dollars per ton, half of this being attributable to improvements in manufacturing. (See Table A5 and A6 for statistics on costs of one of the colony's large producers.)

"Improvements" were viewed with great reverence by Guiana planters of the late nineteenth century. The planters were self-conscious about the need to improve extraction, hence the use of double and triple crushing and the introduction of "maceration," or imbibition. Extraction by the diffusion process was considered too expensive at prevailing low sugar prices to have been worth the slight gains in the recovery of juice, but the attention paid to this innovation was further proof of planter seriousness.[45] Of course, all but a handful of planters opted for the vacuum pan during the period in question, and they showed a willingness to adopt the newest vacuum-pan technology as it became available—namely, double vacuum pans, then triples and quadruples and so on. Clarification was not left untouched, especially since this aspect of sugar manufacture accounted for the color and "bloom" of the highly vaunted yellow crystals.

Planter discussions within the Royal Agricultural and Commercial Society and the public press indicate that capital was virtually the sole constraint on the use of science and technology to reduce factory costs in British Guiana in the 1880s and 1890s. There was need to find extra capital to acquire the best technology to cut production costs, but the depression made it highly unlikely that such capital would be readily forthcoming. Individual estates sometimes cut back on necessary inputs to the point where the policy was self-defeating. For instance, it was reported in January 1885 that the manager of Plantation Wales was not spending one cent more than was absolutely necessary, and his principals feared that he might starve the cultivation by giving up manuring.[46] In the factory, the conflict between immediate savings and long-term investment was all the greater; and the sugar industry as a whole never solved this conundrum. With the exception of the years 1884-86, the worst moments of the depression were reflected in sharp curtailment of new investment. For instance, most planters restricted their 1896 budgets to the bare essentials required to keep the estates functioning, and the investment figures for the 1890s were generally lower than for the preceding decade. The largest annual import of new machinery amounted to $876,460 in 1884. This was not equaled over the next twenty years nor did the average for the 1890s match that for the preceding and succeeding decades.[47] The picture presented by Sandbach Parker seems to be fairly typical of the overall investment pattern. Between 1881 and 1895, the Sandbach estates spent on improvements a total of $1,148,847—equivalent to $9.00 per ton on a production of 127,870 tons. Most of this money went into their new factory at Plantation Diamond in 1884-86. Thereafter, the expenditure per ton of sugar on new machinery (exclusive of cost of erection) fluctuated sharply over the next ten years.[48]

1887	1888	1889	1890	1891	1892	1893	1894	1895	1896
$1.00	$5.07	$2.47	$3.33	$1.59	$1.43	$1.56	$1.35	$0.54	$0.77

The ten-year figures were prepared for the benefit of the West India Royal Commission of 1897 with the intention of convincing the United Kingdom government that the sugar industry in British Guiana was doing all it could to help itself, and therefore deserved help in the midst of depression and subsidized beet sugar competition. A defensive attitude was necessary because several West Indian territories were noted for old-fashioned muscovado processes. As it was, British Guiana and Trinidad did gain for themselves the reputation of being technologically progressive—recognition being afforded by the Colonial Office, Parliament, and influential sugar journals. It also came to be well known that British Guiana was a place in which sugar estates were constantly being amalgamated and transformed into larger and more efficient units. Like technological change, amalgamation was no new feature on the plantation scene during the years under discussion. It had been discernible during the post-Emancipation era, and was effected through the merger of successful estates as well as by the take-over of properties which were otherwise on the verge of being abandoned. These typical capitalist developments were speeded up through the pressure of low prices. Amalgamation was a technique for rationalizing production and decreasing costs. This was immediately apparent in the integration of water systems and the reduction in the number of factories.

Hampton Court, Reliance, Uitvlugt, Leonora, Windsor Forest, Diamond, Bel Air, and Better Hope were the leading examples of amalgamation in the early 1880s.[49] The concept of a huge "central" for the whole of East Demerara was discussed in 1895, but was never actualized.[50] Even so, it was principally due to amalgamation that the standard of what was considered an "average" sugar crop kept constantly rising from about 1,800 tons to about 5,000 tons over the course of the period. Once again, the external market factor was largely responsible for increasing the minima in terms of profitable acreages and sugar-cane tonnages. Efforts were made to halt the decline in the area of total cultivation at the turn of this century. Managers and attorneys at least sought to ensure that their estates should be increased in size and that more of their land should be brought under cultivation.[51]

Amalgamation further exposed the colonial economy to the direct decision making of the metropolitan centers. So long as there were many small resident planters, the relationship with the metropolises was mediated by a variety of financial and marketing organizations. Amalgamation all but eliminated the small resident proprietors, and this was accompanied by the widespread creation of limited liability companies in the United Kingdom, as replacements for the family partnerships that had previously prevailed. In June 1886, Mr. Arnold sold Plantation Columbia and left for the United

Kingdom.[52] He was described as "the father of Demerara planters," and his departure marked the end of an era—there being no independent small proprietor of Arnold's type left in the industry. The large companies which survived into the present century were the Colonial Company, Curtis Campbell, Sandbach Parker, Booker Brothers, H. K. Davson, and Ewing and Company. These entities reinvested accumulated profits and also drew upon investment funds available to them in the London money market. In either event, they were making investment decisions based on the calculation of the rate of interest and the rate of profit on a global scale. The times were not very propitious for Guiana. As capitalism completed its social and political domination of the world, the sugar industry of British Guiana (and the British West Indies) appeared very unattractive relative to other possibilities in Africa, Asia, and parts of the Americas.

That there was a change in Guiana's international status during the years of depression, and the period when capitalism completed the imperialist organization of production, is strikingly illustrated by the calculations and actions of Quintin Hogg. In 1880, Hogg wrote his brother from Ceylon, "On the whole I would rather live in Demerara than in Ceylon, and I would not give Golden Fleece for the best estate in the island."[53] By 1897, however, Quintin Hogg was disenchanted with Plantation Golden Fleece and other properties in Guiana, although the cost of production had been reduced from £20-25 per ton in 1881-82 to less than £10 per ton in 1886-87 (i.e., from as high as $120 per ton in 1881-82 to $48 per ton in 1886-87). When Quintin Hogg appeared before the West India Commission, he still had most of his personal property and shares in Guiana, St. Kitts, St. Lucia, and Jamaica, but he was redeploying his sugar profits to the East Indies. He explained that he was interested neither in further sugar investments (given the bounties and the low returns) nor in opening up other enterprises in Guiana and the West Indies. In the East Indies, Hogg was planting coffee, or alternatively, when the coffee market was unfavorable, tea. The transition from crisis-hit coffee to tea was easily made in Ceylon because the inexpensive coffee plant was written off with little loss, and labor was much cheaper than in the West Indies. Quintin Hogg made his position quite clear to the West India Commission:

> I myself have just gone in for a block of land in the Malay peninsula for putting in coffee, exactly the coffee I should put in Demerara. I pay for my labour there 4 pence or 5 pence per day. What should I go and put coffee in Demerara? My machinery will not serve me, and I should have to pay double and treble for my labour to what I should have to pay in the East.

With a long-term investor like Quintin Hogg minimizing holdings in Guiana and investing in another section of the expanding imperialist economy, it is not surprising that new capital was not enamored of Guiana and the British

West Indies, and that the region commanded an ever decreasing share of world trade.[54]

As already indicated, West Indian planters could not win concessions from the British government in opposition to important domestic interests in the United Kingdom. The hopelessness of the position did not stop the planters from bombarding the imperial legislature with petitions asking for more favorable terms of entry for cane sugar and also for rum. However, the only effective manipulation of international markets came when planters could seize whatever opportunities were offered by capitalist market forces and conflicting national and class objectives within the international arena. Specialization in Demerara yellow crystals rather than muscovado was an initiative that secured profits for the British Guiana sugar industry in the latter part of the nineteenth century of offering a "direct consumption sugar" that was popular in British grocery stores. Demerara yellow did not have to compete against refining sugars, and it did so well relative to refined beet that sellers of the latter at times sought to imitate Demerara yellow crystals.[55]

Demerara yellow also briefly made its mark on the North American market in the 1860s. A market was opened in New York and the Eastern states for high-class crystallized sguar, consequent upon the closing of the Louisiana plantations during the Civil War. However, as had occurred in Britain at a much earlier date, refiners lobbied against high-class grocery sugar that needed no further refinement. This led to a change of tariff in 1872. Thereafter, tariff structures in North America favored the importation of low-grade raw sugars for refining, the grades being defined by color in accordance with the conventional "Dutch Standard." Given the slight freight advantage in shipping to the United States and Canada rather than Britain, plantation owners in Guiana also responded to this new demand. The concentration on producing dark cyrstals for sale in North America became a matter of the greatest relevance to the subsequent history of sugar in British Guiana. The gray refining crystals were also the product of vacuum pan and centrifugals, but they were clarified differently. Both the cost of production and the quality were only slightly lower than in the case of yellow crystals. It was possible to obtain a high polarization of sugar while retaining the dark color held to be characteristic of low grades. Starting in the late 1870s, exporters in Georgetown teamed with certain import firms in the United States of America to exploit the loophole in the tariff regulations. Dark refining crystals equivalent to the middle or upper grades of the Dutch Standard were treated as low grades for customs purposes, thereby evading duty to the tune of roughly 1½ cents on each pound. The United States Treasury Department was not amused. An official complaint was lodged with the British government in 1879, alleging that sugars in Guiana were being prepared especially for the United States market with intent to defraud. Consignments of dark crystals were seized at the ports of entry by injunctions of the Treasury Department, and scores of lawsuits resulted. Charges and counter charges, commissions of enquiry and legal proceedings were part of the complex episode known locally as "The Dark Sugars Question," which was paramount between 1879 and 1883.[56]

United States Treasury Department injunctions failed to stand in court, but planters realized that the market was precarious unless firm agreements could be reached at governmental level. Hence the concern to negotiate a treaty with the United States of America embodying reciprocal tariff concessions. "Reciprocity" became the password for the whole of the two decades following the price fall of 1884 (a period that was also characterized by the most intense competition from subsidized beet). Britain was prevailed upon to negotiate on behalf of the West Indian colonies in 1883-84, but the effort was abortive. The question was not officially reopened until the passage of the McKinley Tariff by the United States in 1891. This measure specifically invited reciprocity, and the British Guiana legislature quickly offered concessions.[57] For British Guiana, as for the rest of the West Indies, the United States market was hailed as the savior during the last years of the nineteenth century, since it rapidly surpassed the "home" market for West Indian sugar in the United Kingdom. This was possible even at the height of beet subsidies since the United States tariffs neutralized the bounties to some extent and since cane sugar was preferred to beet sugar by United States manufacturers of syrups. Canada was next in line to become the major purchaser of sugar from British Guiana. The Canadian market was so insignificant before the turn of the present century that West Indian planters turned down Canadian initiatives to sign reciprocity agreements for fear that these might prejudice their share of the much more substantial United States market. However, Canada dramatically entered the picture in 1903 and rapidly asserted its preeminence as a West Indian sugar buyer. (See table A7). Predictably, the politics of the planter class in British Guiana thereafter revolved around Canada whenever issues of foreign trade and tariffs were being discussed.

Specific market shifts—from Britain to the United States, and eventually to Canada—did not alter the essentials of market dependency. The politics of trade in British Guiana were always reactive and accommodative. For instance, the United States administration was constantly changing its tariff policy in the light of domestic sugar production in Louisiana, the presence of United States capital in certain sugar-growing territories, and the action of European beet exporters. There were important United States tariff acts in 1894 and 1897 which nullified the effects of the brief reciprocity of 1891-93, and there were many years in which West Indian legislatures hopefully dangled tariff concessions to no avail. To a great extent, the opening of the United States market to larger quantities of West Indian sugar in the late 1890s was merely incidental to the United States policy of protection against bounty-fed beet sugar. The 27 percent surcharge which was placed on the entry of beet sugar gave producers in the British West Indies the necessary margin to compete successfully.[58] The sudden expansion of the Canadian market was even more clearly a consequence of forces entirely beyond the control of the legislature in British Guiana. Up until 1902, imports of German sugar into Canada were worth about three million (Canadian) dollars per annum; but Germany refused to admit Canadian agricultural imports under the favorable conditions of the German Conventional Tariff. Canada retaliated in 1903 with penalties on German commodities, including a surtax of 33 percent on beet sugar. It was under these circumstances that the bulk of the British Guiana crop found its way to Canada that year. Once the particular orientation was created, it then become a priority in Guiana and in London to ensure that, irrespective of further changes in relations between Canada and its trading partners, the position of cane sugar would be guaranteed by negotiated preferences.[59]

The fact that the working people took practically no part in resolving any of the above issues is no measure of the importance of external pressures on their day-to-day lives. On the contrary, capitalist slumps and market crises struck at the very fundamentals of working class existence—namely the right to work and the right to earn a living wage. Given that the sugar industry was by far the largest employer of labor in the nineteenth century, and given the limited alternatives available, estate labor that was made redundant by sugar crises was in a desperate situation. Abandonment, amalgamation, and factory modernization all contributed to a shrinkage in the number of employment opportunities. Between 1892 and 1900, the factories of no fewer than forty-one estates were dismantled. Of these estates, twenty-one passed more or less out of cultivation and the remaining twenty were amalgamated with adjacent estates. The situation stabilized somewhat thereafter, but another five estates passed out of cultivation by December 1906.[60] Factory labor was hit hardest by the abandonment of a number of "grinding estates" and by the introduction of labor-saving machinery. Field labor suffered most from underemployment, seasonal unemployment, and the need to relocate or become temporary migrants in search of jobs. All categories of workers as well as peasants together bore the burden of reduction in wage rates, diminution in earnings, and increase in indirect taxation that were features of this crisis-ridden period.

Spokesmen for Booker Brothers accept that the largely political see saw of prices and production brought hardship and a low standard of living as the lot of the colonial laborer. They note that "the two-fold problem of the sea and the floods is still with us," but that "the problems of the world market have perhaps proved the more intractable." For the purposes of the present analysis, it is unnecessary to seek to assign priority between the two sets of factors which have initially been conceptualized as constituting internal and external constraints. Operationally, the two were often merged, because dependency was not simply a matter of foreign trade but was reflected in and supported by the internal socioeconomic structures. In turn, the response to the environment was socially determined as well as being ultimately limited by the restricted freedom of British Guiana. But these constraints were certainly preponderant influences on the lives of the working people at each stage of their development, their weight being most painfully evident when flood or drought coincided with international depression.

CHAPTER 2

The Evolution of the Plantation Labor Force in the Nineteenth Century

> I come from the nigger yard of yesterday
> Leaping from the oppressors hate
> And the scorn of myself;
> From the agony of the dark hut in the shadow
> And the hurt of things.
>
> *Martin Carter*

Endemic slave revolts during the 1820s had taught the lesson that slavery as a form of control over labor was proving uneconomical and unstable.[1] Nevertheless, slavery ended when it did in the West Indies mainly because of having exhausted itself politically and economically in terms of the system of international exchange. That exhaustion brought with it a greater exposure of the local situation to international scrutiny and intervention, but it did not alter the political structures. The extent to which an alteration of legal status was transformed into substantial social change was determined by the class struggle in the post-Emancipation era. Antislavery propaganda supposedly made the Colonial Office more anxious than ever before to act as trustee on behalf of the freed community, but in practice the metropolitan officials did very little to redress the political imbalance between planter and former slave.

In Guiana, planters who had invested in polders, land, slaves, and machinery were not defeated and crushed locally by the slave masses. They remained firmly in control of the post-Emancipation legislature and were confirmed in the ownership of all property except the slaves. Thus, this dominant social class was both able and willing to maintain the realization of profits, while making the minimum of concessions to the newly emancipated population. The latter in turn responded by continuing their struggle with the plantation owners under radically transformed legal conditions but under the same material circumstances. No major shifts in the production process were registered in British Guiana during the second quarter of the nineteenth

31

century. Cutlass, fork, and shovel were the basic tools of the field; and this rudimentary technology was the basis of the piecework or taskwork organization of labor into weeding gangs, shovel gangs, fork-molding gangs, and the like. The element of continuity was especially marked because neither of the two contending classes under slavery proved capable of sustaining a commitment to a modern system of "free labour" in the post-Emancipation era.

Under classic capitalism, labor is "free" in a dual sense, as elaborated upon by Marx. Firstly, the laborer has been divested of ownership of the means of survival. In this connection, the more eloquent formulation is that of the "naked worker" rather than the "free worker." Secondly, the laborer is free to sell labor as a commodity on a market comprising different employers.[2] The worker thereby earns all of his necessary upkeep, although his surplus is of course alienated. This schema of free labor became characteristic of factory relations in capitalist centers of the nineteenth century. The young and growing capitalist system of commodity production was quite capable of extending itself via the master class of the slave society of the Americas, in spite of such precapitalist tendencies as were retained by the slave masters.[3] In the postslavery epoch, planters were bitterly opposed to the untrammeled operation of free wage labor, while the former slaves were equally resistant to that aspect of the free labor system that demanded total alienation of workers from land ownership.

Planters discouraged the mobility of workers. They first devised the strategy of "apprenticeship" to keep laborers tied to the estates on which they had been slaves. On the termination of apprenticeship on 1 August 1838, workers demanded more than employers were prepared to pay and they began exercising a greater degree of independence than the estates would tolerate. The struggle that resulted, and that assumed the form of protracted sugar strikes in 1842 and 1848, strengthened the determination of planters to secure immigrant laborers whose conditions of indentured service excluded the right to seek out new employers and whose wage rates were also statutorily restricted. It is significant that the first experiment in 1838 with Indian indentured labor was terminated by the British government because of substantiated allegations as to the neo-slave nature of indentureship; and ex-slaves were among those who testified that the first Indian arrivals were treated in precisely the same manner as Africans under slavery.[4]

Former slaves immediately mobilized for increases in the basic apprenticeship wages of thirty-two cents per day for general field labor and forty-eight cents per day for common factory hands. Women and children started withdrawing from the fields and there was a general reduction of labor at times when it was most needed. These attempts to lay down terms were met by combination on the part of estate proprietors to restrict wages and introduce intimidatory work codes. An extremely severe code was formulated in December 1841 and was to have been introduced throughout Demerara and

Essequibo. Sugar workers coordinated their opposition in a strike that lasted for twelve to thirteen weeks.[5] Less than three years after being emancipated from slavery, the new wage-earning class was acting in certain respects like a modern proletariat; and the first recorded strike in the history of the Guyanese working class was a success, leading to the withdrawal of the planters' labor code and the continuation of the moderately increased wage rate.

The most acute class conflict of the post-Emancipation decade took place in 1848. Estate owners once more collaborated to reduce wages, and workers again responded by withholding their labor during the first months of 1848. The decisive factor in the eventual defeat of the Creole African strikers was the presence of alternative labor controlled by the estates. In 1846 a total of 5,975 Portuguese were brought from Madeira—this being the highest annual figure for Portuguese indentured immigration between 1835 and its termination in 1882. Having been resumed in 1845, Indian immigration reached the notable figure of 4,019 in 1846, while 1,097 Africans were also landed. Such work as was done on the estates during the 1848 strike was performed by the new immigrants.[6] The planters had found their supply of "bound" laborers. The sugar planters were also given permission by the metropolitan power to use the colony's resources to partially subsidize the importation of their "bound" labor. Within very wide limits, the local legislature was allowed free rein to regulate legal conditions that governed the deployment of labor. This meant that the political hegemony of the planter class guaranteed that the class struggle at the point of production would be conditioned primarily by legal sanctions rather than by the operation of market forces as such.

An indentured laborer was always a recent immigrant, bonded to work on a given plantation for a fixed number of years at a stipulated rate of pay. Consolidation of the immigration ordinances of British Guiana in 1864 confirmed the period as being five years, while allowing for the possibility of voluntary reindenture for another five years. African immigration into the Colony ended in 1864, after having made a notable contribution to labor supplies from the 1840s. Chinese immigration reached its peak in the early 1860s, but ceased in 1866—apart from sporadic entries subsequently. Portuguese immigration was numerically insignificant between 1865 and 1882, although its social implications were important. West Indian islanders added to the variety of migrants reaching British Guiana, and they constituted a factor to be reckoned with during the period under discussion. However, the history of indentured labor is dominated by the activity of the total of 228,743 Indians introduced between 1851 and 1917—the years of uninterrupted annual shipments.[7]

Throughout the 1880s and most of the 1890s, British Guiana continued to be the main destination of contract emigrants from India. Drought, famine, and distress in British India provided the context in which emigration agents and recruiters lured members of the rural population to undertake the journey across the "black water." The importation level of about 4,900 per annum for the decade 1870-79 was an unusually high one. The average was approximately 3,900 per annum for the years 1860-69, 1880-89, and 1890-99; and it dropped to about 2,500 in the following decade. The last indentures in British Guiana were canceled on 15 April 1920. Right up until that moment, the plantation labor force comprised three distinct sections: firstly, indentured laborers who were predominantly Indian; secondly, free estate residents who were usually time-expired immigrants and their Creole descendants; and thirdly, Creole villagers who were mainly African. Each section had its own role, although the proportions were not always the same and important changes were noticeable during the last two decades of the nineteenth century. (For other demographic characteristics of the work force during this period, see table A8.)

By 1880, indentured Indians were already outnumbered by unindentured Indians resident on plantations. Immigrants under indenture comprised less than one sixth of the resident estate population in 1905. (See table A9.) Nevertheless, this form of "bound" labor continued to function as the basis upon which the plantation work force was constructed. They were the lowest paid group of workers. Reform legislation in 1893 stated that after the immigrant had been at work for forty-two hours and had earned $1.50, he could claim leave for the balance of the week. The figure of $1.50 seems to have been accepted as a desirable minimum weekly earning, but this was purely notional. The legal minimum was the provision of taskwork that was worth 24 cents per day and that would have yielded $1.20 in a week of five work days. Estate pay-lists for 1880 suggest that indentured laborers were earning between $50 and $88 per year.[8]

Newcomers to Guiana were the ones at the lower end of the scale of earnings. This was so because unseasoned immigrants were more likely to miss work from illness, they could not complete tasks as quickly as they would do after some experience, and they were not ready to tackle more robust or more skilled jobs such as cane-cutting and punt-loading.[9] However, it must be clearly understood that there was never any increase in the statutory minimum rate for indentured laborers, neither during the duration of a bond nor over the course of indentureship as an institution. By definition, this category of labor was removed from normal market forces and the figure of twenty-four cents or one shilling per day should be borne constantly in mind as the best to which most indentured workers were allowed to aspire as they labored to fulfill the routine field tasks of weeding, manuring, forking and the like.

Weekly earnings were never static, although they fluctuated within narrow limits. The weekly payout to each worker—both bonded and free—depended upon the number of tasks offered, the nature of the tasks, and the speed with which they were completed. Annual reports of the immigration agent-general were not very helpful in the matter of earnings. In a stereotyped and perhaps deliberately ambiguous manner, the reports tended to assert that sufficient work was provided so that the industrious immigrant could have earned at least the legal minimum of twenty-four cents per day and probably more. No attempt was made to come to grips with the many obstacles which stood between this possibility and its fulfillment. Governor Irving (1882-87) censured the immigration agent-general for a lax approach to this question and correctly emphasized the distinction between the *legal rate of wages* and the *actual earnings* of indentured laborers. (For actual estate wages see table A10.) "It is precisely because earnings are not and cannot be regulated by law that they should be the subject of watchfulness on the part of the Immigration agent-general," wrote Irving to the Colonial Office in March 1887.[10] Comments such as these were generated because of the crisis in the sugar industry. They started at the end of 1884, when it was officially being admitted that immigrant earnings "were leaning towards the lower end of the scale."[11] This rather delicate observation was put in a more matter-of-fact manner in the months that lay ahead between the first sharp fall in sugar prices in 1884 and the partial recovery in 1889.

Large numbers of immigrants were imported in 1884 and 1885 out of profits acquired before the effects of the price fall were strongly felt. This numerous indentured labor force was seldom fully employed in the years between 1886 and 1889. Of course, the workers remained legally tied to their respective estates for the duration of their bond, but they had to accept cuts in tasks offered and in money earned. In June 1886, and again in March 1887, the governor reviewed the labor situation on the estates, with the aid of assessments submitted by the district immigration agents. The process of cutting back on tasks and reducing employment had been carried to such an extent on Plantation Bel Air that one of the immigration agents declared that it was a puzzle to him to know how some of the immigrants existed, since he judged earnings "insufficient to support life."[12] When the agent-general was asked to enquire on how many estates the earnings of indentured laborers had fallen below subsistence level, he blustered and fumed in the planter interest and did not carry out the assignment.

The muster rolls at Plantation Bel Air showed an alarming proportion of days when the indentured servants were absent from work. Most of these absences were enforced rather than being the choice of the workers. Under normal circumstances, planters gave indentured laborers as much work as possible and paid higher amounts to nonindentured Indians or to Africans only to the extent that this was unavoidable for certain field and factory tasks. The circumstances of international depression paradoxically made free labor cheaper than bound labor in some instances. Low sugar prices and retrenchment on the estates meant that the general wage rate for free agricultural laborers went down by a third between 1884 and 1886 and began to compare unfavorably with the minimum guaranteed to the indentured laborer. Free labor was therefore being substituted for indentured labor. The governor's explanation of this phenomenon was very much to the point. He wrote (in January 1889):

> At the present moment the market price of free labour is unusually low, and whenever the price of free labour falls below the minimum daily wage fixed by law for indentured labour it is hardly to be expected that pressure will be constantly exercised by managers to compel the indentured labourers to earn even the *minimum* rate of wages.[13]

Since the economic crisis of the 1890s hit employers more severely than ever before, it also affected workers more adversely than ever before. By 1896, indentured laborers were earning pittances not only because of production cuts and fewer offers of task work but also because some planters were prepared to ignore the legal minima. Evidence to this effect was disclosed during the enquiry which resulted from rioting and loss of life on the part of the indentured workers of Plantation Non Pareil in October 1896. Gooljar, spokesman for the immigrants, declared, "Times were very hard . . . we cannot live on the wages we are getting; our stomachs are not being filled."[14] Punt-loaders, cane-cutters, and weeders were not being given sufficient work and the task rates (which had already declined 20 percent compared with 1894 rates) were slashed at the beginning of October 1896. Earnings of indentured field hands were between forty cents and seventy cents per week at Non Pareil—figures which were not atypical for the sugar belt as a whole. The arbitrator of the Non Pareil dispute was the manager of Windsor Forest. With the exception of weeding, he found the task rates at Non Pareil adequate. However, it emerged that he himself had just previously reduced the Windsor Forest rates in a similar manner.

Since the plantations were supposed to provide free housing and medical facilities for indentured workers, this represented another mechanism which raised or lowered living standards. The colonial state was seldom as insistent as it might have been to ensure that planters honored their obligation to provide proper housing and medical facilities for immigrants. An unusually energetic agent-general or an unusually concerned governor tended to expose and partially remedy abuses in this connection; but the two did not necessarily occur at the same time. Complicity between the immigration agent-general and the plantocracy helped frustrate enquiries such as one made by the governor in 1886 requesting a report on deaths that had occurred without the deceased estate residents having seen a doctor in the course of their illness.[15]

Free social services must be added to the earnings of indentured laborers to arrive at their share of the product of their own labor. Yet it was the paucity of these services which constantly gave rise to comment. A report by the medical inspector in 1886 linked poor sanitation on the estates with high

'Nigger Yard,' 'Coolie Yard,' or 'Bound Yard.'
Estate tenement houses, or logies.

mortality. The tenement ranges or logies of the inherited "nigger yard" were unventilated, the water supply was polluted and lavatory facilities nonexistent.[16] Consequently, disease outbreaks tended to assume epidemic proportions. Estates in Essequibo were singled out for unfavorable attention, one of the worst offenders being Plantation Henrietta on the island of Leguan, where residents drank water from a pond dug between the logies in close proximity to feces scattered on the ground. When such cases came to light, the government made demands for reforms or for compliance with existing regulations. But constant reiteration of the same kind of complaint indicates that the situation was generally poor and that proprietors were not persuaded to invest substantially in services for the improvement of the health of the resident estate laborers, in spite of regulations placed on the statute books since the Des Voeux Commission of 1871. Governor Gormanston inherited the administrative responsibility for such problems when he assumed office early in 1888. In one of his first dispatches he remarked: "I have observed with surprise that among the enactments of the Immigration Ordinance No. 7 of 1873 which have been neglected must be included the cardinal provisions of section 119 and 135. Under section 135 no regulations have ever been made, as designed, for the proper construction, arrangement and drainage of the dwellings of indentured immigrants."[17]

Plantation Chateau Margot, East Coast Demerara. Ceased to be a grinding estate in the present century. One of the towers still stands on the site.

It cost during the 1800s on average $82 to introduce a fresh immigrant. An indentured Indian whose contract had expired could claim the right of a free return passage at a cost of another $60.[18] The planter had to meet the outlay on social services as well as the hidden expenses of "seasoning" a fresh immigrant. Against this expenditure, one must reckon the savings in low wages paid to indentured workers and the savings implicit in the lowering of the wage rate for the remaining sections of the labor force.

Estate managers and proprietors sometimes openly avowed that indentured labor was cheapest and best. In October 1886, G. R. Sandbach indicated to his Liverpool home office that labor charges had to be reduced and that the most effective way of so doing was to increase the indentured gang relative to the free Creoles. He explained that "so long as an estate has a large Coolie gang, Creoles must give way in prices asked or see the work done by indentured labourers—and this is a strong reason why the number of Coolies on estates must not be reduced."[19] An English visitor to Sandbach Parker's Plantation Diamond in 1891 was made aware of the three categories of labor—indentured, Indian residents unindentured, and African villagers—and was informed that the indentured were counted most profitable.[20] Yet planters and their spokesmen were also prepared to affirm that immigrant labor was costly. In such cases, they drew attention to the expenses of recruitment, transportation, housing, and hospitals, as well as to the investment occasioned by the seasoning process during the first year of the immigrant's stay. By the turn of the present century, it had become commonplace to emphasize that indentured labor was expensive. The manager of Plantation Cove and John sought in June 1903 to expose what he termed the fallacy of indentured labor being cheap. He calculated that the planters' contribution to immigration added 25 percent to their wage bill.[21] Another important proprietor claimed that in 1910 (when the cost of production of sugar was about $50 per ton), the costs of immigration accounted for $4.80 per ton.[22]

What is significant about this paradoxical presentation of low-wage immigrant labor as "expensive" is the clear admission that indentured labor had as its ultimate function the guaranteeing of planter *control* over the entire labor process, and that this alone justified the continuation of indentureship, irrespective of the cost to the individual proprietor and to the general taxpayer. Of course, planters were determined to use their political power in the legislature to ensure that indentured immigration was not *for them as private capitalists* an uneconomic undertaking. They shielded themselves (with metropolitan help) from the full cost of indentureship. At no time after 1878 did they pay more than two-thirds of the immigration bill; and, at moments of acute distress during the 1890s, the colonial state lightened that load through deferred payments, loans, and grants, and also by transferring part of the monetary burden of repatriation on to the immigrants themselves. The planters would have gone further, if they could. In 1899, and again in 1903, India rejected the proposal made by the West Indian colonists that they be relieved of payment of any portion of the return passage.

Estate production in the Guianas was initiated through the ownership of slaves. The analogy between slavery and indenture has been drawn on numerous occasions. It is one that comes easily, since indenture followed so closely on slavery, and since it can scarcely be denied that hangovers from the slavery epoch were present in the attitudes and practices of the plantation owners. Peter Ruhomon, one of the first Creole Indian historians of indenture, asserts unequivocally that "no trick of sophistry or twist of logic . . . can ever avail to defend the system of semi-slavery paraded under the guise of indentured immigration, under which Indians were brought to the Colony to labour on the sugar plantations, in the interests of a powerful and privileged body of capitalists."[23] More than anything else, it was the regimented social and industrial control which caused indenture to approximate so closely to slavery.

Indentured labor was accessible to its employer all the year round, which was of paramount importance during the most hectic portion of the agricultural year when the canes had to be cut and (shortly thereafter) when a certain proportion of new canes had to be planted. In any given week of the agricultural cycle, the indentured laborer was potentially available for six days. On any given day, the indentured servant could be dragged forcibly from the logies to present himself or herself when tasks were being assigned for the day. Some fifteen hours of work and travel would usually have elapsed before the return to the logies, while the comparable expenditure of time during the grinding season was twenty to twenty-two hours. Besides, there was hardly any scope for objecting to the type of task which was distributed and to the rate of pay considered adequate for the particular job. Legal control of the indentured portion of estate labor gave to employers a remarkable advantage in imposing their version of industrial discipline.

William des Voeux had testified that many planters cynically declared that indentured immigrants on their estates must always be actually at work or in hospital or in jail. Many who should have been in hospital were out in the fields. Doctors in charge of estate hospitals were also employees of the estates, and were prone to certify sick indentured laborers as fit for duty—either refusing them entry into hospital or discharging them prematurely. The courts of law provided the final sanction for ensuring that indentured laborers were available every season, every week, and every day. An unexplained absence was classed as "desertion," and like all other breaches of civil contract on the part of the laborer, absence constituted a criminal offense punishable by a fine or imprisonment.

The fate of indentured servants under the law can be partly ascertained by consulting surviving documentation under "criminal statistics"—e.g., the record for 1881 of summary convictions in the magistrates' courts.[24] The law had that year defined 3,168 indentured workers as criminals because of their struggles with capital at the point of production. The law had further summarily dispatched 532 of these workers to prison and imposed on 1,577 others fines of such severity that they often accepted the option of imprisonment. For those who went to prison, the distinction between convict labor and indentured labor was erased, because they performed their hard labor on the estates on pain of further conviction. No doubt without meaning to do so, officials thereby correctly equated indentured labor with convict labor. Only one other group of summary offenses rivaled breaches of the Masters and Servants Act—namely, offenses against the person. The priority changed in some years, as in 1882, when 3,495 indentured immigrants were convicted for contract offenses and 3,472 persons were convicted for offenses against the person. Besides, summary imprisonment was more often meted out for convictions under the labor laws. (For detailed statistics of convictions and penalties in these and the following years, see tables A11-A13.)

Surgeon-Major Comins conducted official enquiries into immigration in 1891. Although he was strongly in favor of continued indentureship, Comins mentioned that half of the Indians in the Georgetown jail were convicted under the immigration and labor laws.[25] In like manner, the Sanderson Commission of 1910 showed a decidedly proplanter bias but felt bound to draw attention to the high incidence of prosecutions of indentured immigrants for labor offenses. The rate of prosecution and conviction, expressed as a percentage of the indentured population, had been on the increase during the last two decades of the nineteenth century and had reached a peak toward the end of the period under discussion. When compared with other territories using indentured labor, British Guiana was also the worst offender with regard to the use of the criminal courts to enforce the rights of employers against the laborers. The Sanderson Commission Chose the year 1907 to illustrate this point.[26]

	Indentured Adults	Convictions under Labor Laws (no./%)
British Guiana	9,784	2,019(20%)
Trinidad	11,506	1,869(16)
Jamaica	2,832	237(8)
Fiji	10,181	2,091(20)
Mauritius	47,000	1,492(3)

There were exceptional instances when justice was on the side of the immigrants and when court officials felt obliged to disassociate themselves from the general position taken within the legal system. They then incurred the wrath of the planters for revealing what the reality was like.[27] A petition signed by overseers of the East Bank Demerara estates reached the legislature in November 1881. It asked for the removal of Magistrate Hastings Huggins and a tightening of procedures at Providence Court. Huggins replied that Providence Court already had virtually no function other than to discipline immigrants, and he denounced the planter-inspired petition for requesting greater facilities for the punishment of laborers. This magistrate had given sympathetic hearing to applications brought before him by immigrants against employers with respect to disputed wages, and he had refused to exact exorbitant fines from indentured laborers whom he found guilty of breach of contract. Managers and overseers criticized him for unduly lenient sentences such as a one-dollar fine and 72 cents costs, with an alternative of seven days imprisonment—for the offense of one day's absence from work. Huggins explained that this was serious punishment, because an able-bodied male indentured laborer seldom earned more than the minimum statutory payment of 24 cents per day. Therefore, the fine plus costs (totaling $1.72) constituted the exaction of seven days of unpaid labor.[28]

Magistrate Huggins also criticized the socio-economic system as it affected women under indenture. He noted that women often earned between 48 cents and 60 cents for a week's hard work. In a judgment in favor of a female plaintiff who sued for wages, Huggins went so far as to justify equality of sexes before the law. "I know of no principle of law or of equity," he said, "which would justify me in awarding to a female—forsooth she happens to be a woman—for the *same* amount of work, a *less* amount of wages."[29] Understandably, this progressive sentiment earned general acceptance neither in colonial Guiana nor in the colonizing society of Great Britain. Discrimination against female indentured workers persisted because planters assigned women to the weeding gang and other low-paying jobs and because women were given less when they performed the same field tasks as men. Indeed, one of the backward characteristics of indentured labor was the employment of a significant proportion of low-paid women and juveniles—all constrained to undertake arduous and often undignified tasks in order to try and build the subsistence earnings of the family.

Periods of absence from work (when proved in court) and terms of imprisonment were excluded when calculating the five years of the indenture bond.[30] Apart from serious illness, the indentured immigrant placed his labor power at the unqualified disposal of the employer for every working day of the five-year period. This the law guaranteed. The law also helped to create a situation in which planters could increase the intensity of the exploitation of indentured labor by using their power to define a "task." It was common knowledge within the sugar industry that a specific task, such as the forking or banking of a given number of "openings," would vary in onerousness and time required for completion according to the location of the beds, the state of the access dams, and the overall weather conditions.* Experienced managers and overseers were as cognizant of these niceties as the workers themselves, and sometimes they made the appropriate allowances. However, indentured immigrants were vulnerable to coercion from overseers and drivers. Therefore, they often had to accept unfair tasks and a proportionately decreased rate of earning. When a manager authorized a hopelessly unrealistic task (and paid as though it were normative), the immigrant could successfully challenge this before a magistrate only by bringing a manager from another estate to give evidence evaluating the task in his favor. Very rarely did the planting fraternity expose anything other than a common front. Managers could produce overseers, drivers, and other dependents to testify; and evidence given by whites was almost invariably accepted as the truth. One immigration agent-general conceded that overseers made it their duty to secure convictions, and he gave his opinion that "this taking of evidence for granted is the bane of justice, as between class and class."[31]

The significance of the legal and industrial control which employers exercised over indentured workers emerges fully when a comparison is drawn between "bound" labor and the two remaining categories of estate labor. Village labor was furthest removed from legal bondage. The free village movement of the middle years of the nineteenth century gave to the African estate worker a partial independence, deriving from residence outside the plantation "nigger yards" as well as from alternative subsistence activities.

_____

*Two cane rows and two intervening banks or clear spaces formed one opening.

Village laborers could bargain, they could specialize in certain tasks, and they could influence the weekly and seasonal deployment of their own labor power on the estate.

The organizational feature that distinguished village labor was the indepen-dent task-gang. Independent "jobbing" gangs emerged during slavery in the West Indies, being hired out by their owners to planters who were short of labor. The independent task-gang under the leadership of one of the worker members was of course a post-Emancipation development. Creole Africans in British Guiana constituted themselves into task-gangs and negotiated with management to have some control over wages, conditions, and duration of work.[32] They moved from estate to estate in the search for better rates; they haggled over the definition of given tasks; and they sought to use the state of the weather or the necessity of the planters to extract some advantage. Above all, village labor aimed at subordinating the requirements of the estate to the rhythms of village life. Their own garden plots, their minor subsistence en-deavors and their estimate of necessary relaxation came before the time and motion of the plantation. Except in dire necessity, villagers never entered into contracts with the estates—preferring simply to reopen bargaining at the beginning of each working week.

Village labor won innumerable small skirmishes in its confrontation with estate capital. Ultimately, however, capital remained in the ascendancy. The presence of indentured labor and the almost endemic crisis of sugar prices were the factors which principally assisted capital in its domination of labor. Most planters aimed at paying villagers thirty-two cents for a day's task. Although higher than the rate for indentured laborers, this was the payment at the beginning of apprenticeship. It remained in operation well into the present century, being cut with each price fall and being restored or raised only through struggle when labor market conditions allowed.

The elected village councils of the nineteenth century were organs of democratic expression, and they usually came into conflict with the govern-ment department or official entrusted with supervision of the villages. In 1879, the inspector of villages portrayed the councillors as being "a great hindrance to the welfare of the villages," and to substantiate this denuncia-tion, he charged that councillors encouraged laborers to hold out for wages which were higher than those obtainable on the estates.[33] The inference is clear: planters and African villagers had conflicting appraisals of what consti-tuted a "decent" living wage—a concept that must be based on minimum objective standards of physiological subsistence but which in the final analysis is socially, culturally, and historically determined.

Creole Africans (and eventually all Creoles) spurned the planter-initiated version of the living wage. In this respect, they were in a somewhat stronger position than that proportion of the estate labor force, who were bound like serfs. But the fortunes of the two sections were interdependent, because the overall stagnation of the wage rate for Creoles was closely tied to the fact that indentureship altered the market conditions for free labor in favor of the planters. So long as each estate had its indentured gang, then it was fortified to deal with the independent task-gangs. Theoretically, the choice was between not earning or earning the low wages which indentureship permitted. Villagers were forced to compromise. In November 1880, the Governor and legislature were presented with a petition "in the name of artisans, shopkeepers, peasants and labourers," drafted by a Creole African, A. S. Moore. The petitioner graphically depicted the dilemma of village labor attempting to operate in a market heavily influenced by indentured labor. He stated that "peasant labourers hesitate between starvation and the price which these [immigrants] in their serfdom are compelled to take."[34]

The above dilemma was tolerably resolved by estate workers or "peasant labourers," who had a reasonable foothold in the peasant sector and who therefore considered estate wages as a minor supplement. However, African villagers dependent on estate wages took the course of seeking the better-paid jobs, given that there was always a wide variation in payment according to the nature of the tasks in the field and the factory. As was to be expected, remuneration was highest for the performance of skilled tasks. Creole villagers gravitated toward the higher end of the wage scale, mainly because of advantages derived from previously accumulated experience and skill. Even under slavery, skill was recognized and rewarded in the case of artisans and those workers engaged in the sensitive processes of sugar manufacture. A considerable differential existed between the wages of skilled categories and those of the common field or factory hand throughout the post-Emancipation years. In 1884, craftsmen such as blacksmiths, boatbuilders, carpenters, and coopers were earning $1.33 per day or roughly four times the pay of a common field laborer.[35] Pan-boilers were the most distinguished of the skilled hands employed by the sugar plantations, and their high earnings during the grinding season reflected their value.

Between 1881 and 1905 and for many years subsequently, the factory remained a preserve of village labor. Field labor was less popular with Creole Africans, because it was less remunerative. The lowest paid estate job has always been weeding—followed by manuring, forking, banking, and cleaning trenches. Africans were sparsely represented in these occupations by the second half of the nineteenth century. On the other hand, field labor such as cane-cutting, punt-loading and the digging of trenches could offer as much as three or four times the wages for unskilled field labor; and it was in the fulfilment of these functions that African Sugar workers continued to play a strategically decisive role.

After several years residence in the colony, the Rev. H. V. Bronkhurst published a text on the laboring population of British Guiana in 1883. He listed the work done by Africans as the application of fertilizers in the field,

*Characteristic transport of canes in iron punts drawn by mules walking
along the canal dams*

the carrying of bagasse in the buildings, the digging of trenches, and other jobs requiring the use of the shovel.[36] The close association of African villagers with shovel work is not surprising in view of the historical experience of digging canals and making dams; and they enjoyed the reputation of having considerable experience in the use of long-handled shovels to dig heavy lumps of mud and throw them accurately over a distance of several yards to build the parapets. There were also frequent comments on the leading role of African villagers as cane-cutters. They kept their cutlasses in perfect order and they tended to earn 50 percent more than other laborers offered the same tasks at the same rate.[37]

Creole Africans moved away from the fields because most of the skilled and better-paid jobs were available in the factory. For the significant number who remained within the fields, it was necessary to avoid if possible the pittance offered to weeders, just as it was essential to strive to be hired as cane-cutters. The choice facing village labor is well illustrated by the wage rates prevailing in 1889, which was an average or normal year in between two serious slumps. For praedials, the daily rates ranged from 20 to 96 cents: weeders, 20 to 32 cents; shovelmen, 24 to 48 cents; puntmen, 32 to 48 cents; and cane-cutters, 48 to 96 cents.[38]

The ability of villagers to demand higher prices for their cane-cutting specialty resulted in part from their sense of organization and their willingness to withhold labor, even though possessing few reserves to sustain strike action. Reaping gangs usually concluded bargains with management for the cutting of each field. The price accepted by the gang varied with the quantity of canes in the field, the demand for cane-cutters in the district and the priorities of the estate at the given time. For instance, the amount of indentured labor free from other tasks and available for cutting cane would influence the agreed price. Villagers were adept at seizing any eventuality to raise the price of labor. The well-known seasonal pattern of labor demand in the sugar industry was of crucial importance to the hiring of cane-cutters, because the canes had to be reaped at a particular time with minimum delay. For most of the year, estates had a sufficient work force in the persons of indentured laborers, and planters had the upper hand in dispensing jobs and pay to villagers. At crop time, however, cane-cutters were said to have taken advantage of planter necessity. Organized work stoppages were a weekly occurrence, often being timed to coincide with the moment when the supply of cut cane was running short.[39]

Poor conditions of work and wage disputes accounted for the frequent stoppages which punctuated any given grinding season. Conscious of the specter of slave labor, Africans refused tasks when the conditions were particularly unpleasant. Such tasks constituted "bad wo'k" in the Creole idiom; and the chances were that villagers would contemptuously tell the overseer to assign such tasks to indentured immigrants—unless management were willing to offer compensatory payments. For example, many decades after Emancipation, the hardships of reaping cane in an unburnt field gained general recognition in the form of extra payment.[40] Only village labor had sufficient bargaining strength to initiate such improvements.

Throughout the West Indies, disputes arose between planters and ex-slaves over the length of the working week and the supply of labor during the crop seasons. These disputes were at their fiercest where villagers developed partial subsistence alternatives, as in British Guiana. There were two flatly contradictory viewpoints on the question of the number of days on which villagers worked on the estates during the course of any given week. Planters and their spokesmen continually asserted that Africans were unwilling to work more than two or three days per week. Their vehement arguments were made before the Poor Law Commission of 1881, before the West India Commission of 1897, in response to the local Labour Enquiry of 1906, and in numerous other contexts. The Creole perspective was represented in letters to the press and other public protestations. Villagers alleged that they were perfectly willing to hire themselves throughout the week but planters refused to give them more than two or three days work. Both sides oversimplified the complex reality of industrial relations during the period. Village labor could and did work steadily on the estates when the terms of work were acceptable. But the disagreement was so frequent that both the laborer and the planter settled for part-time contracts. Planters in their own class interests determined that African labor was in short supply, since it was not forthcoming on conditions judged essential for the realization of surplus value. Workers in turn discovered that employment opportunities were limited in so far as it was possible to earn a "decent" or "fair" living wage. Starting from these irreconcilable positions, both class protagonists used part-time labor as a weapon.

As already indicated, the bargaining strength of village workers was a factor to be reckoned with during grinding seasons. It was necessary to cut, transport, and grind the canes within a limited time, and there were associated tasks such as the "supplying" of tops for replanting. Depending on the weather and other fortuitous circumstances, crop time might also have been made busier by the need to carry on with weeding, trench-cleaning, and other routine maintenance work. It was not unusual for Africans to turn up on Monday merely to "mark" or assess the work to be done. Assuming that they agreed to fulfill the task, they then returned on Wednesday and worked for three days. Delay was sometimes occasioned by the need to check on alternative estates, if they existed in the vicinity. The late start in the week to some extent compelled the planters to compromise over wages and conditions so as to ensure that, once begun, the cutting would be effeciently concluded without further interruption.

Planters held the upper hand during the slack periods in the crop cycle. Indentured and resident gangs got priority for the small amount of work available, while the villagers were lucky if they received two or three days per week. Tasks were then doled out to them, and it was a form of patronage which was tied to their behavior during the crop season. Besides, even during crop time, planter ascendancy was assured more often than not by Indian indentured labor or by Barbadian contract labor or by the necessities of international depression or by a combination of these factors.

Vital aspects of the impact of Indian indentured labor on African village labor emerged from the detailed evidence collected by the West India Royal Commission of 1897. One of these was the value of the indentured section at key points in the crop cycle. The commission's interview with one articulate overseer proceeded as follows:

Q. What is your opinion with regard to increasing the supply of coolies when there is in the colony at the present time an excess of labour?

A. The supply of labor has no bearing on the sugar industry; the whole origin of immigration hinges on this point. You may have work and plenty of it for a black man and a coloured man, and they will not do it. In planting cane if you leave certain agricultural work over, your crop is ruined. Therefore it is absolutely necessary that you should have bound labour that you can command. . . . Certain kinds of work on an estate could be left to the unreliable work of the blacks, thus leaving the indentured gangs free to do urgent work. There are certain kinds of work which absolutely must be done at certain times—such as replanting in rainy weather—and for this an indentured gang is absolutely necessary.[41]

The hitch in the above strategy was that the indentured gang could not always be substituted for the independent task gang, because they specialized
in different tasks. Theoretically, it is possible to conceive of large numbers of
immigrants covering all aspects of field production. In practice, however,
estates avoided extremely large indentured gangs because they constituted a
burden during the out-of-crop season. There was always scope for free labor
at crop time—and more so since they completed vital tasks quickly. Indentured females mainly comprised the weeding gangs; children took care of the
manuring; and the menfolk were chiefly valued for their use of the fork.
Fresh immigrants were seldom robust enough for punt-loading and few were
adept at cane-cutting, so that substitution in this vital category meant a sacrifice of efficiency. For this reason, planters turned to the import of labor from
other West Indian territories and from Barbados in particular.

British Guiana procured labor from the older sugar territories of the
British West Indies before slavery ended. The inflow averaged approximately
1,075 persons per annum between 1835 and 1846.[42] A new phase of Barbadian immigration into British Guiana was opened in 1863, and it continued
alongside of high imports of Indian indentured labor in the 1870s and 1880s.
Government assistance to planters requiring Barbadian immigrant workers
ceased in 1886, and subsequent entries were infrequent. Even at its peak,
Barbadian immigration was outstripped by Indian immigration by 4 to 1; but
Barbadians exercised a great influence on the labor market as direct competitors to Creole Africans. In fact, Barbadians were themselves Creole Africans
and seasoned agricultural laborers—fully capable of strenuous physical exer-
tion and of performing the skilled task of cane-cutting. Barbadians stayed for
the harvesting season and accepted work schedules, wages, and controls that
the local villagers were rejecting. The changeover from open-pan muscovado
to vacuum pan and centrifugals was most marked during the 1870s and was
completed during the 1890s.[43] Factory operations were concluded within a
shorter period as a result of technological renovation. September through
December became the intense grinding season; and it was at this time that
Barbadians were available. Some planters were dissatisfied with the tendency
of Barbadian labor to return home at Christmas, but this would have adversely affected only those estates which still had a long-drawn-out crop season. In
any event, when Barbadians were at work their labor was appreciated because
it was intense. In 1882, Plantation Uitvlugt boasted a large gang of Barbadian
laborers who worked steadily for six days in the week. Such a gang had
existed for two previous years; and, on the completion of each harvest, they
were rewarded with a feast at which two fat oxen were slaughtered.[44] Since
Barbadians proved amenable to a six-day work week, some local villagers
must have followed suit in the struggle for the fixed number of cane-cutting
jobs. The Barbadian presence added to that of the indentured immigrants in
reducing planter dependency on the most dynamic and aggressive sector of
the estate labor force. The village laborer then had to be satisfied with part-

time employment on terms that he could not easily dictate.

International price falls drove planters to the edge of distraction and drove workers into the abyss of desperation. Ultimately, the external environment was the most powerful sanction on the side of capital in keeping village labor under a tight rein. The fall in sugar prices in 1884 meant more wage decreases accompanied by significant retrenchment as acreages under cultivation were reduced. The management on several estates combined wage reductions with an insistence on short-term contracts that bound the village worker for a grinding season of three months. During these months, the estate guaranteed to provide work every day and to offer hospital accommodation if necessary. Creole Africans contracted to make themselves available to work five days each week; they were to accept weeding if no canes were to be cut; they were to complete the day's task within that given day; and they became subject to various penalties for breach of contract. The rate offered at Plantation Anna Regina in 1884 was 24 cents for a cord of unburnt cane of dimensions 8 ft. x 4 ft. x 4 ft.; while 20 cents was the payment for the same bundle if the field was burnt before the cane was cut. In 1885, the rates offered for unburnt and burnt cane fell to 20 cents and 18 cents respectively; and the following year they were lowered still further to 16 cents and 14 cents—remaining at this level for three years.[45] Each man received a bounty of $5.00 on signing the contract, indicating that planters recognized the inadequacy of the basic wages but were only prepared to pay extra if labor supplies were fully guaranteed at the time they were required by the estates.

An "average" cane-cutter is said to have earned $2.40 per week at the wages prevailing in 1886 at Anna Regina. The management calculated that, over a working week in dry weather, a worker would cut enough canes to make just over a ton of sugar. The ratio of tons cane to tons sugar was not constant and was crudely measured at the time, but it took about twelve tons of cane to produce one ton of sugar.[46] The champion worker at Anna Regina was then one McPherson, who could earn on average $5.00 per week during the cutting season. For him and other workers who proved capable of earning at least $2.40 per week, the management offered a $10.00 bonus in 1888. Others who fell below the average but worked reasonably well received a $4.00 bonus for the season. These niceties could not mask the fact that the rate of exploitation of labor on the sugar estates had been tremendously stepped up after 1884, with earnings of all categories being depressed to a point lower than anything prevailing in the previous half century. As already noted, the late 1880s were years when the rate for independent village labor fell below that for indentured workers. For instance, village laborers at Anna Regina were earning 6 percent less than indentured immigrants in October 1887.[47]

Employers found it unnecessary and expensive to introduce many additional Barbadian workers after 1885, because the economic pressures were such that Creoles in British Guiana had no option but to make do with lowered wages and tight industrial discipline. The Essequibo staff correspondent of the *Argosy* reported favorably on the impact of contracts on village laborers, observing that "they commence work now on Monday morning and work till Saturday, instead of wandering from one estate to another for the first few days of each week looking for 'price.'"[48] From a worker standpoint, the situation improved somewhat in 1889 and 1890—mainly because of the availability of alternative employment in goldfields. Immediately, planters raised the cry of high wages and labor shortage. They demanded more indentured immigrants as well as a new scheme for bringing Barbadians on short contracts. A few Barbadians arrived in 1890-92 as part of this scheme; but a recurrence of international crisis threatened planter profits, and a large part of the burden was immediately transferred on to the shoulders of the working population of estate and village. The greatest threat was retrenchment. Failures and amalgamations led to factory closures and these in turn increased the pressure on the employed sector of the work force. In November 1895, the view was expressed that fewer indentured Indians were required, "as the blacks and others are getting scared at continued abandonments."[49] Amid the evidence of real distress on the part of many employers and the fearful finality of estates being abandoned, village workers were deprived of room to maneuver. Planters were actually able to advance a theory of "social contract" between capital and labor—requiring labor to willingly accept wage cuts in the interests of preserving the industry and their jobs. The following notice posted at Non Pareil and signed by the planting attorney of the estate tells a whole story:

TO THE
MECHANICS & LABOURERS
OF THE ESTATE

Owing to the exceedingly LOW price of SUGAR, the lowest that has ever been known, it is ABSOLUTELY IMPOSSIBLE for us to pay the Old Rate of Wages and Carry the Estate on; I am aware that even the Old Rates were a reduced rate, but under the circumstances there is nothing for it but to still further reduce all round. It is a hard thing to ask, but if the Labourers and Mechanics will cheerfully accept the Reduction there is just a hope for the Estate and nothing more. If they refuse we must close up, and that almost at once. Should Prices rise to a paying level I need hardly say that I will give back what has been cut off.

HARRY GARNETT

September, 1896

The above sign was the prelude to lowered wage rates for indentured immigrants to the extent that employers broke the law in not guaranteeing that a standard task would earn immigrants their twenty-four cents in a working day. It was a sign that meant that the differential between free and

bound labor was erased. This applied both to village labor and to unindentured workers still resident on the estate. The unique role of the latter group
is one that demands greater attention in studies of Guiana's plantations. As
each batch of indentured shipmates received their legal freedom, it was
customary for them to test it by "taking a walk."[50] In most instances, they
shortly returned to the estate on which they had been indentured and entered
into a new relationship with management. They continued to reside in the
plantation logies or were allowed to build houses on estate land. Housing was
accompanied by the privilege of access to free medical facilities; and in
return, the free residents usually contracted on a monthly basis to work for
the estates.

Ex-indentured resident workers were a mixture of new independence and
renewed dependence. Their stay within estate houses—liable to ejection at a
moment's notice—was the cornerstone of their dependence on the estate.
Some might move from "bound yard" to adjacent "free yards," but they
were still within the confines of the old "nigger yard" where paternalism and
quasi-feudalism died hard.[51] On the one hand, they were more familiar with
the work routine and with the society than they were five years earlier on
arrival. They were therefore able to earn more at the same tasks and to
engage in subsistence activities. On the other hand, many tended to become
further enmeshed with the estate authorities because the latter granted them
a series of favors—giving or renting small agricultural plots, permitting the
establishment of retail shops, offering the possibility for grazing cattle or
small livestock. The latter was perhaps the most pervasive symbol of the
ambiguity of resident labor. The worker who "ran a cow" could supplement
his estate earnings and improve the lot of his family. He also had to take
care to remain in the good books of the estate management. In spite of all
ambiguities, it can be said that this section of the work force had progressed.
Their legal freedom was at least partially translated into industrial freedom.

Ex-indentured residents were capable of resisting some of the impositions
which filled the lives of their bonded kinsmen. When involved in controversy over a task or over payment, they were said to display a tendency to "sit
down" until some adjustment was made. They also discriminated against
certain kinds of work, such as punt-loading, which was physically strenuous
and poorly remunerated.

Planters generally preferred indentured labor to free resident labor, for the
same reasons that they praised indentured labor as compared with village
labor. No estate was ever faced with the experience of its entire indentured
labor force becoming free overnight, as in the case of Emancipation; but
managers felt great discomfiture whenever the free resident gangs increased
disproportionately to the indentured gangs. A crisis of this nature occurred
during the 1870s, owing to the abandonment of the device of reindenture.
Up until 1873, each extension of bonded service was obtained by a payment

of $50 to the immigrant concerned. Fifty dollars was a seemingly large lump sum in the eyes of the immigrants and it made the signing of reindenture contracts very prevalent. However, the reindenture bounty was raised to $120 in December 1873 and to $200 in June 1875. Planters could not afford these sums, and reindenture ended as a practical proposition.[52] Protected from being ensnared by another consecutive five-year contract, the immigrant had at least five years of free residence before becoming entitled to repatriation. This was the start of a really significant presence of free ex-indentured resident workers on the estates. As early as 1875, planters started evicting free immigrants from the estates logies in order to make room for fresh indentured workers—thereby clearly demonstrating their preference.[53] Nevertheless, nonindentured residents constantly increased relative to indentured workers, and estate management had to make adjustments accordingly.

Surgeon-Major Comins emphasized in his report (of 1891) that African village labor would not submit to contracts. He was wrong in so far as he overlooked the period between 1884 and 1888 when village labor was often forced to sign disadvantageous short-term contracts, but the gist of his remarks really applied to the resident nonindentured Indians. The latter were held up as persons willing to sign short-term contracts as a normal procedure. Comins also listed eight different fringe benefits which were part of the package that estates offered to nonindentured immigrants.[54]

A number of uncertainties in the relationship between the nonindentured residents and the estate proprietors were resolved during the late 1870s and the early 1880s. Some planters were willing at first to grant concessions to their nonindentured workers and leave it to them to reciprocate voluntarily. For instance, in 1879 Mon Repos was allowing residents to build houses on estate lands and yet retain the option of working away from the estate. The immigration agent-general was of the opinion that this degree of permissiveness should be the norm.[55] However, estate managers did not ignore the leverage which came into their possession. Commenting on the spread of rice farming in Berbice, Comins left no doubt that the object of planters in renting and selling plots of land was to ensure a supply of labor within easy reach.[56] Planters demanded part-time work on their respective estates. They standardized such compromise in the form of written or unwritten contracts, having the protection of the law as landlords and as masters while the nonindentured were of course subject to the inequalities of the same law as tenants and servants. Several witnesses before the Royal Commission of 1897 gave evidence to this effect—none more pertinently than the manager of Plantation Providence on the East Bank Demerara. Part of his interview proceeded as follows:

Q. You have law on your side with the indentured immigrants?

A. With the free labourers too, and the Master and Servant Ordinance is most strict.

Q. I suppose you have a certain hold over *free coolies that reside on the estate*, because if they did not turn out to work you can require them to leave.

A. Oh yes.

Q. Is that a sufficient hold?

A. Oh yes, for that class of men.

Q. Do you give the free coolies who reside on the estate constant employment?

A. Yes, that is part of the contract.

Q. And they work steadily?

A. Yes, I may say with regard to the free coolies that I let each man who can afford it keep a cow.[57]

To place the replies in their correct perspective, notice should also be taken of the preference for indentured labor—notwithstanding the limited freedom of action of the resident laborers. In the same interview, the witness argued forcibly for maintaining the heavy influx of indentured labor:

Q. You give various reasons; you say resident free coolies are not always reliable as they have a tendency to sit down, and they are apt to take dislike to certain kinds of work, and if pressed they give 14 days' notice and leave the estate. However much free labour is in your neighbourhood, you would still want the indentured coolie?

A. Oh yes . . . As I have mentioned, there are some kinds of work [unindentured residents] will not do, and if it did not suit them they would walk off and leave us in the lurch.

Q. *The free coolies who do not reside on the estate*—you do not give them constant employment?

A. We want them occasionally. They will go from one estate to the other, and see which kind of work will suit them best. It is the compulsory conditions of labour that they object to.

Q. They prefer to find their own houses, pay their own medical men, and take their chance of getting work in order that they may be free?

A. Yes.

Like the movement of Africans away from estate residence, the movement of Indians away from plantation housing in the latter part of the nineteenth century did not necessarily prevent the persons concerned from continuing as estate labor. It did mean that this labor behaved differently from residents—both bonded and free. The development of the nonresident Indian labor force in villages reinforces the generalizations concerning village labor and conclusively cuts across identification according to legal status or race. The device of the independent task gang quickly became the common property of both African and Indian villagers, when the latter felt the need to bargain with management for better conditions. In his report for the year

1882, the immigration agent-general referred to independent task gangs among the unindentured Indians. He described members of such groups as "agricultural nomads" who wandered from one estate to another trying to sell their labor to the best advantage; he chided them for being so simple as not to recognize that it was better to work somewhat longer at a lower rate rather than walking many miles to discover a rate which was a few cents higher; and he concluded that they were grasping after shadows rather than the substance of guaranteed housing and medical attention on the estate. Nevertheless, in the course of these submissions, the agent-general at least perceived the possibility that there was virtue in being at liberty to seek the best market for one's labor, and he conceded that these freelance task-gangs might have had a beneficial effect on the price of labor.

As soon as a proportion of free immigrants began to reside in villages and to return to the plantations for employment, they were equated with African villagers with regard to their industrial habits. Comins was well briefed on this point; and he saw evidence of the tendency when he visited estates on the West Coast of Demerara. Indians who had gone into the villages were restricting their time on the estates to about three days per week.[58] Because planter propaganda concentrated on the difference between reliable Indian indentured servants and unreliable African villagers, it obscured the fact that common socioeconomic circumstances produced similar responses—irrespective of race. The findings of the Royal Commission of 1897 helped set the record straight. Thereafter, even the internal memoranda of the Colonial Office demonstrated an awareness that no group of nonresident workers would tolerate the rigid industrial discipline to which residents were subjected. A deputation of the Planters' Association met the governor in November 1897 and pressed for more indentured immigrants, allegedly because neither African nor Indian free labor could be relied upon to do more than a few days per week. This position was relayed to the Colonial Office, where officials saw fit to underline a remark by the leading Corentyne planter that there was little to choose between free persons of the two main races from the viewpoint of reliability and willingness to work.[59] Interestingly enough, the Corentyne was one of the areas of the coast where Indian villages had already taken firm root.

From one region to another and from one estate to another, there were slight variations in the proportions of each category of labor. The bigger and better capitalized estates could afford to requisition more indentured labor, while the proximity of large reservoirs of village labor tended to increase the importance of this element. As a general rule, there was a consistent change in the proportionate makeup of the plantation labor force—with Indian non-indentured resident labor achieving precedence over indentured labor, as well as village labor (African and Indian).

The composition of the plantation labor force in the early 1880s is admirably brought out in a comprehensive description of sugar estates serialized in the *Argosy* in 1883.[60] Plantation Anna Regina was then regarded as one of the finest in the country. It had a resident population of 1,731, of which 1,002 were immigrants from Asia; but it drew heavily upon Creole African village labor found in the villages of Bush Lot, Henrietta, and Richmond— with their combined population of 2,511. Plantations Hampton Court, Reliance, and Affiance were the other amalgamations on the Essequibo Coast which could easily afford indentured labor and which simultaneously retained their access to the "proprietary villages" such as Queenstown. Many Essequibo villages were the result of an enlightened planter strategy of the 1840s, which envisaged that the sale of a small portion of the front lands to the emancipated workers on an individual propriety basis would gain good will and secure a labor force.[61] This calculation proved correct.

In West Demerara, there was the same pattern of interspersed and interdependent estates and villages. The villagers of Good Intent, Sisters, and Bagotville were associated with Plantations Nismes and Wales; those of Den Amstel and Fellowship with Plantations Hague, Blankenburg, and Windsor Forest; and the residents of Anna Catherina (amongst whom a large proportion of Indians were to be found) were employed at Plantations Leonora and Cornelia Ida. Obviously, the large communal villages on the East Coast Demerara supplied part of the labor force of the amalgamated estates which dominated this section of the coast. At Plantation Cove and John, the availability of both indentured immigrants and a large village population enabled this estate to produce the (then) large crop of 1,800 tons in 1882-83. Besides, so long as there were indentured immigrants, there were also time-expired immigrants and some Creole Indians. The same pattern was repeated on the West and East Coasts of the county of Berbice—including the estates watered by the Canje Creek and the Corentyne river.

Occasionally, an important estate failed to maintain a balance between indentured, free residents, and villagers. It was said that expansion at Plantation Albion on the Corentyne was limited by the insufficiency of indentured servants, but that "Albion is fortunate in being next to the villages of Fyrish, Gilbraltar and Rose Hall—the residents of which are the finest examples of the creole race to be seen in British Guiana."[62] However, it was at Plantation Better Hope on the East Coast Demerara that the most unusual circumstances prevailed in the early 1880s. There it was decided that indentured labor should be avoided as a matter of policy. A large proportion of workers were recruited from nearby African villages, and the remainder were free Indians who had served their time on that estate when it used to have a large indentured section or who had served their indenture more recently on another plantation. Better Hope, which incorporated Vryheid's Lust, boasted a crop of over 3,000 tons. Its proprietors were Messrs. Ewing and Company of Glasgow, and their local planting attorney in British Guiana issued an important statement on their behalf in May 1883, explaining the reluctance to hire indentured labor. The Ewings rested their policy on two planks: the substitution of implemental for manual work and the employment of free labor, with preference where possible to the Creole African. In a remarkable departure from typical planter statements, the attorney represented his Scottish principals as follows:

> They recognise duties connected with the possession of land; and so they give employment to the free labourers of different races, all of whom have been introduced to the Colony and can fairly claim, in making a living out of it, to have a share in the labour of the estates; especially do they consider the black creole labourer, as a son of the soil, to be entitled to the offer of such work as he will undertake, and they are not unmindful either that his forefathers were forcibly brought to the country for the gain of the planter of the past and that the planter of today cannot divest himself of *all* the responsibilities incurred by his predecessors.[63]

Since the Ewings (under James Ewing, lord provost of Glasgow) had benefited from slavery in Guiana, they may have been expressing a unique but genuine sense of historical responsibility. However, the firm was in effect guilty of breaking the ranks of its own class, and was vigorously attacked by fellow planters. The latter alleged that Ewings were no more interested in implemental work than other proprietors, that their use of nonindentured labor at Better Hope amounted to the poaching of labor supplies from planters who paid to introduce fresh immigrants, and that the employment of African villagers was simply because the large village of Plaisance offered ample scope to recruit cheaply. The last of these charges had been raised in the legislature in 1882, when a move was made to reduce the acreage tax on sugar plantations from $2.00 to $1.50 per acre—the said acreage of tax being the means by which planters made their contribution to the immigration fund. The proposal came from the Ewings and from R. P. Drysdale (of Plantation Clonbrook) who felt that they should reduce their contribution to the general cost of immigration, while planters using this form of labor would meet more of the costs. At the time, there were 384 immigrants resident at Clonbrook, of whom only 42 were under indenture; while Better Hope had 2,260 nonindentured residents compared to 324 under indenture. The governor was not sympathetic to the view that only estates using indentured labor should contribute to the planters' share of one-third of the immigration bill. He argued that "Messrs. Ewing employ on their estates upwards of 2,200 Immigrants not under indenture; and I need not say that without the continued introduction of indentured immigrants they should lose the undisputed command of this body of free labor and would be exposed to a competition which would largely raise the rate of wages."[64]

Although the approach of the Ewings was challenged in principle, there were a few estates on which indentured labor had in practice given way to free labor. This depended on special circumstances under which the given plantation commanded the market for free labor. For instance, the lower

East Bank Demerara was easily accessible to laborers living in Georgetown. Estates such as Houston and Ruimveldt developed an early reputation for hiring time-expired immigrants who had become inhabitants of Georgetown or its immediate environs to the south. By the end of the century, much of the East Bank could exist on this pool of free labor along with the permanent residents and villagers close to the estates. Plantations Bath and Blairmont counted themselves as similarly fortunate, not because of the proximity of an urban concentration of free workers, but because these were the only estates in the whole of West Berbice. Africans and Indians of the West Coast Berbice had little alternative but to trek to Plantations Bath and Blairmont if they wanted money wages.

This was the rationale which guided their proprietors (the Davson brothers) to inform the West India Commission of 1897 that they intended to encourage rice growing among their unindentured work force. Shortly afterwards they told the Colonial Office that the policy was not well considered because it was found that workers were tending their rice beds at the time that they were wanted on the estate. The Davsons changed their approach and urged the building up of indentured gangs through immigration.[65] Nevertheless, the annual inflow of new immigrants never picked up in the present century to match the levels of the 1870s and 1880s. Therefore, the increase in the importance of the nonindentured resident gangs was never reversed.

Immigration officials presented fairly precise data on the absolute and relative numbers of indentured and time-expired immigrants. Large capitalists such as Quintin Hogg had on their estates a ratio of one bonded worker to three or four nonindentured residents in the 1890s. However, difficulties arise in estimating the total plantation work force and hence the proportion of village laborers. Thoughtful attempts have been made to quantify certain values from the inadequate statistics of the nineteenth century; but estimates of the plantation labor muster still rely on literary sources and approximations.[66] It is clear that the unindentured resident section expanded relative to the villagers, especially during the worst depression years. From 1884 to 1887, the disassociation of Africans from plantation work was accelerated through retrenchment, low wages, and the rise of alternative employment in the goldfields. The process was repeated in 1894-96. By this latter date, many villagers were flocking in desperation to Georgetown, even though their prospects of urban employment were slim. Planters generally concurred that it was unthinkable to lower wages beyond the point reached in 1896.[67] One of their reasons for this seemingly benign judgment was that a further deterioration would probably drive the resident unindentured away from the estates and from estate labor as it had already done for many Creoles.

Indications are that the total plantation work force was declining in the late 1890s and the early 1900s.[68] Indentured and village labor were the components which were being substantially reduced. The exodus of villagers to the goldfields was a constant talking point among planters. A few continued to use Creole labor intensively for three or four months of the year and therefore lost nothing when the same laborers took to the interior for the remaining months. Indeed, they welcomed this development, since it removed the obligation to employ village labor during the out-of-crop season. However, there were several small estates which could not grind all of their cane in one short spell, and these complained bitterly of the shortage of village canecutters.[69]

In effect, the uneven rate of amalgamation and technological change led to contradictions among the planters themselves, as they sought access to the depleted reservoir of village estate labor. The withdrawal of villagers was most marked in Essequibo and in parts of Berbice—notably on the right bank of the Berbice river and on the Canje. African village labor was slowly losing ground in these latter districts ever since the 1860s, a matter to which the Nonconformist churches constantly drew attention since it so directly affected the persons to whom they ministered. Pastors of the London Missionary Society noted that, once displaced from estate labor, villagers tended to move away from the area or at least to cut all connections with the sugar industry.[70] After several decades of this trend, the Colonial Company found it almost impossible to attract African village labor to its estates at Mara and Friends—even at rates substantially higher than other planters in the Colony were paying.[71]

Changes in the composition of the estate work force meant in part the substitution of one ethnic group for another, but they also gave rise to greater homogeneity in terms of industrial experience. The time-expired immigrants had begun to carry out field tasks previously associated only with emancipated Africans and the first generation of their descendants. Shovel work, for example, was taken up more and more by seasoned indentured workers and by those whose contracts had expired. Even cane-cutting was no longer identified so completely with African Creoles or their Barbadian counterparts by the end of the period under discussion.[72] Besides, in spite of specialized functions, all sections of the estate laboring class shared in most of the fundamental experiences of the era. It is essential to reiterate that (with minor exceptions) payment for labor expended was by task rather than by the day or week. Workers of all categories were subjected to increased rates of exploitation by the simple device of increasing the size of the tasks. Workers had no say in appraising a task. Whether or not a task was successfully completed was a matter left to the discretion of the overseer. If he was not satisfied, he withheld or "stopped" the pay of the worker in question. Among old workers who have survived one or other of the forms of estate employment, no grievance was expressed as universally or as feelingly as that of the "stopping" of their expected weekly earnings when they approached the estate pay table.[73]

After 1896, the wage or task rate stabilized at the low level to which it had been driven by international depression. To economize further, planters reduced the amount of work which was offered. The alternative response of mechanized agriculture (with a stable and better-paid work force) which was hinted at by the Ewings was never seriously pursued in the colony as a whole. Although factory modernization continued where possible, technological stagnation characterized the field routines—resting as they did on the basis of cheap indentured and time-expired resident immigrant gangs. In a certain sense, planters were correct in affirming that external supplies of labor guaranteed the survival of the sugar industry in British Guiana during its most difficult years. However, it is also true to say that the availability of subsidized external sources of labor simultaneously guaranteed the persistence of backward hand-husbandry and of heavily supervised work routines associated with the plantation as a unit of production[74] Above all, immigration rapidly created a labor surplus which made unemployment and underemployment endemic in the late nineteenth century. These were scourges that affected primarily the Creole and free sections of the laboring population, but from which even the indentured working people were not protected.

CHAPTER 3

Crisis and Creativity in the
Small-Farming Sectors

We wanted land as it should be:
hard and firm; the trees deep-rooted. . . .
Edward Braithwaite

Rural wage earners in Guiana in the nineteenth century were so close to the land that they have often been imprecisely designated as peasants.[1] The dynamics of peasant farming cannot be understood without constant reference to the plantations, but it remains essential to distinguish between self-employed farming and estate wage labor. Land acquisition by the emancipated population during the 1840s represented the search for some degree of ownership and control of the means of production, the better to cope with planters both on and off the estates. Each piece of land purchased and each village settled gave to the Creole Africans involved a small measure of independence which frustrated the planter strategy of intimidating workers because they lived in estate housing.

As is well known, many slaves in Guiana and the West Indies had access to small provision plots. The planters of Demerara and Essequibo proposed in December 1841 that these provision grounds be withdrawn, that hogpens be destroyed and that no fishing be permitted in the canals of the estates.[2] These were the threats brandished before workers who contemplated resisting wage decreases and increased workloads. The measures of victimization had something in common with those fashioned at an earlier epoch by landed proprietors in Europe, who were making the transition from feudalism to capitalism by depriving the farmer serfs of their customary rights to the land. But while the European enclosure movement created a landless proletariat to enter into new relations of production based on new instruments of production in the factories, the object of planters in Guiana was to increase the dependency of workers by enmeshing them in a series of reciprocal ties reminiscent of feudalism. A fine was to be imposed for absence from work on the estate on which one was resident; while refusal to comply with regulations was punishable with summary eviction from estate houses. Each proprietor wanted a set of laborers bound to his estate and hence secure from distraction by better offers elsewhere. Being small and well organized, the planter class readily agreed to avoid competition among themselves. The workers, too, had to show discipline and organization in order to survive, hence the important strikers of 1842 and 1848. Confrontations with the planters suggested to the Creoles that their freedom could not be guaranteed by wage labor alone.[3] As they sought to secure parcels of land, this in itself led to sharper conflicts with plantation capitalists, who would not stand idly by and allow the diversion of any significant proportion of their labor force.

The movement of free blacks into villages—"the free village movement"— became a reality in spite of powerful opposition by the planter class and the colonial legislature. Allan Young's informative study of local government notes that land policy was carefully shaped toward keeping black people landless. Yet ex-slaves managed to purchase lots on the front land of estates and sometimes acquired abandoned plantations in their entirety, at highly inflated prices. After a decade of freedom, the number of Creole Africans resident on the sugar estates had fallen to 19,939 while the villages and settlements numbered between them 44,456 persons. Allan Young concludes that "the important point is the fact that the freed apprentice had surmounted the initial barrier of a restrictive land policy to emerge as a landed proprietor."[4] This emphasis is misdirected. The writer seizes upon a legal relationship, namely, that of proprietorship. But he fails to pursue the social implications of evidence which he himself presents with regard to the sharp class struggles of the 1840s—in terms of figures showing that more than 7,000 persons in proprietary villages owned freehold plots of only ¼ acre to 5 acres, while in communal villages scores of ex-slaves jointly owned each particular property of 100, 200, or 500 acres. One does not become a "landed proprietor" in any socially meaningful sense with a holding of between ¼ acre and 5 acres or with a tiny part-share in communal lands. One might conceivably be classed as a peasant or small farmer on such a basis—in the event of owning sufficient agricultural land to produce subsistence and perhaps a limited surplus for sale.

Three broad occupational subdivisions became discernible within the ranks of the emancipated population. There was a small group that remained exclusively tied to the estates. Secondly, there were those who obtained a material base on the land, sufficient to exempt them from wage labor. Thirdly, and most importantly, there was a large number who fell into an area of overlap between the wage workers and the provision-growing peasantry. Wage workers and their families lived in the villages and practiced small-farming away from the plantation. The incomplete crystallization of an independent peasantry was reflected in the incomplete separation of workers from peasants. This proved to be a long-term rather than a temporary feature of class delineation in Guiana.

It has been argued that the plantation/peasant clash was the principal contradiction in Guianese society during the period in the nineteenth century when sugar was produced without slave labor.[5] This approach is valuable in illuminating planter commitment to a monopoly of land, labor, and capital; but it tends to identify the villagers solely with the peasantry and thereby underplays the significance of full-time and part-time Creole African plantation workers. A more comprehensive explanation requires that one pinpoint the fundamental contradiction as that between capital and labor on the estates; as a derivative, capital usually sought to negate the village political economy, both as an independent peasant alternative, and as a provider of supplementary subsistence which might strengthen the bargaining power of one of the categories of plantation labor.

The censuses of 1881, 1891, and 1911 indicate that the rural population was becoming more and more villagized. For the former slaves and their descendants, this did not necessarily mean that farming away from the plantations had become more buoyant. On the contrary, there was ample evidence of crisis, stagnation, and decline among Creole African peasants for most of the second half of the nineteenth century. A number of contemporary observers in the 1880s recognized that the exhaustion of the peasantry had its roots in an earlier period. For instance, the report of the inspector of villages in 1881 referred to the previous remarkable efforts of villagers in raising capital for lands and housing. He correctly linked the difficulties of Afro-Guianese small farmers with the exorbitant land prices demanded of former slaves, and he conceded that the parties who purchased estates had expended all their ready capital and had no means of working the land.[6] Their plight was all the more serious because of the heavy financial demands of polder agriculture. Under these circumstances, each setback exposed the prevailing weakness of the small-farming sector and further militated against any profound recovery.

The record of setbacks during the period in question is as dismal as it is repetitive. Official sources that were not usually sympathetic to peasants and subsistence farmers are nevertheless replete with accounts of disasters caused by eroded front dams, blocked kokers, broken back dams and the effects of the "twin seasons" of "parching drought and flood." Nonconformist churches were particularly close to the rural Creoles and helped to chronicle their sufferings. In January 1879, spokesmen for the London Missionary Society commented on the droughts which had impoverished the people; and in March 1887 their reports highlighted the flood that drowned hundreds of sheep, cattle, and goats and destroyed most of the cassava and plantains.[7] Such seemingly mundane episodes contributed to the precariousness of peasant existence. Besides, the effects of international depression penetrated

Rev. F. C. Glasgow, London Missionary Society
and Congregationalist

swiftly and deeply into the nonplantation sector—a reminder that the villages never constituted an independent economic system or even a coherent economic subsystem.[8] Because of retrenchment, unemployment, and lowered wages, farm produce could only be bought by workers at ridiculously low prices. The Rev. F. C. Glasgow spoke on behalf of his fellow countrymen before the West India Commission of 1897. With his base at Bagotville, he was in a good position to observe the decline in the amount of money circulated by the West Demerara sugar industry and the consequent difficulties which farmers had in disposing of their produce. Darnell Davis, then a senior government officer who had a long and close connection with supplying Blue Book statistics, was also ideally placed to pronounce on the crisis in the countryside, which he attributed mainly to the fall in sugar wages from approximately $5 million per year in good years to about $3 million during the depression of 1896. Finally, one could scarcely overlook the evidence of Z. A. Lewis, the Pomeroon small farmer who was the only member of this class to appear before the commission in Guiana. Lewis testified that the market for food crops was glutted, and that peasants were subject to price falls that matched (and surpassed) those of sugar. He cited tannias, which in 1895 sold for upwards of $2.40 per bag but which were then being offered at 56 cents per bag.[9]

No political force existed that could redistribute social surplus to Creole Africans engaged in peasant and subsistence farming. A governor like Henry

Irving or a commission such as that of 1897 might advise that priority be given to supporting a peasantry, but these exceptional proposals were not energetically implemented. As already noted, public spending on drainage, irrigation, and sea defense was approved with planter interests in mind. There were no inputs into the promotion of peasant crops in the conventional areas of credit, transportation, and marketing. Not surprisingly, there was little interest in the scientific study of "ground provisions," even after the establishment of the Botanic Gardens in 1880 and the conduct of original research on cane seedlings. A major plantation disease made its presence felt throughout the last six or seven decades of the nineteenth century, but it received no scientific attention—although Schomburgk described it as early as 1840 and called for an investigation. Schomburgk wrote as follows:

> For some years past an extremely peculiar disease has introduced itself into the *Musa* plantations; this has become particularly dangerous owing to its having proved so infective that if one shaft is attacked the whole plantation follows suit and perishes. Unfortunately, one has not found any remedy for this "Worm" disease as the Colonists call it.
>
> When the tree is attacked, its outward appearance immediately shows it and the whole plantation has to be cut down to prevent the further spread to others. The disease itself starts from the innermost vascular bundles which take on a brownish colour intermixed with a number of blackspots. This decomposition of the sap soon extends to the whole shaft. The growth of the plant as well as that of the fruit is arrested and a resinous oxidation renders the latter absolutely uneatable. If the same piece of land is going to be replanted, suckers from a healthy plant must be used, because experience has taught that even the suckers contain the diseased material of the mother plant. Ten years ago the pest was completely unknown, but at the present time has gained such strides that it becomes the serious duty of the proprietors to have enquiry made into its origins on scientific lines.[10]

Schomburgk's description is generally considered to be the first clear indication of the incidence of Moko, or bacterial wilt disease—a bacterial vascular disease somewhat similar to the more widely known and dreaded Panama disease. Scientific literature on the subject identifies the first serious outbreak of the disease in Trinidad in the 1890s, when it almost wiped out the Moko plantain from which the name derives.[11] However, it seems clear that long before the Trinidad outbreak, Moko disease violently attacked and hindered the development of the peasant plantain industry in British Guiana. Soil conditions were unfavorable to plant growth and extremely favorable to the disease. There was inadequate drainage and high soil moisture. When investigated locally in the 1930s, Moko disease occurred both on the frontland clays and on the pegasse or humus that overlay an impervious clay stratum.[12] It is also known to be likely to occur in soils of reclaimed low-lying areas; and it is striking to find that when villages in East Demerara opened up second depths of empoldered land in the late 1860s and 1870s. it was only a matter of a few years before the ravages of plantain disease were felt.[13]

Fortunately, peasants and the community at large had accumulated a store of practical wisdom in dealing with this and similar crises. As Schomburgk had already noted, farmers were aware that all replanting required suckers from healthy plants—rather than seemingly healthy suckers from diseased plants. They were also aware that the radical treatment of destroying an infected plantain estate was necessary to prevent ruinous spread. By the 1880s, it was common knowledge that the spread of the disease was facilitated by the tools, such as shovels, which might have come into contact with diseased plants; while fallowing (including flood fallowing) was also recognized as a technique in disease control.[14] Such measures were scientifically investigated and applied in Central America in recent times, when Moko disease began to pose a threat to commercial production of bananas by large companies. But Moko disease has inflicted far more losses on peasant crops of plantains and bananas than on large commercial plantings.[15] The peasants of British Guiana are to be numbered among the earliest victims—and this at a time when planters did not see fit to divert any social surplus to an attempted solution of the problem.

Inactivity and discriminatory legislation on the part of the planter legislature was also reproduced through the many statutory bodies that operated at the regional level. The road boards were among the chief offenders as far as the peasantry was concerned. When the Wakenaam Road Board met in May 1882, it recommended that no funds be allocated to repairing the dam and road at Palmyra. This estate had just been abandoned, and had fallen into the hands of the government, but the board's decision automatically cut off the villages of Ridge and Concordia from the rest of the island. In this instance, the road commissary was sufficiently concerned about the injustice of the decision to see that it was reversed.[16] It was precisely when there was the occasional official intervention and criticism that one gains an insight into the customary procedure. One year after the above Wakenaam incident, the road situation in the neighboring island of Leguan gave rise to a petition before the legislature. The chief commissary was frank in his criticism of how the planter-controlled road boards normally operated. He commented:

> To my mind the situation is susceptible of being thus formulated—The road to a sugar estate must be kept open, that to a village may not. So thoroughly was this understood by the person who was placed in charge of Pln. Richmond Hill by the Acting Administrator-General that during his management a portion of the Good Intent [village] road was taken to make up a breach in the [estate] dam.[17]

Since each estate was responsible for maintaining the stretch of road along its own facade, the coastal road had all but disappeared in some areas where several plantations were abandoned during the earlier part of the century.

Where provision growing replaced sugar, the villagers made valiant efforts to patch the roads; but it was a losing battle. The new economic activity was usually confined to the frontlands and did not yield the surplus necessary for upkeep of the main road—which so often served as a line of defense against the sea. The desperation of small farmers manifested itself in the many and futile petitions reaching the legislature. Sometimes they complained against the road boards. In at least one instance, a village which had no board protested the arbitrary actions of the commissary and demanded the appointment of a board.[18] Time and again, petitions arrived from owners of cattle farms and coconut estates asking to be relieved of payment of road tax. These emanated from areas such as Mahaica and Mahaicony where sugar and cotton plantations had all but become a thing of the past by the early 1880s, and where small capitalists had established commercial farms. There were times when circumstances were entirely beyond the control and means of lot-owners and cultivators. The poor state of major drainage channels, like the Grand Canal and the Canals Polder, were examples of the strain that could be placed on road maintenance. At Stanleytown, West Bank Demerara, villagers complained of the expense entailed by having to "smouse" or erect makeshift dams to try and keep the overflow of the blocked Canal No. 2 from rushing over the road and on to their provision beds.[19] At Bagotville, village rates and taxes were swallowed up by upkeep of the public road along a facade of 100 roods. In addition, villagers were responsible for another 750 roods on the south side of Canal No. 1, although proprietors on both sides used the roads.[20] Their proposal for change was backed by the relevant government officers, but official action had to await the planter legislators.

The Road Ordinances of 1876 and 1878 were particularly objectionable. They compelled owners who had bought estates with bridle paths to change these into carriage roads, to cover all roads with metal (burnt earth), and to restore certain quantities of road-building material at the roadside every year. Among such properties were the free villages that were subdivided into lots, leaving each proprietor with two or three roods to keep up. Village economies could not stand the cost, and fragmentation of responsibility made matters worse. To keep his share of road under repair, a villager would have to ensure that drainage was adequate, and such an imposition was totally unrealistic. Richard Whitfield, a liberal lawyer of the times, wrote in 1873 strongly criticizing the Government with respect to village roads and related matters. He charged that the complex village problem of roads, drainage, and agriculture had been reduced by the government to a series of restrictive bylaws. As part of this analysis, he observed that "to drain a single acre, a whole district must be drained, and yet our existing law exacts from the owner of a half-acre lot or less the conditions that it should be well drained; in other words it attempts to compel an impossibility."[21] W. S. Turner, a commentator who indicated no great love of African Creoles, nevertheless hit upon the injustice of the road taxes in relation to peasantry and cultivators other than sugar capitalists. He stated (in 1885):

> It is difficult to conceive a system more completely calculated to strangle the struggling landed proprietor than the old road system, not the least of its many vices being that it often placed the thrifty and the industrious at the mercy of the idle and the improvident; thus tending to demoralise and degrade the whole of our agricultural population and at the same time to prevent the small capitalist from investing in the land.[22]

Antipeasant legislation may have sought to compel an impossibility, but compel it did. Enforced sale of property and speedy eviction were sanctions that were provided within the Roman-Dutch law governing immovable property. The road boards or the road commissary carried out maintenance works on any given road and then charged these against the properties concerned. Failure to repay the government led to swift retribution in the form of parate execution sales. Parate execution—the ability to levy on property and sell at public auction—was an extraordinary and drastic remedy peculiar to Roman-Dutch law. On a certificate by a public officer that money was due to the government, the court issued parate execution against the property of the debtor.[23] Apart from the central government, there were other public bodies authorized to recover debts in this manner—the town and village councils, the Central Board of Health, the road boards and the sea defense boards being the most significant.

Large numbers of persons were evicted from their small-holdings through parate execution. In the early 1880s, the government itself recognized that the situation was intolerable, and the full weight of the law was not brought to bear on those who could not comply. The governor and legislature, along with a road commission, engaged in discussion of this issue between 1880 and 1884. They agreed that small cultivators lacked the finances, labor and appliances for road building; but it was only in 1884 that a road ordinance finally relieved small proprietors of the burden of road maintenance. Even then the issue was not dead. As late as 1890, the legislature still sought to recover arrears of road taxes that had accumulated before the legislation of 1884.[24]

Proprietors of cattle farms, coconut estates, provision estates and the like protested when the government insisted on collecting arrears of road taxes. They contrasted themselves unfavorably with the actual villagized peasants, alleging that officials victimized them as small capitalists while temporizing with village communities for fear that the latter would create unrest.[25] Government agencies did refrain from legal action against entire village communities, one notable instance being the waiver by the East Berbice Sea Defence Board in 1898.[26] But large numbers of individual peasants were proceeded against, as attested to by the notices of execution sale which appeared in the *Official Gazette*. In July 1887, a correspondent of the newspaper *Echo* bitterly denounced the practice. "The Inspectorship of the Villages means the inspecting of the knocking down of property by the Marshal's hammer at Execution sales," he wrote.[27] The element of vituperation in this statement probably represents the subjective response of many African Creoles. On the other hand, the objective importance of this technique was confirmed by renewed legislation. Between 1901 and 1904 the government took the step of providing itself with a general power of recovery by parate execution sale in respect of claims due to the colony. Thereafter, ordinances restored the previous situation in which the power to issue execution was specifically given on application in each individual case.[28]

Parate execution sales for road and village taxes had a notable impact on particular localities. The abominable conditions of drainage and sea defense at Fyrish drove village proprietors before the marshal. In his report on this village proprietors before the marshal. In his report on this village for 1878, the inspector of villages expressed regret that at a sale of execution for rates, he had to buy several lots, the owners having said that they had no intention of paying any more taxes.[29] El Dorado Block in West Berbice was another problem area. The population suffered from the overflow from Weldaad and adjoining estates that lacked back dams or outlet kokers, so that water from the Abary river came across the sidelines. By 1889, frustrations gave rise to a movement against rate payment—those who abstained allegedly intimidating those who did not want to do so.[30] The result was that several properties in this district passed into the hands of the Central Board of Health in 1890. A third (and the most poignant) example was that of Craig, which was a dying village in the 1870s. The population was down to 395 in 1881 as compared with 425 in the census of 1871 and 528 in 1861. Craig villagers were reported as refusing to pay rates in 1885, because their drainage was defective and water overflowed from Hope estate on to their backlands. The government proceeded to acquire several of their lots at execution sales. At the same time, it was remiss in its obligation to build a back dam to protect the village lands. By 1894, there was no improvement in rate collection and little or no work was being done by the Central Board of Health in the villages. The river dam was gradually being washed away and the public road was in danger of being carried away also. The Central Board of Health had resold much of the backlands that it acquired in rate sales, but only two of the lots had been bought by villagers.[31]

Difficulties in retaining land were sometimes occasioned by private capitalists. Plantations were likely to act in an overbearing manner in any disputes over land with neighboring villages. A notorious instance was the seizure of land by Plantation Diamond from Mocha villagers in Canal No. 3—an injustice that was perpetrated in 1883 and only partially redressed by the courts in 1887.[32] A similar aggression against the backlands of Enterprise village (Berbice River) was conducted by the Colonial Company, which took advantage of the fact that the villagers did not have a transport in their possession.[33]

When peasants and subsistence farmers managed to hold on to their land titles, and when crops were not ruined for lack of infrastructural investment, they faced a further acute problem—that of praedial larceny. Court records provide a partial view of this social ill, since the majority of offenders escaped arrest and prosecution. The director of prisons was among those who observed that the hard times of international depressions usually led to an upswing in the incidence of praedial larceny before the courts and of convicts in prison as a consequence. In 1885 (a year comprising twelve months of depression), the number of prisoners committed was 7,195—showing a large increase on the preceding year's total of 2,250 prisoners. Many people deliberately got themselves sent to jail for petty offenses, while others committed praedial larceny simply to obtain food. There were 636 imprisonments for praedial larceny in 1885, as against 163 in 1884.[34]

One response to praedial larceny was to impose the penalty of flogging, which in the early 1880s meant public flogging. Late in 1880, Magistrate Huggins was the subject of controversy for refusing to hand out sentences of flogging as indiscriminately as most planters would have liked. Bascom of Plantation Cove & John and Struthers of Plantation Melville reproved Huggins for encouraging plantain stealing through a refusal to order corporal punishment. In his defense, Huggins adverted to his own remarks in court to make it clear that, while in principle reluctant to order flogging, he had done so because of increasing theft of growing crops. Huggins also pointed out that many estates grew plantains and were fostering their own self-interest with this punitive legislation. The governor countered by stating that flogging as a penalty for praedial larceny had been instituted by Ordinance No. 22 of 1862 in consequence of murders committed by proprietors of plantain estates on persons caught in the act.[35] Flogging as a penalty was challenged both ethically and because its deterrent value was doubtful. The Colonial Office was forced to take a special interest in the problem because questions were raised in the House of Commons. When this occurred in March 1881, the most recent information in the possession of the secretary of state for the colonies was for the year 1879. In that year, there were 1,043 cases of praedial larceny reported to the police; 189 prosecutions ended in conviction, and there were 32 instances of flogging. In contrast, Trinidad had one flogging, while such punishment was not inflicted in Jamaica, Antigua, or Barbados.[36]

In September 1898, it was agreed that the practice of flogging for praedial larceny should be partially relaxed. The argument for its retention was that the crime was more serious in its social consequences than would appear from the mere value of the property stolen. The colonial state also gave itself a pat on the back by stating that "the owners and cultivators of the plots of

plantains, cassava, etc. which are the subject of these depradations, belong to
the class of small proprietors and occupiers whom it is the policy of the
government to encourage and protect."[37] Throughout these discussions of
the 1880s and 1890s, officials implied that the demand for severe punishment
was coming from the peasants. This was probably correct, since those suffering directly were unlikely to have taken the detached view that plantain
thieves were victims of social misery. For once the law was seemingly on the
side of the peasants and small producers, but of course praedial larceny could
not be remedied by floggings or imprisonment. Provision stealing continued,
and it was a major disincentive to the pursuit of small farming.

An issue of greater significance was the placing of legislative obstacles in
the way of land acquisition. The government owned extensive areas of
coastal backlands which could readily be empoldered, quite apart from the
huge areas of crown land in the interior. Immediately upon total Emancipation, the legislature restricted the sale of crown lands by high prices and by
the large amount of land which was set as the minimum purchaseable. Indeed,
the partisan use of planter political power was nowhere more blatant than on
issues concerning the availability of land to the peasantry. As early as 1861,
the planter-inspired ordinances had achieved what Alan Adamson appropri-
ately terms "the legislative encirclement of the peasant" by raising the price
of crown land on the coast to a minimum of $10 per acre, while the mini-
mum size which could be bought was 100 acres.[38] The latter figure was
reduced to 25 acres in 1890, but this remained outside the reach of peasants.
Almost the whole of the period in question was characterized by complaints
around this issue and by lack of remedial action.

The chorus of Creole complaints on the land question came before the West
India Commission of 1897, and their report contrasted the situation within
Guiana with the rise of a sturdy peasantry in territories such as Jamaica.
Consequently, the Crown lands regulations were amended in 1898, making
concessions relevant to the opening up of the interior as well as to the conduct of agriculture on the coast. Land prices and sizes were reduced and so,
too, were the expenses incident upon acquiring title. Under the new enact-
ment, 144 land grants were processed in the year 1900-1901 compared with
37 issued during the fifty years after Emancipation.[39] There was a clearly
discernible speed-up of peasantization during the first years of this century,
although it came too late to be of benefit to Creole Africans who had by then
moved after different economic pursuits in the struggle for survival.

As so often happens in situations of land shortage, some amount of
squatting developed on crown land and had perforce to be tolerated. This
took place in many riverain areas, in coastal areas beyond the sugar belt, and
in coastal areas back of larger villages. In the latter instances, the land was
euphemistically said to have been acquired by "absorption."[40] Nevertheless,
the scope both for squatting and for land-buying activities in the nineteenth

century was narrowly circumscribed by the poor drainage. As a result, the principal legal relationship of cultivators to the land was tenancy and leasehold rather than freehold.

Much of the discussion of the peasantry in the mid-nineteenth century and thereafter assumes that they were small freehold landowners, having either individual title to land or an inherited share of communal property. In practice, there was an ever increasing number of villagers who were either landless or owned insufficient land to engage in peasant production. The majority of the rural population acquired that status of tenant farmers. For instance, at Bagotville in 1896, the five hundred ¼-acre lots were owned by about 250 persons, while the total village population was 2,403. (For original prices and appraised value of land in this year, see table A14.) Landless villagers therefore rented land from proprietors absent in Georgetown and elsewhere.[41] Landlord-tenant relations also developed within the Indian community. But being the major owners of polder land, the estates were the principal agencies for renting or leasing land to peasants on a short-term basis. The typical tenement farm was a lot having a facade of 3 roods and a depth of 750 roods. The typical short-least was for a period of three years on a monthly rental basis. After an initial down payment, the first six to fourteen months constituted a period of grace while the tenant farmer established his crops. Rents ranged between fifty cents and two dollars per acre per month, although the most common figure was one dollar per month.[42] Riverain areas were popular with tenant farmers, but land hunger within the empoldered coastlands was sufficiently acute for land tenancy to establish itself throughout the coastlands. Those estates which dropped out of sugar production almost invariably came to certain arrangements with villagers in the neighborhood with respect to the renting of land. This operation was profitable to the planters concerned, and it also held back the development of an independent landowning peasantry.

The small size of landholdings, the ever-present risk of drought and flood, and the lack of capital in this sector were among the factors that forced the choice of provision growing rather than the planting of permanent crops like cocoa and coffee. Short-term tenancies also reinforced this crop choice. Whitfield (1873) denounced the land tenure contracts as being overwhelmingly in favor of the landlords.[43] Even so, the planters of the 1880s strengthened their legal control over rural tenements. The Small Tenements Ordinance of 1880 added another dimension to the recovery of possession of tenements for the nonpayment of rent. Once the landlord gained judgment in his favor, he could levy on the growing crops at a value ascertained by the (planter-aligned) magistrate of the district. The attorney-general justified the measure by alleging that most tenants were "indolent and poor" and that the recovery of rents by the salable assets was unlikely.[44] W. F. Haynes-Smith, then the attorney-general, was himself a large landowner in West Demerara. The law did specify instances where tenants were to receive rent remission and relief, and it also insisted that the landlord was responsible for the maintenance of the main drainage and navigation trenches. But peasants were unable to defend or realize these rights in court. Instead, the matters that came up for adjudication were mainly landlord actions against tenants for improper use of tenancies and for recovery of rent. The courts were not mere rubber stamps for the interests of individual proprietors, several of whom lost cases against tenants and against villagers for trespass and the like. But defense of property by the courts was of course sacrosanct, and the social background of the magistracy made it as unlikely that they would be propeasant as it was unlikely that they would defend the indentured contract laborer against the plantation employer. In 1889, the Supreme Court ruled on appeal that plantain suckers did not constitute growing crops for the purpose of compensating a tenant unless the said suckers were the product of the tenant's labor.[45] On the face of it, such a ruling was reasonable, given that suckers generated spontaneously from the parent plant. However, the tenant was exposed to the real risk that at the moment of eviction, he might expect little or nothing for the value of the labor put into a field where there were suckers and young plants. Knowledgeable observers claimed that disputes that led to eviction of lessees constituted one of the reasons why more land was not in provision.[46]

Implicit in much of the earlier discussion is the overwhelming importance of drainage to subsistence and peasant farming. According to the report of the inspector of villages, the installation of a new drainage koker in 1894 was all it took to get the villagers of Golden Grove, Nabaclis, and Victoria to begin replanting abandoned backlands. Conversely, deterioration of drainage facilities could put an abrupt end to farming. John Gomes Fernandes petitioned the legislature in 1889 because the government altered the drainage of Danielstown and inadvertently shut off his estate, Fear Not. Fear Not had long ceased to be a coffee or sugar estate, but John Gomes Fernandes was the latest in a line of owners who rented land to provision farmers. The blocking of the drainage led to his tenants abandoning the land and caused him to lose $300 per month in rent.[47] It is not difficult to imagine similar sequences, which occurred with regularity but were unreported, because they were small-scale and commonplace. Occasionally, reverses happened on a scale large enough to affect land tenancy in the entire district. Such was the case with the Canals Polder of West Demerara during the 1880s.

Canals No. 1 and No. 2 quickly acquired the reputation of being the foremost provision-growing district in the postslavery era. The small-farming community supplied most of the needs of the city of Georgetown in respect of vegetables, fruit, and provisions; and Creoles were willing to pay high rents for farmland there.[48] However, drainage slowly deteriorated, and after several dry years in the late 1870s, disaster struck in the form of floods in 1880 and

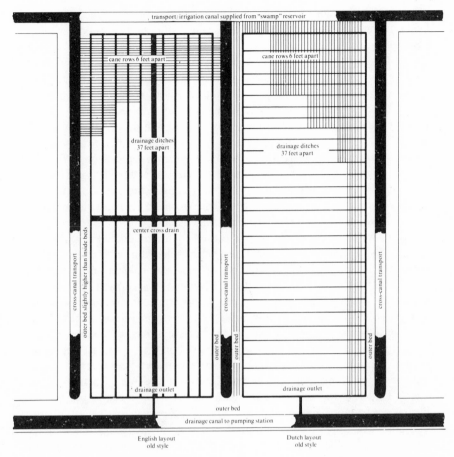

Typical drainage pattern in Guyanese plantations, late nineteenth century

again in 1882. Up until 1879, there were thirty-one estates on Canal No. 1 with 8,588 acres let to tenants. This figure was reduced to 490 acres by January 1883. Of the thirty-one estates, seven were actually villages and six others were in cane. This meant that eighteen estates supplied the bulk of rented land, and fourteen of these were up for sale.[49] Plantations Ostend, New Soesdyke, Endeavour, Mes Delices, Sans Souci, and Bordeaux were among those advertised for sale. The names attested to the mixed European ancestry of the first colonists on the Canal—estate proprietors who failed in their efforts to maintain the cultivation of cocoa and coffee. Without some assistance, the peasantry was also doomed to failure. As it was, the legislature held out some promise to the residents of the district in the form of a polder development scheme.

The Canals Polder Scheme as resolved by the legislature in December 1885 was the first of its kind in Guiana. It came at a time when works for the improvement of village drainage and sanitation were afoot. But the Canals Polder Scheme was on an unprecedentedly large scale, aiming at securing through drainage and irrigation the use of 21,000 acres at an estimated cost of $165,000. Crown lands comprised 8,356 acres within the projected empolder, the remainder being the freehold land which was precariously farmed up until then. The enterprise began with the clearing and redigging of Canals No. 1 and No. 2. People immediately began flocking to the area. Unfortunately, the works became bogged down. Costs escalated to twice the original estimate, and failure to complete the polder as designed meant that capital and labor were totally wasted or even proved counterproductive. The *Argosy* reported on 8 January 1887 that recent rains had hit the Canals Polder extremely hard. As part of the Polder Scheme, the colonial civil engineer had dug a water path to connect the Boerasirie and Hubabu Creeks, but there were no dams or stop-offs for protection; consequently, the new water path caused water to sweep down on the Canal farms. In conjunction with disastrous floods, there was scarcity in years of drought.[50] Many of the cultivators of land within the Canals Polder lived on the West Coast Demerara or at any rate looked to the populous coast as a market; this meant that the lack of properly maintained waterways between the West Coast and the Canals Polder was a serious liability. Cultivators were forced to pay toll to Plantation Leonora and to the Boerasirie Conservancy for the use of the only available canal. The result of these many shortcomings was an out-migration of Creole Africans from the Canals Polder in the last two decades of the nineteenth century and the loss of its preeminence as the purveyor of agricultural provisions to Georgetown.

Traffic of small boats or bateaux across the Demerara River from the farms to Georgetown was economically important in its own right. So long as the West Bank Demerara could supply foodstuffs, it was at least guaranteed rapid and relatively cheap transport to the country's major internal market. This was one of the reasons why the Canals Polder continued to lead in the supply of mangoes. In 1889, the Georgetown clerk of markets found it convenient to concentrate the sale of mangoes at the Stabroek market, with a wharf easily accessible to Demerara river craft. Between 15 February and 28 February of that year, Stabroek handled nearly ten thousand baskets of mangoes at an average weight of about 60 lbs. per basket.[51] The only comparable influx of fruit was from Clonbrook (Mahaica), and that was made possibly by rail transport. Between 16 June and 24 June 1890, the Demerara Railway carried nearly seven tons (15,680 lbs.) of mangoes from Clonbrook to Georgetown.[52] Only the East Coast Demerara had access to rail transport throughout the period under discussion. This was a marginal advantage over other regions. Rail freight was so expensive that sugar planters made strenuous efforts to have the rates reduced.[53] No wonder then that plantain farmers found the rates prohibitive and stuck to using carts for transport to the city when they could not dispose of their produce in the populous villages and plantations of the East Coast Demerara. Beyond Mahaica, there was no rail extension until 1900. Besides, the population was sparse and cart transport to Georgetown tedious and expensive, disadvantages that contributed to the West Coast Berbice being an economically backward area even by Guianese peasant standards of the nineteenth century.

Only Plantation Bath survived as a sugar estate in West Coast Berbice into the last two decades of the nineteenth century. Those who could not be employed at Bath trekked to Blairmont or further afield, residing during crop season on estates away from home. The Church was one of the social agencies which urged West Berbicians to stay at home and till their land fully. They were apparently prepared to do just that, provided that crops such as arrowroot could earn them some cash. During the 1880s, the primary schools at Lichfield and Belladrum were still accepting fees in kind.[54] Sporadic and ad hoc measures were taken to deal with the problem of distance from sizable markets. For instance, the local Anglican rector personally organized a nonprofit collection and agency service in 1886. But such solutions could not be long-lasting, and evidence from similar church sources bewailed the crushing poverty of the area in the last years of the century.[55]

To the major problems of the peasantry of the period, one must also add a long list of secondary grievances that affected production and the well-being of this large section of the population. Many small farmers sold their own provisions and protested having to buy huckster licenses.[56] Many had to acquire bateaux for water transport, and again they paid taxes, although sugar estates were granted exemption from payment on punts. Farmers at Soesdyke on the Demerara river drew attention to the small but objectionable burden of having to take out gun and dog licenses when these were essential in isolated areas. It is not difficult to appreciate the feelings of these farmers that added taxes were unacceptable in the light of the fact that "farmers time after time suffered losses by water, wind, disease and insects destroying their provisions."[57]

Peasant history (with the rare exception of peasant revolts) proceeds not from one great turning point to another but through a series of cyclical patterns, reflecting the dominance of the environment, the stagnation in technology, and the slow rate of change in the overall social structure. These characteristics direct that historical reconstruction should accord due attention to the minutiae of difficulties in the peasant existence. Moreover, the awareness and discussion of these difficulties reached a high point during the

1880s and 1890s, even if the problems themselves were typical of those that went before and after. One of the consequences of years of futile debate was the sense of frustration that laid the basis for riots in 1889. A second consequence was that small farmers supported the demand for political reform that gave rise to the new Constitution of 1881. In this sense, intense contemporary discussion of the peasant problem was a historical phenomenon in its own right.

Preoccupation with the catalog of peasant woes is also a desideratum for evaluating all efforts within the small farming sector—both those that were nullified and those that registered in the form of increased production. The Poor Law Commission of 1881 was informed as follows:

> In 1847, there were comparatively few [Creoles] living in the villages, but now there were comparatively few living on the estates. The village lands are cultivated now to a great extent, and a great many people are engaged in growing provisions, and the best fruit of that is that there are to be seen now in all parts of the Colony, more particularly on Saturdays, markets for the sale of vegetables of all kinds in all villages and in the front of sugar estates where people reside, and that consequently the whole population and more particularly the Indian population have now the means of procuring these vegetables with the greatest ease, whereas formerly they had to walk miles to procure them. The people grow sufficient provisions to support themselves but they do not grow a sufficient quantity to reduce the price over the whole colony.[58]

This testimony came from a colonist who was a planter in 1847 and who served as a stipendiary magistrate and as the inspector general of police. It is an informed appraisal of increased peasant production—something that tends to go unrecorded because it is difficult to measure subsistence.

Official sources paid little attention to positive peasant initiatives, but the crown surveyor compiled an unusual statement showing the state of village cultivation for the year 1886.[59] (See table A15; for data on the village economy in 1902, see table A16.) Cultivation was most varied on the West Coast Berbice, with small acreages of arrowroot in addition to the regular range of provisions: namely, plantains, cassava, yams, tannias, sweet potatoes, eddoes, and corn. Hopetown, the largest village of the district, planted arrowroot, castor oil, and coconuts, along with mixed provisions. The search for more variety was undoubtedly linked with the difficulties of finding estate employment in West Berbice, to which attention has already been drawn. The situation was slightly more favorable in parts of Essequibo, where sugar estates were in existence. Villagers sought to extract the most out of their rural markets. Both sweet cassava and the toxic bitter cassava were under cultivation, and villagers specialized in the making of cassava bread and casareep (sauce). Oral tradition emphasizes the role of the women of Queenstown in this process and the sale of these products at the then functioning estates of

Anna Regina and Golden Fleece.[60] On the East Bank of the Essequibo, the specialization was in plantains, using abandoned sugar lands but aiming at markets on Plantation Philadelphia and others that lay along the West Coast Demerara. The backlands in this area were slightly higher and better drained, and the peasants were prepared to clear new lands as soon as the plantain disease established itself. In this way, they maintained a reputation during the early 1880s of being able to unload large supplies of plantains and other vegetables thrice weekly at the Boerasirie Creek bridge.[61]

One of the interesting developments was the emergence of the Pomeroon as a leading center of food production. The district was long known to be fertile—ever since the days of Dutch rule—and it attracted post-Emancipation settlements of free Creole Africans. By the 1870s, it was already known as a rather cosmopolitan area that was popular with ex-indentured Portugese and to a lesser extent with ex-indentured Indians. Without estate wages as an element in their survival, Pomeroon farmers had of necessity to cultivate on a reasonably large scale and to ensure that they transported to Georgetown by water. The district was mentioned before the West India Commission of 1897 as the main supplier of the Georgetown market. New farms had begun springing up in the Pomeroon around 1878. Some of these were pioneered by squatters, who were not given land titles until 1890. The owners were not the typical peasants and subsistence farmers of the villages; rather they were medium-sized proprietors with as much as 100 or 150 acres, and many claimed that they would not wish to exchange their positions for the liabilities of a sugar estate.[62]

Market gardening understandably developed in close proximity to the city of Georgetown. In 1883, Plantation Houston was described as "the most desirable sugar property in the Colony."[63] This superlative was bestowed because Houston made a great deal of money from renting part of its land on short leases. The system followed was periodically to throw a number of fields out of cane cultivation and rent them to small farmers for plantains and other provisions. Houston at that point had 165 acres in plantains as compared with 922 in canes and 912 uncultivated. Plantation Peter's Hall lay just beyond Houston and was slightly farther from Georgetown; but it was also an estate that rented land to small farmers for the same reason. The Colonial Company owned six estates with a total of 18,548 acres of empoldered land in British Guiana in 1896, out of which it rented only 140 acres. Peter's Hall accounted for 123 of the 140 acres rented.[64] Tenant farmers vigorously pursued land rentals from the estates on the lower East Bank Demerara because there was no other available land and because their surplus was readily marketable.

From the foregoing, it is clear that Guianese who were committed to a full-time peasant existence, or even to a part-time cultivation, demonstrated both persistence and initiative in their attempts to make farming economical-

La Penitence: Bridge between Georgetown and the East Bank Demerara estates

ly viable. In Guiana, as in the West Indies, the emancipated population planted not only provisions and fruits, but also coffee, cotton, and cocoa. These crops seldom reached dimensions that merited mention in the annual Blue Book statistics, after having collapsed as plantation crops by the middle of the nineteenth century. Peasants were interested in these crop choices, but any reestablishment would have had to overcome the heritage of, and reasons for, previous failure. An excellent case in point was provided when a representative of the London Missionary Society prevailed upon his church members to resume cotton cultivation at Fryish on the Corentyne in the 1860s. They earned an income until the slump after the American Civil War caused prices to plummet and wiped out commercial cotton growing both on estates and on peasant farms.[65] Nearly forty years later, strenuous but unsuccessful efforts were made to revive cotton growing on the Corentyne and other parts of the coastlands. An association called the Berbice Cotton Growers' Committee was formed in June 1903; several hundred pounds of seed were distributed, and numerous inducements were offered. Yet only four acres were actually planted. The director of lands attributed the failure of the experiment to "the long established distaste on the part of the ordinary creole farmer to embark upon the cultivation of other than edible products."[66] The explanation is essentially correct, but it needs to be emphasized that the seeming conservatism on the part of the peasants was deeply rooted in a bitter experience of the disaster that attended such initiatives when the state machinery was not prepared to sustain their efforts.

Only the sugar industry could count upon the assistance of the colonial state to ensure its survival, in spite of numerous vicissitudes. This suggested to some Creole Africans and to some planters the possibility of a nexus in the form of peasant production of cane for grinding by the plantations. Peasant cultivation of sugar cane had been tried in a few instances immediately after Emancipation, but it lapsed, and the reintroduction of cane farming by peasants dates from the 1870s. William Russell, the "sugar king," was the originator of one of the earliest suggestions that the villagers should grow cane for grinding in the factories. His specific proposal in April 1872 was that the villagers of Beterverwagting should produce cane for the factory at La Bonne Intention (L.B.I.). In reporting the scheme, the *Working Man* advised that it should be given a trial in the hope that it would lead to a point at which "our creole peasantry see that THEIR INTERESTS ARE MORE CLOSELY BOUND UP with the large staple of export than MERE DAILY WAGES." [67] The annual report on agriculture took cognizance of peasant cane farming for the first time in 1879, but the operation had begun several years previously, with Afro-Guianese on the lower East Coast Demerara as the pioneers. Canes grown at Beterverwagting went to Plantation La Bonne Intention, while Plaisance cane farmers dispatched theirs mainly to Plantation Geodverwagting. In 1879, several villagers at Victoria, Ann's Grove, and Two Friends planted canes on their backlands, after securing a promise that grinding would be done on Plantation Clonbrook. At the same time, the possibility was also being considered at Sister's Village on the West Bank Demerara, and the inspector of villages was apparently lobbying that the manager of Plantation Wales should agree to take off the cane. In 1881, Bagotville farmers turned to Plantation Nismes, while Den Amstel and Fellowship were willing to plant if the factory at Windsor Forest would consent to grind.[68]

Small increases in peasant cane production were registered in 1880 and 1881. The estimated peasant production of cane in 1882 was sufficient to yield 1,000 hogsheads (900 tons) of sugar, which was half the output of any efficient producer among the sugar estates then grinding.[69] By 1886, commercial cane farming was still confined to the county of Demerara—with the exception of Aberdeen village on the Essequibo coast and Rosignol on the West Bank Berbice, which had 39 acres and 12 acres respectively under cane. In spite of the preponderance of mixed cultivation, the sugar cane crop must have loomed large in the monetary calculations of many small farmers. For instance, Bagotville had 44 acres under sugar as compared to 129 under plantains; Arcadia on Canal No. 3 had 100 acres of cane and 99 of mixed provisions; Ann's Grove assigned 136 acres to sugar cane and 243 acres to other crops, while at Beterverwagting 185 acres were devoted to cane as compared to 39 acres under provisions and fruits.[70]

Cane farming constitutes one of the rare economic avenues opened up by
the Creole African peasantry; and they would probably have embraced it
more warmly were it not for certain obstacles. The main stumbling block in
the formative years was a guaranteed buyer for the canes in the form of a
"grinding estate."* If a factory manager agreed to purchase, it was necessary
that farmers be offered long-term arrangements to afford them security in the
new enterprise. Cane farmers soon found that they were no less exposed than
sugar workers to the exploitation and arbitrariness of plantation proprietors.
On some estates, farmers' canes were priced according to the amount of sugar
indicated by the polarization of the juice. A transaction of this nature, in
which 29 hogsheads (23 tons) of sugar were expected, involved a payment of
$1,650 to the farmers. This meant that the estate paid approximately $57 for
the juice equivalent of one hogshead of sugar at a time when vaccum pan
sugar was averaging $96 per hogshead (of 18 cwt.) on the market.[71] Besides,
management benefited from the value of the by-products, namely rum,
molasses, and bagasse. Rum and molasses brought immediate monetary
earnings to the factory; while bagasse was rapidly being substituted for coal
in the more modern factories and effected a major saving, with the price of
coal at $7 per ton.[72]

During the early history of cane farming, disputes arose over the weight
of cane supplied by the peasants, the quality of their cane juice, and the
number of tons of cane which yielded one ton or one hogshead of sugar.
Factory owners exercised what amounted to absolute and unilateral powers
to resolve these sensitive issues and to determine whether the grinding (and
hence cultivation) of peasant cane should continue. Cane farmers felt that
they were forced to accept disadvantageous terms. When there was a changeover from payment by weight of canes to payment by polarization, peasants
were extremely suspicious, in spite of reassurances that this was a more
accurate and a fairer means of assessment.[73] An additional problem, which
sometimes proved overwhelming, was that of transportation, which required
the existence or construction of canals running from the village backlands
to the particular factory and the provision of punts at appropriate times.
Farmers at Beterverwagting complained that it was costing them $14 per
hogshead to fetch their canes to La Bonne Intention. The estate management
was also enxious to avoid the circuitous transport system, which entailed
head porterage across dams. Failure on the part of the government to attend
to the water connections precipitated a temporary cessation of the grinding
of farmers' canes at La Bonne Intention in 1881. Plantation Better Hope took
a similar step in 1884 in relation to farmers of Plaisance and Sparendaam,
after getting no response to their suggestion that estate punts would fetch the
cane if the government gave permission to build an aqueduct. Ann's Grove

*"Grinding estate"—term used to identify an estate with its own factory.

villagers reported a more frustrating experience. There, the villagers agreed to put in at their own expense an aqueduct to link with the Clonbrook factory. But the village administration was taken over by the Central Board of Health and the project was stopped.[74]

Both acrimony and distress surrounded the termination of the relationship between cane farmers and the management of any given estate. A small but very poignant piece of evidence to this effect was provided when the Central Board of Health sued Abel Ameo of Plaisance for $24 to recover arrears in rent. When the case was heard early in 1883, Abel Ameo stated that the land on which the rent was due was abandoned as a consequence of the notice received from William Russell that he would no longer take canes from farmers.[75] Cane farmers must have been thoroughly disenchanted with factory arrangements throughout the county of Demerara in which the industry was established, because there arose in the early 1880s a remarkable movement to acquire small sugar mills—usually worked by wind power and producing muscovado sugar. Individuals and groups that favored this idea needed credit to purchase and establish sugar mills. The government was the principal source to which they turned for assistance, and that assistance was consistently denied them. Between 1880 and 1883, a series of requests from would-be mill owners before the legislature with regard to loans in the vicinity of $600 to $1,000 were all turned down.[76]

Planters were divided in their views on the utility of cane farming. William Russell continued to be a proponent of the idea, in spite of his many rooted prejudices against the Creole African peasantry. C. L. Bascom of Cove and John and R. P. Drysdale of Clonbrook (both members of the legislature) were among the prominent proprietors connected with cane farming. Perhaps they judged that the peasant contribution allowed for a more effective utilization of the extra capacity of the modern equipment then being installed in the factories.* However, the proposal to have independent cane mills was less attractive; and one finds Drysdale voting alongside the planter lords, J. Booker and H. K. Davson, against requests for loans for such enterprises. Only very rarely did the government take steps to encourage cane farming in this period. The governor announced in May 1884 that he proposed joining the East Coast Demerara villages, so that peasants could carry their cane to the factories. An aqueduct was constructed between Plaisance and Better Hope, and the waterway between Beterverwagting and La Bonne Intention was completed.[77] This belated and inadequate assistance in 1884 came just as the sugar industry fell victim to an international capitalist crisis. Declining prices severely and adversely affected cane farming. Factories obviously offered less for peasant canes when the price of sugar went down on international markets. Payment for cane juice was reduced from 3 cents

*In effect, peasants were resuming cane cultivation on lands previously abandoned by the plantations.

per gallon in 1884 to 1½ cents per gallon in 1886.[78] The few village cane mills that were set up had a poor rate of extraction and produced muscovado, which sold for less than vacuum-pan sugar, so they certainly could not afford better prices to cane farmers.

The earnings of most cane farmers were meager. L.B.I. paid out $4,243 to cane farmers in 1877, and in 1880 the figure climbed to just above $5,000. The latter payout gave to the farmers sums as tiny as $1.89 for a season's labor and usually no more than $25.00.[79] Obviously, farmers must have made some rough calculations of the cost-benefits of cane cultivation. The *Colonist* of 2 November 1883 reported that many who had tried it on the West Bank Demerara were of the opinion that cane farming did not pay—at least not when the farms were some distance from the factory and costs were incurred in carrying the canes from field to riverside, and from there to the estate concerned. On the other hand, the factory payment was considered worthwhile if one sought to acquire money in a lump sum. Peasant cane cultivation continued under adverse conditions during the depression of the 1880s. It was on the decrease during the 1890s and reached its lowest point during the depression of 1895-97. A representative of the Colonial Company told the West India Commission that the company was offering land to cane farmers in Guiana at a nominal rent of $1.00 per acre per annum, and that it was willing to purchase the crop at $2.40 per ton. Yet only two farmers took advantage of the offer and not more than 10 acres were taken up. This was at a time when the same company was engaged in grinding large tonnages of peasant cane in Trinidad. There was a slight revival of interest in cane farming at the turn of the present century. In January 1902, the Victoria-Belfield Agricultural Society added its voice to the clamor for an end to beet-sugar bounties, and in the process it claimed credit for the resuscitation of peasant cane farming.[80] Peasant canefields were then estimated at less than 700 acres. Tentative as these beginnings undoubtedly were, the new economic activity had come to stay.

When cane farming and opportunities for estate labor decreased during moments of deep economic crisis, they were replaced by participation in subsistence activity. Unemployed and underemployed workers devoted a portion of their time to the cultivation of provisions. The inspector of villages noted this in his report for 1885, and regarded the hardship as a blessing in disguise in so far as it renewed interest in the land. The Creole African population started paying greater attention to their backlands, and for this reason a larger amount of taxes was collected in 1886 than in any previous year. The conventional response to prices was subordinated to, though not entirely negated by, the necessity to merely subsist. In 1888, artisans on the Essequibo coast were turning to farming because of unemployment. Since most of their product was intended for home consumption, the market price was not a decisive factor. Nevertheless, the price for their surplus provisions must have been reasonably remunerative to allow villagers to rent land from the estates, and there would have been some response, however sluggish, from farmers such as those in Berbice who, in December 1888, experienced a sudden rise in the average price of a bunch of plantains from fourteen cents to thirty cents. The *Argosy* later specified that there was a great rush by Essequibo laborers to lease backlands for provision growing, because of the scarcity of provisions.[81] The inference as to good prices was confirmed by the reverse trend in 1894-95. In these years the price of ground provisions fell, and (together with a lessened demand for labor in the goldfields) this helped estates to recruit their full complement of villagers. Plantains dropped from 36 cents per bunch to 16 cents per bunch between 1894 and 1896. Poor prices for agricultural produce went far to explain why the village backlands in 1898-99 were abandoned or tilled only in a perfunctory manner, with a few notable exceptions such as Golden Grove and Nabaclis.[82] Plantains had in the meanwhile won external markets in the Caribbean. Exports in 1886 amounted to 26,047 bunches, as compared with 5,751 bunches in 1885—the first year of exportation. Some of this was due to the increased cultivation of plantains by sugar estates on land taken out of sugar cane. Unfortunately, when the economy once more fell back into a slump in 1902, the West Indian market for plantains all but disappeared.[83]

General patterns in the performance of small farmers prevailed, with slight differences from one part of the coastland to another. One major variable was the decline of sugar estates in any given region. Residents of the Essequibo islands, for example, saw the closure of one estate after another until the final disappearance of sugar manufacturing in 1905. This process (wherever it occurred) left part-time and full-time wage workers "living from hand to mouth on the produce of their small garden holdings."[84] Estate collapse encouraged out-migration. Both plantation and peasant sectors lost Creole African labor that moved toward the towns and the hinterland. At the same time, the immigrant population, which was by then the principal source of estate labor, also stepped up their contribution to subsistence and peasant farming. The end of reindentureship and the increase in time-expired immigrants marked the start of a dynamic contribution by immigrants to the nonplantation sectors. From the mid-1870s, the immigration agent-general reported that Indians were spreading out and were turning to a variety of occupations: cultivating provision farms, tending cattle, hiring out as domestics, setting up as hucksters, and driving carts. The census of 1891 enumerated 579 East Indian peasant proprietors. Apart from these, thousands of estate laborers had by then obtained small plots of land both on and off the estates. The process was accelerated by international depression, since small food gardens became essential in the face of mass unemployment and lowered wages. The proliferation of economic activities and the resort to subsistence farming were reminiscent of the behavior of Creoles after slavery. In this instance, however, the principal food crop was rice rather than plantains.

Africans from rice-growing areas of the Upper Guinea Coast had sown rice in Guiana since slavery days and continued to do so after Emancipation.[85] But the modern rice industry was pioneered by Asian immigrants, who introduced new techniques, new varieties, and a seriousness which reflected the importance of rice in their diet. When Asians started growing "wet rice" on the low-lying coastlands, water for irrigation purposes was the main problem.* For the most part, rice farming was therefore established on the front lands of functioning sugar estates or on abandoned sugar estates where the drainage was still intact. Canal bottoms were found especially suited to rice nurseries. Of the several nuclei of rice farming that emerged along the coast in the 1880s, the least developed were on the East Coast Demerara, where cultivators used patches of savanna fortuitously cleared by bush fires following the dry periods in 1882, 1883, and 1884. These were squatters on crown land, who obtained water supplies from the water path running aback to the Lamaha conservation. Settled cultivation was carried on in the Abary district, where Indians had acquired the estates of Novar and Dundee in 1883, and at Plantation Prospect on the East Bank Berbice. In both instances, Indian proprietors made a success of rice cultivation in spite of uncertain water supplies. Leonora was another pioneer locality. Rice was sown there by Chinese and Indian immigrants from the 1860s, but the initiative ended in 1872 and the cultivation later had to be reestablished.[86]

The best rice cultivation of the 1880s was said to have been that on rented land at Plantation Anna Regina. Chinese immigrants devised ingenious irrigation practices, "liberating" water through bamboo stems from the estate supplies. During this same period, the Indian role in the expansion of rice farming on the Essequibo coast is seen from the fact that they were allowed to lease 30 acres in 1884, and by 1887 they were planting 300 acres at Anna Regina, although the rent rose from $6 per acre per year to $24 per acre per year.[87] On the upper Corentyne, Chinese and Indians displayed similar enthusiasm for rice farming and proved to be quite innovative. The manager of Plantation Skeldon addressed the Royal Agricultural and Commercial Society in April 1881 on the rice industry of the upper Corentyne. He observed of the Chinese:

> In lot 72 or Hong Kong they have peculiar arrangements that I have not seen anywhere else for husking and cleaning their rice, of which they have about 100 acres in cultivation, independent of what the Coolies and Blacks have. The arrangement I refer to is in the shape of a conical hat and made of stone. Around this and enclosing it to within about a quarter of an inch

*Africans on the Canje and Berbice rivers had previously cultivated the "dry" upland variety.

The early rice industry. Threshing by hand before the era of mechanization at the turn of the century.

a wicker case is placed of similar shape. This is made to revolve by a simple system of ropes and levers and as the rough grain passes between the stone and the casing, the friction detaches the husk from the kernel. The winnowing separates the bulk of the husk from the grain and the cleaning is completed by the rice being pounded in a large-sized mortar, the pestle of which is fixed to the end of a long lever which is easily worked by the foot. The Coolies, who have from 200 to 300 acres of rice in cultivation, have been simply using the mortar and the pestle for cleaning the grain, but they are copying the Chinese plan very fast.[88]

In its initial stages, the rice industry received little support from the colonial government. However, the ex-indentured immigrants were able to take advantage of certain conditions which placed the planter class on the defensive: notably, international depression, the right of return to India, and the rise of a lobby demanding promotion of "minor industries."

It was with the coming of the depression of 1884 that the manager of Anna Regina offered contracts to free Indians to halve the rental on ½-acre plots, on condition that the beneficiary should work for three days in a week on the estate at the lowered wage rates. The estate was therefore solving its acute economic problems at very little real cost—if any. At nearby Plantation Coffee Grove, the management rented out frontlands that were some two feet below the level of water in the navigation trenches, and that were almost useless for canes because the cultivation was extremely susceptible to becoming water-starved. The Indian peasantry was then left to cope with the myriad uncertainties of polder husbandry, along with other disincentives, such as the plague of rats which hit the Essequibo rice fields in 1886.[89] Given international depression and severe beet competition, both workers and employers seemed to have concurred on the need for subsistence food production to ease the distress of retrenchment and lowered wages. By 1897, rice cultivation was officially estimated at 15,500 acres. The survey was incomplete, but it clearly indicates rapid expansion during the depression, since estimates up to 1893 gave no more than 2,500 acres under rice.[90] The abandonment of a number of sugar estates was partly responsible for the leap in acreage, and it was also still the policy of functioning sugar estates to make deals with their resident unindentured work force around the question of rice beds. The opening of third depths on most estates meant that cane cultivation could be pursued on the new lands while the exhausted frontlands were deployed to bind a portion of the workers.

Indian immigrants derived some advantage from the existence of India as an external reference point. The colonial state in India had perforce to recognize a responsibility toward its own citizens on the issue of emigration. The manner of their withdrawl from Indian society and their possible reentry into India were equally pertinent. Besides, their treatment as Indians and human beings in a new land influenced the permission given to recruit in India. These considerations aided the emergence of an Indo-Guianese peasantry in that planters decided to open up lands to time-expired immigrants rather than allow a large exodus of repatriates. The decade of the 1880s started with a wave of repatriations, and the rate continued to be high for the rest of the century. Of the 2,340 Indians who registered repatriation claims between January and March 1880, there were 1,679, or 71.75 percent, who had not been resident in the country for eleven years. In other words, adult immigrants were claiming on behalf of themselves and their children the right to free return passage as soon as it became due at the end of ten years in the colony.[91] A committee of the legislature investigated the problem in 1880, in 1888, and again in 1895. One proposal which gained credence among planters was that of establishing settlement schemes, where Indians relinquished their repatriation rights in return for free land grants. From this thinking emerged the settlement schemes at Huis t'Dieren (Essequibo Coast, 1880), Helena (West Coast Berbice, 1897), Whim (lower Corentyne, 1898), Bush Lot (West Coast Berbice, 1898), and Maria's Pleasure (Essequibo, 1902). At times, the view prevailed that government-organized settlement schemes in lieu of repatriation were unnecessary, but in practice, this view also favored Indian small farmers, because the solution was seen in the preparation of well-drained empoldered land for sale to rice growers at cheap prices.[92]

During the 1890s and at the turn of the present century, planters were under considerable pressure of public opinion to pay attention to industries other than the venerable sugar industry. The advocacy of minor industries was one of the planks of the reform platform—leading to constitutional change in 1891. The issue of minor industries received mere lip service for many years, although action was taken to subsidize a short-lived rice-milling firm in 1897. After the West India Commission recommended more decisive action in establishing a peasantry, rice farming received some measure of legislative assistance. The relaxation of restrictions on the acquisition of crown land in 1898 was a fillip to rice farmers, and so too was the creation of a technical service that distributed new seed types under an Agricultural Board from 1900.

The fact that rice peasants were mainly part-time estate workers was by no means incidental. A rice-farming group of subsistence farmers and peasants was permitted, if not promoted, because their existence was judged compatible with the labor demands of the sugar industry. It was the proprietor of Plantation Melville who in 1880 served as spokesman for Indian enquiries as to the possibility of getting Plantation L'Amitie (West Bank Mahaica) as an immigrant settlement. The idea won the approval of the crown surveyor, who stated:

> It would be desirable that the lands granted should not exceed a certain quantity per man or family, and that they should be in as close proximity to the sugar estates on which the immigrants have served their time as practicable, in order that as the quantity assigned each man or family would not occupy the time of either himself or his family exclusively they might be able to work on the sugar estates occasionally, so that their labour would not be entirely withdrawn from the estates. The proposed settlement at l'Amitie is well adapted to carry this out.[93]

In marked contrast, Indians at Princess Carolina on the Demerara river were given short shrift when they petitioned for land rights, because they were beyond the sugar belt and were seeking to be independent. One planter in the legislature denounced the petitioners as "squatters of the worst description," and he dismissed Princess Caroline as "a harbour of refuge for immigrant deserters."[94]

Surgeon-Major Comins has already been cited in the discussion of time-expired immigrant workers to indicate that the latter were tied to estate labor by various inducements. The offer of rice beds was the greatest of these inducements, and its importance was constantly on the increase. Doubts were from time to time expressed over the clash between rice harvesting and cane harvesting, and some planters swung against the acceptance of rice farming for this reason.[95] But this was a secondary issue. Time-expired immigrants and large sections of the population were demanding economic opportunities other than estate wage labor. Planters found themselves forced to choose between the proximity of rice farming (whatever its shortcomings from an estate viewpoint) and the possibility of schemes that might disperse labor to other parts of the colony. It was in this context that the manager of

Plantation Skeldon firmly opposed the encouragement of settlers in the hinterland and urged that government assistance be given to immigrants who were rice farmers. He went to the trouble of conducting his own census of households and inhabitants between No. 64 village and No. 79; and he found the population (in 1880) to consist of 1,161 free Indians, 499 blacks, 163 Chinese, and 79 Portuguese. He also recorded the number of Indian and Chinese villagers who turned up to work on the two nearby estates in a sample week.

	Mon.	Tues.	Wed.	Thurs.	Fri.
Skeldon	43	162	297	331	302
Eliza and Mary	104	135	159	97	113
Total	147	297	456	428	415

The total adult Asian population was then 908 in the villages mentioned, and the manager expressed himself satisfied with the average daily turnout of 368 persons, or approximately 40.5 percent of the potential.[96]

Most Indian rice farmers were dependent on the estates or on other land-lords, and they included a large group which Lesley Potter accurately de-scribes as a "paddy proletariat," contending that between 1895 and 1920 a large proportion of Indian rice growers fitted more closely the definition of "proletariat" than that of "peasantry." The paddy proletariat included estate residents growing rice on estate land as well as those who grew rice elsewhere; and, at the end of the period under discussion, about one-third of the rice was grown on sugar estates.[97] By this date, too, rice had definitely established itself as an export crop, although what mattered most was its contribution to the domestic market. The spurt in production in 1894-97 registered mainly as a fulfillment of subsistence requirements. The Blue Book for 1897 con-tained little that was encouraging on the economic front other than the story of rice. It noted specifically that in Berbice production already went a long way towards supplying local consumption and it looked forward to the time when Guiana would grow rice for its own needs and export the surplus. The immigration agent-general also drew attention to the good rice harvest at the end of 1897 and to the fact that on some estates immigrants stored up enough rice to last their respective households one year—calculating one bag to last a man and wife one month. This latter figure is more significant than other seemingly more impressive data, such as the jump in rice exports to 3,474,572 lbs. in 1906 and the doubling of this quantity the following year to outstrip imports for the first time. The estimate of household rice stocks kept by small producers suggests greater consumption among the most deprived sections of the population, while the overall figures indicate in-creased per capita consumption for the country at large.[98]

The general health of ex-indentured immigrants was reported to have been extremely poor in the early 1880s, when the movement from the estates was in its infancy.[99] Improvements were noted by the time of the Mortality Commission of 1906, and these had much to do with increased production of food in the small-farming sector and the attendant rise in consumption among laborers as a whole. It was striking that among Indians in the countryside who breastfed and used cow's milk when substituting, the fall in infant mortality rates was pronounced—dropping by 12 percent between 1895 and 1904 to a figure of 182 per thousand.[100] The availability of milk and meat came about because livestock was being reared on numerous small and medium-sized farms.

According to the rough calculations, the total number of livestock slaughtered per year showed continual growth from the 1830s through the turn of the century, from 2,308 in 1832; 5,147 in 1852; 11,478 in 1872; 25,596 in 1892; to 57,950 in 1912.[101]

Although the figures given are little more than intelligent guesses, the literary sources attest to the increase of cattle farms, especially in Mahaica-Mahaicony, West Berbice, and the Corentyne. They also indicate obliquely that Creole Africans were raising more livestock and were therefore losers in time of flood and drought. Above all, reports of the immigration agent-general drew attention to the swelling tide of livestock ownership among Indians, several of whom managed to buy a cow before their indentureship was actually ended. Unlike the rice industry, the coastal cattle industry received little attention and no accolades. But its growth in the later nineteenth century was impressive, and further confirms how the creative efforts of rural working people filled the interstices of the plantation economy and guaranteed their own survival in a period of protracted crisis.

CHAPTER 4

Socioeconomic Differentiation:
On the Coast and in the Hinterland

> There runs a dream of perished Dutch plantations
> In these Guiana rivers to the sea. . . .
> History moved down river, leaving free
> The forest to creep back, foot by quiet foot
> And overhang black waters to the sea.
>
> *A. J. Seymour*

Economic Diversification

Peasant farming contributed in a small way to making the colonial economy of British Guiana more differentiated. Food-producing and food-exporting sectors were added, along with allied distributive services. But sugar's decline as a proportion of total exports in the last two decades of the nineteenth century was due primarily to the broadening of the economy to exploit the productive capacity of areas in the hinterland of the coastal strip. (see table 17.) The elements of economic differentiation included the consolidation of the timber industry, the pioneering of diamond mining, and above all, the revival of the gold industry. By 1897, sugar had fallen to 70 percent of total exports, but calculated on the basis of exports other than gold, it accounted for 94 percent, a figure that would have brought British Guiana into line with the other West Indian sugar monocultural percentages: Antigua, 94 percent; St. Kitts, 96 percent; and Barbados, 97 percent.[1]

Ever since the Dutch resolved upon coastal agriculture in the mid-eighteenth century, the Guianese economy had turned its back on the hinterland. Economic possibilities there were known to exist. Sometimes they were exaggerated and romanticized, but no agency took practical steps to enlarge the coastal economy in the direction of the interior for most of the nineteenth century. On the contrary, planters viewed the hinterland as a potential competitor for labor and sought to dissuade free blacks from

Greenheart Logs transported from the Essequibo River to Wismar on the Demerara River

moving in that direction in the 1840s, just as they had earlier sought to fore-
stall slaves from escaping into the bush. The economy of British Guiana was
a classic example of a colonial economy in its failure to use resources that
were readily at hand within the domestic environment, while relying on the
importation of goods that could have been supplied by those very resources.
Contemporaries were aware of this contradiction and often expressed dissatisfaction with the state of affairs.[2] The buildings of Georgetown, New Amsterdam, and other towns were made of wood, but for the most part that wood
was not cut from the forests of Guiana. The same could be said for the furniture in the houses. Imported American white and yellow pine were much
favored in the early 1880s, being used for exteriors, flooring, furniture, and
planking of bridges. Not surprisingly, the local timber industry was then woe-
fully undeveloped, and such as it was, it had grown mainly in response to
external demand which centered around the greenheart species to the exclusion of almost everything else.

Greenheart exports started in the 1850s and were closely tied to the
construction of docks and canals in the United Kingdom. The building and
rebuilding (after fire) of the Liverpool landing stage dictated the tempo of the
timber-exporting industry in the early 1880s. The good orders of 1882 were
not repeated; instead, greenheart too suffered from the price collapse and
depressed commercial conditions of the second half of the decade. The annual report on exports in 1886 drew particular attention to the decrease in
exports of timber and shingles and to the depression in the woodcutting
industry. A partial recovery took place in 1889 because of large orders from
the Manchester Ship Canal and from piers at Ostend and Buenos Aires. Ship-

ments fell short of the level reached in 1882, but the special size ordered for the ship canal brought a better price two dollars per cubic foot).[3] After a long period in the doldrums, there was another spurt in demand in 1895-96, owing to specific projects in Scotland, the Orkneys, Holland, and France. However, by this date the greenheart industry had stagnated. Cataracts on the Essequibo river restricted operations to an area which had already been worked over two or three times, leading to the disappearance of the best trees.[4] Indeed, the industry had earlier experienced difficulties in getting the large-sized greenheart which was in demand for the Manchester Ship Canal. Even during the early years of this century, the excellent stands of timber above the cataracts were hardly used, because more access roads or railways would have been required. The *Chronicle* of 20 August 1903 reported that timber from the coastal reaches around Supenaam, Groete Creek, and Bonasika was hard to obtain. These areas had previously had a good reputation for mora and greenheart. At the time, the best timber was being shipped by the firm of Sprostons from Wismar, since they used the only existing interior railway to transport logs from the Essequibo side of the watershed between the Demerara and Essequibo rivers.

Balata constituted a minor but unique tree product. It was regarded as the best of the natural caoutchouc substances in the manufacture of telegraph wires. However, total dependence on a foreign market once more meant that the growth and performance of the industry could not be locally planned. Starting in 1860, the tapping or "bleeding" of balata from bulletwood trees proved profitable for only a few years before price and demand declined steeply. There was some revival in the early 1880s, and by 1883 the price of balata on the English market was thirty cents per pound as compared with six cents per pound some years before. This price was soon to fall as part of the general price movement during the downswing in the business cycle. Output rose from 47, 295 pounds in 1884 to 80,942 pounds in 1887, at the same time that earnings actually dropped. Nevertheless, the industry became firmly established. Output of balata advanced by 200 percent in 1888 and reached its peak in 1903 when even Venezuelan balata was sold via the Georgetown dealers.[5] (See table A18).

The only other local species popular with woodcutters and featured on the international market was wallaba. It was exported to parts of the Caribbean in the form of staves, shingles, and charcoal, and these products retained some vitality in periods of economic distress. For instance, there was an overall decrease in export in 1881, but the market for shingles remained constant, while the fall in the export of coals was attributed to increased local consumption. Charcoal exports stayed remarkably constant at about 60,000 barrels per annum (worth just over $30,000), whereas shingles went down in the 1890s and by 1904 had reached the level of a mere $7,360.[6] Since there was a domestic demand for both wallaba shingles and charcoal, the social

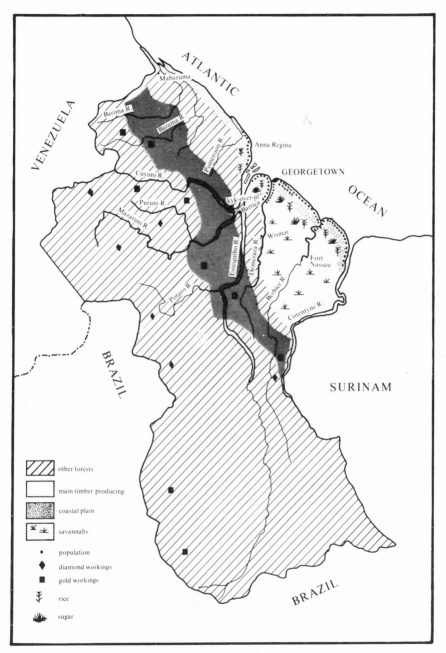

National resources of British Guiana, c. 1900

significance of these products was greater than suggested by the meager export earnings. Galvanized roofing was introduced in 1880, but this failed to stop the expansion of demand for shingles, which were increasingly fashionable as roofing on the estates, in the countryside generally, and among the Portuguese in particular.[7]

A local and supposedly informed publication in 1885 stated that buildings were boarded with white pine or American lumber because the colonists possessed no cheap softwoods suitable for the purpose.[8] The explanation was simply not true. One of the more positive trends of the late nineteenth century was a start toward the utilization of native woods. The church community was one that expressed frequent concern over buildings and materials. Their places of worship, their schools and all related residences were subject to high maintenance costs because of the relatively rapid decay of wooden buildings in tropical conditions. Consequently, their records reflected a growing willingness to use local woods where these offered advantages of convenience, lower cost, and superior durability. As early as 1872, an interior mission station of the United Society for the Propagation of the Gospel at Moruca on the Pomeroon was remodeled by stripping the white pine from the floor and replacing it with crabwood, while the roof was rebuilt of hardwood rafters and wallaba shingles. At Skeldon and Orealla (at the other end of the coast), U.S.P.G. reports for 1883 indicated that they were using silverballi boards sawn at Plantations Eliza and Mary, as well as bulletwood to replace pitch-pine frames.[9] However, in the construction of the Anglican cathedral of St. Georges in Georgetown, the use of local woods was elevated to a matter of policy. In 1889, the building committee for the cathedral expressed a preference for local woods and particularly for greenheart boards for the exterior. The roof was close-boarded with American pine, and some Honduran cedar went into the interior furnishing. But the exterior and flooring were of greenheart while simarupa and silverballi gave a touch of class to the vaulted ceiling.[10]

By 1880, there were two steam sawmills in Georgetown and one up the Demerara river. The range and quantity of their output could not have been very great. At this date, Stipendiary Magistrate Michael McTurk was a notable advocate of the variety and value of the woods of British Guiana, but this was a lonely voice and there was indifference toward sponsoring the local softwoods and hardwoods in building and furniture making. As late as 1902, the administration was unable to answer a query from the Colonial Office as to the existence of certain woods in the colony. On this occasion, the governor observed:

> It is so clearly unsatisfactory that we should be without complete and suitable specimens of all the woods of this Colony on a sufficient examination, that I am making arrangements for a collection to be made slowly but on a proper scale at the Government sawmills at Christianburg. . . . I

Building in wood. The Victoria Law Courts in process of construction, 1884.

am also having reprinted Mr. McTurk's lists of woods collected for the local and Paris exhibitions in 1878.[11]

McTurk's pioneer reports were probably subjected to the "gnawing criticism of the mice" during the last two decades of the nineteenth century, and there is little evidence of official initiatives to assist the timber industry to exploit the full range of forest species. Any expansion of output of local woods was due solely to commercial calculations that a domestic market did exist. The population was expanding, Georgetown was growing, and rebuilding was based not just on rapid deterioration but on the frequent fires which beset the city.

On October 1887, it was proudly announced that Messrs. Park and Cunningham, well-known upholsterers in Georgetown, had taken another step in the direction of using local products. Observing the suitability of the wood of the simarupa for making Venetian blinds, they procured a supply and found it superior to the then commonly used Spanish poplar, yellow pine, and willow. The substitution of the local product was given its first vindication in the manufacture of blinds for the Victoria Law Courts.[12] Smith Bros., another large firm, was soon afterwards offering local lumber of better quality than imported pine at cheaper rates. Not all of the business ventures of this type proved successful. The response from carpenters was not over enthusiastic, since they discovered that the dressing of local woods demanded a lot of work. Nevertheless, when a sawmill failed in 1893, it was quickly replaced by another (at Vreed-en-Rust) producing mainly crabwood, silverballi, uraballi, and simarupa.[13] It is true that the colonial attachment to

American pine was hard to break, and the quantity of imports of this commodity kept rising at the turn of the century. On the other hand, imports of boards other than pine were falling as a consequence of the increased availability and use of local number. The emphasis on local woods was reflected in the revenue. By 1905, timber was yielding increased royalties, although greenheart royalties were less. The chief producers were local capitalist firms like Sprostons, Bugle & Co. and J. I. Matthews.

Bugle was the largest of the concerns dealing exclusively in timber. When orders were won for the Manchester Ship Canal in 1889, Bugle was responsible for 3,300 of the 6,000 loads contracted for, followed by Sprostons with 1,000, Bookers with 600, and a number of other smaller operators. Bugle was actually a family firm which possessed its own wharf in Georgetown.* It associated with Sandbach Parker & Co. to export its timber. Sandbach Parker and Booker Bros. advanced working capital to Bugle to ensure that when chartered vessels arrived, the timber would be cut and waiting in Georgetown. Mr. C. Bugle (senior) died in 1889 after thirty years of close business collaboration with Sandbach Parker, and his son took on the same role until 1904 when relations deteriorated. Sandbach Parker sought a new woodcutter whom it could sponsor, while Bugle strengthened an alliance with Thom & Cameron.[14]

Most woodcutters in the late nineteenth century obtained their wood from the Essequibo. There were also attempts to expand the timber industry in Berbice. W. J. Phillips, former manager of Springlands Estate, received in 1905 a grant of 100 acres on the left bank of the Corentyne, about 17 miles south of Skeldon, to establish a sawmill and woodworking factory. The wood used was crabwood, and by installing an American band saw of 24 feet perimeter Phillips expected to produce 2,000 to 3,000 square feet of board per day for domestic consumption and for export.[15]

The forests were deemed to be crown lands, and the rights of the indigenous Amerindians were totally subordinated to those of coastal business interests that obtained woodcutting grants. On ungranted crown lands, Amerindians were prohibited from felling trees above a certain girth, and in practice this meant no more than saplings for poles and staves. From time to time, the authorities seized both the wood and the boats used to transport timber allegedly above the specifications.[16] The balata industry was also closed to Amerindians. Under clause 8 of the Amerindian Regulations of 1904, they were banned from bleeding balata or rubber on crown lands or on their own reservations. Therefore, those Amerindians who were increasingly drawn into the timber industry were restricted to the role of wage earners and were exposed to the vicissitudes caused by the fluctuations in price and external demand. It was estimated that some 1,500 men were employed in

*There is a Bugle Street in Georgetown which is located in a wharf area still identified with sawmilling.

felling timber in 1895, the majority being Amerindians receiving piecework pay at three to five cents per cubic foot cut and squared.[17] Notwithstanding the employment of Amerindians in tree felling, the production of timber products was viewed as an attraction to coastal labor. The balata industry, for instance, began as the province of African Creoles and Bovianders* on the upper reaches of the Canje, but it soon proved an attraction to plantation workers. The activity was mainly concentrated in Berbice, having intially been extended from Suriname. Unemployed "peasant-laborers" moved seasonally from the coastlands and made their way into the hinterland of Berbice or Suriname to tap balata on behalf of local and foreign capitalist companies. The timber industry proper also drew laborers from the coastlands in addition to exploiting Amerindian labor. It did not take long for immigrants to seek out the prospects in the interior. In the 1860s and 1870s, the best laborers in the timber industry were the Kru from the West African Coast, who were already familiar with boats and with logging.[18] Chinese and Portuguese ex-indentured immigrants earned reputations in the bush for their excellent charcoal pits. Only the Indian immigrants were not noted for withdrawing their labor from the coastlands. Even so, planters were far from satisfied with the labor attraction posed by the woodcutting industry, and they were definitely alarmed at the large number of coastal workers who made their way to the goldfields.

The census of 1881 identified more than 3,000 woodcutters and other laborers concerned with timber, charcoal burning, and the like. Employment in these spheres suffered as a consequence of the poor export performance of timber; and the number of woodcutters declined appreciably by the end of the decade. Meanwhile, the category of gold seekers had become quite important, and there was a definite movement from woodcutting to gold prospecting. In April 1887, officials of Sandbach Parker were alarmed by reports that Bugle had stopped woodcutting and was about to employ his men in gold. This did not prove entirely true, but the employees themselves were deserting timber for gold. Gold (and even balata) offered greater attractions than cutting timber. At least 10,000 persons must have passed through the goldfields in any given year between 1891 and 1893, although considerably fewer reported goldsearching as thir principal activity. Reports in 1896 estimated between 11,000 and 12,000 persons employed on various gold concessions.[19] The numbers dropped soon afterwards, but then came the fillip of commercial diamond finds on the Mazaruni and elsewhere. They overlapped with alluvial gold deposits and, although some prospectors worked diamonds to the exclusion of gold, the two generally reinforced each other as economic ventures. It was because of the attraction of these two high value commodities that in October 1901 the Governor estimated that "prob-

*Boviander—Word of Creole-Dutch origin, referring to upriver residents who were usually of mixed African-Amerindian ancestry.

ably 50,000 persons are directly and indirectly dependent for their subsistence on gold and diamond mining in various parts of the country."[20]

In spite of the El Dorado legend and the undoubted stimulus provided by the search for gold in the Americas, the gold industry in British Guiana was pursued with remarkable lack of vigor in the years before the prospecting and mining of alluvial gold became the principal hinterland occupation in the mid-1880s. African slaves and Bovianders had mined gold under the direction of the Dutch in the mid-eighteenth century. After the move to the coastal plantations, Dutch planters were apparently so fearful of any competition to their plantation labor supplies that they closed down gold-mining operations entirely. Nothing was revived until 1864 when a small capitalist company sought concessions in the North-West. Several problems—including a disputed border with Venezuela—contributed to this British Guiana Gold Mining Company remaining nonoperational and losing its concession in 1867. Meanwhile, a gold-mining industry was being firmly established in Cayenne, and it was from that direction that energy flowed into British Guiana. Henry Ledoux, merchant of Georgetown and vice-consul of France, applied for gold exploratory rights early in 1880, pointing out that gold was already found in Cayenne in a zone between 4° and 5° latitude.[21] Government licenses for prospecting were issued that year, and cognizance was taken of a small amount of gold exported to the value of about $4,800.

Gold production started after discoveries in the Pomeroon district, and was extended through successful finds on the tributaries of the Essequibo—the Puruni being one of the first to acquire a reputation. By 1889, the Puruni Placers were yielding less, but there were new finds in the Cuyuni and Potaro as well as on the Barama in the North-West district. Two years later, the Barama in turn was eclipsed by the Barima.[22] Local entrepreneurs recognized the potential for quartz mining, but there was insufficient capital available, and limited success attended efforts to attract foreign investment. The reports on the mining sector for the year ending April 1895 noted that up to that date there had only been "scratching," with no shaft anywhere reaching 200 feet. Indeed, it was rare to go below fifteen feet. Gold production for 1896 amounted to 120,107 ozs., out of which the three new quartz mines accounted for just 6,458 ozs. The high point had been reached by 1893 and production never recovered, although the districts of Essequibo and Potaro forged ahead. Diamonds were also unsteady, with the cost of transportation to the upper Mazaruni being prohibitive.

The not unfamiliar picture of gold rush followed by decline came to be known at Bartica and Morawhanna—serving the Essequibo rivers and the North-West, respectively. Bartica (then known as Bartica Grove) became an entrepot for balata bleeders and gold diggers. A light railway was constructed between the Demerara and Essequibo rivers in 1896, cutting the time of travel to Bartica from three or four days to nine hours. Then came the decline in the gold industry and Bartica did not recover until a new diamond boom in 1920.[23] Nevertheless, quite apart from the ups and downs, the emphasis should correctly be placed on the value created by gold mining during the period under discussion. The 1905 review of the gold industry stressed that notwithstanding the primitive alluvial mining, earnings totaled $28,276,919 between 1891 and 1904—with gold averaging $18 per oz. on the London market.

There was a flurry of legislative and administrative attention designed to provide regulations for gold mining, and a committee of the legislature dealt with the subject in November 1886. Even some planters showed concern for the welfare of the gold industry, because of the depressed sugar market between 1884 and 1887. Gold was the only commodity in Guiana which was not adversely affected. Local banks were able to use gold as a means of exchange with the United Kingdom, merchants were delighted at the amount of money put into circulation, and working people were relieved by the offer of wage employment. It was partly fortuitous that gold should have been rediscovered in the period of agricultural depression. But there was a definite connection between the state of the coastal economy and the rate of expansion of gold mining in the bush. The crisis of plantation employment after 1884 induced Creole Africans to seek their livelihood beyond the littoral, and there was direct correlation between estate unemployment and a rapid increase of manpower on the goldfields. Conversely, a drop in the demand for labor in the interior in 1894 benefited estate employers.

The census of 1881 treated gold seekers as a fixed occupational category. Thereafter, although the data was not readily forthcoming, increasing output may be correlated with increased employment. Official scrutiny of the movement of goldfield labor began in 1887. Between January and June 1887, just over 1,500 laborers registered with other government officers so as to proceed to the goldfields. It was calculated at the time that the annual wages of miners, boatmen, and various dependent categories amounted to not less than $33,600.[24] Within the next few years, production tripled and the value of this new sector to the work force was proportionately enhanced. A few gold miners were probably devoting their time fully to prospecting, but the bulk were coastal Creoles who were essentially short-term migrant workers in the bush, and this accounted for the large numbers who resided in the bush over a given year. Rarely did anyone stay in the interior for more than a few months at a time. They exercised their choice as to whether they preferred to be home for Christmas or whether they wanted to be present on the coast between September and December so as to take advantage of crop season employment.[25] Their calculations had also to include the state of the weather and the volume of water in the rivers and creeks. Generally speaking, the employment pattern in the bush retained a casual and seasonal pattern derived from, and eventually subordinated to, the already widespread Creole life-style of part-time wage earning on the coast.

Throughout the 1880s and early 1890s, planters represented the attraction of gold as a threat to plantation labor supplies. They complained from Essequibo in 1890 that the best of the cane-cutters were flocking to the Barima and that several new "Coolies" would be needed to fill the place of one of these seasoned laborers.[26] This was the response of the majority of planters. The price crisis had eased somewhat by 1889 and the Guiana sugar industry had stabilized itself. Planters immediately highlighted the gold-diggings as the principal obstacle in the path of sugar expansion. They fell back on their stock rationalization that there was labor shortage and that indentured immigration should be stepped up. Such was the position adopted by planters meeting under the auspices of the Royal Agricultural and Commercial Society in 1890. Their views were endorsed by the government,[27] and the colonial secretary's report on the Blue Book in 1892-93 appraised the situation with planter orthodoxy when it observed:

> The one shadow on the present outlook is the scarcity of labour, which is making itself felt more and more. . . . Dependent as the sugar estates are on the Villages to supplement the indentured labour, which is barely sufficient for cultivation purposes and wholly inadequate to the demands of the manufacturing season, the planters view with great concern the steady drain on this source created by the freer life and higher wages of the diggings.

Yet the occasional planter had already begun to express an opposing viewpoint. The manager of Plantation Anna Regina influenced a comment in the *Argosy* of 24 January 1891 to the effect that the large numbers of laborers who had left the coast since the Christmas holidays were no loss, because their services were not required at this time. The manager of Plantations L'Union and Aurora immediately countered that he still had need for village labor in the months to come and that he had suffered during the past grinding season from the absence of his regular Creole African cane-cutters. Anna Regina, he claimed, was favored because it could afford a bounty to attract the majority of the greatly reduced body of village labor. The manager of Plantation Taymouth Manor gave a further spirited rejoinder:

> As a planter on the Coast, it is *not* a relief to me to see so many men leaving to go to the Gold Diggings. I would rather they had not gone, and would have been glad of their labour to trash 600 acres of canes on this estate, which work had not been done owing to labour not being available. [Trashing canes is the work cane-cutters generally do when cane-cutting is not going on.] I should also like them to have been here to cut these canes later on. Estates which by means of a bounty or otherwise obtain for a few

months an undue proportion of the labour supply of the coast, and then wish the people to shift for themselves for the balance of the year, *may* feel their absence a relief; but an estate such as Taymouth Manor which employs its labourers regularly from 1st January to 31st December cannot do so.[28]

As indicated in an earlier discussion of plantation labor, the differences in technology from one estate to another affected planter responses to the question of village labor. Only the more advanced factories could adopt the intensified crop season and dispense with much labor thereafter. But the short crop season was becoming the norm during the last decade of the nineteenth century. This forced Creole African labor to develop in a many-sided fashion. They were accustomed to artisan work, day labor on the sea defenses or the village roads, provision farming, the making and selling of cassava bread, and the huckstering of foodstuffs—in addition to their days of estate labor. Into this typical annual labor cycle, many villagers resident on the coast integrated gold and diamond seeking or the collection of balata. For many others who were already driven to the towns, the trip to the bush supplemented a precarious existence on casual employment opportunities.

Gold seeking may have been viewed as a get-rich-quick exercise, but in reality it was an extension of the exploitative pattern of the sugar plantation. Payments to laborers varied from thirty-two cents to sixty-four cents per day, plus food. These rates were better than estate wages, but were offset by hardships and by hazards to life and health. Besides, gold miners also suffered wage reductions during the depression which started in 1894, while the depression of 1902 was worse in this respect. Because of gold earnings, some villagers could repair and enlarge their dwellings or make small investments. Very often, however, prospecting was the equivalent of the lowest form of subsistence. This was particularly true with the rise of the "pork-knockers" in the 1890s. The pork-knocker, tributer, or fossicker, was self-employed within small teams of three to five men. These teams operated with a minimum of shelter, a minimum of food, and little capital other than the tools required to make the sluices, battels, and toms. After a few weeks, they brought down what gold they had managed to procure.

Some pork-knockers entered into a relationship with petty speculators who supplied them with provisions in return for two-thirds of the find. Because of high transport costs, the average cost of production on a placer was between 50 percent to 70 percent of the value of the gold—a proportion which went up on poor placers.[29] One official was convinced that pork-knockers did not know what the real costs were, because "if they calculated the "value of their labour they would not go up at all."[30] The fact that they went up at all was surely an indication that better could not be done. The tendency to independent pork-knocking received its initial impetus during the depression years 1894-96, when a number of small mining companies went bankrupt. Former employees therefore decided to work for themselves on abandoned claims and in new areas. The tendency was accelerated with the next economic crisis in 1902, which completed the demise of several gold syndicates. The increase of diamond seeking at this time also accommodated the pork-knocker in his quest to gain a living on the basis of his own tools and labor.[31]

Whether the search was for gold or diamonds, the uncertainty was tremendous, and even the minimum replacement of living labor was not always possible. At Potaro during Christmas 1895 and the dawn of the New Year, there were several sickly, starving, and sometimes moribund laborers unable to obtain passage to Bartica. Under normal circumstances, the returns were hardly better than subsistence, as is admirably illustrated by the presence of a modified "truck" system under which the pork-knocker handed over his small findings to a shopkeeper near the claim—in order to obtain food and supplies to keep himself alive and to be able to acquire another small parcel of gold—to exchange with the shopkeeper. Little wonder that many who sought their fortune in the bush returned empty-handed to their villages.[32]

As with all migrant labor in various parts of the world, that to the bush in British Guiana placed a severe strain on the community of provenance. There was an added burden on those who wished to maintain good husbandry on village lands, because proper care of drainage was impossible when many lot owners were absent. Women and children were left destitute when the waters of the Potaro and the Mazaruni claimed royalties on the lives of miners and boathands. At the best of times, women were forced to carry on with household tillage for months while male labor was unavailable.

Taking the household as a unit, it is all the more clear that village labor covered an extremely wide spectrum, from domestic service through to the panning of gold in stream beds. Examples of the combination and overlap of farmer and balata bleeder or sugar worker and diamond seeker were extremely common.[33] They support the contention of this analysis that fromer slaves did not simply become peasants after Emancipation. They became instead potential members of a free labor force and were amendable to numerous forms of labor. Pressures generated by international depression caused Indian workers to use rice farming to enhance monetary earnings, while Africans resorted to the bush for their survival and created a new economic sector. Admittedly, the gold and balata industries were structurally no better than the sugar industry in terms of domestic linkages; but village labor had laid the groundwork for the economic exploration of the hinterland, and this ranks as a decisive and lasting contribution to the political economy of Guyana in modern times.

Social Stratification

All workers on the coast and in the interior remained under the shadow of the plantation, and it is important to stresss the factor of continuity in the hegemony exercised by the plantation.[34] Yet it is equally essential to recognize the measure of change in the structure and composition of output implied in the reduction of sugar's share of exports from 98 percent to 71 percent over the period 1880-1904. In social terms, large numbers of workers had to make major adjustments in their lives. Differentiation of the economy (and the crisis in sugar) meant greater stratification and greater social mobility—both upward and downward. For instance, craftsmen who had long been at the top of the plantation hierarchy suffered a dramatic worsening of their socioeconomic standing during the years under discussion. Because of relative privilege and security, artisan occupations attracted unskilled labourers and youths anxious to "learn a trade and better themselves."* Many West Indian migrants were also classed as artisans or mechanics. The census of 1891 recorded 13,693 mechanics and artisans, an increase of 4,147 during the decade. Very few among these maintained the traditional preeminence of the artisan within the laboring class. The majority had to hustle for a hand-to-mouth existence and many could not avoid the ravages of unemployment. The inspector of villages indicated that carpenters, coopers, and other tradesmen could not find work during the year 1879. That same year, the acting governor informed the Colonial Office that the colony was overrun with artisans.[35] From this point onwards, their predicament was protracted and intractable, and it was clear from investigations following the disturbances of 1905 that the downward slide of artisans had not been halted.[36]

The Poor Law Commission of 1881 heard a great deal of evidence on the plight of artisans. A good carpenters received one dollar per day in 1840, but in 1881 he got only eighty cents per day. Besides the work available for the many was less than it had previously been for the few. The fallen wage rate must therefore be seen in conjunction with fewer available work days.[37] Estate amalgamation left fewer factories, while modernization lessened the demand for regular factory workers by as much as 40 percent or more. When economic crisis hit the sugar industry in 1884, the position of carpenters, coopers, masons, coppersmiths and the like further deteriorated. There was new machinery to be installed in 1885, but there were also cutbacks in what planters considered expendable overheads—such as the building of laborers' houses, repairs to immigrant hospitals, and even upkeep of houses for man-

*Oral sources.

agers and overseers. An artisan who was adversely affected might become a peasant in the countryside. Alternatively, many moved to Georgetown in October 1882 to consider the depression of their trades. Their plight was intensified by the introduction of steam-driven machinery by the Demerara Wood Working Company and by the importation of bags to package sugar in place of locally made hogshead barrels.[38]

Comprehensive data on the decline of the artisanry emerged from the hearings of the West India Royal Commission of 1897. Several witnesses of varied backgrounds emphasized that there was less work and lower wages for artisans and that their material condition had definitely declined over the years. E. A. Trotz,* himself a carpenter, brought before the Commission a petition signed by 200 carpenters, masons, engineers, bricklayers, builders, porters, and carters. This stated in part:

> We mechanics have experienced of late great financial reverses in this Colony, brought about by a steady decrease of employment which began in a marked degree since the year 1878. . . . As tradesmen we were often employed to build houses for managers, overseers, machineries, labourers, etc. Since the decline of the sugar trade and the amalgamation of many of the sugar estates, there have been thrown out of employment many mechanics, artisans and labourers; and with the introduction of labour-saving machineries, megass logies and other buildings utilised in former methods of manufacture had to be abandoned. Although we have little or no work to do, yet we are bound to submit to increased taxation, for be it remembered that the imported goods most heavily taxed are those made use of by the poor man: namely, flour, rice, pork, beef and such like things.
>
> We, as a classs of men, are labouring under great disadvantages, as it is often thought by the well-to-do of the land that we are well-fed and so forth, because hitherto we have struggled to keep body and soul together. Therefore, it stands to reason in their estimation that we have need of nothing. . . . Not so your honours, for many a man and woman of the lower order of the population have often endured hunger for a day or two rather than beg.
>
> We are willing to work and need help, as will readily be seen by the fact that many carpenters, blacksmiths and others from want of work have been driven into the gold-fields.

The artisan delegate also indicated that fifteen to twenty years earlier (1877-82), every "dry goods" outlet in the city of Georgetown had an ironmongery department, but these had all gone to the wall through the declining purchasing power of the tradesmen.

Mechanics went to great lengths to remain respectably poor. To endure hunger rather than beg or become dependents of the Poor Law Boards—such

---

*For earlier activities of this worker leader, see chapter 6.

was the code of these proud workers. Unemployed craftsmen had to cross a social and psychological barrier before accepting any common laborer's job. As the Reverend Mr. Ritchie (Presbyterian) put it to the West India Commission, "After a man becomes a carpenter's boss he is not supposed to go down from that, except under very great pressure." The authenticity of such observations is borne out by wider comparisons, since independent craftsmen took precisely the same dignified stand in England when faced with redundancy in the course of the industrial revolution.[39] Reminiscing in 1897, one manager of many years' experience recalled the days when the estate took care of its skilled craftsmen in and out of crop and guaranteed them employment in good seasons and bad, because there was still a relationship of personal dependency, personal obligation, and concern.[40] However, the rise of a rationalized capitalist plantation unit was a feature of the late nineteenth century—marked by the disappearance of resident planter-owners and the dominance of the limited liability company. The latter had no time for factory employees outside of the grinding season, and even the pan-boiler who was cock of the walk when producing sugar, was reduced to a casual during the out-of-crop season.[41] Of course, the Guiana situation had its own peculiarities. In contrast to England, there was no overall technological and industrial transformation which might reintegrate artisans or their children as skilled members of a new community of factory workers. That is why some trekked to the interior for mere subsistence, while others no doubt joined the ranks of the not so respectable poor who lived off petty crimes in the city of Georgetown.

A minority of artisans preserved both their dignity and a level of material existence above the common laborer. The fortunate few were those classified as carpenter bosses, factory engineers, pan-boilers, dispensers, painter-contractors, master wheelwrights, joinery foremen and so on. In February 1889, one journalist remarked on a tendency on the Essequibo coast for some Creoles to beautify the surroundings with flower gardens. He viewed this with great pleasure, modified only by the realization that the common laborer was not involved; and in citing the example of Mr. P. Hastings of Johanna Cecilia (a young master mason), the reporter added, "He belongs to a class above those whom I wish more particularly to encourage in this matter."[42]

Privileged artisans constituted a small percentage of the growing number of persons who were perceived to have been incorporated into intermediary strata in the 1880s. It was a process which received frank public approval, as instanced by a newspaper correspondent who wrote in December 1880: "Of late we have observed several indications of the growth of a middle proprietary class, a thing greatly to be desired."[43]

Because they were rising above the mass, the members of this new class were not nameless or faceless. On the contrary, they were boldly named as upstanding persons in the community. They were men like John Allick, described as a wealthy and respectable farmer of Victoria, who possessed several acres of provision lands and who patronized the railway by regularly forwarding a large quantity of farm produce to Georgetown; John Griffith of Plaisance, who owned valuable landed property and who spent $2,700 as a down payment on a small sugar mill in 1883; Thomas Henry Shepard of Stanley Town, West Bank Demerara, who farmed thirty-two acres of canes and provisions in Canal No. 2 and bought his own sugar mill; Pharaoh Chase of Nabaclis, who was able to set up a wind-driven sugar mill in 1880 without financial assistance; and Mr. William Parkinson of Rome, East Bank Demerara, who acquired a similar sugar mill around the same time.[44]

It is widely recognized that peasant societies having a relationship with a market economy usually proceed irreversibly toward stratification based on dispossession of the many and accumulation by the few. Inequalities in land holdings were present among the freed population of British Guiana in the 1840s, but they became more marked as communal land was partitioned and as the impact of parate execution sales became felt.[45] Leading landowners within the villages were of course commodity producers. When half a dozen small proprietors jointly acquired Plantation Triumph in the 1870s, they sought to maintain the estate as a commercial concern in their own interests. Where the purchase price may have been too onerous, it was sometimes possible for a middle-class Creole to obtain a valuable property on long-term lease. Such was the case with Plantation Foulis, of which Alexander Ross took control in 1870, persisting with sugar manufacturing for nearly twenty years and paying acreage tax like any other planter. If and when new economic opportunities arose, the small group of propertied villagers were the first to benefit. The extension of village expolders was proceeding during the 1870s, albeit more slowly than the extension of the plantations to second and third depths. Cornelius Kryenhoff contracted to pay an annual rental of $3,500 to the government for the lease of the second depth at Friendship. Part of this was recovered by subletting the land to provision farmers at $1 per acre per annum, while part of the payment was met from his activities as a cane farmer. The name Kryenhoff came to be remembered by villagers of Buxton/Friendship simply in the form of "the Kryenhoff empolder."[46]

Cornelius Kryenhoff came from respectable and well to-do parents in Friendship. After having been educated by the African Methodist Episcopal Church, he was taught the skills of a cooper. He became overseer of Friendship village under a revised Village Ordinance of 1873, and it was from this strategic position that he leased the land from government in 1878. One hundred and twenty acres were reserved for his own use and put under cane. The cane was sold to an established factory, and Kryenhoff lost heavily when in 1886 the price he received dropped from 3 cents per gallon of juice to 1¾ cents per gallon. He then bought from the government the cane engine at Triumph and transferred it to Friendship to start processing his own sugar. However, the exodus of plantain farmers from the leased land placed a

Windmill at Golden Grove, East Coast Demerara. James W. James, proprietor.

further strain on his finances and he appealed successfully to the legislature for a reduction of the rent to $2,784 per annum.[47] Kryenhoff, who was "colored" rather than black, apparently inherited certain tangible assets and property from his father. Mrs. Margaret Burns was in a somewhat similar position. In the mid-1880s, she was the leading Creole lady in Berbice, with a fine store on the Strand and several other properties, including a cattle ranch. The same advantages of inheritance did not apply to Mr. James W. James of Golden Grove, who was a "self-made" man. Son of a laborer, James learnt a carpenter's trade, and in 1873 he started planting canes. These he squeezed with a wooden lever working in a hollow log—a construction of his own making—and he boiled the juice for household use. Later on, he extended his cultivation, and in 1876 he bought an old manual vertical mill from an estate in No. 2 Canal. Steady progress was registered in the form of a windmill (1878) and a set of iron rollers (1885). James had only ten acres of canes of his own, but he purchased farmer's canes by the ton at the mill door. In 1891 he bought 476 tons and crushed a total of 540 tons.[48]

To survive, members of this embryonic class had to exploit village labor and immigrant labor. As landlords and employers, they had exploitative relations with tenants and displayed towards workers attitudes which were necessarily those of the capitalist class. For example, Kryenhoff appeared before the Labor Commission of 1890 and justified hiring fifteen Indians out of a gang of thirty laborers because black people would not work on Mondays.[49] He also became involved in several court cases, bringing actions for alleged trespass or for eviction of tenant farmers.[50] Mr. James W. James was still around in 1906, and gave evidence that Africans did not care to work except at their own price, which he could not afford and still make common process sugar at a profit. Therefore, when he wanted assistance he had to employ Indians.[51] The stark reality is that this petty capitalist was subject to the economic laws of the system as a whole. With poorer equipment and a less readily marketable product, he had to be more uncompromising in the extraction of surplus value from labor. As he became differentiated from the mass of village laborers, James took advantage of the lowering of the wage rate brought about by the operation of state-aided immigration, although his fellow villagers at Golden Grove and elsewhere were raising desperate cries against the same state-aided immigration.

Immigrants also contributed to the emergence of a land-based middle class. While thousands rented or purchased small garden plots there were a few who acquired land in sufficient quantities to become landlords and employers. Portuguese immigrants led the way in this regard. Portuguese immigrants were freed from contractual obligations at a very early date, or where such obligations existed, they were tacitly waived. Consequently, the Portuguese never labored under the same disabilities as indentured Indians and Chinese.[52] Starting in the 1840s, the Portuguese received considerable assistance from planters and government. Creole blacks were discriminated against while Portuguese were promoted to carry out the functions of retail distribution in town and country. Portuguese hucksters seized this opportunity and rapidly established a near monopoly of retail commerce.[53] They owned the bulk of the "salt goods shopes," "dry goods shops," and "rum shops": that is to say, shops selling basic imported foodstuffs, cloth, and alcoholic beverages, respectively. The Portuguese community was itself stratified, possibly in part a consequence of the transfer of social differences from Madeira. The prominent Portuguese businessmen in Guiana during the last quarter of the nineteenth century could be described as the commercial wing of the emergent Guianese middle class.

It is less generally recognized that Portuguese preeminence in shopkeeping was matched by their ability to buy land in the villages as well as in the towns. Portuguese were outstanding as market gardeners on the lower East Bank Demerara, they were grantees or squatters on Crown Land in the Demerara and Pomeroon river districts, they were prominent in the leasing of second depths of villages on the East Coast Demerara, and they were able to purchase a few of the many estates which abandoned sugar cultivation in the last years of the nineteenth century. A number of the Portuguese provision farmers operated on a scale large enough to be awarded government contracts to supply plantains and other provisions to institutions such as the

Georgetown hospital. Other Portuguese landowners engaged in the leasing of land or in cattle rearing. As landowners and shop owners, they had a definite presence in the rural areas, and the best house in the village almost invariably belonged to a Portuguese.[54]

Portuguese settlers on Crown lands on the rivers had as their purpose not merely farming, but more so the felling of trees and the burning of charcoal. Creole Africans complained bitterly at the time of the Poor Law Commission (1881) that they were being elbowed out of woodcutting by Portuguese entrepreneurs, because the latter could afford to provide rum and foodstuffs for their workers.[55] At issue was the intermediary role between the Georgetown timber merchant and the actual workers who cut the trees and squared the timber. It was apparently not very lucrative during the 1880s and 1890s, and Michael McTurk held that woodcutting agents (as distinct from timber merchants) barely subsisted.[56] Nevertheless the Portuguese benefited from legislation that was expressly designed to deter Creole Africans from withdrawing from the plantation labor market. An ordinance of 1861 placed the price and size of timber grants beyond the reach of small riverain settlers, who therefore remained upriver only if they accepted wage employment from the Portuguese merchants who could afford the annual licenses.[57]

It is clear that the Portuguese business community, with its access to credit, was able to effectively infiltrate sectors of the economy that were not directly controlled by the plantations. On the coast, this meant retail merchandising and market gardening; while in the interior, shopkeeping was combined with the hiring of woodcutters, the employment of gold miners and the staking of pork-knockers. Many of these remarks also apply to the tiny Chinese segment of the immigrant work force, whose rise into the ranks of the middle class was closely tied to shopkeeping, woodcutting, and entrepreneurship in the goldfields. There could have been few households unfamiliar with the name Ho-A-Hin(g) in the late nineteenth century. He was clearly an aggressive and not so petty capitalist who owned land, rumshops, and grocery stores in East and West Berbice and who was one of the foremost pioneers of the gold and balata industries. The same sort of profile is presented by Ho-A-Shoo, who came to Guiana in 1874 and had become one of the wealthiest of the Chinese shopkeepers in Georgetown before his death in 1906. Above all, the career of Wong Yan-Sau (better known as J. H. Evan Wong) admirably illustrates the rise of Chinese businessmen as an integral aspect of the diversification of the economy and the rise of the middle class. Starting as a storekeeper, Wong came into possession of plantations and large tracts of land on the Demerara and Essequibo rivers.[58] These proved to be invaluable not simply for gold, but later for bauxite as well.

Indian indentured immigrants were far too numerous to have been promoted en masse to provide specialized intermediary services like the Portuguese and Chinese. Consequently, the rise of Indians within the middle class was a process in which the few differentiated themselves from the many. As soon as ex-indentured immigrants started moving away from estates in large numbers in the 1870s, there were comments that some individuals were acquiring wealth. In a dispatch of August 1879, the governor noted the upward mobility of "shirtless Coolies," who were becoming land owners, landlords, cab proprietors, storekeepers and the like. The dispatch also remarked that an Indian racehorse owner had visited from Trinidad and has caused quite a stir, suggesting that this order of property-ownership was then beyond the reach of the Indian middle class in British Guiana.[59]

The highest remittances to India were sent by cattle-keepers, shopkeepers, drivers, and cart owners. The most likely bases for differentiation of the Indian immigrant community were cattle rearing, rural landlordship, retail shopkeeping, moneylending, and commercial rice farming. Very often, two or more of these activities were correlated and combined by a particular individual or family. Very often, the particular individual or head of family who succeeded in accumulating was a "driver" or task-gang foreman. Within the estate hierarchy, the authority of the manager and overseers had to be buttressed by workers chosen from within the rank and file. From the days of slavery, it was not uncommon to select and coopt from within the mass of slaves. The term "driver" persisted from the slave epoch, although it was occasionally replaced by the Hindi word "sirdar." Like some of the slave drivers before, an indentured driver could sometimes rise above his equivocal position and offer real assistance to workers under his immediate control. More usually, however, drivers were incorporated into the plantation system with higher rewards and more fringe benefits, so as to guarantee that they would be effective NCOs. Most drivers sought not simply to maximize profits for the owners but also to secure material advantages for themselves directly from the task-gang members. They stopped workers' pay, engaged in favoritism and patronage, set up usurious credit and pawnbroking services, and recouped loans on a "truck" or "trust" basis in their own shops. Some of these practices were exposed by the Des Voeux Commission, and Europeans sometimes appeared to be hostile to the trend. For example, Bronkhurst wrote critically:

> Some of the old Coolies long resident on the estate know too well the art of imposing on the newly arrived ones, in spite of all remonstrances and watching on the part of overseers and managers of estates. They generally provide themselves with bags of rice and other things necessary for the sustenance of life, and sell them at famine prices; and also lend money at heavy interest to the new Coolies, and thus make haste to become rich, and indeed in a very short time they become possessors of shops, farms, etc. Hylandum, Muniswamy, Paul, Sivapadam, Pokhoye, Suklall (up the Demerara river) and others are great speculators and own valuable properties in town and country districts.[60]

Yet estate authorities tacitly supported practices which confirmed ᴛne usefulness of their drivers in the chain of command, and many of the activities of
the drivers were carried out in collusion with overseers.

Both money lending and land speculation attracted comment from time
to time. Rates of interest were usurious, as is inevitably the case with loans
to poor people. One driver on the Corentyne collected 8 cents per week on
every dollar loaned. It is unlikely that his debtors ever conceptualized this as
interest to the tune of 416 percent; but even if they did they would have had
access to no other source of credit that was less exploitative.[61] Indian cultivators were glad to avail themselves of opportunities to rent rice lands from
their fellow Indians, even where the rents were high and the drainage inadequate. Coastal land was obtained by Indians either from sugar estates in process of abandonment, through special government schemes, or at parate
execution sales. Blocks of land purchased by Indians were sometimes farmed
by their new owners, but they could also be subdivided for purposes of speculation. Letter Kenny (the eastern three-quarters of Lot 16 Corentyne) was
sold by the government in 1887 for just over $1,000 to Gundoora and
Ramburran. The latter divided his half-share with Sreegobind, driver at Port
Mourant, and these three rented and speculated with the lots comprising
the first and second depths of the estate. This operation was fairly standard,
and it drew close scrutiny only because Gundoora petitioned the legislature
in 1900, claiming to have been unjustly deprived of part of his land.[62] Gundoora arrived in Guiana in 1856. A study of land-buying patterns among
Indians has shown that length of stay in the Colony was a significant variable.[63] Those who worked on and around the estate for many years had the
opportunity to become drivers, to raise cattle, to grow rice, or to engage in
other means of petty accumulation such as was impossible on wages alone.
The elements of class formation were discernible in the persons of landlords
in the midst of rice tenants and of farmers with hundreds of head of cattle
alongside the owners of one animal or two.[64] Many examples to this effect
were cited for the Corentyne, but the trend was visible on all parts of the
coastland. Moving eastward from Georgetown, Comins felt it necessary to
comment on Sukhanut of Leonora, a wealthy shopowner and former driver;
on the head driver, Edun, at Philadelphia, who had cattle farm and provision
ground valued at $15,000; and on Chand Khan, the second driver at Phila-
dephia, who had a cattle farm of 500 acres. At Maryville, Leguan, in the
midst of poverty and decline, one Indian shopkeeper operated on such a
scale that his fellow Indians on the estate owed him $6,000.[65]

Indian immigrants came from a subcontinent wʰᵉrᵉ specialization and the
division of labor were highly developed. The disparaging term "Coolies"
had its origins in the description of laborers or *kulis* working for hire in India
itself. Most of the indentured "Coolies" were agricultural laborers with no
particular specialization. However, there were many with craft skills and there

were a few with caste, educational, and other distinctions that could be put to advantage in the society of adoption. A breakdown of data according to caste indicates a much higher than normal proportion of Brahmins and Kshattriyas (Chatris) among land buyers before 1900, demonstrating that the land buyers were a privileged minority in more ways than one.[66] High caste status and the job of driver each separately provided advantages which were transformed into class mobility. Clearly, therefore, when the two were combined in one person, that individual was specially favored. Such was the position of Ramsaroop Maraj and Resaul Maraj, who were "sirdars" at Hampton Court and Leonora respectively, during the 1890s, and who subsequently achieved prominence in land ownership and commerce.[67]

The end of reindenture and the movement away from the estates allowed for the surfacing of retained skills—as confectioners, entertainers, scribes, carpenters, and blacksmiths. Material rewards accruing from such pursuits were undoubtedly meager in many cases. One scholar correctly portrays the process by stating that the petty exploitation by drivers merely allowed them "to become a little less poor."[68] Even so, accumulation on a small scale by immigrants on and off the estates constituted the first movements of the process of social stratification within this ethnic community. Some occupations offered greater opportunities for accumulation and mobility. Gold- and silver-smithing was one such, and the "Madrasis" Kassie Pattar and Periannan were named as outstanding in this connection.[69] Another significant occupational group comprised Indians who served as "compounders," or (male) nurses, on board immigrant vessels and those who were recruited to act as interpreters for the immigration department and the courts. These formed the base for the first generation of the professional Indian middle class in British Guiana: namely, civil servants, lawyers, and doctors of medicine.[70]

In an evaluation of the ethnic strands that went into the making of the educated middle class, attention has to be paid to its Indian component, whose barely perceptible beginnings in the nineteenth century foreshadowed major developments at a later date. However, the educated middle class in the latter part of the nineteenth century was black and colored. Creole laborers had placed a great deal of value on educating their children in the post-Emancipation period. The educational facilities of church and state were limited, but they were utilized for what they were worth, and the consequence was a generation of young black people who completed primary school and who had varying amounts of exposure to teacher training and secondary education. They sought employment as primary school teachers, as clerks in the private commercial sector, as dispensers on the estates, and as junior members of the colonial civil service. By 1883, Creole clerks were to be found in every place of business in Georgetown, whereas ten years previously that would have been a rarity.[71] Within the next two decades, the educated stratum in the society consolidated its position through higher education and (to a lesser extent) through intermarriage.[72]

Inevitably, the upward mobility of the black and brown middle class brought them into conflict with white incumbents in jobs that indigenous persons identified as rightfully theirs. In many instances, it seemed all the more galling to the new educated elite that positions were filled by incompetent or inexperienced Europeans whom native Guianese had to teach or prop up. Conversely, white government officials seldom concurred in a favorable estimation of the middle class and adopted a very contemptuous attitude in trying to keep the locals at bay. When C. J. Braithwaite was dismissed from the Census Office in 1881, he charged racial discrimination. Governor Kortright not only ignored Braithwaite but seized the opportunity to generalize that a mistaken confidence in fitness to hold public office was a common failing in men of Mr. Braithwaite's class. A few months later, the same governor returned to the theme in rejecting an application from another black man, "who belongs to that class of men who are continually raising the cry of being excluded from office solely on account of colour."[73] A black man in the commissary's office allegedly stole some rum and became the subject of a governor's dispatch in July 1882. He was represented as the measure of moral turpitude for the race as a whole, with the governor offering the gratuitous remark that "like the general run of men of his class, when the temptation of opportunity assails them they cannot effectually resist it."[74] Governor Irving was also prone to infer the racial factor in appraising the performance of officials, as in the case of Commissary Haly in 1887. This individual was cleared of a number of charges of falsification and misappropriation, but the governor insisted on adding to the report that Haly was largely imbued with an impractical temper and the sensitiveness of his class on the score of race or color.[75]

Interestingly enough, Colonial Office officials were able to distance themselves from the bigotry which was only too often evident in the governors' dispatches, and they were prepared to correct glaring discriminatory decisions. One colored Creole referred his grievance to the Colonial Office when passed over for promotion in favor of an inexperienced white with important social connections in the local social hierarchy. Giving his decision in July 1895, the colonial secretary was advised by his officials that the candidate in question might well have been "a bumptious brown man," but this was insufficient reason for them to ignore what otherwise appeared to have been an unquestionable claim.[76]

Numerous examples can be cited to illustrate the painful growth of the black educated middle class in a society still suffering the racial hangovers of the slavery epoch, and indeed such experiences were later to constitute an integral part of the colonial situation on several continents, so that Guiana and the West Indies can be regarded as prototypes. One clear-cut instance to this effect was the resolution of the native-expatriate conflict within the framework of the Church.

The London Missionary Society was the first religious organization to dispatch missionaries to work among the slaves of Guiana. It was also the first to respond to sentiments for the appointment of "Native Pastors"—a decision made more palatable from the metropolitan viewpoint because it coincided with the need to reduce the expense of sending European missionaries.[77] Once appointed, the Native Pastors had to fight for respect within the Congregational churches. Messrs. A. Jansen and J. Levi, the two pioneer colored pastors, had to protest their exclusion from the District Committees which governed the church locally.[78] Fortunately, the European superintendent of the L.M.S. stations in Berbice from 1868 to 1884 was Rev. Dalgleish, a man with the foresight to realize that a local ministry had not only to be tolerated but also encouraged.[79] The Revs. J. R. Mittelholzer, J. E. London, J. S. Simon, Fenton, and W. Isaacs were all recruited in Berbice in the late 1860s and 1870s,. Their education was closely tied to the church and their advancement within the church and the society preceeded *pari passu*.

By 1880, when the L.M.S. headquarters confirmed its decision to disengage from support of missions in British Guiana, there was already a sizable cadre of local pastors, some of whom were sons of the first generation of pathfinders. The situation was not as favorable within the Wesleyan Methodist church. This latter society was still committed to advancing both funds and pastoral personnel from England, although it had started the training of West Indian pastors in Jamaica in 1877 and although both the Reverend Mr. Bronkhurst and Superintendent Greathead went on record as being confident of the prospects and capabilities of local ministers in Guiana. The Reverend Mr. Downer (of New Amsterdam) sought a transfer from the Methodists to the Congregationalists in March 1881, apparently influenced by the type of postings and the lack of advancement for himself and other Guianese in the Methodist church.[80] The local ministers protested vigorously when one of their senior members, the Reverend Mr. Campbell, was not appointed at Kingston Methodist church. Campbell himself complained feelingly:

> The manner in which I have been treated with respect to my appointment to Kingston and kindred actions of the Committee have given rise to the very painful conclusion by the native brethren that the Committee have unwittingly allowed themselves to support a procedure calculated to alienate the sympathies of the native ministers and the people of our church, who are exceedingly sensitive on such subjects . . . with respect to invidious distinctions of race, etc.[81]

William Claxton, the black founder of Methodism in Guiana, also added his opinion that Campbell's treatment had done much to alienate black and colored people.[82]

The truth of the matter is that the middle class was consolidating itself. Its members not only wanted to be clerks, teachers and ministers but they expected to rise to the top of those categories as well as qualifying themselves for the revered professions of medicine and law. The more advanced the social differentiation, the more likely it was that members of the educated middle class would hit against the ceiling constructed by white colonists. The church in this instance was serving as a microcosm of the whole, because Kingston church was a prestige appointment in the leading residential section of Georgetown. White pastors were prepared to countenance blacks in the rural districts but not as the persons responsible for the Kingston circuit. They claimed that a black face in the latter circuit would cause the Methodist church to lose status in the eyes of whites and even among some of the entrenched middle-class browns and blacks.[83] The Anglican Church did not have this problem. It just would not have been contemplated that a native minister would have filled any of their senior urban establishments. A Creole who reviewed the life of the Rev. J. R. Moore, a black Anglican Priest, caustically remarked that Moore was banished first to the Corentyne and then to the howling wilds of the upper Berbice, and was brought to the procathedral in Georgetown only to preach the sermon of the Emancipation Jubilee in 1888.[84]

The influence of the churches as employers was magnified by church control over schools. Teachers and headmasters came under the authority of denominational boards, headed by a manager appointed by the respective church. The rise of the middle class can only be effectively chronicled and analyzed in relationship to the schools.

To complete primary school was a major achievement. The individual in this category was qualified to become a pupil teacher and to proceed upward through several "certificated" grades. When young scholars completed this phase, they were immediately appointed headmasters of primary schools. Such an appointment lifted the individual out of the working class. The position of headmaster of a primary school must be viewed as constituting the cornerstone of the black and brown middle class. Biographical data on a number of prominent lawyers show that they filled the posts of headmaster as the first step in a professional career. A. B. Brown, Samuel E. Wills, McLean Ogle and many others were all young headmasters before they left the country to study law in Britain. Alternatively, when a headmaster remained on the job for many years, he became an active force within the middle class, responsible for the training and shaping of many others who would subsequently become professionals. This was the role of Cornelius B. Carto of the L.M.S. school in New Amsterdam; while Dan E. Sharples of St. Thomas primary school was the acknowledged doyen of the Georgetown middle class.[85]

Queen's College was founded in 1844 as the elite (Anglican) grammar school. As a church school and (after 1877) as a nondenominational government institution, Queen's College undoubtedly became the fulcrum of the Guianese intelligentsia. A Roman Catholic grammar school opened in 1866, floundered for some years, and revived in 1880 to the point where it was considered on a par with Queen's College. Together, these two secondary schools catered mainly for the education of Creole whites, Portuguese, and sons of the established brown middle class. However, when the emergent black Creole professionals of the late nineteenth century looked to a post-primary alma mater, it would usually have been Bishop's College, the first teacher training institution in the country. Bishop's College started as a theological seminary in 1851, but its most fruitful years were as a government normal school between 1877 and 1882.[86] Many years later (in 1922), J. A. Barbour-James alleged that Bishop's College was closed, not for economic reasons as the government claimed, but to cut the flow of able black alumni who were competing successfully for jobs.[87]

For many individuals, therefore, the church and the primary school were inseparably linked and functioned objectively as the doorway from working-class to middle-class status. Because these were such far-reaching social institutions, they provided the framework within which persons rapidly became conscious of themselves as part of a given social stratum—the proof of this being their constant campaigning to expand education and to remove the barriers within church and state that hindered the advance of brown and black members of the educated middle class. Their response was naturally positive when one of their members scored some mark of distinction. In 1895, two young Creole scholarship winners left to pursue studies in medicine and law, one as the holder of the prestigious Guiana Scholarship. They were praised at a meeting of the Congregational Union in glowing terms: "Both of these gentlemen have set wholesome examples to their race . . . a small link in the chain of possibilities of the Creoles of this Colony."[88] One has to guard against the simplistic interpretation that the members of this first generation of educated churchmen and headmasters were merely advancing their own private interests; the socially significant fact is that their mobilization helped guarantee the reproduction and expansion of the middle class as a whole.

Headmasters had charge of both rural and urban schools. But on the whole, they were recruited from the villages, with the East Coast Demerara and the environs of New Amsterdam being heavily represented. The rise of the middle class was a movement of urbanization only to a limited extent in this period. Rural postmasters and dispensers on the estates were also key elements of the middle strata and exercised in their village communities an influence which was far greater than the actual difference in earnings between themselves and the direct producers. It seems probable that their articulateness and their quest for political roles in local and central government helped to induce a sort of "white back-lash" against the brown and black middle class. William Nicholas Lynch (Vincentian in origin) was one of the most successful barristers of the nineteenth century. He was black and big in stature, and William Russell was said to have referred to him as "a good shovelman spoiled."[89] This was a white response to a section of blacks whose education must have rankled all the more since the planters were not distinguished as men of letters.

Feeling their social position to be challenged, whites began to draw certain social distinctions more rigidly. For example, the plantations pursued a reactionary policy and discontinued the hiring of young colored overseers.[90] This defined the estate hierarchy as the unquestioned preserve of foreign capital, expatriate appointees, and creole whites. The civil service was only slightly less blatant in establishing how high the native middle class could aspire and where they would be tolerated. At the very end of the century, the governor still operated on the presumption that educated blacks could make good rural postmasters but nothing more.[91] Approached from another perspective, the firm line in employment had its counterpart in the sharp demarcation between the local social clubs. Robert Tenant, M.P., wrote of British Guiana in 1895:

> Society may be said to be divided into two classes by a hard-and-fast line, separating those who are invited to Government House from those who are not. . . . There are two clubs, one patronised by the higher officials, professional men and merchants, and the other by clerks in the public offices and the leading shopkeepers.[92]

Yet there was clearly an objective need which was met by the emergence of the middle class, and for this reason even the plantocracy welcomed them—in their proper place. The differentiation of the economy ever since Emancipation meant that new social layers had to be entrusted with supervisory and intermediary roles. It is for instance noteworthy that Chief Interpreter Veerasawmy was appointed superintendent of the Huis t'Dieren Indian settlement scheme; and at times during the 1860s and 1870s, village overseers were appointed from within the ranks of the Creole Africans. The government machinery and the state as a whole was expanding to cope with hinterland development, the rice industry and the distributive sector. It was therefore necessary to recruit an indigenous middle class.

Many members of the emergent professional middle class would have called themselves "self-made" men, and there is a measure of truth to the claim. Thomas Hubbard, chief clerk in the Customs Department in 1886, was the only surveyor and measurer of shipping in the country. He was totally self-taught and without certificates, but his excellence was vouched for by the comptroller of customs.[93] Of course, many proceeded to acquire the certificates that were asked for as the test of competence. John Monteith Rohlehr left the colony at age twenty-eight to pursue medical studies in

*Veerasawmy Mudaliar, chief interpreter of the Immigration Department
and Zamidar of the Huis t'Dieren Land Settlement, established by the
government during the 1880s*

Canada. In 1887, he classed himself among the Creoles who had first to work
so as to secure finances for professional studies—"and this class the last few
years show to be greatly on the increase."[94] Among the better-known per-
sonalities in this category were the Reverend Dr. London, who took to
medicine after serving as a pastor; A. B. Brown, who traveled the road of
headmastership in Guiana followed by the Middle Temple in London; and
Patrick Dargan (a Creole of "mixed blood") who worked as a clerk until
he could manage to do the bar in London. Yet in the final analysis, this
stratum was what it was because of the immense pressure for change exerted
by the dispossessed masses, especially in the sphere of education and in support of openings of employment for their educated sons. The Reverend Mr.
Campbell and other black Methodist pastors under the sympathetic Superintendent Greathead, were backed by petitions signed by working class
individuals like Joseph Oliver (a lay preacher at Trinity) and Cornelia Burnham (a Sabbath-school teacher at Bedford).[95] Similarly, John Rohlehr's
career became the concern of working people when the colonial regime refused to appoint him to the government medical service. The "respectable
poor" of New Amsterdam were among those who demanded that Dr. Rohlehr
be employed so as to serve them.[96]
    So long as they were in business, the middle strata exploited their fel-
lows in the respective racial groups and promoted values derived from the

planter class. And yet, the vertical ties (including family ties) were such that they could in most instances identify as men of the people. Kryenhoff, the village capitalist, was also a village elder and served as village chairman. He was appointed justice of the peace by the colonial authorities, but he was also first president of the British Guiana Native Progressive Union, which counted among its founders in 1887 other prominent members of the rural middle class such as S. W. Ogle (landowner), R. Carter (dispenser) and the Rev. J. P. Taylor.[97] Reports of the inspector of villages refer from time to time to the contributions made by village proprietors to get certain jobs done—a loan of $275 to dig sideline trenches, an advance of $300 towards a new koker, a loan of $400 for a fresh water canal. Acts of racial solidarity with the masses were carried out by Africans as well as by Portuguese proprietors. On the estates and within the new Indian village settlements, the same pattern was discernible. One can reasonably surmise that Parahoo, described as "an Indian nabob" and the leading cattle owner and butcher in Berbice, would also have been active in promoting the welfare of his muslim coreligionists, just as the Brahmin landowners constituted an integral part of the Hindu community; and just as the handful of educated Indians in the Immigration Office assisted their countrymen who were bound to the estates. The point is well illustrated by an unsigned letter from a Corentyne Indian who had been head driver for sixteen of the twenty-eight years he had lived in Guiana, and who leased 400 acres of land, which he rented out. The letter read as follows: "Though I am head driver on a sugar estate, I am an East Indian, a Maharaj, I take a great interest in my fellow-people, I would not see them wronged."[98]

Life in the villages and on the estates cannot be chronicled without reference to the activities of these well-to-do elements who joined their fellows in the search for better schooling, improved conditions for land husbandry, additional sanitary and medical facilities, and so on. The energies of working class and peasant families, the moral force of large mass of people, and the actual political mobilization of the working people were required to help create for the middle classes the conditions of accelerated development. The middle layers had not yet been brought into fundamental conflict with the base from which they had emerged.

CHAPTER 5

The Politics of the Middle Classes
and the Masses, 1880-1892

> ... like a root
> stopped by a stone you turn back questioning
> the tree you feed. But what the leaves hear
> is not what the roots ask.
>
> *Martin Carter*

In the Hands of the Planter Class, 1880-1887

At several junctures of this study, it has been necessary to allude to the planter-dominated legislature. This institution loomed large in the problems of sea defense and drainage, in the allocation of land, in the determination of industrial relations, and in much else. An understanding of the scope and development of politics in the late nineteenth century must be premised on a clear appreciation of the political power of the planters vis-à-vis the metropolitan authorities and in relation to other classes and strata inside the colony of British Guiana.

In each of the "old colonial systems" of white settlement, contradictions arose between metropole and colonists. The early history of the Guiana colonies under the Dutch predisposed toward a resolution of this contradiction in favor of metropolitan interests. When the affairs of the Dutch in the Guianas were firmly in the hands of one private company or another, government was merely a matter of administration carried out by company officials. However, more and more colonists were encouraged as private settlers over the course of the eighteenth century, and they sought means of giving expression to their views as property owners, taxpayers, and militia. Consequently, the structures of colonial rule under the Dutch companies and under the Estates General were modified to permit some degree of representation in the organs which enacted, administered, and adjudicated the laws in Berbice, Essequibo, and Demerara.[1]

From the moment that planters were given political voice in the legislature, it became the principal locus of disputes between resident colonists and colonial officials on a range of issues and particularly around questions of finance. Prior to the British takeover (the "capitulation" of 1803) the planter colonists had acquired de facto control over the imposition of taxes and over revenue expenditure. The planters were remarkably successful in presenting their own constitutional interpretation of settler rights to the British colonial authorities thereafter. The Dutch capitulated to the British as a result of military and naval defeats, but the settlers did not lose under the articles of capitulation. The British agreed firstly, that the representative principle had become customary and legal under the Dutch regime and secondly, that the British crown would respect all antecedent Dutch usages. Minor constitutional changes were effected in 1912 with a view to ensuring that British settlers were better represented.

Under the cover of defending time-honored usages, planters extended and consolidated gains that had been won during the latter part of Dutch colonial rule—and then primarily in Essequibo and Demerara rather than in Berbice, where company rule was very strong. The Constitution that united the three colonies in 1831 derived most of its features from Essequibo and Demerara and thus favored the planters. Thereafter, the Guiana planters rode out the crisis years of Amelioration, Emancipation, and Apprenticeship. Their privileges might have been cut back, given that this was a period when the powers and functions of the imperial government were being extended and were more scrupulously exercised against the background of militant antislavery activity. But planters in Guiana emerged in the post-Emancipation era as a stronger force in the constitutional and political spheres. The proof of this came in their ability to raise and use public funds in their own interest and to deny revenue to the British governor and his administration if they so chose.

All local laws and ordinances were formulated in the British Guiana Court of Policy. The Court of Policy and Justice, as it was called in Dutch times, was a forum within which officials and planters sat together on terms of near parity. The governor presided and had with him four senior officials and four colonists. In addition to its primary legislative function, the Court of Policy closely supervised the administration in the fashion of an executive, and it also judicially resolved matters such as licensing and civil service appointments which came before it on appeal through petition. The colonists in the Court of Policy were chosen by the College of Electors (Kiezers), a seven-man electoral college which represented resident planters and private merchants, as distinct from the company. From 1812, members of the Court of Policy were joined by six "Financial Representatives" to constitute a Combined Court. Given the clear majority of elective members over ex-officio appointees, the Combined Court was the political fulcrum of planter power. It was in the

Combined Court that revenues were raised and disbursed, and it was around this institution that the "Civil List" disputes raged.

Starting in 1835, the Combined Court voted the salaries of all government officials under an authorization which lasted for a period of five years. This crucial money vote was known as the Civil List and went along with the much smaller Clergy List. After the first Civil List had expired in 1840, a second was passed only after a clash between the governor and the planters. The latter successfully attached certain stipulations to the Civil List before it was voted in 1841 for a period of seven years. The next time round, the dispute was even more serious and left the Colony without any revenue vote for some time. Again, the planters were able to carry their position and confirmed that the power over the purse would be used to achieve far-reaching political demands. From 1853 to 1882, the granting of the Civil List involved no political turmoil. It was renewed for seven-year periods, so that the authorizations expired on the last day of the years 1861, 1868, 1875, 1882, and 1889. However, in the meantime, the Colonial Office unsuccessfully raised the suggestion of a permanent Civil List. The suggestion came in 1856 and was not put to the vote within the Court of Policy until 1874. The planters might have conceded if they had been given absolute guarantees about indentured immigration. Since these were not forthcoming, the motion was defeated. The question was mooted once more in 1882 in a modified form, the Colonial Office having requested that the salaries of the judges should be permanent, and should become free of the control exercised by the Combined Court. Once more, the planter electives stood firm in defence of a privilege which politically confirmed their socioeconomic hegemony.[2]

In the articulation of their interests, planters were assisted by a declining but still valuable West Indian presence in the British Parliament in the latter part of the nineteenth century. According to one count, there were in 1872 some twenty to twenty-five members of Parliament with a West Indian connection.[3] The West India associations of Glasgow and Liverpool lobbied Parliament and the Colonial Office, both directly and through the West India Committee in London, to which they made financial contributions. Sandbach Parker was a major influence in the Liverpool group; while for the entire period of this study, one or another member of the Ewing family was at the helm of affairs in the West India Association of Glasgow. The effort to elect parliamentary spokesmen for plantation sugar was apparently in abeyance, but it was reconsidered in Glasgow in 1880, when beet sugar competition demanded more positive action.[4]

The Civil List disputes were quite virulent, and they seemed to have resulted in the unqualified victory of the planters over metropolitan authority. Yet the scenario of Civil List conflicts could lead to misleading inferences. The Colonial Office was never bested in terms of sheer strength. At all times, the Colonial Office had huge reserves of real power upon which it could call if it so wished. Orders-in-Council were available to change the Constitution of the colony; and the political authority of the governor could have been buttressed in a number of cases to override planter opposition. Recent scholarship has found little evidence to suggest that the metropole was prepared to give substance to the theoretical claim that the Colonial Office was exercising "trusteeship" on behalf of those sectors of the Guianese population outside of the planter class. One inclines to the view that the planters' successful assertion of their relatively smaller power reflected the absence of fundamental antagonisms between themselves and the imperial state.

Much has been said of the peculiarities of the representative system of British Guiana, as inherited from the Dutch colonial superstructure.[5] The maintenance of these constitutional peculiarities, like the retention of Roman-Dutch law, ultimately attests to their compatibility with continued colonial exploitation and with the basically unaltered relations of production. There was no disguising the class nature of the Court of Policy, the Combined Court, and the College of Electors. Planter representation was direct and unmediated, and it rested upon an extremely narrow franchise. Until 1891, the franchise in the countryside remained at three acres of land under cultivation or a house of $96 annual rent; occupancy for three years of six acres of land under cultivation or for one year of a house of $192 rental; or an income of $600. In the towns, it was a house property worth $500; occupancy at an annual rental of $120; or an annual income of $600. In addition, the franchise was restricted to adult males who passed a literacy test. These were the electors who were entitled to choose financial representatives in the Combined Court as well as members of the College of Electors, which nominated the unofficial members of the Court of Policy.

During the slave era, candidates for membership of the Court of Policy were required to own no fewer than twenty-five slaves. Subsequently, the qualification became ownership of no less than eighty acres of land, at least half of which had to be under cultivation. By custom, individuals were eligible as electors and financial representatives if they had eighty acres of land. An alternative qualification prescribed in 1849 was an annual income of $1,440. Large commercial interests tended to enter the political arena through the College of Electors or the Combined Court. But the planters were so close to the large import-export merchants and to the sugar brokers that their differences were insignificant. Representatives of the mercantile houses became members of the College of Electors; they chose planters as members of the Court of Policy; and the same mercantile interests entered the legislature as financial representatives—sitting with planters and officials to constitute the Combined Court. To close the circle of political power, former members of the Combined Court tended to become members of the College of Electors if they were available at the moment of one of the rare vacancies.

R. P. Drysdale, planter and first chairman of the Reform Association

Vacancies to the College of Electors were created only on the death of one of its serving life-members, so it was easy to maintain this organ as a seat of conservatism. The Constitution actually allowed the anomaly of a person being elected simultaneously to the Combined Court (as a financial representative) and to the College of Electors, although in practice this did not occur after 1849.[6]

The high property qualifications automatically limited the field for candidates to the legislature. Besides, there were fewer colonists both qualified and willing to serve. Therefore, a rota of the same names appeared and reappeared over a span of time—until death or permanent retirement from the shores of Guiana removed one planter personality or another. J. E. Tinne and S. Booker were two of the more substantial citizens who retired from the Court of Policy (and the colony) by the end of the decade of the 1870s; G. R. Sandbach and J. H. Booker continued to form part of the honor roll of the Court of Policy into the 1880s. A few members were independent local landowners—notably, C. L. Bascom, Howell Jones, Arthur Brand, Thomas Mulligan, E. T. Henery and R. P. Drysdale. Several others were connected with English family concerns, which were then in process of being transformed into limited liability companies. In the latter case, what is significant is that the company representatives were not mere employees; they were shareholders and part owners resident in Guiana and qualified to be termed members of the planter class in their own right. Occasionally, such a person lived on and managed a single estate; but more usually, he would have charge of a group of estates as a "planting attorney." J. W. and R. K. Davson, H. T. Garnett, Allan McCalman, Andrew Hunter, and William Russell fitted into this category. Prominent financial representatives included A. W. Perot (merchant importer), I. H. de Jonge (sugar broker) and Hugh Sproston (entrepreneur in industrial engineering and transport).[7] In addition, it was usual to chose as financial representatives the "Town Agents" of large plantation companies or the planting attorneys who were not themselves managers of estates.

Quite apart from the entrenchment of their rights through the Constitution, planters objectively expanded their political power in the immediate post-Emancipation era, because the sphere of government action had enormously expanded. Slavery, like feudalism, meant a certain coincidence of economic and political power within the domains of the plantation. On the other hand, the "Free Society" obliged the central government to administer matters on a wider basis. The Combined Court was committed to raising public funds and could tax all citizens. Imposition of heavy indirect taxes on the former slaves was one of the new and crucial lines of policy in the mid-nineteenth century. The taxes were then deployed primarily to advance planter interests.

The greater the development of the working classes and the intermediary strata, the greater the likelihood that other bases of power might have countered the constitutional authority of the planters. As it was, the planters were the ones who benefited from informal sources of power outside the legislature. For instance, the domination of several statutory boards was of decisive importance. Drainage, Sea Defence, Health, the Lamaha Conservancy, the Vlissingen Commission, the Board of Villages, the Vestry Boards—all of these were planter preserves. Against the background of a plethora of sources of direct power, it seems almost superfluous to add that planters had tremendous political *influence*, deriving from social contact and consonance with officials of various branches of the civil service and judiciary—not excluding the governor himself. Yet this influence was significant in that it averted potential conflict between the metropolitan-appointed officials and the planters, and blunted the edge of any official policies aspiring toward better treatment of the working people. In theory, the indentured population were supposedly wards of the imperial state; but the existence of this large and politically passive sector strengthened the position of the planters. Paradoxically, it afforded planters a pretext for affirming that other sectors of the work force should not have the franchise, because this would add to the disadvantage of indentured immigrants.[8]

Having indicated the formidable array of political powers in the hands of the planter class, it is equally imperative to identify the possibilities of change inherent in the system and the period in which these possibilities began to realize themselves. The political power of the planters within the Guianese political context seemed unshakable and immutable, but of course this was not really so. Their constitutional strength derived historically from their identity as colonists—that is to say, locally resident independent property owners and taxpayers. The independent local planter was inexorably being squeezed out of existence by changes in sugar technology and in the organization of plantation production in the last quarter of the nineteenth century. Firstly, plantations were becoming larger capitalist ventures because of amalgamation; and secondly, family holdings were being superseded by limited liability companies. Thomas Daniel and Son of Bristol was regarded as a conservative planting house. When they reincorporated as a limited liability company in 1886, it was an indication of how far this irreversible process had advanced.

Officials of the large plantation companies began to replace the part owners and planting attorneys of the earlier era. These officials were expatriates and employees rather than Creoles or family members with a lasting commitment to residence and property in Guiana. The politically active class of resident planters was therefore in frank decline, and it was this class around whom the Constitution had developed. Until 1871, Sandbach Parker and Company of Demerara and their parent company, Sandbach Tinne of London and Liverpool, were directly represented in the Court of Policy by J. E. Tinne. Thereafter, the Tinne members of the firm maintained their interest by the occasional visit to Guiana, but more so by lobbying in England.[9] Charles Sandbach Parker also remained in Liverpool, and the company employed managers and planting attorneys who were seldom large landowners in their own right. In like manner, John McConnell retired from the Court of Policy in 1871. His son, F. V. McConnell visited the company holdings in Guiana mainly to pursue his interest in the bird species of the country.[10]

The career of William Russell, the "Sugar King" of the nineteenth century, illustrates that attrition suffered by the class of resident planters. Russell was associated at one time or another both with Sandbach Parker and with the working team of McConnell and Booker Bros. But he quickly outgrew the status of a mere employee and became a significant landowner with minority or majority shares in several estates. In the 1870s and very early in the 1880s, Russell sat in the Court of Policy alongside many substantial family owners from Britain and several local planters. Before his death in 1888, Russell saw the withdrawal of the long-term resident members of the Sandbach, Tinne, McConnell, and Booker families. They were not replaced. He also saw the estates of several of the local planters "going under," with obvious consequences for the political strength of the class.

When faced with the depression in the sugar industry in the 1880s, Howell

Jones (member of the Court of Policy) pressed for small planters to receive government help on the grounds that they were "the backbone of the colony."[11] As a statement on socioeconomic reality—made by a notable member of the declining class—this assertion was an anachronism. The government prudently did not become tied to subsidizing the small estates of local planters. The plantation companies also began to distance themselves from their smaller counterparts. They ceased to extend easy credit; they discouraged new partnerships of the type that was customary in the ownership of many estates; and they foreclosed on the helpless resident planters.

Charles Bascom of Plantation Cove and John (another member of the Court of Policy) was quoted in October 1885 as saying that Quintin Hogg was trying to put the screws on him by demanding payment for estate supplies on a monthly basis rather than quarterly, as had been the practice before. He appealed to Sandbach Parker as an alternative supplier of the necessary plantation inputs, but Sandbach Parker said that their hands were full.[12] In fact, the local firm received orders from their London principals that they were to make no credit advances available to any owner or manager outside the Sandbach estates. They were still using William Russell as a planting attorney, but he was growing older; and by March 1887, Sandbach Parker were contemplating dispensing with planting attorneys. Their aim was to ask their paid estate managers to make most decisions in conjunction with a commercial "town agent," rather than under the supervision of another planter.[13]

Some of the smallest sugar estates in Guiana were to be found in Essequibo. In 1883, Plantations Sparta, Coffee Grove, and Lima had under cane cultivation 65, 71, and 104 acres respectively, along with uncultivated tracts of 162, 377, and 806 acres. Their owners were therefore qualified to be members of the Court of Policy and the Combined Court. But muscovado estates of this type were either being abandoned or they were being bought to become parts of larger entities. In 1842, there were thirty-seven such estates on the Essequibo Coast. In 1883, it was observed that "Mr. Winter of Coffee Grove and Mr. Arnold of Columbia are alone to represent the condition of those days."[14] On 26 June 1886, the *Argosy* wrote what can almost be regarded as the obituary of the small resident planter class, when it announced that Arnold, the father of Guiana planters, had sold out to the larger property of Plantation Taymouth Manor and was off to England.

Attrition in the ranks of the local planters was accompanied by the rise of a Creole middle class in the towns and in the countryside. This was a situation that offered prospects of political change. Instead of mere supplication, the disenfranchised sections of the community could raise resolute demands, and at times they felt strong enough to engage in confrontation. The demands for a more representative political system encompassed urban and village institutions, as well as the organs of the central government.

The Village Scene

To live in a village was to open up the possibility of participating in a political process which was by no means totally under planter control. Villagers exercised choice of their own, no matter how difficult it may have been to cope with the problems of maintaining roads, sanitation and so on. During the early phases of post-Emancipation history, villagers in British Guiana were uniquely free, judged by standards prevailing in the West Indies. A comparison between Jamaica and Guyana has helped to underscore this point. As one scholar put it:

> Up until 1844 the villagers were left to function without any explicit interference or control in their administration by the governor or the legislature. From the middle of the 1840s to the middle of the 1860s, no clear colonial policy emerged as to how to deal with the general problem of the new villages. [This] provided an opportunity of escape from the tyranny of the plantation in Guiana much like the physical movement of black freedmen to the mountains of Jamaica. The free village of Guiana was more outside the pale of government than the mountain settlement of Jamaica.[15]

Allan Young, pioneer historian of local self-government in Guiana, highlights the rapid and widespread adoption of voluntary contractual "Agreements" to constitute independent villages in the early 1840s. The agreement signed by shareholders of Victoria Village entrusted management to an elective committee with not less than seven members who were at liberty to co-opt other members. A monthly subscription of one guilder (32 cents) was to be collected from each proprietor to defray the cost of repairs to bridges, kokers, dams, and trenches. The committee functioned also as a tribunal of first instance in the determination of all offenses under the agreement. When the *Times* of London described the proprietors of Guiana's communal villages as "little bands of Socialists," this was in effect a reference to the cooperative self-government characteristic of those villages.[16]

The local government situation in Guiana in the mid-nineteenth century was not one that the central government could have tolerated indefinitely. It was often alleged that the villages "failed" during this early period. Undoubtedly, their record was no great success story, but they at least "muddled through," as N. E. Cameron justly observes.[17] From a colonialist viewpoint, the key problem with the villages by the 1860s was that local government was no longer acceptable under a class different from that which controlled the central government. Consequently, the central legislature intervened as problems arose; and it sought to supervise village life, particularly in areas adjacent to sugar plantations. The first definitive Village Ordinance appeared in 1866. It instituted a Central Board of Villages that could bring settlements under its authority and that exercised the power to levy taxes. Before a village could become incorporated, it had first to be partitioned and a local Board of Superintendence appointed. Another ordinance in 1873 provided for the administration of the 18 villages which had been partitioned. The claim was that rural sanitation and public health were deteriorating. In 1878, the government created another legal instrument of control in the form of a Central Board of Health, since villagers were ostensibly unqualified to have elective local authorities managing a matter of such importance as public health. The Central Board of Villages exercised authority over 18 villages, while about 200 remaining local authorities were subject to the Central Board of Health.[18] Members of the planter class were appointed to these boards, and the inspector of villages was their principal functionary.

The state had to resort to coercion to overcome village freedom in the 1860s. Conflicts surrounded the practical questions of drainage, roads, sanitation, land titles, and the incidence of taxation. Reconstitution of the villages as part of the colonial order was a task which fell to the lot of Governor Hincks (1862-69), during whose regime violent and tenacious struggles took place in Buxton and Friendship. The Central Board of Villages and its overseers met opposition not only on the East Coast Demerara, but also in West Berbice. There were riots at Ithaca in 1867 against the enforcement of rates. Many villagers were arrested, but the protests at least forced a redress of grievances. Properties were classified, rates equalized, an L.M.S. pastor placed on the local board of superintendence, and a village overseer appointed with a less authoritarian definition of his duties.[19]

In the early 1880s, the planter legislature was still allowing several villages to practice elementary democracy in electing their own councils, although the Inspector of Villages was not responsible to the villagers for the expenditure of rates levied on the appraised value of lots in the village. His budget was extremely small, and the attitude of the plantocracy was that village programs must be implemented solely on the basis of such rates as were raised. Government loans were obtained with great difficulty; they were inadequate, limited to a few villages, and made strictly recoverable. Apart from defending their right to choose their own administration, leading elements among the rural masses had to struggle for the right of their villages to have access to the social surplus. The planter class was vigorously opposed. They insisted both on levying rates within the villages and on preventing the disbursement of public revenues for village purposes, although villagers contributed to the general revenue through indirect taxes and licenses. Where villagers had a choice, they at times refused to incorporate under the Village Ordinances, because they received no subventions and seemed only to expose themselves to the repaciousness of rate-gathering and the threat of parate execution.[20]

Local government came under review by Governor Irving in 1882. This forceful governor was critical of planter refusal to recognize the distinction between a money-earning sugar estate and a village where scarce revenue came from provision growing. He echoed sentiments of the Creoles that problems of road maintenance, sanitation, drainage, and agriculture had to be resolved at a national level and that the legislature had a responsibility to advance grants for these purposes. Irving was also highly critical of village governments, and attributed to them the failures that (from his own analysis) should have been laid at the doorstep of those who controlled political power in the state. He emphasized that loans to village councils were frequently bad debts, that the rates were imperfectly collected, that the said rates were largely expended in the cost of their own collection and management, and that essential work in the villages was left undone.[21]

Irving's sociopolitical values as they emerged from his dispatches were those of a "benevolent despot" with an a priori hostility to any exercise of democracy on the part of a colonized people. In an analysis of the British Guiana Constitution, he argued against the Colonial Office introducing an Executive Council, since it might arouse the then dormant public discussion on the representative principle. With specific reference to village government, Irving affirmed: "It is not I think surprising that the attempt to create representative institutions and to establish local self-government amongst the negro rural population should have proved a failure."[22] Irving indicated that villages in Guiana were functioning as quasi-municipalities and urged that this measure of local self-government should be abrogated. He anticipated the specific objection that villagers paid taxes and therefore ought to be represented. Let local taxation come to an end, if necessary, he said, provided that the colonial state took firm control at all levels. As it turned out, political rights were withdrawn from the village communities while village taxes remained. The Governor claimed that blacks were not interested in political rights—they simply wanted good drainage under the central government. Apparently, Irving carried out some soundings of opinion on this subject, and cited specific support for his schemes as coming from the large village of Plaisance.[23] By Ordinance 20 of 1883, village autonomy was replaced by the bureaucratic rule of the Central Board of Health.

There was coherence to Irving's policy. He urged that the upkeep of roads outside the sugar estates should become the responsibility of government; and having deprived villagers of political power, he was prepared to campaign on their behalf against the sugar planters of the legislature. But there was also an element of marked ambivalence in the same policy. The administration conceded that the peasantry contributed largely to the general revenues in the form of licenses and indirect taxes, and yet it wished to disenfranchise these taxpayers. Paradoxically, the governor held out as a threat against the planters the fact that there was a growing body of public opinion which could not be ignored.[24]

Paternalism might have been acceptable to some villagers if it had been a practical success. Residents of Ann's Grove and Beterverwagting petitioned to extend Irving's term of office because they felt that his village ordinance needed to be given time for its implementation and they feared that a successor might not continue the program of drainage and village development.[25] The popular press was also broadly supportive of this governor, since he argued that there were interests other than those of sugar planters that had to be given attention. The weekly *Echo*, which focused primarily on the rural areas, favorably reviewed Irving's tenure when he was leaving in December 1887. But the *Echo* was not satisfied by good intentions. It argued that his village scheme did not confer the anticipated large benefits. Roads and bridges were put in slightly better order, while sanitation and other matters remained almost the same. Besides, there was no functioning system bequeathed by the Irving administration, so that on his departure things quickly deteriorated.

Scholarly evaluations of Irving's policies range from negative to merely lukewarm.[26] From the viewpoint of popular democracy, things reached their lowest ebb. Nor can it be said that his schemes really resolved the material problems of village life. Loans were made available to renovate drainage pumps at Plaisance, Buxton, and Beterverwagting; the sea defenses of Queenstown on the Essequibo coast were reconstructed; and several villages were linked to fresh-water conservancies in East and West Demerara. But the amount of $25,000 for rural expenditure was so small that it had to be concentrated on about half of the twenty incorporated villages. This sum was reduced to $15,000 in 1889 and to $10,000 in 1890. Another weakness was bureaucratic centralization in Georgetown, which led to serious delays in the execution of plans. In his report for 1890, the inspector of villages was clearly annoyed that there was yet no back dam at Craig, although it had been estimated yearly ever since 1886. This was the kind of shortcoming that stimulated the search for more local freedom in the years after Irving's departure.

The demand for local self-government was revived between 1888 and 1891 within the context of the failure of the government-controlled incorporated villages. People readily perceived that their efforts could hardly prove less effective than the intervention of the central government. In August 1889, the residents of Lodge actually defended their road against the inspector of villages and the commissary of roads. They prevented these officials from inspecting the road and placed across it a paling with a notice saying that no vehicle was to ply there. A police squad was required to remove the paling and to protect one individual who was actively assisting the authorities. The government had never carried out road repairs or any other work in the incorporated village of Lodge. Residents were left to do the best they could; and that is why they defended the road as their own property.[27] Nearly a year after the fracas, the same situation persisted, although villagers were paying the rate of 2 percent of the appraised value of lots and some had lost their property for nonpayment.[28] To protest vigorously, as people did in Lodge and also in Belladrum around this time, was to run the risk of being imprisoned and of having one's house lot fall under the marshal's hammer. The fact that protests continued was an indication of the desperation of the rural population and evidence of strivings on their part to make some input into the political decision-making process.

At a meeting of the Central Board of Health held in January 1890, it was decided to declare Sparendaam a Sanitary District. The villagers held a meeting at which the proposal was rejected. The *Echo* then took up their cause and argued it within the framework of democracy and efficiency in village affairs.

> The incorporated villages being on the average in a worse condition than those unincorporated, while they sustain the extra burden of taxation and pay for sanitary conveniences which they certainly never get. In the matter of Sparendaam, we question the power of the government to deal in so peremptory a manner with the people who, as a matter of fact, can better manage their own affairs. Let it be in a manner that shall commend itself to common sense. What is wanted is less interference with the people and a wise oversight of what they do in sanitation.[29]

The charge that many incorporated villages were in worse condition than those that were unincorporated was well founded. From 1888, the cycle of accretion had blocked many drainage channels on the East Coast Demerara. Incorporated villages were among the sufferers, and government help was seldom forthcoming. Ann's Grove and Two Friends petitioned the legislature on this subject in April 1891. Both villages had been incorporated for over twenty years. Periodically, and particularly since 1888, floods in the back-lands had destroyed cassavas and sweet potatoes and even the fruit-bearing trees for which the district had a fine reputation. Officials conceded the justice of these complaints.[30]

Shortcomings of the independent village governments in the mid-nineteenth century had to do with lack of finances and the inability to pay for an administrative structure to implement projects. Central government intervention, when it came, was not carried out on a scale to transcend these short-comings. Therefore, the way seemed clear for a reassertion of self-government. Nowhere was this more fully grasped than in Victoria village. The people of Victoria had refused to become incorporated when this was first proposed under Governor Hincks. They valued their own independence, and maintained during the 1870s and 1880s a political system close to the original agreement of democratic socialism. There was revived discussion of a government takeover of Victoria in October 1887, and this provoked an immediate petition of dissent.[31] But the government did not expedite its reply. In March 1888, it was observed that several months had elapsed since the proprietors of Victoria had petitioned to be allowed to remain "free villagers" and to exercise their former government. They asked that their village council be empowered as a body corporate to sue and recover all rates due. Government's delay in replying had made it impossible for the inhabitants to go ahead with their water scheme arrangements, with trench digging, roadmaking, and other measures for sanitary improvement. The legislature did declare Victoria a Sanitary District in June, but stayed their hand in executing the decision.[32]

Victoria villagers remained on the alert. There was a well-attended public meeting in the community in May 1891, after the attorney-general again gave notice of a bill to declare the village a Sanitary District. Anxiety was heightened by the poor condition of the neighboring incorporated villages. Victoria was ultimately incorporated in July 1891, the event being preceded and followed by a storm of petitions, backed by some fracas in the village to discourage workers employed by the local authority.[33]

A new scheme was soon produced to reform local government in the colony as a whole. In 1892, the Gormanston administration permitted the establishment of village councils with a majority of elected councillors. The years 1882-92 have been described as a period of reaction in local government, introduced by the centralizing efforts of Irving and ending with the reforms of Gormanston. The principal interpretation of these phases has totally identified policy shifts with the respective governors, and argues that "the village reforms [of 1892] were born in the mind of one man only, and that was the Irish Viscount who was governing the Colony."[34] But Viscount Gormanston was no democrat. His hostile attitude toward constitutional reform between 1888-91 will shortly be illustrated. The little-known historical work of the Guyanese scholar N. E. Cameron is much closer to the mark when it places the local government concessions of 1892 within the larger context of popular agitation for constitutional change.[35]

In justifying the grant of village democracy in 1892, the government drew attention to the increase in population and education. The latter had been raised by villagers and the popular press for many years. Creole demands were influenced by the educated element, but they were cast in a broad democratic form. For instance, in April 1890, Queenstown village petitioned the governor that there should be quarterly balance sheets and that the books should be open at all times to the inspection of the rate payers.[36] The inspector of villages in his report for 1890 also attested to the demand from below for democracy, and he advised as follows:

> The villagers complain that they never know how their rates have been expended. I think that this desire on their part to become acquainted with the receipts and expenditure is an indication that they take some interest in their affairs which should be encouraged. If the government undertake to work the villages and levy a rate, it is surely their duty to inform the people how that rate is expended, and such an account would also show that their rates do not pay their expenses.

The government had certain views drawn to its attention by the press, by petitions, by official administrative reports, by campaigns for nonpayment of rates, and by the well-organized protests emanating from Victoria village. The Gormanston proposals, therefore, were the reflection of administrative experience, and this was made clear by the attorney-general, who was responsible for sponsoring bills in the legislature. In an address to Plaisance villagers in October 1892, the attorney-general explained the local government bill as the result of experience and as a draft which had the attention of the Central Board of Health for many months, in addition to commanding the personal interest of Governor Gormanston. The attorney-general criticized Irving's Village Ordinance and contrasted it with the then current 1892 proposals.

> I confess it seems to me that [the 1882] Ordinance was passed upon a wrong principle. It was too centralised. It did not provide for the carrying on in the locality of necessary and useful works at the required moment of time. If a plank comes off a koker door, you don't want to be running off to a department in Georgetown to get it put on again. The main idea of this [1892] Ordinance is that there shall be a large measure of local self-government for the villagers, that is, that the villagers shall manage their own affairs, with a central controlling body looking after them, supervising them, and keeping them in hand, and securing uniformity of administration throughout the Colony. Now this idea that people should manage their own affairs is one that is developing very much just now, I may say throughout the world, and more recognized and acted upon.[37]

In effect, therefore, the democratic tendency at home and abroad led, at this conjuncture, to some small beneficial results for local self-government.

The 1892 ordinance was more in accord with the aspirations of the people. Villagers hailed it as "the self-government ordinance," and the Rev. F. C. Glasgow commended it to his fellow Congregationalists for allowing "self-management and self-reliance."[38] Yet the central government rather cynically withdrew all subsidies for rural development. No attempt was made to repair capital equipment, such as drainage engines, for handing over to the new authorities in working order. The question of access to the "national" surplus was far from settled as far as the village communities were concerned.

Long before the achievements and setbacks of the 1892 Village Ordinance, villagers had realized that "the question of how much food goes into the kitchen is never decided in the kitchen." The Combined Court was the place where financial allocations were made. The village political activists of the 1860s were among the first Creoles to petition that they be directly represented in the legislature.[39] This proposal was dismissed without consideration when it was made in 1871. But seventeen years later, the circumstances were more favorable. Over the last years of the 1880s, a broad cross section of nonplanter interests combined their energies to seek elective representation in the legislature so as to stand some chance of determining the allocation of surplus produced within the colony.

Constitutional Reform of the Central Government

The several constitutional crises of the nineteenth century in the form of the Civil List disputes were essentially disagreements between planters and the imperial state; and their only consequence was the adjustment of the relations between these two, without allowing other classes to participate in the exercise of political power. In the 1880s, the recurrence of the periodic intraclass disputes involving planters and the governor was fraught with new possibilities. On the face of it nothing had changed, because planters were the majority inside the Combined Court. But in the wider society, socioeconomic changes had reduced the numbers of resident planters and increased the importance of commercial and middle class occupations. Hard times for urban and rural working people had heightened the awareness that social adjustments could be made only after some measure of political power was conquered.

The year 1887 was one of troubled relations between the Governor and the legislature. A report of the medical inspector had exposed rampant abuses within the indentured system and had incensed planters to the extent that their representatives refused to carry on with the business of the legislature unless the report were withdrawn. This the governor refused to do, and he proposed constitutional reform to resolve the deadlock. He was frank in recognizing that the planters were esconced in the legislature and that matters must inevitably grind to a halt when there was a clash between the planters and himself. In October 1887, the governor informed the Colonial Office that a moderate installment of reform should be contemplated as a salutary lesson to the planters and as a means of satisfying the democratic movement outside of the legislature. But, he warned that

if the Government were to temporize and the elective members of the legislature were not to be made aware of the true nature of the conflict in which they have embarked, there would be danger not only of mischievous interruption of public affairs, but risk of a political agitation in the country against the dominant class which would be prejudicial to the interests of the Colony and might become a source of embarrassment to her Majesty's Government.[40]

Subsequent governmental despatches returned to the same theme. Their advice was that the colonial secretary should act quickly at a time when the colony was free of political excitement. It was suggested that the College of Electors be abolished and that direct elections be instituted to choose six electives to the Court of Policy. The number of official members should advance from four to five, leaving the governor with the power of dissolving the legislature. A moderate reduction of the franchise from $600 per annum to $480 per annum was also proposed, but the property qualification for electives was to remain at eighty acres of land, out of which at least forty acres were to be under cultivation. These tepid proposals sought to conciliate disgruntled planters, who in turn began to speak the language of constitutional reform.

By the middle of 1888, even the Planters' Association had forwarded a memorandum accepting constitutional changes. Theirs was a purely defensive reflex in the face of hostile statements in the press and the knowledge that the colonial power was contemplating some reform—if only to strengthen the crown at their expense. Planters stuck to the College of Electors and conceded nothing except the inclusion of two electives qualified in terms of urban property or rentals, thereby hoping to mollify commercial interests. The Colonial Office commented that planter suggestions contrived the appearance of reform without any of its substance.[41] But the executive in London and in Georgetown wanted compromise with the local ruling class. The transfer of the controversial medial inspector was a gesture in this direction, and there was reason to expect that the Civil List* would readily be passed when it came up for renewal at the beginning of 1890.[42]

Meanwhile, the public agitation the governor feared had already begun. Demands were raised for abolition of the College of Electors; transformation of the Court of Policy into a House of Assembly with ten electives; lowering of qualifications for electives to $1,440 per annum; lowering of franchise from $600 to $300 per annum for urban voters; appointment of a Speaker from among the electives; electives to have the right to introduce legislation; and regular (biennial) elections. Proposals along these lines were forwarded to the secretary of state for the colonies as early as May 1886, after having been passed at a Georgetown public meeting of April that year. This was acknowledged in the House of Commons in response to a question by a member of Parliament.[43] These small beginnings were fanned by the disputed report of the medical inspector.

*The existing Civil List had been passed in January 1883 and was due to expire after seven years on the last day of 1889.

Planters, too, sent their missives to the Colonial Office and to the British Parliament in a fight against constitutional reform. Henry K. Davson, owner of Plantations Bath and Blairmont, was a leading spokesman on the constitutional issue, and his letters to the Colonial Office were buttressed by those of the West India Committee and the West India Association of Glasgow, both of which were presided over by proprietors with major interests in British Guiana. Norman Lubbock of the Colonial Company was then chairman of the West India Committee. When he went to Guiana at the end of 1889, he chaired a meeting of planters and had talks with the governor. There emerged a very clear conservative position uniting all sections of the planter class and meeting most of the demands of the Executive for a modicum of reform to prevent far-reaching reform.[44]

In reviewing these matters, the Colonial Office tended to adopt a broad comparative approach in the light of experience elsewhere in the colonial empire. Senior officials advised in January 1890 that the decision on the Constitution should bear in mind that there was a Reform Association which wanted to sweep away the present Constitution and start *de novo* somewhat on the Jamaica model. The democratic proposals of the Reform Association were judged dangerous because of the experience of Jamaica, Mauritius, and Malta, where there were elective majorities. One adviser raised the bogey of crown colony government, but since this was likely to prove difficult of implementation, he urged instead "the skilful use of the terror" of an extended franchise. This was a threat to keep planters in line so that they would grant the Civil List and approve moderate reform.[45]

One of the most striking aspects of the constitutional wrangle was the role of Governor Gormanston (1887-93). Gormanston's dispatches either played down the importance of mass manifestations or they provided sponsorship for planter documents. Thus, in August 1889 he enclosed an extract from the local press giving the proposals of the Reform Association, but urging that the group was insignificant. Shortly afterward, he sent under confidential cover and with strong approval, minutes of the Planters' Association which deprecated agitation for extension of the franchise and abolition of the College of Kiezers.[46] Gormanston worked in close collaboration with planters who knew the proplanter views that he had expressed in England even before his appointment.[47] Confirmation of this came from planters themselves. W. H. Sherlock, member of the College of Kiezers and planting attorney of Sandbach Parker & Co., wrote his head office in Liverpool in August 1889 explaining that Gormanston had requested an interview with himself and Alexander Barr of the Colonial Company. What Gormanston communicated at this interview was reported as follows:

He told us at the outset that personally he was and had been averse to any changes whatever—that he had even deprecated the mild proposals of the

Planters' Association a year ago which were intended to meet the first cry
for reform. Since then the subject has been pressed on by the Colonial
Office, and as often discouraged by him in reply. But by last mail he got
a despatch which demands that the people should have a larger representation. Lord Gormanston now feels that he has no choice in the matter and
that he is now reluctantly compelled to comply with the request of the
Colonial Office and to put before it a scheme for the alteration of the
constitution. Before doing so, he was anxious that proprietors here at
home should be taken into his confidence.[48]

Gormanston actually sidetracked directives from the Colonial Office, so
that he could avoid any substantial concession to the reform groups. For
instance, Colonial Office functionaries seriously contemplated granting the
right to secret ballot, but the governor opposed and fenced with the issue in
such a way that it could not become a reality.[49] He was unequivocally defending what he conceived of as the interests not simply of resident planters,
but of the plantation companies.

Against the background of the power of the planter class taken as a whole
and the concurrence of the chief executive, it is not in the least surprising
that the actual constitutional amendments of 1891 were very limited. The
planters conceded that property qualifications be altered to admit representation of large commercial interests. They also agreed that the urban income
qualification for the franchise be dropped to $480 per annum; and they had
little choice but to accept the abolition of the archaic College of Electors. But
the Court of Policy was enlarged by only three electives, and they were
balanced by the appointment of three officials. The governor (rather than a
Speaker) remained the head of the legislature, while the executive functions
of the Court of Policy were transferred to an Executive Council that the
governor and planters firmly controlled. The reform agitators were sadly
disappointed. Ironically, the new Constitution was to come into effect on
Emancipation Day, 1 August 1891. The *Reflector* commented that they had
asked for bread and received stone.[50]

Scholars reviewing the 1891 Constitution have generally agreed that it
made no immediate impact on political life. The first elections under the new
Constitution took place in 1892 and produced a legislature hardly different
in composition from the previous Combined Court. Indeed, only three of the
eight seats available were actually contested. Yet there is also agreement that
1891 was a new beginning in Guianese political life because of acceptance of
the principle that the legislators were to be chosen directly by an electorate.
The consequences of this new beginning were realized within the political
system over the next two decades (especially after secret ballot was conceded
in 1897); and its long-term significance can be judged from the fact that when
another major constitutional change took place in 1928 planters had already
completely disappeared from the Court of Policy.[51] Their replacements were

mainly brown and black professionals who successfully contested elections in the 1890s and more so during the early part of this century. The "coloured" lawyer Patrick Dargan in many ways epitomized the political generation of the 1890s who made their presence increasingly felt until 1928. Viewed by a Guianese patriot (around 1909), Patrick Dargan was seen as "the product of the Constitution of 1891, which released new forces in the political life of the country and gave to public-spirited colonists their opportunity."[52] The same political phenomena could of course be viewed from a planter perspective. After H. K. Davson played a key role in trying to keep the 1891 Constitution as moderate as possible, he later denounced the post-1891 changes as having brought into being nonwhite representation in the Court of Policy. He stated (in 1908): "I do not believe that in any Colony of the Empire the white element should be subject to the coloured, whether it be black, brown or yellow."[53]

Davson was being histrionic when he spoke of the white element having been made subject to the "coloured" in British Guiana at the date in question. He overlooked the growing power of the plantation companies such as the one which he himself controlled. The principal shareholders in these companies visited Guiana occasionally, but it was not necessary for them to be locally resident and to take personal oversight of the local legislative apparatus. Their economic and political base was in the United Kingdom; and they were adequately represented within the colony by their planter attorneys on the Executive Council and by the governor. Besides, the same planter attorneys continued to supervise the important statutory boards dealing with drainage, sea defense, irrigation, roads, and local government. The altered composition of the legislature in the years before World War I did not seriously affect the fundamental colonial order. At best, the changes after 1891 had introduced a political embryo that would grow into a movement for self-determination in the distant future. The reform movement leading to the Constitution of 1891 displayed characteristics of an incipient "mass" organization with discernible class objectives; and for this reason it merits closer reexamination than might be accorded it on the basis of the meager concessions contained in the Constitution itself.

Middle-Class Leadership of a Popular Front, 1887-1892

The limited constitutional concessions of 1891 were in effect adjustments made by the Colonial Office, the West India Committee, the governor, and the planter representatives of the Combined Court. But virtually all strata within colonial Guianese society were united in the demand for more fundamental reform, recognizing that the anachronistic Constitution failed to accommodate the many socioeconomic developments of the nineteenth century. The movement for reform was organized as a popular front, and to some extent may even be described as "populist," with the various strands drawn together through common opposition to the landlord class, which embodied large-scale capital.

During the 1870s, there was a revival of awareness of the need for reform to break the legislative monopoly of the planters over the economic benefits of the years of relative prosperity. By the mid-1880s, the feeling was strengthened in the context of economic recession; and the misfortune of widespread flooding was added to general economic distress at the beginning of 1887. The democratic thrust received its first organizational expression in the birth of a Political Reform Club in 1887. This Reform Club aimed at mass mobilization and succeeded in collecting 4,647 signatures for a petition which was dispatched in December 1887. Correspondence was entered into with the Anti-Slavery Society and with a few members of the British Parliament.[54]

The Reform Club made its appeal in broad terms, while its leadership was always demonstrably middle class. Its history can most readily be traced in the contemporary press, much of which was dedicated to the articulation of mass grievances by the emergent middle class. Only the *Argosy* was an unwavering voice of the planter class. The *Chronicle* and the *Royal Gazette* were capable of being liberal, and most other publications were to the "left." The *Creole* and the *Working Man* assumed the mantle of spokesmen of the middle and lower classes during the 1870s, and the same role was later played in the 1880s by the *Villager*, the *Echo*, and the *Reflector*—with the *Liberal* joining the ranks in the 1890s. These latter were all small newspapers run by practicing journalists who also doubled as job printers and producers of stationery. They were the cutting edge of the middle class and were also in contact with the grievances of wage earners and small farmers. These sections of the press carried on profuse and abrasive criticism of the governor, senior civil servants, and the judiciary.

The inept Colonial Hospital, the medical service as a whole, and the system of education were all topics to which the popular press returned time and again to score telling points. Nor can it be said that they were merely destructive in their criticism. Suggestions flowed from the editors and from the correspondents whom they encouraged. News from the Caribbean and farther afield provided a sense of what was possible in a wider world. There must have been a fruitful interaction between what is loosely termed "public opinion" and the views of these combative journalists representing a Creole and antiplanter consciousness. The colonial regime by its actions recognized and deplored the democratic contribution of the press. The trial of the Guianese lawyer De Souza, on a charge of contempt, became a genuine *cause célèbre* in 1888. The courts not only dealt harshly with De Souza for having criticized the judges, but they also seized the opportunity to convict two editors who reported on the proceedings.[55] Such repression served no

*D. M. Hutson, lawyer, politician, solicitor-general, and one-time chairman
of the Reform Association*

useful purpose. By this date, the numerous flows of criticism had already
merged into the single stream of "Constitutional Reform." The mood of the
middle-class journalists was well expressed by the bold comments of the
Echo, which described the Court of Policy as a mimic parliament and declared, "it would be almost impossible to supersede this government with
anything more inherently ridiculous."[56]

The prime mover in the Reform Club was David Thomas Straughn, then a
journalist with the *Chronicle* and later to become the owner and publisher of
the *Liberal*. His father, Richard Straughn, was a Barbadian who settled in
Guiana in the 1830s and who became a well-known cabinet maker and
upholsterer in Georgetown. David Straughn served as the articulate and
courageous secretary of the Reform Club. The post of president was taken
up by D. M. Hutson, a well-to-do (brown) Creole attorney at law who was a
prominent member of the professional middle class. W. H. Hinds, editor of
the *Echo*, gave considerable support on the journalistic front and in the
villages of the East Coast Demerara. J. A. Murdoch brought the influence
which came from being established as a lawyer since 1868 as well as from the
fact that he inherited property from his Scottish father, who owned Plantation Good Fortune on the West Bank Demerara.[57] A third lawyer in the
vanguard of the movement was J. Van Ryck de Groot, who was elected
financial representative for New Amsterdam in 1887. To the lawyers and

journalists, one must also add the schoolteachers. They included J. D. Fileen, who ran the Alexandria Grammar School, T.F.R. Elliot, the local poet, and S. E. Wills, who was a primary school headmaster at Plaisance until February 1888, when he left to study law in the United Kingdom. Where anonymity surrounds some of their activities, their social class was nevertheless discernible. At a Reform Club meeting at Plaisance, the village overseer, two druggists, and a schoolteacher shared the platform with W. H. Hinds. Many of the same names and occupations appear in a number of other social movements of the time, and it is clear that the reformers were more than a random collection of individuals. They were prominent in promoting literature and music; they were in attendance at the debates of the Churchmen's Union; they were active in benefit societies and lodges; they formed a cooperative building society and a cooperative trading venture; and they were the organizers of the Emancipation Jubilee on 1 August 1888.

Some of the middle-class adherents of the Reform Club looked to their social superiors rather than to the disenfranchised working people for leadership. The view was expressed that the Reform Club lacked the weight and prestige to mount an effective challenge to the colonial order. This explains the invitation to Robert Pate Drysdale to become chairman of a new Constitutional Reform Association. Drysdale was a man of property. He came to Guiana from Scotland in 1843 as a plantation employee and himself became a planter. The crisis of the small estate owners caused him to give up sugar planting and to concentrate instead on mercantile business in Georgetown. As chairman of the Reform Association, Drysdale was expected to lead the attack against the monopolization of political power by the planter oligarchy. Some doubt was cast on the resoluteness with which Drysdale could proceed.[58] But he certainly fitted the bill as far as middle-class respectability was concerned. Chairman of the British Guiana Mutual Fire Insurance Society, treasurer of the British Guiana Churchmen's Union, president of the Royal Agricultural and Commercial Society, member of the Combined Court and oft-time mayor of Georgetown—these were the qualifications of R. P. Drysdale.

Drysdale became identified with reform in 1889, and the Reform Association was constituted on 15 July of that same year. The transition from the Reform Club to the Reform Association retained many elements intact, including the continued presence of D. T. Straughn on the executive.[59] However, there was also a shift in the center of gravity in both racial and class terms. The young black professionals were partly superseded by merchants who were usually either brown or white. The honorary secretary of the Reform Association was William Cunningham of the Creole upholstering firm of Park and Cunningham. Other local firms that were represented include Smith Bros. and J. Wood Davis, both of which engaged in wholesale and general merchandising. J. B. Woolford (a Creole white lawyer) and W. Howell Jones (the Creole white planter) were influential recruits into the ranks of the movement. Then there were the Portuguese, who were not defined as "whites" within the Guianese context and who were still struggling to gain rights as citizens.

Although initially pampered by the planters in their efforts to advance in business, the Portuguese community by this date was open to attack from the planter class.[60] They were particularly anxious to counter planter maneuvers to deem them "aliens" and to keep them permanently disenfranchised. They needed a measure of political power to defend and extend their business interests. They wanted crown land opened up for commercial farming, gold mining, and timber operations; they were unhappy that so much of the public debt was incurred on account of immigration; and they resented it when planters paid low wages and then sniped at the Portuguese merchants for profiteering. For these reasons, several prominent Portuguese businessmen became staunch supporters of the Reform Association.

Ironically, Portuguese participation in the reform movement came swiftly on the heels of the anti-Portuguese riots of 1889. The event must have shaken even the most liberal of the Portuguese businessmen—judging from remarks in the Portuguese language newspaper *O Portuguez*. The editor wrote feelingly that he recognized revolution as a principle of civilization and he conceded the validity of revolt as an instrument against powerful authorities, but he would not accept that there was any justice in the damage inflicted on the persons and property of the Portuguese in Guiana.[61] This same editor had previously preached a form of Portuguese cultural nationalism which verged on chauvinism. He habitually denounced the fact that many Portuguese fraternized with Creoles, lived with black women, and abandoned the Portuguese language in favour of Creole English.[62] Yet, these very social features may have contributed to the ability of the Portuguese to make common cause with the Creoles of various strata. In any event, Portuguese persistence in aligning themselves with the populist movement indicates that they considered themselves to have had profound differences with the planter class.

Because commerce was largely to be found in the city of Georgetown, it followed that the city played the dominant role in political agitation. It is no coincidence that William Cunningham was secretary of both the Reform Association and the newly formed Georgetown Chamber of Commerce. The tempo of political life within Georgetown was first stepped up in relation to municipal elections. Having captured the Georgetown Town Council, the middle class used this as a base for their assault on the central legislature. At the same time, business interests were the hub of a network which extended across the country, so that the economy of the coastal countryside and of the hinterland was also reflected in Reform positions. This emerges clearly with respect to what was known as the "Minor Industries" question. "Minor Industries" was an umbrella term that covered virtually every kind of production other than sugar. In practice, it tended to be identified with the gold and timber industries and with *export* crops other than sugar.

Local merchants anxious to participate in the expanding gold industry of the late 1880s tried first to break the plantation monopoly of land and labor which strangled so many of the alternative industries that were promoted by small capital. Hardly was there a reform meeting at which the question of the gold industry was not touched upon. The reform movement expressed concern at the failure to expedite a settlement of the border dispute with Venezuela, because that dispute held up gold mining. It drew attention to the poor communications that were such a heavy liability to economic exploitation of the hinterland. The names of merchants noted for dealings with the hinterland continually came up in relation to the Reform Association. Besides, several members of the professional middle class were hopeful that they might obtain a more substantial material base by associating with entrepreneurship in the gold industry.[63] "The Rights of the People are our Cause"—this was the motto of the *Nugget* newspaper, which was launched on the auspicious date of 1 August 1888. A *Gold Mining Gazette* was also started as a special weekly edition of the *Echo*. In both instances, the connection was explicitly drawn between gold mining, the formation of a middle class, and the need for reform.

The fact that the gold industry excited Georgetown businessmen was in no way surprising. However, the equally intense attention given to a banana industry in the late 1880s constitutes one of the byways of Guianese history. At this time, the Jamaica banana export industry was already firmly established and helped to foster the hope that British Guiana, too, could readily become a large-scale producer of bananas. The first obvious hurdle to be crossed was the indifference of the planter legislature to the promotion of small farmers. The initiative clearly had to be taken by commercial firms that were not closely tied to sugar brokerage. In 1888, Captain E. T. White began negotiating to start a banana industry in Guiana with the object of export to the United States. Captain White was a Creole white Bahamian settled in Georgetown and engaged in import trade. He set up a liaison with Charles Baker of the Boston Fruit Company, who had achieved a great deal with regard to peasant-based banana exports from Jamaica. Hundreds of Guianese peasants and commercial farmers attached their signatures to a petition drafted by Captain White on the sponsorship of a banana industry, but it was actually mislaid in the government secretary's office.[64] Captain White became a prominent member of the Reform Association and meetings of the council of the association were held in his home. Although the banana project ultimately proved abortive, it provided significant motivation to the reform movement.

It is at times necessary to infer the existence of class motivation, even when the protagonists protest to the contrary. In this instance, the middle class was conscious of itself and had nothing to hide. Both the Reform Club and the Reform Association emphasized what they termed the "intermediary classes" of society. Their reform petitions directed attention to the growth of middle strata; and the existence of new social groups was offered as the principal justification for remodeling the constitution.[65] Public opinion in Guiana was very conscious of West Indian parallels in the constitutional field. As early as October 1887, the *Echo* editorialized that recent reforms in Jamaica and Trinidad were an object lesson that crown colony government would be useless, and that the way ahead lay through increased constitutional representation. Thereafter, there were constant comparisons made with Jamaica, Trinidad, and Barbados, and a common thread in these analyses was the feeling that representation in the West Indies was the consequence of the rise of an indigenous middle class.[66] (See table A19.)

Working People and the Political Process, 1887-1892

If, as already adduced, the middle class led a genuinely popular movement, it follows that there was some role played by workers and peasants. Reform was influenced by the fact that wage earners, common artisans, and small cultivators did not simply remain passive, but set out to be seen and heard advocating a radical position. The reform petitions which were presented to the legislature and forwarded to the Colonial Office had an extraparliamentary dimension. It was precisely this extraparliamentary dimension that gave vigor to the reform petitions.

Starting with the occasion of the disputed medical report, reformers pointed out the need to transcend the politics of the planters and the Governor by taking issues directly to the public. The Reform Club organized a series of public meetings in town and country. The Georgetown Town Council building became a sort of political capital. The first public meeting of the Reform Association was held there on 26 August 1889, and it was the venue at critical stages of the struggle. For instance, a public meeting convened on 10 January 1890, after it was confirmed that the Colonial Office had authorized a new constitution. At this gathering, there were 2,000 persons present and no standing room.[67] Smaller public meetings were held at business premises and in buildings belonging to the church and the lodges. Nor was the countryside ignored. The press carried notices of large meetings which took place along the East Coast Demerara and at Lonsdale and Hopetown villages' in West Berbice. Essequibo seemed largely left out of the movement, but the Reform Association claimed in September 1890 to have established a branch in Essequibo as well.

Nonconformist churches also provided an important bridge between the middle classes and the working people, especially in rural areas. Congregational ministers served as chairmen of branches of the Reform Association in Berbice and on the West Coast Demerara. The Congregationalists openly endorsed the reform objective of direct representation to replace the "present one-sided system of Government which favours a certain section of the community to the detriment of the others."[68]

From an electoral standpoint, there were three types of persons in the audiences attracted by the reform platform: first, a few who were qualified to vote under the existing limited franchise; second, a larger number who hoped to obtain the vote if the qualification was lowered to $300 per year; and third, a group who would not have qualified even if the reform proposals had been acceptable to the colonial government. The few eligible voters were a special concern of the reform movement, because they often failed to register, and it became a priority to register all who were legally entitled to exercise the franchise. There were a few dozen rural residents who were enfranchised because they owned three acres of land under cultivation. First the Reform Club and then the Reform Association urged those who had not bothered to register to make good the oversight. Registered voters for the whole of Guiana were as few as 715 in 1880. This number rose to 1,306 in 1884, mostly because of persons qualified by virtue of urban property or rentals. The registration drive from 1887 onwards included rural voters, and this proved decisive when Drysdale died in September 1890 and his seat as a financial representative in the Combined Court was contested by D. M. Hutson on behalf of the Reform Association.

The by-election of 1890 was most unusual. Technically, the post of financial representative was filled by direct election, but it was customary that planters and merchants simply agreed on a candidate and he was returned unopposed. But when Hutson's candidature was announced, the planters shopped around for an opposing candidate until they found Mr. R. Allan. The election to replace the deceased Drysdale as financial representative for Demerara was the first to be contested in twenty-five years. Besides, it was a new departure to witness an electoral confrontation in which candidates stood for an agreed position, almost verging on a party position. D. M. Hutson addressed himself to the electors as follows:

> As a colleague of your late Representative on the Council of the British Guiana Constitutional Reform Association, I have consented to a request that I should place myself before you as a candidate. It shall afford me pleasure, as a creole of the Colony, to follow in the footsteps of your late respected representative in the endeavour to bring about Political Reform on the lines of the Association's programme. I am in favour of direct representation, reduction of the franchise and vote by ballot, and I pledge

myself by all legitimate means to work for the attainment of these and other collateral reforms.[69]

Following on the above, it was logical that Hutson should have an organized campaign and that the Reform Association considered itself responsible for that campaign. Voter registration and public meetings in Georgetown, Belfield, Friendship, Sparendaam, and Den Amstel were the main features of this by-election.

The 1890 Demerara electoral register comprised a mere 240 voters out of 120,000 inhabitants. Of these privileged few, 155 went to the polls on 13 October 1890, and victory went to Hutson, by 85 votes to 70. There was jubilation. There was also sober reflection. D. T. Straughn had proposed the candidature of Hutson with the Reverend F. C. Glasgow as seconder. When the victory was won, it was Straughn who mounted the platform and fearlessly exposed the corruption, bribery, and intimidation carried on by the planters. Much of this corruption was possible because of the open voting, and Straughn argued that this proved definitively how essential it was to win the secret ballot in the proposed new Constitution. He elaborated:

Coercion and intimidation failed to be effectual with the villagers simply because they have their "three acres and a cow" to fall back upon, but if this election was for another county or had been held in Georgetown, it would have resulted differently. We would never have succeeded in getting our candidate returned, because poor clerks and other such like dependent inhabitants would have succumbed to coercion and intimidation. On polling day at one of the polls certain villagers were threatened that if they voted against Mr. Allan a stop-off would be put in the cross-canal of the adjoining estate and their drainage would be impeded. These villagers nevertheless fearlessly recorded their votes for the Reform Candidate. Other villagers were told that they will be made to repent the refusal to vote for Mr. Allan . . . the remark was to convey to the minds of the people that they will not get work from the estate any more—because when challenged the reply was that the Reform Association was not going to feed the people. Information also reached me that a Head Overseer gave the people in a certain estate to understand that any employee who voted for Mr. Hutson must be immediately discharged. Mr. Hutson got a vote or two from that estate notwithstanding.[70]

Perhaps the most decisive grouping within reform meetings was that of those who would acquire the franchise if monetary barriers were lowered. How many persons would be enfranchised by a lowering of the qualification from $600 per annum to $480 or $300 per annum? This question was posed by the Colonial Office to the governor, who responded by supplying data on estate earnings.[71] His information is summarized in the accompanying table.

Employment	Earnings (per annum)
Head Foreman Engineer	$960
Head Pan-Boiler	$720
Triple Effect Pan-Boiler	$600
Pan-Boiler	$340-540
Engineer	$364-480
Dispenser	$240-420
Schoolmaster	$336
Head Foreman Carpenter	$312
Boat Builder	$312
Blacksmith	$225-230
Carpenter	$225
Cooper	$225
Cane-Cutter	$176-250

As far as estate employees were concerned, only pan-boilers, "engineer" mechanics, dispensers, schoolmasters, and foremen in the construction area would have been enfranchised by the lowering of the qualification to $300. Government and private service in town would have accounted for several others—especially schoolmasters, postmasters, and clerks. As a guide to actual numbers, it should be noted that a list of persons liable to militia duty roughly approximated to the sort of persons for whom the Reform Association sought the franchise. The Militia List was first compiled in 1891, consequent upon the Militia Ordinance of that year. It sought to identify all males between the ages of eighteen and forty-five who had certain property qualifications or an income qualification of not less than $350. For Georgetown, it listed some 650 persons, some of whom undoubtedly were already in possession of the vote under the old Constitution. Those who had expectations of the vote and who formed the backbone of the reform constituency would have included sanitary inspectors, clerks, bookbinders, tailors, shopkeepers, cabinetmakers, wharfingers, printer-compositors, druggists, and schoolmasters.[72]

It is highly significant that some persons who supported reform did not command an income of $300. Blacksmiths, carpenters, coopers, and cane-cutters earned no more than $250 per annum on the estates, according to the governor's calculation above. Yet, such persons attended reform meetings. Artisans were particularly active in writing to the popular press. Many backed the reform demands, although they would not personally receive the franchise of $300 per annum that was being demanded. By implication, such persons were conscious of the overall social and economic benefits that might derive from a new political system. Their presence within the reform ranks was ample testimony to the conviction that life in Guiana would improve when the bottleneck of the exclusive constitution was bypassed.

The support of low-income working people confirmed the omnibus character of the reform movement. At all times it incorporated a wide range of social grievances and aspirations. An end to state-aided immigration, the opening up of crown lands, state assistance to minor industries, the development of the hinterland, the advancement of Creole civil servants, justice for village communities, and the improvement of medical and educational services—these were all objectives of the reformers. Hardly any were exclusively middle-class goals. Different emphases were placed by different social forces within the popular front. One contribution to the discussion of education stated: "Upon the Reform of our rotten system of government hinges every question affecting the welfare of the public and more especially of the poorer classes; but few questions are so absolutely dependent upon Reform as that of Education."[73] Some working people saw education as a priority, while others placed their hopes in agriculture or mining. Small peasants of the coastal villages were eager to see the launching of a banana industry, while wage workers in the goldfields were no less committted to the development of the hinterland than were the local entrepreneurs. Large public meetings were held on questions such as a proposed banana steamship service to the United States and on the need to reassert the frontier vis-à-vis Venezuela. The working people in attendance indicated that the resolution of these matters affected their livelihood.

Working people also demonstrated support on issues that did not offer them any practical benefits but which were defined as being part of a struggle for justice. The conviction of the barrister De Souza on contempt charges was taken up by the reform movement; and it was the disenfranchised masses who swarmed around the courtyard and virtually invaded the courtroom.[74] The right of a lawyer to speak critically about the existing judiciary was perceived as part of the rights of the colonized to speak freely on the conditions of their exploitation. Similarly, working people gave invaluable support to radical journalists who exposed acts of discrimination against individuals. The refusal on the part of the government to register the black Berbician, Dr. Rohlehr, as a medical practitioner, led to countrywide protests until a special enabling act had to be passed by the legislature in 1890.[75] The Fred Wills case was not as famous. He was the black assistant sanitary inspector of the Port of Georgetown. His dismissal for alleged misconduct in June 1889 appeared to have been an instance of crass racial discrimination, and the press rallied to his defense.[76]

As political reform gathered momentum, every public issue was potentially contributory to the democratic tendency. Civil service examinations was one demand, better pay and conditions for dispensers was another. Contemporaries readily recognized that reform was fed by numerous streams, and they sought to illustrate how completely the national life found itself in contradiction with the existing constitutional forms. In its own inimitable style, the *Echo* of 4 May 1889 editorialized:

The City of Georgetown, the Town of New Amsterdam, the rural districts cry "Reform." Our Minor Industries of all kinds call o. "Reform." Gold fields and miners seek Reform. The hampered banana industry echoes "Reform." Our mighty and almost never trodden forests with their giant trees throw back the echoes, "Reform," "Reform." Even sugar, the darling cause of our present ludicrous form of constitution, cannot refrain from joining the tumultuous strains and gently whispers, *"Mild"* Reform, *Mild* Reform."

"Mild Reform" prevailed, as far as immediate constitutional change was concerned. In terms of wider political change, however, the reform movement had generated energy and consciousness which carried forward into the long struggle of the middle strata and the masses against planter domination.

▬

CHAPTER 6

Resistance and Accommodation

questioning
the whole threshing floor of the earth, trying to discover
the meaning of this vast disorder . . .
perhaps even rebelling at finding no answer.
Aime Cesaire

Struggles of the Indian Immigrant Work Force, 1884-1903

Each day in the life of a member of the working population was a day on which there was both struggle and accommodation. Struggle was implicit in the application of labor power to earn wages or to grow crops, while accommodation was a necessary aspect of survival within a system in which power was so comprehensively monopolized by the planter class. Some persons resisted more tenaciously and consistently than others; but there was no simple distinction between those who resisted and those who accommodated. Moments of struggle and moments of compromise appeared within the same historical conjuncture, but ultimately, resistance rather than accommodation asserted itself as the principal aspect of this contradiction.

It takes a very jaundiced eye to read a people's history as a record of undiluted compliance and docility. Such an interpretation with respect to slavery was never comfortable in the light of numerous examples of slave rebellion and revolt.[1] Similarly, when the myth of docility was transferred to indentured immigrants, it clearly conflicted with the evidence of resistance. The dialectic of accommodation and resistance is in many ways most readily perceptible within the history of the East Indian immigrant population.

The long tenure of Agent-General Crosby came to an end in 1880, having lasted for twenty-two years. Crosby stood in the tradition of colonial paternalism, and worked to uphold the reputation that his office served the indentured laborers *in loco parentis*. However, this was too liberal for the

151

plantation system, and the governors under whom Crosby served gave him little support. There has emerged out of the Crosby era the picture of the Indian having childlike trust in the Immigration Office and using this institution as the sole means of obtaining justice. It is a commonplace in Guyana that all subsequent immigration agents came to be colloquially referred to by immigrants as "Crosby." But the emphasis on the real or imagined remedial actions of immigration functionaries tended to obscure the self-liberating activity of indentured laborers. Dwarka Nath, for example, completely overlooked this dimension in his first study on indentureship (1950) and only repaired the omission in a recent work (1975).[2]

Where resistance has been perceived to have occurred, its assessment has been unsystematic. Peter Ruhomon was not entirely sanguine about the helpfulness of immigration officers. While eulogizing Crosby, he notes that Crosby's successors were mainly concerned with planter interests. But Ruhomon only haphazardly assembles data on what he calls "tragic events"—that is to say, loss of life resulting from industrial disputes on estates.[3] The "tragic events" were undoubtedly dramatic, but they provide only one of the many indicators that tell of the existence and extent of protest by the "bound" laborers.

One of the ways in which indentured immigrant resistance can be ascertained and approximately quantified is through recourse to the record of cases under the Immigration and Masters and Servants' Ordinances. Immigrants regularly went before the courts as victims of a legal system which brought the force of law directly on the side of the planters. The high incidence of cases under the labor laws was itself proof of restlessness, absenteeism, and noncompliance among the indentured workers.* W. Alleyne Ireland, an overseer, published his observations on "the history of the East Indian immigrant." He recognized that the frequency with which immigrants were prosecuted did not tally with their reported docility. He put it thus: "As to the immigrants submitting like blind men to their employers as willingly as one would desire, the annual reports of the Immigration Agent-General show that between 1874 and 1895, sixty-five thousand and eighty-four indentured immigrants were convicted of breaches of labor contract."[4]

Without necessarily intending legal redress, immigrants walked to see "Crosby" to ask his favorable intervention with their employers. This technique was not as submissive as it appears at first sight. The right to break off work and to have access to the agent-general or to a subagent was one for which immigrants had to fight, and one that planters did not yield without a struggle. Early in January 1882, Narain Singh went to "Crosby" to complain about his wages. He was advised to go to a magistrate who would summon the

---

*Prosecution of immigrants took place to the extent of one in five being brought before the magistrates' courts under the Immigration Ordinance.

manager of Plantation Providence, to which this immigrant was indentured. Instead, it was the manager of Plantation Providence who summoned the immigrant, charging "that he being under indenture . . . did on the 4th day of January, 1882, without lawful excuse. refuse to begin certain work assigned to him." In this instance, the magistrate struck the case off the list, and his decision was upheld by the Court of Review.[5] An even more effective tactic was that of resorting to the immigration agent *en masse*. It was not uncommon to see fifty or sixty indentured laborers with their shovels and forks in Georgetown, taking their case directly to the officials.[6] In effect, indentured bondsmen had opened up a channel of demonstrative protest which virtually constituted a picket line—with the tools of their trade as pickets—to bring their grievances to the public gaze.

Sporadic acts of violence on the estates were at one end of the spectrum of assertiveness by indentured and unindentured Indian labourers. The appointment of the Commission of 1870-71 stemmed, not so much from the letters of William des Voeux, but from bloody clashes between police and indentured workers at Leonora on the West Coast Demerara. Shortly afterwards (in 1872), low wages on Plantation Devonshire Castle on the Essequibo Coast led to mass protests, followed by indiscriminate police fire that killed five and injured seven persons.[7] The Leonora and Devonshire Castle episodes were among those that conditioned planter and official attitudes toward Indian estate labor. They were fully aware that their dependable laborers could prove volatile and violent. The (acting) governor dispatched a statement of caution to the Colonial Office in September 1880:

> We must remember that these uprisings are not rare, and we must remember that on some occasions they have been attended with loss of life— And we must remember that the agricultural implements placed in the hands of the Coolies constitute them at any time an armed force; . . . One serious Coolie disturbance would so demoralize the principal labour power in the Colony that a loss would result from a money point of view, to say nothing of other consequences.[8]

Violent protests were occasioned by many specific and local grievances, such as overbearing behavior by management, disagreements over tasks, sexual exploitation of women by overseers, the "stopping" of pay, and so on. Violence was usually (though not always) a last resort, and it generally arose out of concerted action that amounted to strikes. Consequently, the relative frequency and seriousness of violent incidents over the years is a rough guide to the underlying socioeconomic situation, and to the trauma brought on by the vicissitudes of international trade between 1884 and 1902.

Strikes and possibilities of violent clashes did not materialize during the opening years of the 1880s. From 1879 to 1883, the indentured population was quiet, mainly because of relatively good returns from sugar. The wage bill of the sugar industry was approximately $5 million per annum, and it jumped to $6.5 million for the large crop of 1883.[9] It was not until the crisis of 1884 that violent labor confrontation became a characteristic of the estate scene.

The Immigration Report for 1884 made light of the fact that there were only five minor strikes among Indian estate workers. But with the continuation such manifestations, the 1885 report sounded a more carping note. It observed that for several years there had been no serious disturbance of the peace by immigrants combining together to forcibly call attention to matters which unsettled them. But, it continued, since 1884 there had been a reversion to "this unsatisfactory way of seeking redress for imaginary grievances." In spite of several arrests (especially in Berbice), indentured immigrants continued their agitation. Thirty-one "strikes and disturbances" occurred in 1886, fifteen in 1887, and forty-two in 1888.[10] This latter year was obviously a peak of discontent and worker manifestations.

Starting in May 1888, estate disturbances intensified from June through August. Plantations Enmore, Non Pareil, Mon Repos, and Hope were affected on the East Coast Demerara. On the other side of the Demerara river, Versailles and Met-en-Meerzorg were hit. Indentured laborers stated that they acted as they did because of the prevailing low wage rate, which never recovered after 1884, and which was further depressed from 1886. Strikes and disturbances fell to twelve in 1889 and to two in 1890, which was one of the few prosperous years in the long trough of depression.

One might expect violent demonstrations to keep step with the violent fluctuations of the economy. In a sense, this proved true with the occurrence of a spate of disturbances in 1894-95, and for another ten years thereafter. During each of these years, there were ten or more disturbances. The most serious of these were listed by the police in their dossiers, the record being as follows:

1894—Leguan, Farm (E.B.D.), Success, Skeldon, La Bonne Mère.
1898—Golden Fleece, De Kinderen, Cornelia Ida, Nismes, Goedverwagting, Mon Repos, Cane Grove, Melville, Blairmont.
1900—"More strikes throughout the Colony over wages, with assaults on overseers and drivers." The most serious were at Blairmont and Peter's Hall.
1903—Leguan, De Kinderen, Wales, Diamond, Peter's Hall, Success, Cane Grove, Friends.
1905—"Another busy year. Strikes occurred at Lusignan, Non Pareil, Friends, Leonora, Wales, Vriesland, Marionville and Springlands."[11]

Planters were realistic enough to realize that given the economic hardships, protests might have been more numerous and forceful. They themselves commended workers for patiently accepted wage cuts over the period 1894-96.[12] But this "patience" was not left entirely to chance. Estate management devised techniques to punish resistance and reward self-effacing behavior. Cooption was an important aspect of control and, as hinted previously, the driver was a key figure in this regard (see above, chap. 2). A satirical work published in Georgetown in 1890 was not very wide of the mark in stating that a worker qualified for promotion to the status of driver by being docile, and by always siding with the overseer.[13] Having got the job of driver, it was then possible to act overbearingly toward fellow workers. An informed observer told the West India Royal Commission of 1897 that indentured laborers were afraid of being abused by drivers and were sometimes assaulted by them. He added that drivers had a certain number of men always on their side—presumably prospective drivers who were toeing the line to ensure their own advancement.[14]

Fresh arrivals were the most malleable of the sectors of plantation labor, and planters specially favored the continual influx of new Indian immigrants. The exceptionally large number of new immigrants introduced between 1877 and 1881 must have had a dampening effect on the struggles of their more seasoned counterparts. Whenever recent arrivals participated in a strike or riot, the administration deliberately played down their involvement by attributing it to inexperience. Conversely, immigrants of longer standing were accused of misleading their newly arrived countrymen. In the administration of justice, a consistent policy was worked out to give substance to the affirmation that a laborer of a few months standing would never protest violently unless confused by more mature mischief-makers. Newcomers who rioted were treated leniently by the courts, or sometimes not brought before the courts at all. Six freshly indentured East Indians who took part in the Plantation Success riot of February 1895 were deliberately excluded from the subsequent indictment; the colonial state instead concentrated its ire on seasoned immigrants. For participation in the same riot at Plantation Success, twenty-eight senior immigrants were found guilty and given prison sentences ranging from twelve months to eight years, accompanied by corporal punishment.[15]

Planters opportunistically overplayed the distinction between new and old indentures; but it seems likely that time-expired immigrants *were* in a better position to articulate grievances. A remarkable example to this effect was the immigrant Bechu, who astonished planters and colonial officials with vigorous and sustained attacks on the abuses of indentureship. Bechu, a Bengali, arrived indentured to Plantation Enmore in 1894. He was physically unfit for heavy manual labor, but performed a number of domestic and light duties until his indenture was discontinued in February 1897. His defense of the members of his class had begun as early as November 1896, when he wrote his first letter to the press. His denunciations included substantial allegations of immoral exploitation of Indian females by overseers, instances of the callous turning away of time-expired immigrants from estate hospitals, active discouragement of those seeking repatriation, and numerous examples of planters breaking the labor code by their treatment of indentured laborers. Bechu's exposures sometimes led to remedial action such as the dismissal of offending overseers, but he also became the target of a campaign of vilification carried out by planters and by important sectors of the colonial administration. This redoubtable fighter was twice tried on one charge of libel after accusing Plantation Enmore's manager of causing the death of an immigrant by turning him away from the estate hospital when he was desperately in need of attention.[16]

Bechu himself was quite conscious of the implications of the struggle that he was waging, and of the fact that he was fighting the ruling class within a particular system of production. He ably explained as follows:

> My countrymen like myself have had the misfortune to come to Demerara, the political system of which colony has very appropriately have divined and defined by Mr. Trollope under a happy inspiration as "despotism tempered by sugar." To these twin forces, the Immigration system is as sacred as the old system of slavery in former days, and for one in my humble position to have ventured to touch it with profane hands or to have dared to unveil it is considered on this side of the Atlantic to be a capital and inexpiable offence.[17]

Bechu was attributed high-caste status by planter observers. It had become an article of faith among planters to assert that upper-caste Indians were the real troublemakers on the estate, and that without them the "Coolies" would be peaceful. They said that Oederman, a Brahmin, was one of the ringleaders of the Devonshire Castle disturbance of 1872; and planters continually returned to this theme.[18] The Sugar Planters' Association wrote the immigration agent in Calcutta in 1889, urging that he exercise care to avoid recruiting upper castes, while Alleyne Ireland spread the word that

> on each estate there are a small number of them who are incorrigible rascals, sowing the seeds of discontent and insubordination and ever ready to promote ill-feeling between the labourer and his employer. It is to these men that we must look for the cause of the riots that have occurred from time to time: the cowardly assaults on overseers and managers, and the larger number of cases that go before the magistrates for decision. It is an unfortunate fact that amongst the East Indian Immigrants there are a few men of some education and ability who, arriving in this colony ostensibly as agricultural labourers, devote their talents to the work of inciting their uneducated fellow-countrymen to acts leading in some instances to the most serious consequences.[19]

Planters pounced on any indication that a "high caste" Indian might have been involved in a given disturbance, but the occasions do not stand out as being strategically or statistically significant.[20] One must reiterate that the spirit of rebellion was both generalized and random. It revealed itself within the ranks of the outwardly placid Indian women whom management, as well as male workers, apparently expected to remain isolated from social decision making. The sources are almost silent on this crucial issue, but women certainly had specific grievances that would have called forth protest. During the 1890s, there was increased awareness of the adverse conditions under which indentured females worked—including field labor performed in advanced stages of pregnancy.[21] From time to time, estate disturbances started in the weeding gang, which was essentially the women's sphere. During the major disturbance at Plantation Friends (Berbice) in 1903, a key role was played by the veteran indentured woman worker Salamea. One driver testified: "I know a bound coolie woman named Salamea. She has been on the estate for three years. I heard that she told her shipmates on the Thursday to go fight. She was at Friends before and she went to Calcutta and returned to Friends. Salamea, I hear, urge the coolies who had assembled to fight."[22]

Many of the violent responses of indentured workers were highly personal, and were directed toward identifiable members of the plantation hierarchy. Indian drivers and European overseers were the supervisors who came most closely into contact with immigrant workers on a day-to-day basis. They were the ones who acquired reputations for callousness or for stopping pay or for engaging in victimization. An indentured field worker or group of such workers could decide to settle personal scores with an overseer or driver "aback" in the cane fields. But it more often happened that industrial conflict provided the opportunity for Indian laborers to attack estate subalterns or the manager himself.

Most overseers were young Scotsmen, themselves bonded for three years, and the community of overseers developed an inordinate fear of being personally assaulted by Indians who used their tools as weapons, or went into action with hackia sticks.*[23] Such attacks represented an extremely rudimentary stage of class struggle. They were born of desperation rather than hope, given the overwhelming power of the plantation system into which the immigrants were integrated. An outbreak of one estate rarely ever sparked off similar protests elsewhere, so the system was never remotely in jeopardy. Yet planters almost invariably reacted as though they faced a major threat. Tragic episodes on the estates tended to follow the same general pattern wherever they occurred. Firstly, a small incident arose, directly affecting a few workers comprising a given task gang. Secondly, the plantation and state authorities overreacted; so that thirdly, there was a physical clash with the mass of workers rallying behind the most outspoken in their midst.

*Hackia or akia—a local hardwood.

Standard estate procedure required that for every strike or stoppage the "ringleaders" be identified. Removal of these persons was to be effected immediately, and there was a strong school of thought that such troublemakers should be banished and relocated on another estate.[24] However, the very act of removing workers from the midst of their workmates and families was seen for what it was: namely, arbitrary and crude victimization. Consequently, attempted removals were themselves an incitement to riot, The colonial authorities know all this, but generally placed their faith in force. The police were sent in numbers to enter situations that did not require their presence. Once more, it was provocative action by the authorities which would lay the basis for a scenario in which the police opened fire.

Planters referred to the "Coolies" as docile, and they also described them as violent—since stereotypes leap over even such glaring internal contradictions. The particular stereotype of the murderous and ungovernable Coolies was activated as a virtually self-fulfilling prophecy, given the heavy-handed, authoritarian responses of those in power. When workers sought to protest peaceably, they were backed into a position of frustration and violence. The Plantation Non Pareil disturbances of October 1896 offer several insights into this general process.

Harry Garnett, a well-known planting attorney associated mainly with Curtis, Campbell and Hogg, was the manager of Plantation Non Pareil in October 1896. He claimed that incendiarism took place in the cane fields on the seventh, eighth, and ninth of the month; and he asked for the transfer of five of the indentured workers identified as promoting grievance claims. Matters got out of hand on 13 October, when four of these men were arrested on returning from a deputation to the Immigration Office. The police party making the arrest was under the command of Captain de Rinzy, who was to achieve long-lasting notoriety as a trigger-happy police officer. When the Non Pareil crowd tried to stop the arrest of their fellow workers, de Rinzy's squad opened fire without bothering with the formalities of reading the Riot Act. Two workers were killed on the spot, while three others died soon after of injuries received. The dead included Jungali, a militant among the workers. Fifty-nine persons were wounded in the hail of police buckshot.

The indentured immigrants on Plantation Non Pareil were not averse to bargaining with management to reach a compromise. Their wages had been illegally lowered below the statutory rate. This they were prepared to tolerate, if they could get cheap rations and if they were allocated provision farms. They had wanted to negotiate with the manager and with immigration officials. The governor of the day practically disassociated himself from the way the Indians at Non Pareil had been treated. He claimed to have issued instructions as follows: one, that arrests were only to be made in the ordinary course of the law and with proper warrants (issued by a stipendiary magistrate); two, that immigrants who wished to come to town to lay their case before the immigration agent-general were in no way to be interfered with; and three, that armed force was not to be used for removal of any immigrant. Captain de Rinzy broke each of these instructions, but he was acting within the planter milieu and according to certain accepted norms. For instance, he was guided by the word of the estate manager on all questions, and he obtained warrants from a local justice of the peace, another planter. Ultimately, his order to fire into the crowd was vindicated as self-defense in the face of a riotous mob.[25]

The persistence of the authoritarian colonial culture meant that it was only a matter of time before there would be another clash resulting in serious casualties. On the morning of 6 May 1903, an indentured gang which was half-banking at Plantation Friends struck work and marched to New Amsterdam with their implements.* They had been earning $1.00 per opening; they claimed $1.44; management offered $1.20 and refused the compromise of $1.28 which was acceptable to the workers. The manager got one driver to swear that certain laborers had threatened his life, and these men were immediately charged and removed. This time, the Riot Act was read. Six workers were killed and seven seriously injured. Ironically, they were shot down outside the Magistrate's Court at Sisters, whence they had proceeded to seek justice. The court subsequently dispensed its class justice by convicting four "ringleaders" for threatening the overseer and sentencing six to twelve months each for rioting. Two more were given six months each and told that they were being treated leniently because they had recently arrived and had obviously been misled.[26]

The regional immigration subagent responsible for Plantation Friends was disciplined after the shootings on charges of indifference to the problems of the indentured gangs, and because, on the night of the killings, he was lying dead drunk and stark naked in Sisters' court room—apparently not an unusual form of diversion for this particular bulwark of state power.[27] He was too undisciplined and he had bungled too much for there to be a cover-up. Yet he, too, had contributed to the development of a policy in which indentured resistance was met with preemptive force by the state apparatus acting on behalf of the plantation capitalists. As one group of indentured workers put it. "they only spoke about their bellies for something to eat."[28] One can scarcely avoid falling back on the hackneyed phrase—"We asked for bread, they gave us bullets."

When Bechu of Enmore appeared before the West India Commission of 1897, he had explained that indentured workers submitted tamely to abuses for fear of buckshot, and that taking into account the recent Non Pareil incident, people were really frightened to make complaints against their employers. It may well have been that each peak of resistance gave way

---

*Half-banking—preparing the rows for the replanting of cane tops.

to a moment of paralysis induced by the murderous reprisals of the colonial state—until such time as the events passed into a tradition of resistance which was itself a morale booster.

Industrial and Social Struggles of the Creole Working People

Village workers were the most advanced section of the plantation labor force, and among the most developed working class elements in the country. In comparison with indentured workers, village workers had much more scope for resistance at the point of production and in the wider social arena. Besides, their wage nexus with the estates was not compounded by other dependency relations arising out of tied housing, pasturage and rice beds. Consequently, their industrial position was also better than that of the free Indians still resident on the estates (see above, chap. 2).

Close and constant supervision maintained productivity in the slave era. Nevertheless, the slave population had devised a series of tactics that partially frustrated the labor process. To produce sugar without slaves entailed many of the same supervisory problems. First and foremost, the class struggle was waged between free workers and plantation managers around the question of how much could be extracted from the laborer in any given work situation. Experienced (Creole) workers used certain stratagems to lighten their work loads and to artificially speed up the completion of tasks. In this connection, young overseers were warned as follows:

> The cane cutters change the trash in cutting from the trash bank to the clean, and if great supervision is not used will leave canes hid under the trash to save them carrying them out. . . . Make the punt-loaders throw the cane lengthways into the punts and not across. They will try to load the two ends first; and then they will fill up the middle by throwing canes across the punt so that though it appears full it has very few canes in it.[29]

The above practices were sufficiently effective to jolt planters into involving the law as a deterrent. On 13 July 1880, an interesting labor case came before the judges on appeal. Four Creole Africans challenged their conviction on a charge of breach of contract by commiting fraud and deception while cutting cane. The conviction by the magistrate was quashed on a technicality, the prosecution having united in one charge the two offenses of "breach of contract" and "practising fraud and deception."[30] However, the impression remained that substantively, the law was available to planters for use against workers who sought to redefine the amount of labor that should go into a given task.

In the factory, workers were in the advantageous position of having moved from piece work to remuneration for time spent in the expenditure of their labor. Factory production, unlike production in the fields, was not overwhelmingly dependent on minute supervision. Even so, workers in Guianese sugar factories sought to get the better of management in ways analogous to the tricks of the field hands. For instance, accidental breakages often occurred, sometimes forcing the factory to shut down for many hours in the midst of grinding. Disgruntled factory hands assisted this process by deliberately leaving pieces of iron on the cane carrier.[31] A dissatisfied work force (and one that was experienced) was clearly likely to intensify its efforts to reduce the exploitation of its own labor, and individuals resorted to actual sabotage in some instances.

The greater the skill, the more predictable it was that a category of labor would accommodate only on terms that went some way toward satisfying their demands. Pan-boilers represented the extreme of this tendency, possessing as they did a store of knowledge denied to the factory overseer. They were the elite of the Creoles within the factory, and factory managers accorded them a grudging respect. The tempering of the cane juice was generally left entirely to the head pan-boiler. In the *Overseers' Manual*, the factory overseer was advised to check on the pan-boiler about one hour after granulation—but "let him do it with tact as pan-boilers do not like being interfered with. It is almost needless to say that the tricks and unjustifiable resources of our professional pan-boilers in Demerara are legion."[32] Pan-boilers produced; and that is why they were left alone to respond to the most advanced technology which the sugar industry had to offer.

The attitude of the pan-boilers highlights an objective of working-class struggle that might otherwise be easily overlooked: namely, the search for dignity and self-fulfillment on the job. Skilled field hands among Creole Africans and free Indians also took pride in their work—that is to say, in their proficiency with cutlass, shovel, and fork. To distinguish oneself among the leading cane cutters must have been a matter for congratulations, quite apart from the bonus that would be earned. Research in the modern period indicates that a valued skill and the ability to "hold down a work" give the laborer prestige among his peers; and this would appear to be a long-standing feature. One observer in the 1880s had this to say about shovelmen: "A robust shovelman earning his eight or nine bitts a day enjoys his work, swaggers about the distance he can throw the 'dirty' from his shovel and considers a piece of trench work he has dug and pared (especially if it be round a corner) a work of art, which it is."[33] Attitudes such as the above presumably redounded to the benefit of employers. Was this accommodation or resistance? The answer lies partly in an understanding of the fact that the process of winning recognition was one of struggle. For instance, skilled field hands such as cane-cutters and shovelmen adopted a principled stand that they would refuse any work other than their specialization. The rationale lay largely in the awareness that a lesser task would be paid at a lesser rate, irrespective of the person performing the labor. But that was not all. Over the course of the nineteenth century Creole laborers had developed a conception of themselves that was incompatible with an increasing number of estate jobs and, ultimately, with field labor as a whole—*given the terms on which estate labor was organized*.

The deep economic crisis of the 1890s accelerated Creole alienation from sugar estate labor. The Rev. F. C. Glasgow, a pillar of the Creole community, told the West India Royal Commission that the system of sugar production in the country did not suit free labor, and that the blacks on the whole did not like estate work. Under cross-examination by the commissioners, Glasgow elaborated. "The system of working sugar estates in peculiar. Even the coolies themselves, when their time is expired, do not like to go back. . . . Free people cannot be depended on, if the thing is to be carried on as it is now. The thing must be changed. The whole system must be discarded; sugar estates are carried on almost in the same way as they were a little after slavery or during slavery." When Creoles alleged that they were driven off the estates by intolerable conditions, planters strenuously denied this. Yet planter arguments support the conclusion that Creole workers genuinely felt that they derived neither adequate pay nor any other satisfaction from their association with the sugar fields. In July 1903, Murray of Plantation Port Mourant insisted that throughout his eighteen years' experience as a planter he could not get blacks to sign contracts. In part, this was because they wished to be free to bargain for higher wages; but it was also because the contract was uncomfortably reminiscent of slavery. Murray faithfully reported this sentiment in the Creole idiom: "Me fader an' me grand-fader bin ah slave befo' me, an' me sah neba make contract fo' wo'k pon suga estate."[34]

By the turn of the century, antipathy to estate labor was undoubtedly a cause of withdrawal from the estates. Village workers strove, not merely for amelioration, but for transformation of the plantation society. They therefore rationalized their replacement on the estates by Indians, and their inability to change estate conditions. But on moving away from estate labor into other occupations, they found an equally pressing necessity to defend their interests as workers, peasants, and small craft producers.

Working people outside the plantation sector were able to develop organizations that both catered to their immediate needs and assisted them in coming to a clearer understanding of their class interests. Before the century ended, workers' associations and farmers' associations had come into existence. However, in tracing the genesis of working-class organization, priority should be given to the Friendly Societies and Lodges.* The movement to establish Friendly Societies was burgeoning throughout the 1880s; these

---

*Also referred to as Benevolent Societies and Benefit Societies.

groups had as their primary function the provision of benefits in times of sickness and death. The report of the surgeon-general in 1884 drew attention to the creditable efforts of Friendly Societies in Berbice in reducing the number of sick persons who would otherwise have had to seek hospital relief at the expense of the government. At the same time, these societies paid attention to the general condition of villagers and urban dwellers. Their intimate identification with the African community was demonstrated at the Emancipation Jubilee on August 1888, when they staged a magnificent and mammoth parade of costumed members through the streets of Georgetown.[35]

Like the small Nonconformist churches, Friendly Societies provided a forum within which the membership could discuss the socioeconomic situation in its relation to the immediate issue of the maintenance of subscriptions and of buildings and their paid staff. In addition, Friendly Societies and several of the Lodges had characteristics reminiscent of European guilds. A Benevolent Society for printers was formed in 1854, and a Teachers' Benevolent Society was in existence from 1852.[36] These organizations did not necessarily survive unbroken through the decades; but they became very integral to the consciousness of workers and farmers, and they represented a stepping stone to a type of craft union. Thus it was that the Teachers' Mutual Improvement Society in existence in 1888 was soon afterwards referred to as the Teachers' Association. It functioned as one of the earliest of the prototype trade unions in Guiana, undertaking the task of bargaining collectively with the state and church management over pay, conditions of work, and educational reform in general.[37]

The Bakers' Association came into existence from 1888 as a union of employees of bakeries, and it was described as being on a footing similar to that of other Benefit Societies. In June 1890, a Guianese Patriotic Club and Mechanics Union was in the process of being formed under the guidance of E. A. Trotz, a carpenter of 80 Croal Street who later became the artisan representative before the 1897 Commission. Among other objectives, this mechanics union aimed at securing employment for its members and at guarding their rights from invasion by nonmembers.[38] In 1890, printers and compositors in Georgetown also started a union. No details have come to hand on this last-named venture; but one presumes that it was also a quasi-guild, protecting a group that was growing in importance as the press expanded.

The class struggle had to be fought with whatever limited weapons were in the hands of the working class. Its principal characteristic was still spontaneity, as illustrated by the anti-Portuguese riots of March 1889. On that occasion, popular anger was fanned by racial discrimination at the judicial level. Over the preceding months, Creoles had taken note of the tendency to treat very lightly the taking of a black man's life. A Portuguese had been fined a mere $24 for wounding a black man so severely that he lost "two buckets of blood"; the wound ultimately proved fatal.[39] The conviction and execution of another black man for the murder of his Portuguese wife might have passed without comment, were it not for the very different treatment later meted out to a Portuguese charged with the murder of his black wife. In the latter case, the chief justice, in summing up at the trial, warned that justice should be done irrespective of race. The jury convicted, and the judge imposed the mandatory capital sentence. But the governor commuted the death sentence, and the black community seethed with anger.[40] The incident that actually precipitated the violence of 1889 was petty to the point of caricature: it was a dispute between a black boy and a Portuguese man in the Stabroek market over a "gill bread."* The working people, as consumers, erupted against the most accessible agents in the hierarchy of exploitation—not the plantation capitalists nor the big import-export firms, but the small shopkeepers. The event was analogous to the enraged attacks by sugar workers on overseers and drivers on the estates.

Within a year of the anti-Portuguese outburst, the popular movement seemed to have raised itself to a more disciplined level. This was the moment when reform agitation was at its peak, and the masses were involved in it. Perhaps the existence of the Reform Association suggested to the working people that organized action could be utilized in other spheres. Be that as it may, there was a spate of strikes, called by the fledgling Benefit Societies or by ad hoc groups of workers within a given trade or enterprise. It began early in August with a strike among lightermen of the port of Georgetown and spread soon after to the stevedores on the wharves.[41] Government printers at the *Chronicle* may have benefited from the formation of the union of compositors and printers in July, and they went on strike in mid-August. At the same time, coopers also withdrew their labor. New rates of pay were demanded by several groups of workers, and where their requests were not favorably met, stoppages resulted. The grooms of the city and the bakers were among those who had cause to strike. When the bakers came out, employers acceded to their demands and then promptly passed on their rise in costs to the consumer by reducing the size of the one-cent loaf, which was the fare of the poorest classes.[42]

Some employers sought to use the law to bring workers in line. On Wednesday, 20 August 1890, E. J. Collins, a compositor, found himself charged before the sheriff by the proprietor of the *Chronicle* with having left his employ on the eleventh of August without tendering due notice. However, even the state functionaries in the courts can be touched by the hot breath of working-class anger and are wont to tread more cautiously. What was at stake was the right to strike—a nodal point in the relationship between

*A loaf of bread worth a penny or two cents.

capital and labor. The magistrate suggested an out-of-court settlement, stating that "it was a matter between employer and servant and affected many people."[43] In a parallel case, five tramway conductors were brought to court for breach of contract when they went on strike. The case was dismissed.[44]

It is highly probable that workers and other social classes in Guiana were influenced by their English counterparts, and by the tremendous struggle which was then begin waged on the English labor front. The historic dock strike began in London in September 1889. This event was covered in the local press, along with many other incidents of worker militancy in the principal capitalist centers. When the press in Guiana spoke of "an epidemic of strikes" in 1890, they pointedly adverted to both the local and international dimensions of this epidemic. One can posit a connection at both the objective and subjective levels. Guiana had long been part of the international division of labor—ever since slavery—and the working class of the nineteenth century was in a position to recognize its affinities with labor elsewhere. The much publicized strikes of dock workers at places like the London West India docks must have brought to the fore the similarity of class interests, and hence the possibility of stepping up the local class struggle through strikes. When the *Royal Gazette* first reported the London dock strike, it noted that "West Indians will be interested in being reminded that intimately associated . . . upon the Dock Directors' Committee is Mr. Neville Lubbock."[45] It may seem purely coincidental that Lubbock needed to travel to Guiana one year later to supervise one of the areas in which his capital extracted labor surplus. But the links between the exploitation of English dockers and West Indian plantation workers were not accidental. If the *Royal Gazette* found the connection intriguing, the sugar estate employees of Mr. Lubbock's Colonial Company and other Guianese workers were certainly capable of deciding to follow the lead of the London dockers.

When considering the international dimensions of the working class, it is self-evident that proletarian organization in Guiana was weak and underdeveloped throughout the nineteenth century—reflecting the lack of proletarian development on and off the dominant sugar estates. There were no institutions that consciously sought to unite large cross sections of the local working class. In 1872, a Working Man's Club was formed in Georgetown, apparently in close association with the *Working Man*, a newspaper run by a printer tradesman, and one that urged combinations of wage earners.[46] E. A. Trotz touched on this question of trade unions when he informed the West Indian Royal Commission: "I think we are very much discouraged in the method of banding ourselves together as a body of mechanics. There is no trade union amongst the people; there is just the chance of catching work wherever you can."[47]

Having made the unfavorable comparison between Guiana and the then proletarianized parts of the world, it remains true that the organizational initiatives of the 1890s marked an advance within the local situation. Creoles on the estate had created the independent task gang as their instrument of liberation. Creoles outside of the estate were displaying even greater mobility and organizational flair. This was most noticeable among urban workers. But before the end of the century, part-time and full-time farmers were also coming together to establish farmers' associations. A farmers' association was started at Mara in Berbice in 1898, and this institution spread quickly into Demerara and Essequibo Farmers' associations sponsored agricultural exhibitions. At the opening of the Victoria-Bolfield Horticultural and Industrial Show in 1898, the chairman was at pains to point out that the exhibition was promoted, not by the sugar planters, but "by men more or less connected with the peasant class." The full implications of this statement would not have been lost on his audience. They knew that planters had, until then, received subventions to exhibit sugar products both in Guiana and abroad. In such exhibititions, the so-called "minor products" of the peasantry would either not have been there, or they would have been relegated to the status of sideshow oddities.

One of the objectives of the farmers' associations was to lobby for financial and technical assistance; the absence of such assistance had always been the bane of peasant farming. The associations were formed against a background of the governor having recently poured cold water on proposals from the Commission on Banana and Fruit Growing which reported to the legislature in March 1895.[48] Obviously, considerable political pressure had to be applied if the peasant organizations were to win any concessions. Realistically, therefore, Creole villagers virtually united the agricultural movement with the movement for the creation of larger and more viable local government entities.

In the decade between the Village Ordinances of 1892 and 1902, politics at the local government level were very vibrant. Village councils allegedly encouraged factionalism and opportunism, but this was merely one of the consequences of the fact that peasants and rural workers were part of a democratic process. One of its dynamic manifestations was the movement toward a common front embracing all village councils. The first Conference of Village Councils took place at Plaisance. Its principal resolution was directed towards the colonial treasury, requesting a subvention of $20,000 for village development. Although the legislature was then devising means for liberally assisting distressed plantation owners, it turned down the appeal. The unified village movement then fell somewhat into abeyance until 1901, when it was revived in the form of the Village Chairmen's Conference.[49]

The Village Chairmen's Conference was given its initial direction by James McFarlane Corry, a magistrate's clerk and the chairman of the village council of Den Amstel and Fellowship. Corry was a Congregationalist, founder President of the Y.M.C.A., and a close friend of other middle-class pillars such as the Reverend Dr. London and A. B. Brown.[50] It was the same leadership that had appeared in the Agricultural Improvement Societies, and they worked toward the same objectives: namely, the betterment of Creoles with house lots and farm lands, as well as the improvement of village conditions generally. The social significance of independent village institutions can be judged from the data concerning the number and size of the villages. By 1902, villages numbered 214, of which 96 were in Berbice, 66 in Demerara, and 52 in Essequibo. The village population had nearly doubled since 1848, rising from 44,456 to 86,935 persons in this period. The value of village property had increased, over the same years, by half a million dollars; and there were 13,969 proprietors owning 77,234 acres.[51]

But the question of village self-government was not definitely settled by the 1892 Village Ordinance as had been promised. Under the 1892 ordinance, there was an area of uncertainty in the boundary between the powers of the village council and the powers of the central government, and consequently, an area of potential conflict. A clash in 1898 was resolved in favor of the Beterverwagting Village Council; but Ordinance No. 12 of 1902 reasserted the authority of the central government. The issue had very little to do with the efficiency, or lack of it, of the democratic village organs. True, villagers had not achieved a great deal during the 1890s without funds, but they had operated with enough distinction for the colonial secretary to give them mild praise in the very memorandum that prepared the ground for rescinding village freedom.[52] One contemporary publicist made an intriguing assessment: "Local self-government has been seriously curtailed because the villages began to show that they understood what it meant."[53]

Creole Villagers protested bitterly against reactionary interference by the government. From early in 1901, letters to the press condemned the proposed new village ordinance, but the government went ahead and annulled such village freedom as existed. The only possible way of raising the challenge to a higher level was by a more radical attack on colonial government per se; and the working people of Guiana laid the basis for such a challenge in the years 1900 to 1905.

Forging New Political Weapons

When "Mild Reform" was actualized after 1891, the masses gained little or nothing. The handful of artisans and workers who were enfranchised must have found electoral politics a most frustrating experience. After the contest for the seat of a financial representative in 1890, Straughn had expressed grave misgivings about the absence of a secret ballot, and his words proved prophetic when the 1892 elections were fought under the new Constitution. In West Demerara, J. A. Murdoch of the Reform Association contest against Alexander Barr, a leading planter attorney. Barr won by thirteen votes; but the association collected evidence of 12 percent of the registered voters having been deterred from voting at all, while others were coerced into voting for Barr at the open hustings. William Griffith, engineer at Plantation La Jalousie, made a deposition with regard to his dismissal immediately after he had voted for Murdoch.[54]

Planters had a number of weapons to add to intimidation and victimization. They controlled registration and preelection procedures, and they had the backing of the courts. In October 1891, it was reported that the planters were withholding registration forms and preventing their distribution.[55] The registrar himself was refusing to register village proprietors who qualified in terms of property but were not literate in English; and he insisted on the appointment of stipendiary magistrates as revising barristers of the electoral lists, knowing the proplanter records of the stipendiaries. Consequently, the total registration for the whole country was only 2,045—an increase of only a few dozen over the previous unreformed electorate. It was an achievement when the Reform candidate, Farnum, won over the influential planter, Luard, in East Demerara; but the court stepped in to declare the poll null and void on a technicality. At the new election for this seat, J. B. Woolford represented reform against the same planter, and a defeat was sustained by the reformers. Luard received the votes of 130 overseers, while 32 of the 185 village voters were constrained to vote for the planter candidate. The *Liberal* stated that "any villager who, having a vote, gives it to the planters or who even fails to give it against them is a traitor to his class and to his own interest."[56] However, the really remarkable fact is that many villagers (as panboilers, carpenters, etc.) cast their ballot publicly against the planter class in spite of the near certainty of victimization. This indicates that the small segment of the working class that was enfranchised in 1891 was called upon to take the greatest risks on behalf of the de facto popular alliance across class lines.

Because the politics of the 1890s were the politics of a popular front, it is possible to recognize some tensions and rifts deriving from divergent class interests. With the renewed onset of economic crisis in 1894, the new middle-class spokesmen compromised considerably with the planters with whom they were sharing the legislature. Together, the commercial middle class and the planters presented to the Colonial Office certain schemes that asked for help for the gold and sugar industries. The sugar barons agreed that government should underwrite a loan of million for the opening up of the hinterland; but in return they exacted support for their own proposal that the general revenue should bear the entire cost of indentured immigration for the next five years.[57] The plan did not go through in its entirety,

*Water Street looking north. Buildings on the left have access to
the Demerara River.*

principally because the Colonial Office saw it as a "log-rolling lobby" of
sugar and gold interests, to obtain loans which the metropolitan government was unwilling to advance. However, on balance, the accommodative
middle-class tendency betrayed hopes which were aroused by the reform
campaign. Concessions to planters in the financial sphere meant the neglect
of social services such as primary education, and at the same time the burden
of taxation was further shifted on to workers and peasants through indirect
taxes.[58]

The Executive Council which was brought into being by the 1891 Constitution was carefully guarded as a preserve of the local representatives of the
plantation companies. With electives supposedly articulating popular interest,
the governor (and Executive Council) seemed to have given up any claims to
trusteeship, and spent a large proportion of their time discussing the purely
coercive functions of the state. The police were reorganized to constitute
what was called a semimilitary force; and a militia came into being in 1891.
Both were designed to replace the West India regiment, which was withdrawn. Border disputes party justified the boosting of the armed forces, but
they also avowedly directed against any internal threat, after the upsurge of
violence in Georgetown and on the estates in 1888-89.[59] The rural constabu-
lary was conceived with estate uprisings in mind, while the regular police and
the militia would have been called upon to quell any overt actions in Georgetown, where unemployment had created an explosive situation. In 1895,
the possibility of riots was taken very seriously indeed. Police reports drew

attention to the reduction of wages in Georgetown and in the goldfields. The words was out that the blacks were dissatisfied with their lowered wages and that they intended to rampage and burn down Water Street (the main commercial center). There was evidence in March 1895 of increased gangs of unemployed standing around Water Street with sticks. They were given to making threats, and some of them had been charged and convicted in the magistrates' courts. Besides, the authorities were greatly alarmed at the expression of views that "there are plenty of Police and Volunteers in favour of the poor."[60] Nothing came of the governor's fears of imminent disaster in 1895; he may have overreacted when he demanded the presence of the warship *Buzzard*.

Witnesses before the West Indian Royal Commission of 1897 dismissed the possibility of urban violence when questioned on this point.[61] By this date, those who still pursued the reform ticket had won a victory when the governor reconsidered his opposition to the introduction of the secret ballot.[62] Nevertheless, the legislature ceased to be the principal focus of popular politics by the turn of the century. Instead, a radical restatement of the protest movement took place within the Creole community. The new politics combined a number of old and new features in a novel manner. Largely from newspaper sources, one derives the following constituent elements:

1. unflinching criticism of the colonial government in public forums;
2. publication of a newspaper organ to carry agitation beyond indoor meeting places;
3. involvement of working people in financing the newspaper;
4. use of public forums and newspapers to advance a consistent policy on fundamental issues;
5. establishment of community organizations to provide for regular public discussions;
6. a call for the creation of trade unions; and
7. launching of a political organisation for the furtherance of the above objectives.

Many of the persons who subscribed to public political action had gained their organizational experience in the Friendly Societies and Agricultural Associations, or directly from the church, which was the matrix of the first two. The London Missionary Society remained close to the Creoles in the post-Emancipation era; and the semi-independent Congregational churches which inherited the mantle of the "Mission Church" were at all times solidly entrench among the rural and urban working people. Indeed, the Congregationalists were distinguished by ministering to working people and *to no other class* in any significant way. Methodism was also quite militant, but the Methodist churches sought their membership from a cross section of the community and seemed inhibited from taking certain positions.[63] The Congregational churches provided the political movement with a physical base, in terms of schoolrooms and churches to be used as meeting places. Less tangibly but more importantly, this branch of the Nonconformists contributed a cultural and moral force for political change. The Rev. F. C. Glasgow, who so ably presented popular grievances to the West India Royal Commission of 1897, was a prime example of "a son of the soil" who was prepared to mobilize Congregational ministers and laity to fight the oppressive conditions under which Creoles still labored at the turn of the century.

Militant political protest was dramatically launched from the very pulpit of the church with the arrival of the Rev. H. J. Shirley from England in July 1900 to take charge of the New Amsterdam Mission Church. In less than eight weeks, the *Chronicle* reported an "Extraordinary Speech by Mr. Shirley" at Providence Congregational Church, Georgetown. Among other things, Shirley affirmed:

> The church should be alive to the fact that its safety and prosperity depended on the contentment, enlightenment and general goodwill of the toilers and the masses of the people. . . . As he moved in and out among the people, his difficulty was to find anybody contented unless they happened to be connected with the Government. He never was anywhere where there was such an undercurrent of discontent. What was simmering in his mind was the thought that that Government about which nobody had any good to say could not have much good in it. (Applause). . . . The burden of taxation fell on the poor and it was meant to fall on the poor. (Loud applause. Mr. Shirley had again to call for silence.) . . . First the Government does not care much about the people; secondly, the people at home (in Britain) knew next to nothing about them; and thirdly, the people here did not realise themselves yet. . . . He was driven to the conclusion that it was the intention if possible to KEEP THE BLACK AND COOLIE RACES IN IGNORANCE. (Loud applause). They should break no law but they should organise themselves and revive their political associations. All the labourers and all the employees of the colony from the clerk to the coolie should FORM TRADE UNIONS so that no employers should be able to dismiss a man for asking simple honest justice. . . . Break no law but exercise the right of free speech, and agitate, for it is both legitimate and imperative.[64]

After the above declarations, Shirley was attacked by spokesmen of the establishment as a "socialist demagogue." But he persisted. A few months later, there was a rumor that he was under police surveillance and would be locked up for inciting the people.[65] In response, Shirley pointed out that there was nothing new or extreme in what he was saying. In addition, he adroitly remarked that words were superfluous when the working people had "enough to incite them in actual occurrences"—like throwing thick, heavy sugar for twelve hours at just over a penny an hour, or digging a drain one foot deep for three roods and earning nothing because the overseer refused to approve the task performance.[66] Before and after Shirley's stay (which ended with a warm-off in July 1903), an extremely progressive stance had been adopted by several Nonconformist church leaders, both European and Guianese. What made Shirley somewhat unique was that he entered the situation with a class consciousness developed in England where the modern proletariat was carrying out trade-union and party struggles. His real contribution was not so much the denunciation of existing ills in Guiana as his emphatic call for the self realization of the working people through agitation and organization.

A Young People's Improvement Society was formed in New Amsterdam in October 1900. This fitted into the existing pattern of Benefit Societies and into the emergent trend of Agricultural Improvement Societies. In addition, the Young People's Improvement Society used on in four of its weekly meetings for the purpose of explicit political discussion. These sessions were addressed by Shirley, by Berbicians like Dr. Rohlehr, and by speakers invited from elsewhere like J. A. Barbour-James, chairman of Victoria Village. Other Young People's Improvement Societies were founded over the course of the next three years. But in the meantime, New Amsterdam had become the virtual political capital of the country. Their next step was the publication of a penny weekly, edited by Shirley and supported by Dargan, Thorne, Wood Davis, A. B. Brown, T. B. Glasgow, Dr. London, Dr. Wills, C. E. Farnum and J. S. McArthur—to name the most prominent of the middle-class radicals. This weekly, the *People* newspaper, was registered in September 1901, after the share capital of $20,000 was underwritten by public shares. The object was for this newspaper to be owned by the common people, and to be sold at a penny so as to bring it within reach of the section of the public for which it was intended.[67]

While the *People* was advocating working class objectives in a general way, primary-school teachers were organizing themselves to promote their specific interests as a section of the working class. The inadequacies of the colonial education system was a perennial question in Guiana and the West Indies. By 1900, the grievances of Guianese teachers spilled over into one of the periodic outbursts against the system, because the new Education Code introduced that year was held to be very unsatisfactory. Both teachers and parents wanted an education board and a regular monthly stipend for teachers in place of the grants per capita. Teachers operated on two fronts: they mobilized the public to forward a giant petition to the Colonial Office, and they entered electoral politics through the process of pledging support to those candidates who committed themselves to rectifying the shortcomings of the Education Code.

Payment by results made teachers into virtual task laborers just like any estate laborer. Teachers, too, could have their salaries "stopped" or withheld. Besides, their earnings were small and their job security was arbitrarily determined by school managers. If teachers stood out in any way from the general run of workers, it was because they constituted themselves into a teachers' association. They had a quasi-union when other workers did not; and this fact gave teachers vanguard status within the working class. They forced the appointment of another Education Commission in April 1902; and one year later, they prevailed upon the public to resume commerorating August as Education Day, in the interests of the children and the community at large.[68]

Being articulate, teachers were also in the forefront of those who responded to the *People* as a unique organizing tool. During the elections of October-November 1901, there was reference to a loosely defined group variously called "the Progressive Party," "the Progressive Association," or "the People's Party." These terms did not describe a formal entity; rather they were appelations which connoted opposition to the formerly dominant interests in the legislature that had come to be called "the Planter Party." Individuals who were supposedly united in opposition to the planters did not always find themselves on the same side of any given division. However, structural development soon followed and the People's Association was born. Its first executive included S. A. Robertson, chairman of the Teachers' Association, along with several of the radical spokesmen of the legislature and the Georgetown Municipal Council. One of the major elements in the policy of the People's Association was its opposition to state-aided indentured immigration; this was a restatement of a position that had been abandoned by several of the middle-class liberals in the 1890s. More than the earlier Reform Association, the People's Party was a proto-party with well-defined positions; and its leadership sought to use the limited constitutional arena to advance popular demands.[69]

Working people were present in the legislature by proxy after the relatively successful intervention of the "Progressives" in the elections of October-November 1901. Their representatives were somewhat more resolute than some of the brown or black middle class who had entered the legislature after 1891. Still, they made little impact on the colonial executive, and less on the quality of life in Guiana—at a time when workers were reeling from a protracted and formidable assault on their living standards. The political leaders who had agitated and organized a "mass" base were far from achieving (or perhaps even conceptualizing) the degree of power required to neutralize the planters or to alter the manner in which Guiana was buffeted by international capitalist forces.

CHAPTER 7

Race as a Contradiction among the Working People

> Out of the sea-bed of my search years
> I have put together again
> a million fragments of my brothers' ancient mirror . . .
> and as I look deep into it
> I see a million shades of fractured brown,
> merging into an unstoppable tide. . . .
>
> *David Campbell*

The perception of race in nineteenth century British Guiana was almost inseparable from the distinction made between Creoles and immigrants. Since Amerindians were excluded from the coastal political economy, African descendants portrayed themselves as the indigenous section of the work force, while workers of other races were deemed immigrants. But with Indian immigrants constituting such an overwhelming numerical majority, the term "immigrant" came to be synonymous with "Indian" (and was so used in offical documentation such as the reports of the immigration agent-general). The two main groups of involuntary immigrants—African and Indian—having arrived at different times, had developed competing interests. More important still was their own conviction that their interest conflicts. The Africans, blacks, or Creoles, as they may variously be called, shared and articulated definite views on immigration and on immigrant Indians.

There was a remarkable unanimity and consistency in Creole views on immigration throughout the period under discussion, from the random petitions of the 1880s to the more structured protects of the People's Association between 1903 and 1906. Africans opposed Indian indentured immigration in defense of their own self-interests. When Creoles met formally or expressed their views in the press, their principal concerns were the basic issues of employment, wages, and the price of food; and, almost invariably, they came around to the question of state-aided immigration, identifying it as the phenomenon which reduced employment, lowered wages, and in-

174

creased the cost of living through the incidence of taxation designed to meet the one-third of the immigration expenses borne by the colonial state. State assistance to indentured immigration was particularly galling because Creole taxpayers were subsidizing their own retrenchment. They also objected to the expenditure approved by the Combined Court with regard to ancillary immigration services. Indentured Indians received inadequate medical attention, but estate hospitals were an advance on no hospitals at all, which was the situation in the villages. Creoles therefore protested the funding of estate medical staff from public finances for the benefit of immigrants alone.[1]

Creole approaches to immigration were self-interested, but they were not merely selfish. Objectively, the free African wage earners were engaged in a level of struggle which was higher than that of other laborers on the estates. Free workers were fighting against the backward-looking tendency of landed capital to extract surplus through legal coercion reminiscent of feudalism. Consequently, the opposition to indentureship was entirely compatible with espousing a more rational political economy. Planters averred that Indian indentured labor was cheap. Creoles responded by stating that, had they been granted increased wages, planter expenditure would have been less than the overall cost of immigration. Many working people perceived that the institution of "bound" labor had a great deal to do with controlling the laborer. It is interesting that Africans were aggrieved by the use of resources to bolster the police force and the prison service so as to keep immigrants in check.[2]

Anti-immigration petitions usually offered counterproposals for reorganizing the colonial economy, urging the need for economic diversification if Guiana was to be something more than a collection of plantations. It was submitted that some proportion of available public resources be channeled to the peasantry, as part of a process of diversification from sugar. The entire community outside of the planter class and the immigrants was mobilized by the argument that subsidies for immigration could be deployed to sponsor minor industries, build roads in the interior, provide teacher training, and so on. For that matter, black people were usually careful to add that the abolition of state-aided indentureship could be a blessing for Indians themselves. After the end of reindenture in the 1870s, the presence of free Indians became a crucial factor in Guianese society. In 1880, blacks noticed that many ex-indentured labourers were unemployed, after having been driven out by fresh batches of indentured immigrants. In the course of anti-immigration presentations, the effort was made to state categorically that no ill will was being directed against Indians as such, but rather against the manner of their introduction and the attendant evils of the system.[3]

In May 1903, Creole Africans of the People's Association drafted a major petition against state-aided immigration to the secretary of state for the colonies. None of the arguments were novel by this late date, but the cogent presentation took account of recent social manifestations such as the tremendous unemployment affecting workers in both of the main racial groups. Indeed, the petitioners pointedly drew attention to the unflagging planter insistence on more indentures in the face of unemployment among the unindentured Indian workers as well as the blacks.[4] One of the planter responses was that Indian immigration was benefiting the country because unindentured Indians remained good workers or became good settlers. The People's Association alluded to the spuriousness of planter arguments that on the one hand attributed laziness to Africans who withdrew from estate labor, and on the other hand extolled the diligence of Indians who did the same. The association further contended that all workers schooled in the plantation system were equally alienated, and the free Indian was reluctant to continue with the semislavery of the plantation, unless induced by increased wages. Planters held that ex-indentured Indians were making a major contribution to the expansion of the population. This was a rider added opportunistically to their main premise that what was good for sugar was good for the country. In addressing the Colonial Office, the People's Association formulated a shrewd hypothetical comparison with Britain itself:

> An adequate conception of the injustice of state-aided immigration, as it obtains in British Guiana, might be gained by imagining the British workmen on a strike for higher and fair wages being taxed to pay for the introduction of *foreign* cheap labour, and the government justifying it on the ground that what would in such case be essentially a grant to capitalists was merely a grant to increase the population of the country.[5]

The People's Association incorporated several references to immigration in a manifesto published in 1906. In alluding to the magistrates' courts, the manifesto condemned the imposition of oppressive fines—"especially against immigrants for breach of regulations."[6] Views such as these, expressed by the most radical of the black leaders like A. A. Thorne, coincided with the opinions expressed by liberal Europeans from time to time. William des Voeux, for instance, never lost his interest in exposing the injustices of indentureship. While in France in 1894, he saw a newspaper report on a proposal to relieve planters of their two-thirds share of immigration costs, and he was moved to forcefully state his objection that the Creole laborers were being taxed to bring in competitive labor.[7] Darnell Davis, who early in his career as a public servant had served as secretary to the Des Voeux Commission, was also a forthright critic of indentured immigration—although as acting colonial secretary in 1894 he was unable to sway official views on this subject.[8] Many years later, Thomas Summerbell, M.P., told the Sanderson Commission (1910) that he considered indentureship as bordering on slavery, and that the time had arrived for its abolition. This was the position which Creole Africans had consistently been taking; and it is significant that Summerbell was reflecting the views of the (Creole) Working Men's Association of Trinidad.[9]

Joseph Ruhomon, author and editor of the People

Sympathy toward Creoles did not necessarily mean hostility toward immigrants and vice versa. The Rev. H. V. Bronkhurst (Methodist) was one of the
few missionaries of the nineteenth century who worked among Indians.
Bronkhurst, who remained in Guiana from 1860 to 1889, was Dutch on his
father's side and Indian on his mother's. In general, he sided with Indians in a
paternalistic manner, but he was not anti-African. He was convinced that by
the 1880s immigration had outlived whatever justification it had in terms of
boosting scarce labor supplies.[10] Bronkhurst dedicated his work to further-
ing good race relations, and the same may be said of the Rev. H. J. Shirley.
Shirley set up his base among black Congregationalists, but he also expressed
pro-Indian sentiments. Even when back in London in 1904, he wrote the
Daily News from his church in Markham Square deriding some current opinion which tried to paint a blissful picture of the lot of Indians under indenture.[11] One of Shirley's close coworkers was Joseph Ruhomon, who came
from the first generation of educated Guianese Indians. As a journalist,
Ruhomon began voicing public concern for the well-being of his countrymen
at least as early as 1894. He later became editor of the *People* newspaper
through which he helped the circulation of Creole views against indentured
immigration. Later still, he remained in the forefront of the movement for
better conditions to be granted to immigrant workers.[12] The point at issue
is that anti-immigration was not incompatible with a pro-Indian position, and
it certainly did not connote racism. Ultimately, the most weighty testimony
is that of the Indian Bechu. In his letters to the press and in his evidence
before the West India Royal Commission of 1897, Bechu exposed the evils
of indentureship and *opposed the further introduction of indentured Indian*

immigrants. In 1900, Bechu was one of those who wrote to the press to counter the criticisms made by conservatives against Shirley.[13]

The Creole-Indian immigrant antithesis at times took the form of an African racial confrontation. Differences in culture constituted obstacles in the way of working class unity across racial lines. Indians lived mainly on the estates. As they became more concentrated in the 1890s, their residences were often set apart from the African villages founded after Emancipation. This partial separation undoubtedly contributed to perpetuating differences in religion, language, and customs.[14] Nevertheless, the process of "Creolization" was already evident among Indians in the final quarter of the nineteenth century. Their food, dress, speech, and funeral customs were undergoing transformation under Creole influence.

In the present study, "Creole" describes anyone of immigrant ancestry who is locally born. Used without qualification, the word "Creoles" refers to persons of African or part African descent; but "Creolization" refers to an indigenizing experience, and it encompassed all racial groups. One of the more evocative uses of the word "Creole" in a Guyanese context is its association with the "Creole gang"—that gang comprising children who did manuring and other light field tasks as soon as they were physically able so to do.[15] Each Indian born on the estate or growing up as a child there would inevitably have passed through the Creole gang.[16] It was the earliest socializing *work experience*; and work experience was one of the imperatives of indigenization. Africans and Indians marked out the same "tasks" between the dams and the drains, and they faced the same vexations from overseers "aback" and at the pay table. Besides, residential separation must not obscure the fact that each group at different times came to understand what it meant to be at the total mercy of the planters in the plantation logies of the "Nigger-yard" and "bound-yard."

When Indians left the estates (residentially or occupationally), they carried with them the mark of the plantation, as did the Creole African forerunners. Reference has already been made to statements of concern by planters in the 1880s, when ex-indentured Indians were behaving as emancipated Africans had previously behaved. The same cry of anguish came from planters throughout the period under discussion. A report of 1910 put this matter very pointedly when it quoted an observer saying of Indians, "If you have them on the estate, they work; as soon as they go out to the villages they get just like the people in the villages."[17]

Africans and Indians brought to Guyana large fragments of the culture of their respective continents. This is beyond dispute, as is the fact that Indian immigrants in the nineteenth century sought to relive wherever possible their ancestral experience.[18] But the Creolizing experience was a counterforce, especially in so far as young Indians were concerned. Contemporaries commented increasingly on Creolization in the 1880s and 1890s as the phenomenon became more obvious. For instance, in March 1891 the editor of the *Argosy* affirmed that "every year sees growing up around us a population of Creole coolies who know nothing of India save what they heard or read of it, and who do not seem to crave for any closer acquaintance with it; and the presence of this large and yearly extending class, goes far towards making the East Indian coolies regard this land as belonging to themselves."[19]

Taken in its broadest sense, the "culture" of the racial fractions of the working people included their work environment and their responses to capital at the point of production. In these critical areas, Africans and free Indians were on common ground. There were also areas of interaction in other social spheres, with striking results. Firstly, the behavior of the Indian immigrants was influenced by Creole African practices in areas as significant as funerary customs. Secondly, the Creoles were culturally interpenetrated— so much so in the field of dietary habits that rice was rapidly becoming the staple of all racial groups in the 1890s. And thirdly, both major racial groups responded in like manner to certain aspects of the culture of the dominant Europeans: notably, to the game of cricket and to the institution of the rum shop. Bronkhurst's writings are a superior source of information on these matters. He recognized the younger Indians to be a new generation of "Hindu-Guyanians"—an apt term, which foreshadowed the concept of "Indo-Guyanese." Curiously, he chastised the Afro-Guyanese for participating enthusiastically in Indian "Tadjah" ceremonies and for independently celebrating their own "Tadjahs."[20] *

The evidence of this early period does not sustain the picture of acute and absolute cultural differences coincident with race.[21] It would be more accurate to contend that the existing aspects of cultural convergence were insufficiently developed to contribute decisively to solidarity among the working people of the two major race groups. The obverse of this race-class conjuncture is that the development of class forces and class consciousness was inadequate to sustain unity of the working people across the barriers created by legal distinctions, racial exclusiveness, and the separate trajectories of important aspects of culture. There were in effect two semiautonomous sets of working class struggles against the domination of capital—the oné conducted by the descendants of ex-slaves and the other by indentured laborers and their fellow Indians. Pursuing their legitimate aspirations, these two ethnically defined sectors of the laboring people could and did come into conflict with each other.

Serious African mobilization against indentured immigration proclaimed itself distinct from anti-Indian sentiment. However, the fine distinction was

---

*Tadjah (correctly *taziyah*), the pagodalike structure carried in the annual Muslim festival of Muharrum, dedicated to Hosein. In British Guiana and Trinidad, "Tadjah" or "Hosein" attracted non-Muslims from among both Indians and Africans.

eroded in practice. Frustration of Creole African claims by planters and officialdom inevitably led to anger and resentment being expressed directly against the Indian sections of the work force. Evidence of this tendency can be culled at many stages of the history of indentureship. During the early 1870s, there was much talk about the violent nature of Indians, brought on by their increasing opposition to indentureship and their resort to personal or group violence on a number of occasions.[22] A paper like the *Working Man* illustrated a confused aspect of Creole African working-class sentiment when it denounced this violence and made it appear as though it posed a threat to African workers.[23]

Creoles sometimes argued that they deserved more because they were more "civilized" than Indian immigrants—the yardsticks of "civilization" being the outward trappings of European clothing, language, and general deportment.[24] It is intriguing that the view of Indians expressed by Creoles was part of the planter stereotype of the Indian immigrant. Planters created the Indian stereotype called "Sammy"—taking the venerable "swamy," steeped in a centuries-old tradition of religious philosophy, and reducing him to a mishmash of self-contradictory attributes: violent, childlike in dependency, hardworking, thievish, admirably frugal, and miserly to the point of self-neglect.

Sometimes the propaganda of racist categorization boomeranged painfully on planters themselves. William Russell was extremely anti-Creole, proimmigration and (avowedly) pro-Indian until 1869 when indentured workers rioted at Plantation Leonora while it was under his charge. Russell barely escaped with his life on a fast horse, and this dampened his enthusiasm somewhat—Indians being thereafter described as "an un-appreciative race that had turned upon the English in India and mercilessly butchered men, women and children."[25]

Nineteenth-century propaganda on the Indian under indenture was in fact a repetition of the caricature of the African under slavery. The redoubtable Kwesi, having his origins in the fast-developing Akan polities of the eighteenth century, was in the West Indies a being called "Quashie": indomitably lazy but cutting tons of cane and producing when workhorses failed in the Demerara mud; docile but requiring the amputation of his limbs to discourage resistance and flight.[26] After slavery, Quashie grew more lazy. True, he cultivated more provisions than ever before and he hazarded his life in the toil of the bush, but he never really worked satisfactorily—on the sugar estates—and therefore civilization was threatened.

When Quashie reproached Sammy with having come to undercut established plantation labor, the answer was readily forthcoming: "Yes, you rascal neegah man: me come from India dis forty-six year: supposing me and me matty no come dis side fo' work, you rascal neegah been a starve one time."[27] This retort could have had no basis in the experience of the Indians.

They were in no position to know whether Africans were starving before indentured immigration got under way. But it was one of the self-evident truths of planter propaganda that the whole country would have been ruined had not the estates been saved by indentured immigration; and in that eventuality, the "lazy nigger" would certainly have starved. As for the crudities of the typical African estimation of Indians, it is not in the least surprising that these should have been heavily influenced by prevailing planter misconceptions, given that even Creole African self-images were conditioned by white racist ideas. Ideological confusion and psychological oppression were as crucial to the maintenance of the plantation system as were the administrative controls and the final sanction of the police force. In a heterogeneous society, the impact of racist perceptions was obviously magnified, and its principal consequence was to hold back the maturing of working class unity by offering an explanation of exploitation and oppression that seemed reasonably consistent with aspects of people's life experience.

In British Guiana, as in Trinidad, Martinique, and Jamaica, the principal objection made by African descendants to the waves of indentured Indians was that they were a threat to employment. In 1846-47, indentured immigrants were unwitting strikebreakers on the Guianese sugar estates; and in Creole eyes, this image was retained for a long while. From memories of his childhood in the early years of this century, one black Guianese worker recalled the then prevailing attitude to Indians: "I often heard men grumbling about the Indian coolies who were brought over to work on the plantations for the sake of cheap labor."[28] This kind of socialization indicates the deeply ingrained nature of the Creole characterization of Indians as persons who undermined the quest of Africans for employment at decent wages. Another closely related aspect of the image of Indians in Creole African eyes was that they were pampered planter proteges, who were given housing and medical facilities. In this connection, evidence drawn from a subsequent period is a useful indicator of retention of ingrained attitudes. Oral interviews of blacks born in the 1890s have demonstrated their deep-rooted feeling that planters discriminated in favor of Indians.[29] From this standpoint, it was but a short step to direct racial animosity.

Racial contradictions notwithstanding, the predominance of Indians on the estates was a fact of life by the late nineteenth century. It was also clearly irreversible, since time-expired Indians were in the majority and repatriation was not very vigorous. Certain racial adjustments took place on the sugar estates in terms of the relative specializations of Africans and Indians. It was off the plantations that further tensions arose around the issue of employment. Creoles regarded the village as their preserve, given that opportunities for employment arose in and near the village on the roads, sea defenses, and so on, and they were very resentful when Indian labor entered these spheres. A number of small incidents attested to this fact. In January 1883, Cuffy

Bristol found himself before the magistrate at Mahaica. Bristol and other Africans at Belfield refused to work on the sea dam for less than forty-eight cents per day. They were threatened that Indians would be brought in, and an altercation ensued with the foreman on the site. Cuffy Bristol told the magistrate that black people were the village proprietors and must do village work in preference to Indians.[30] In like vein, the Combined Court was questioned in May 1886 as to why indentured immigrants were being employed to dig trenches for the East Coast Water Scheme when Creole laborers were being refused work.[31] The availability or nonavailability of land for peasant farming was another major issue that proved racially divisive. The white-dominated plantation society was unrelenting in its vindictiveness against Creole small farmers. Without displaying any greater love for time-expired Indian peasants, the system nevertheless found it advisable to accommodate some Indian demands for land. This was done at the expense of Creole Africans—sometimes quite literally by replacing one group by the other. Parate execution sales facilitated the concentration of rural property in fewer hands. Simultaneously, it sparked off a transfer from Creole Africans as a group into the hands of Indians, Portuguese, and Chinese. This process was particularly noticeable on the Corentyne—affecting the villages numbered 57, 58, 64, 67, 69, 70, and 71 in the 1880s and transforming Rose Hall from a predominantly African into a predominantly Indian village by the early years of this century.[32] When they owned the land, African peasants sold fresh provisions to Indian sugar workers of the Corentyne district; but as the land changed hands, Indians entered into effective competition as food growers and hucksters—virtually reversing the roles of buyer and seller.[33] Reports of changes in land ownership also come from the East Bank Demerara in the 1890s. After land was taken for nonpayment of rates in Craig Village, it was usually repurchased by Indians.[34] Some of these lands were lost to Creoles after many years of frustrating experiences with respect to roads and drainage. They expressed the fear that their village would be taken over by Indians and they harbored "grudge feelings" on this account.

When lands were sold for nonpayment of rates and taxes, the colonial government simply sold to those who could afford it out of trading profits or from accumulated savings. Indentured and unindentured immigrants had to practice considerable self-denial in order to save. From an Indian perspective, all land purchases were legitimate and helped in a small way to meet a great need. Politically, the planter class succeeded in interposing another set of landowners between itself and its traditional villagized African antagonists of the post-Emancipation era. Planters also diffused the social pressure for a more egalitarian distribution of social funds—at least for a short while before the villagized Indians joined the chorus for greater governmental attention to the basic drainage, irrigation, and sea defense services. Indians who had spent at least ten of the best years of their working lives laboring for the sugar capitalists were demanding a permanent stake in the society as a matter of right. In the narrow coastal economy, their rights clashed with those of Creole Africans.

After Emancipation, Africans in Guiana were in effect describing themselves as "natives" and they claimed rights to the land deriving from priority of settlement and their long history of exploitation. Creole Africans spoke of Indians as immigrants making a sojourn in this country, even at the end of the nineteenth century when that sojourn in some instances had already been transformed into permanent residence and had given rise to a generation of Creole Indians. When African rights to the land were overlooked and preferance seemingly given to Indians, this automatically increased racial tension. The estates were expanding to take in the third and extra depths of pegasse backlands which had previously been used for plantains and provisions (as in the Canals Polder), while they were freeing exhausted front lands from cane and renting to rice farmers. Translated into racial categories, this meant displacing African small farmers with Indian small farmers.

The struggle against plantation landlordism became incredibly convoluted, and different sectors of the laboring population turned on each other in the quest for the limited acreages of drained polder released by the planter class. This was amply illustrated by the projects for settling times-expired Indian immigrants in Guiana in lieu of their repatriation passages. These projects involved Indians bartering their legal right of return for a small parcel of land. Many within the Indian community saw this as giving up their birthright, and they either resisted it or at least insisted on a land grant of some significance.[35] Of course, planters were committed to the scheme so as to fob off pieces of land costing less than they would have paid for repatriating the individuals concerned.

The first government attempt at settling Indian immigrants was in 1871 at Nooten Zuil, an estate which was no longer under sugar cultivation and which by then was leased to Africans. The project failed because Indian small farmers refused to accept the proposed allocation of a mere 1½ acres for provision grounds and 1 acre as a house lot.[36] But it is significant that when Indian settlement at Nooten Zuil was proposed, the interests of Africans leasing the land were ignored. The same pattern was repeated with regard to the Helena settlement of 1899. The three northern sections of the seven into which Plantation Helena was divided were partitioned among immigrants who had originally been indentured on the lower part of the East Coast. They were therefore strangers, and for quite some time they did not take up their allotments. Instead, they leased them to the same Africans who had been renting the land before. Creole Africans had been given no option to become settlers after Helena failed as a sugar estate and became government property. They valued the land highly, because it was sandy and had better natural drainage than the generality of coastal land.[37] Whatever the

stated purposes of the legislature in sanctioning such arrangements, the objective consequences must have included a legacy of racial bitterness.

The Indian settlement scheme that was started at Huis t'Dieren on the
Essequibo coast in 1881 was designed to counter the rush for repatriation
that was then worrying the planters. The manner in which Huis t'Dieren was
started engendered sharp racial conflict in the locality.[38] Plantation Huis
t'Dieren came to an end more abruptly than most. Its boiler exploded with
fatal results in 1879. It was decided to abandon the estate, and the adminis-
trator-general stepped in. The African presence on the estate is attested to
by the fact that at the time of the explosion the female megass loaders were
blacks, a job category that elsewhere was already associated with Indians.[39]
When the Government started distributing the land to time-expired Indian
immigrants in 1881, there were eighteen Creole blacks with leases on the
land, and there were still fifteen African-born laborers in the logies.* Chief
Interpreter Veeraswamy, who was appointed overseer of the settlement, advised the government that Indians did not want to live in close proximity to
blacks and that the latter had to be ejected from the estate. This could not be
put into practice without the use of force. The blacks tried to prevent the
cleaning of the trenches. Ameerally, the driver in charge of the operations,
was also a rural constable. He attested one man and in turn was set upon
and beaten.[40]

The Huis t'Dieren situation was hardly conducive to unity between the
peasantry of the two ethnic groups, and planters used it to their advantage.
William Russell—after his Leonora horse-riding experience—urged that a few
black people should be allowed to remain at Huis t'Dieren, as they would in
all probability prove a check to the coolies in cases of disturbance or uprisings.[41]

African-Indian conflicts were recorded in a random fashion, mainly in
the form of newspaper reports of the incidents. The clashes were brief and
usually without fatalities. At Leguan during the early 1880s, there was strife
between the African villagers of Reserve and Indians of Ridge, the government having decided to drain Ridge and make it available to Indians.[42] There
was no reports of violence around this Leguan dispute, although the quarrel
probably simmered on for some time. It was simmering resentment that was
occasionally brought to a point of violence by some relatively insignificant
action. In February 1881, a row involving a Creole African youth began at
the Plantation Albion paytable. He was sent to the Fyrish police station, accompanied by an Indian rural constable and three other Indians. Meanwhile,
his father ran to Fyrish and rang the chapel bell, which called out both
Fyrish and Gibraltar villages. A Creole gang then attacked the party on the
way to the police station, but failed to prevent the surrender of the arrested
boy. Management at Albion claimed that overseers had to stop the Indians

---

*I.e., they were introduced as part of post-Emancipation immigration.

leaving the estate to pursue a vendetta when they heard of the Fyrish-Gibraltar attack.[43] Be that as it may, the incident petered out. In March 1890, the roles were reversed: it was because an African rural constable had arrested an Indian at the Providence road market that three days of racial tension were experienced in this part of East Berbice.[44] At other times, the details were lost in the reporting. One is simply told that on 18 July 1881 there was a serious affray between Indians of Plantation Goldstone Hall and the villagers of Good Banana Land.[45]

Piddling as they undoubtedly were, the above incidents are not to be dismissed without careful scrutiny. There is a conceptual problem attached to their evaluation. Were they primarily racial clashes or can they be explained as contradictions among the people springing from the inability of the colonial capitalist economy to satisfy the demands of the majority of the producers? When outsiders are introduced into any situation to modify the terms of labor to the disadvantage of local labor, there are clashes between the locals and the strangers—including "strangers" from a few miles away. While Africans were having their conflicts with Indians in Guiana, one learns that (in England) Ipsden men were attacking harvesters brought in from Woodstock, and Hardmead farmhands were assaulting replacements brought in from Chicheley.[46] One is not encouraged to think that these were racial clashes or even regional clashes. In Guiana, there is a risk of the purely extrinsic aspect of the phenomenon taking procedence in its interpretation.

It was possible for labor disputes or land disputes to take place between two sets of Creole Africans. There was always an element of dissension within villages and between villages.[47] The *Echo* of 29 October 1890 reported that laborers at Hopetown, Golden Grove, and No. 28 villages had obtained work at Blairmont estate and had rejected the proposal of their fellow Creole villagers at No. 5 that they should jointly hold out for an increase in rates of pay. On Saturday, 25 October, residents of No. 5 waylaid and beat the "offenders" from the villages in question. As would be expected, each racial group had its own internal divisions. Indians did not constitute a homogeneous group. They too faced problems deriving from religious, linguistic, cultural, and social differences brought from India. Any division within the working classs could be turned against their own interests. Some planters were conscious of the range of identities masked by the term "Indian immigrant," and they deliberately mixed their indentured servants to prevent unity of purpose.[48] Immigration Agent-General Crosby was in 1881 urging the importation of Madras (Tamil-speaking) Indians. He presented the difference between Madrasis and other Indians as one of "race," and he further contended that the "natural" antipathy of the races concerned would stand in the way of "combination." The *Colonist* newspaper published and endorsed the above view, adding that "the natural antagonism between a Madras and a Calcutta coolie is almost as intense as between a Moslem and a Chris-

tian."[49] These views underscore the point that contradictions between laborers did not always have a racial dimension, in the commonly accepted
sense of the term "racial." By the same reasoning, conflicts between different
race groups were not necessarily "racial"—although disputes were always
potentially more explosive when racial identification was involved. (See tables
A20-22 for data on the changing ethnic composition of the population.)

The conditions of economic distress that characterized the period might
have helped establish a small base of shared consciousness of common deprivation. But the greater likelihood is that the unfavorable economic environment exacerbated racial ill will—around issues such as unemployment, taxation for immigration purposes, land acquisition, and so on. Appearing before
the Poor Law Enquiry Commission of 1881, Creole blacks expressed sentiments primarily against the Portuguese rather than Indians, in so far as economic competition was concerned (see above, chap. 4). During the 1880s,
Creoles enthusiastically looked to the hinterland as a sphere of employment,
and Indians were absent from this sphere. But by the mid-1890s, the plantation economy was plunged into deeper crisis than ever before, and the hinterland sectors were not vibrant enough to save the situation or redress the
balance. Creole blacks therefore returned to the expression of animosity
against "outsiders."

The comptroller of customs included in his report for 1900-1901 a review
of the value of imports for the previous twenty years. The quinquennial
averages showed a substantial decline for the period, from $9,192,312 in
1881-85, $7,983,768 in 1886-90; $8,180,256 in 1891-95; and $6,439,992
in 1896-1900. He argued that even if the goods had become cheaper, the
overall value should not have dropped when the population had increased
by 35,000; and he concluded his anlysis by affirming that the reduced consumption had to be attributed to reduced wages and earnings—amounting in
some instances to a 50 percent contraction in the purchasing power of the
mass of the people.[50] The conclusion that derives from the impersonal statistics of the Blue Books was independently part of popular consciousness
through hardship. One Creole writer, J. Van Sertima, dramatically expressed
this by imagining a working-class woman before the royal commission:

> Distress is no' de wu'd, Sah. Times is too ha'd now. Dis time en' like befo'
> time, 'tall 'tall. When a was a young gal growin' up. you ax a young man
> fo' someting, he gie you tree or four shillin' and tink nutt'n 'bout it.
> Now if he gie you a sixpence, he want to ax you a question. Times is too
> brown. Look at de stores, dem en' half as much ʼas dey yewst to be. Sah,
> po' pe'ple, dey seein' hell pon dis ert.[51]

Interestingly enough, Van Sertima's working class character pointedly drew
attention to the class nature of the society when she observed that, in spite
of the prevailing distress, the propertied class still passed by in their presti-

gious carriages, unconcerned with making any sacrifices. This Creole character was also a mouthpiece for disparaging or hostile remarks against Indians and all other "outsiders."

Barbadians were still entering the country in the late 1880s and 1890s on short contracts or as free immigrants. Their reception by Creoles indirectly provides an insight into the relations between Creole Africans and Indians. Van Sertima quoted prevailing anti-Bajan sentiments: "Creole say he will do de wuk fo' two shillin', Bajan step up say he do if fo' four bitts an' a ha'f."*[52] Many years previously, Rev. H. V. Bronkhurst had affirmed that Creole blacks displayed the same animus towards all labor competitors, irrespective of whether they were Hindus, "Bajans," or "islanders" from elsewhere in the West Indies.[53] Nevertheless, the prejudice against Barbadians virtually disappeared over a period of time. The small numbers of permanent Barbadian settlers were comfortably incorporated into Afro-Guyanese society. Few Barbadians entered between 1886 and 1917. Meanwhile, the Indian population was being augmented substantially from outside—to the point where it became the largest ethnic sector, and Creole ire therefore concentrated on Indians as the ones who were supposedly "taking the bread out of their mouths."[54] Barbadians were of course Creole Africans in their own right, which helps to explain their ready integration after the initial hostility based on labor competition. Barbadians dispersed into the same kinds of activities as local Creoles. They preferred urban and village life, and they joined Creole blacks in the goldfields.

Living together and sharing the same culture, Creole Africans of Barbados were able to develop solidarity with their Guianese counterparts in industrial and social struggles. When Barbadians completed contracts and settled in Guiana, they joined the class struggle on terms similar to local residents. Planter awareness of this fact was always a disincentive to long-term Barbadian immigration.[55] Barbadians, as laborers and artisans, introduced new Lodges and Benefit Societies and contributed to the articulation of working-class and middle-class views in the popular press.[56] In all of these spheres, the coming together of Indians and Africans was delayed until a date more recent than the period under discussion.

Meanwhile planters took advantage of the possibilities of manipulating existing racial separation or tension between Africans and Indians. The notion that races should help police each other was at the center of the racially divisive policy of the colonial state. The conquest of the Amerindians was followed by the employment of these native Guianese to track and recover runaway slaves. Later, they pursued escaped prisoners in return for a bounty. Africans and Indians were not actually paid a bounty to keep each other in check, but they were both encouraged to negate each other's efforts to

*One bitt = 8 cents.

challenge the socioeconomic system. Early in the history of indentureship, planters recognized the practical value of having a working population segmented racially; and they never lost sight of the opportunity of playing off the two principal races—by using one to put down any overt resistance by the other.[57] J. E. Tinne forthrightly summed up this experience when he appeared before the West Indian Royal Commission. "The two peoples do not intermix. That is, of course, one of our great safeties in the colony when there has been any rioting. If the negroes were troublesome every coolie on the estate would stand by one. If the coolies attacked me, I could with confidence trust my negro friends for keeping me from injury."[58]

Although planters were willing to exploit racial differences, none of the African-Indian clashes of the nineteenth century came anywhere close to large-scale communal violence. This is a matter of note, when one considers that on several occasions communal violence embroiled African Creoles and Portuguese immigrants. Commutation of the death sentence on a convicted Portuguese was held to be proof that he had *bought* his life—something which neither Africans nor Indians could accomplish.[59] Their common deprivation was a bond; and at the same time these two races had not developed any relations of mutual exploitation.

The weight of present scholarship inclines toward portraying Guyana as a society in which racial division and conflict have been in the ascendancy over consensus and class action. Whether this is true or not, the question also arises as to whether the society is best elucidated by those paradigms based on the perception of cultural pluralism. The evaluation of pluralist theory with respect to its ideological underpinnings and general applicability lies outside the scope of this work. Instead, one would like to review briefly the notion of Guyanese *history* as one that is ridden with racial conflict. As indicated earlier, my contention is that the case for the dominant role of racial division in the historical sphere has been overstated, and that scholarship on the subject has accepted without due scrutiny the proposition that Indians and Africans existed in mutually exclusive cultural compartments. The problems of interpretation lie not only in the marshaling of the evidence but, more fundamentally, in the historical methodology that is applied. In the present context, the complex relations between past and present have been treated in a deterministic fashion.

The occurrence of violent racial conflict in Guiana on the eve of independence has been used as a springboard for historical enquiry. This is legitimate if it is nothing but a recognition of an important moment in history, requiring to have its antecedents traced. It ·is indefensible when the assumption is made that all previous development was nothing but the unfolding of the theme of racial conflict. With the skimpiest evidential base, one Guyanese scholar (writing in 1970) affirms that "events [moved] inexorably towards culture conflict as more and more immigrants poured into the country."[60]

In this instance, contemporary conflict serves both as starting point and as goal, so that the author reconstructs much of the substantive history under the rubric, "The Precursors of Conflict." Such an approach is guaranteed to discover precursors of conflict and *nothing but* precursors of conflict. When the determinism is not as obvious as in the foregoing example, there is still a tendentious element introduced into discussion because of a particular assessment of the more recent racial competition. For instance, a recent dissertation on indentureship found no significant evidence of racial violence, but the author strained after the following conclusion: "That no violence broke out between the two groups was due more to the fact that each group tended to go its own way, than to any feeling of cordiality between them."[61] Why should cordiality become the antithesis of "violence"? A more straightforward conclusion (supportable by the evidence) would simply by that antipathy and racial separation were part of the conjuncture in the late nineteenth century, but did not give rise to violence under the conditions of the period.

The racial dimension to contradictions among the people established itself in the nineteenth century because of a variety of factors: notably, the sustained volume of state-aided Indian immigration, the residential separation of the two main racial groups, the mutual unintelligibility of some aspects of nonmaterial culture, the slow rate of diversification of the colonial economy, and the conscious manipulation of the society by those who had state power. Subsequently, there arose a further set of variables that were political in nature and that profoundly affected race relations. Until the elections of 1906, the quest for political representation was restricted to Afro-Guyanese and Portuguese. Political rivalry between Africans and Indians led to the politicization of ethno-cultural differences. Ultimately, communal violence came about in a context of both local and international class struggle. The specificity of the early 1960s can scarcely be used to characterize the entire history of Guyana. On the contrary, one sides with the judgment of a Guyanese labor spokesman. H.J.M. Hubbard, who wrote (in 1969): "It is by any standards a remarkable fact that in a competitive semi-feudal society such as British Guiana with restricted social and economic opportunities and less jobs than potential workers, very few serious physical inter-racial conflicts arose between the ethnic groups constituting the population."[62]

CHAPTER 8

The 1905 Riots

> were some who ran one way.
> were some who ran another way.
> were some who did not run at all.
> were some who will not run again.
> And I was with them all,
> when the sun and streets exploded,
> and a city of clerks
> turned a city of men!
>
> *Martin Carter*

The Event and Its Causes

Riots and disturbances punctuate the history of the British West Indies. Most were minor phenomena with little significance beyond the small circle of lives touched by a brief explosion of social violence.[1] But there were times when the disaffection was more wide-ranging and the scale of violence larger; and when the level of consciousness and organization of the participants carried these elements forward into a moment of challenge to colonial authority. In different degrees, these characteristics were present in the riots of November-December 1905 in the county of Demerara.

The 1905 riots are often referred to as the "Ruimveldt Riots," because several workers from Plantation Ruimveldt were among the first to lose their lives in the violence. But other sugar estates on the East and West Banks of the Demerara were significantly involved, while Georgetown remained—throughout—the hub of activity. Being close to the city, Plantation Ruimveldt was understandably first to respond to the agitation in Georgetown. Thereafter, social unrest became evident on other East Bank estates, and then on the estates of the left or West Bank which were in constant contact with Georgetown and with East Bank plantations like Ruimveldt and Diamond. In most instances, the estate strikes started and remained within the precincts of the factories. Sugar boilers, porters, stokers, and other building hands were the workers involved. When the unrest spread, it moved logically to Creole cane-cutters who were friends, relatives and neighbors of the factory hands in the villages. But it was the Georgetown stevedores who provided the spark of rebellion when they decided to take a stand on the question of the wage rate, which had stagnated for nearly three decades.

Each shipping firm in the city of Georgetown retained a nucleus of permanent stevedores, but most of their needs were met by the hiring of casual "outside" laborers who received two guilders, or 64 cents, on completion of a day's work of ten and one-half hours. One of the major complaints of these laborers was that they were paid pro rata on the basis of the daily wage when work ran out before the day was finished. Stevedores contended that they were willing to work the full day of ten and one-half hours and should receive a full day's wage when available tasks were completed. Alternatively, if they were to be paid for part of a day, the hourly remuneration should be far higher than the prevailing six cents per hour. A second sore point among the waterfront workers was that "boys" earned 48 cents per day (16 cents less than grown men), but adults were often categorized as "boys." In the final analysis, workers were convinced that wages had remained at a low level for far too long. On Sunday, 26 November, the New Colonial Company offered a special rate of 16 cents an hour to have laborers complete the loading of a steamer. This was a practical demonstration of the value of their labor, and it precipitated strike action to back demands that wages be raised to that level.

The dramatic moments of the 1905 riots were on 30 November and 1 December. However, a diary of the entire event would span the period from 28 November to 6 December. It was on Tuesday, 28 November, that a strike was called on the wharf of Sandbach, the "boys" refusing to take less than sixteen cents an hour. There was no disorder. Workers who came off the job got together in groups and discussed the matter quietly. On the following day, Wednesday, 29 November, the number of strikers increased considerably. All of the shipping firms were affected, and the strikers were vociferous and demonstrative. From early in the day, a large group of about three hundred young stevedores marched under a banner that read, "16 cents an hour or no work."[2] They moved from place to place and persuaded others to withdraw their labor all along the waterfront. Other strikers congregated in groups of fifty to sixty at various points in the business district. Meanwhile, porters employed by Ruimveldt estate (East Bank Demerara) began a strike at midday. The scene was set for an alliance between urban workers and sugar estate workers—an alliance which was a distinguishing feature of the 1905 riots.

On Thursday, 30 November, masses of people took to the streets in Georgetown. Those who were on strike set out to persuade others of their fellow workers to likewise cease labor. Sometimes force was required. That

Thursday morning, domestics were dragged out of private houses, while workers at the Railway Goods Wharf were threatened and pushed off the job site. By afternoon, crowds roamed the business center, and some looting took place at pawnbrokers' and jewelers'. Most businessmen hastened to close their premises, but the scale of intimidation and larceny was very restricted, and, interestingly enough, there were no cases of arson.

The police response, when it came, was not to criminal acts but to what they interpreted as social rebellion. The inspector of police claimed that a large crowd of some fifteen hundred persons in front of Bookers' Wharf had stated an intention to prevent anyone working. There was no indication that they were bent on looting or damaging property. The strike was joined that evening by bakers who left their jobs because of a pay dispute and staged a march down Carmichael Street. The colonial state had but one answer to this escalation of industrial action: to declare parts of the city "proclaimed areas" and read the Riot Act.[3] The Riot Act was read around 6:00 P.M. that Thursday at four different points of the city of Georgetown. The crowds dispersed, but instead of going home, people gathered that night in animated groups in Bourda, Alberttown, Wortmanville, and Albouystown.

"Fore-day morning" on 1 December found the Ruimveldt factory grinding. It began to consume coals, cane, and human labor from 4:00 A.M. However, work came to a stop by 5:00 A.M, and after "dayclean," cane-cutters joined the factory hands to confront the manager, who not only rejected their wage demands, but sent for the police, alleging that he was assaulted and that the workers were rioting. At 7:55 A.M., the police and a detachment of artillery were in position at the Ruimveldt bridge, over which the East Bank workers were about to cross to link up with Georgetown and La Penitence workers who were assembled on the other side. The Riot Act was read, and the police opened fire when the crowd failed to disperse. Four workers were seriously injured. Their bleeding bodies were taken first to Government House and then to the Colonial (Public) Hospital. Word of the Ruimveldt shooting flashed through the city of Georgetown, which was already in a state of tension. According to one report, "three-fourths of the population of Georgetown seemed to have gone stark staring mad."[4] In spite of the Riot Act, thousands converged on the streets in the western part of the city from the Parade Ground to the Public Buildings. A hostile crowd invaded the Public Buildings, forcing His Excellency the governor to take refuge behind locked doors in the Court of Policy hall. They rushed up and down the galleries and stairs of the Public Buildings looking for the inspector-general of police, who was rumored to have threatened to shoot down more people. One man was killed by police fire in the vicinity of the Public Buildings. As the police regained control of the western section of the city, the crowds were forced east of Camp Street, where they vented their anger on individual members of the ruling class who crossed their paths. The dead and the dying in the Colonial Hospital attracted many rioters to that part of the city. Along the length of Thomas Street, the police patrols were showered with stones and other missiles. They responded with rifle fire; and before the day was done, the toll rose to seven dead and seventeen critically wounded.

Predictably, the newspapers labeled Friday, 1 December 1905, "Black Friday." On the next morning, the population of Georgetown was extremely bitter but more cautious, moving in groups of no more than a dozen or so. Strikers repeated the exercise of invading the Railway Goods Wharf to dissuade laborers there from working. They also continued attacks on persons closely identified with the system of exploitation. The women in particular were said to have resorted to stone throwing, and a band of women attacked the police station in Hadfield Street that Saturday at midday, scattering the prepared meal which was being carried in. But several were arrested; and increased police and vigilante activity caused street manifestations to disintegrate into knots of a mere four or five persons. It was outside of Georgetown that the disturbances grew in scope and intensity after the shootings on "Black Friday." The sugar estate areas of the East Bank Demerara were all affected. In the wake of the Ruimveldt shootings, the deputy manager of Houston had been stoned, while the carts of Plantations Farm and Diamond were robbed of their groceries. The porters of Diamond demanded on Saturday, 2 December, an increase from thirty-six cents per day to forty-eight cents per day, while sugar curers asked for fifty-six cents instead of the forty cents per day that they were then receiving. A mixed force of twenty-seven police and special constables was sent to deal with these wage demands at Plantation Diamond.

Sunday was of course a day of rest for most workers. This did not apply to the tram conductors who chose Sunday, 3 December, to strike for more pay. A tram conductor who had been employed for less than a year earned five cents an hour, while those with one year's service or more received six cents an hour. The following Friday morning, estate workers again had an opportunity to demonstrate their grievances and their militancy. The porters and girls at Peter's Hall struck for higher wages, which meant that every estate on the East Bank Demerara had been affected by the industrial unrest. At the same time, factory workers on the West Bank Demerara decided to seize the chance to press their wage claims. The first group of workers to make this decision visited Plantation Nismes and called out the workers. Schoonord, Wales, and Versailles followed in quick succession. For the first time in decades, managers were forced to sit down by their own employees. At Schoonord and Versailles, the managers were prepared to negotiate, but the colonial state was not. The forces of repression had been immeasurably strengthened by the arrival of two Admiralty vessels. H.M.S. *Diamond* was a fast third-class cruiser of 3,000 tons, with a crew of 300. It had been commissioned one year earlier, and it was dispatched from Barbados. The

British also sent H.M.S. *Sappho*, an older second-class cruiser of 3,400 tons, which arrived from Trinidad with its crew of 272 men plus a contingent from another cruiser then in Port of Spain. The bluejackets from the *Diamond* and the *Sappho* were used to arrest the so-called ringleaders of the strikes on the West Bank Demerara.

If the strikes were to grow to epidemic proportions as the governor feared, then they would next have affected the east and west coasts of Demerara. The governor was advised by police security that bands of men came from as far as Plantation Hope on the west coast and the island of Wakenaam on the east, trying to stir up strikes and rioting among the Afro-Guyanese laboring population. If this was true, then nothing came of their agitation.[5]

An alarm was soon raised by a disturbance in the hinterland among gold miners at Peter's mine in the Puruni river district. About 225 laborers employed by this American-owned quartz mine struck work on 12 December. Payment for laborers working underground then ranged between sixty-four cents and $1.20 per day, and the men were proposing $1.50 a day. When this was rejected, the men demanded to be paid off, and the company accepted this with respect to 67 of them. The official reaction at Bartica and in Georgetown was that the miners' dispute was an indication of "strike contagion." However, once more selective arrests and victimization put an end to all manifestations.

By Tuesday, 5 December, the streets of Georgetown were back to normal, but the wharves continued to be at practically a standstill, particularly with regard to the employment of "outside" labor. The withholding of labor persisted on a few estates. Nevertheless, the end was in sight; and on Wednesday the sixth, the governor reported that all was normal in Georgetown and in the rural areas, with the exception of the West Bank factories where a few stokers had not yet returned to their jobs.

The collapse of the waterfront strike in Georgetown was dictated by sheer want, since the workers had no means of surviving without employment. Obviously, there were no strike relief funds; and in place of such a mechanism, a group of workers found themselves scrambling for a few coins and cigarettes thrown down by the mayor. It seems as though he intended to be charitable, but the result was thoroughly degrading. In any event, a handout like the mayor's was far from adequate. When workers surrendered to necessity and broke the strike, they did so with a sullenness born of the conviction that their demands were just, and that justice for workers was unobtainable.

The events of 1905 must be placed in the context of the sustained and unrelenting pressure brought to bear on the living standards of the working people ever since the depression of 1884, and more so since the acute depression of 1894-96. In the late 1880s, wages recovered briefly from their low rate in the period 1886-87. There had been no major upheaval in the city of Georgetown since 1889. Nevertheless, it should be recalled that in 1895 the colonial authorities were particularly concerned that urban workers and unemployed might resort to violence. Ten years later, wages were lower and unemployment was greater than ever. The recommendations of the Royal Commission of 1896-97 had had no impact on people's lives, and when the populace took to the streets in November-December 1905, it was in a desperate effort to deal with the endemic ills of low wages and high unemployment.

Most of the year 1905 passed by without social protest of an unusual kind. There were several small work stoppages and strikes occurring mainly on the sugar estates; but it does not appear that the authorities considered that the situation was building to a climax or that there was the possibility that "things were ·getting out of hand." What should be borne in mind was that the distress of the working people was at the time being publicly aired. Throughout the month of November 1905, a Mortality Commission was sitting in Georgetown and taking public evidence. Witnesses referred to a range of social and environmental factors which were responsible for high mortality, and especially for high infant mortality, in the countryside and in Georgetown. Sanitation and sewage disposal in Georgetown were frighteningly poor. The pit latrines or cesspits were cleared from time to time by a piece of equipment referred to as an "odorless excavator," a name which proved to be a masterly euphemism. Quite apart from the asphyxiating smell, there was a direct threat to health because the contents of the latrines floated in the flooded yards in the rainy seasons. It was the poorer classes who had to wallow in that filth and to crowd into the many-roomed tenement houses in which tuberculosis was on the increase. They could do no better. Lengthy correspondence in the *Chronicle* back in February 1902 had clearly indicated that overcrowding of families into single rooms was inevitable, given that even a single room consumed in rent at least 25 percent of the three or four dollars which a poor man might earn in a week. The mortality commissioners eventually concluded as follows: "We are of the opinion that the excessive mortality in the colony occurs chiefly among the poorer classes of the community . . . and the high rate among the poorer classes is in part due to the absence of adequate measures of sanitation; overcrowding in rooms, in ranges of tenement rooms and in tenement houses. . . . It is also due to poverty."[6]

The mortality commissioners were drawn from the ruling class. In a circular manner, they attributed the distress of the poor to poverty. The poverty was explained in large part as due to ignorance and laziness. In other words, poverty was the fault of the poor. Such social analysis was not unusual at the time; however, the enquiry did illustrate the hard facts of social existence for the large number of persons who were to participate in the riots of 1905.

Some of the authorities were certainly aware that deplorable conditions in many parts of Georgetown (whoever was at fault), were the breeding ground for potential violence. Henry Kirke, an experienced magistrate and sheriff of

Demerara, had commented on the subject a few years previously. "Let anyone walk through the yards which lead out of lower Regent Street, Lombard
Street and Leopold Street in Georgetown, and let him ask himself how he
could expect respectable law-abiding citizens to be raised therein."[7] Kirke
was concerned with narrow, antisocial violence, but the conditions that he
perceived and that were noted by the Mortality Commission were such as
would encourage much more sweeping violence.

When the rains fell, Georgetown residents waded among floating feces;
when casual laborers obtained two days' work per week, the entire earnings
could barely cover the rent and keep away the bailiff's cart; when mothers
gave birth, they stood a 30 percent chance of burying that child before the
first year was up, given an infant mortality rate of 298 per thousand. Besides, the Mortality Commission had been sitting for nearly one month
before the outbreak of the riots. The witnesses were not telling the poor
anything that the poor did not know, but they were placing before the
authorities common experiences that were otherwise hidden; and the poor
were reminded of the intolerable nature of that which they tolerated from
day to day. One witness referred to the houses of the poor as "dog-houses";
another expressed his amazement at the capacity of laborers to do hard
manual labor from 6:00 A.M. until noon, fortified merely by a cup of "sugar-
water" and a few biscuits.

Apart from sharing their living environment, many rioters had a special
nexus with the stevedores. The casual or "outside" laborer was poised uncer-
tainly between unemployment and employment. Every day, large numbers of
"outside" laborers would assemble near the wharf gates and try to catch the
eye of the wharfinger. The majority received work only for a few days a week
and were permanently underemployed. Young men out of work were recruits
for the "centipede" street gangs; they also spent a lot of time playing "Cheefa," a Chinese gambling game which was comparable to the "numbers" game
of U.S. cities. Up until 1905, the government offered no solution beyond
arresting "centipedes" and "Cheefa" gamblers. One correspondent in the
press indicated his awareness that the colonial authorities were not exercising
any social responsibility. He stated: "I have often wondered at the supineness
of the Government in permitting so many men to go on existing without any
visible means of livelihood."[8]

With hindsight, it is easy to see that the unemployment, poor wages,
atrocious living conditions, and the consequent riots of 1905 should all be
placed within the context of the protracted crisis since 1884. But, in addition, it is of overriding importance to note that Georgetown workers themselves made a conscious connection between their current misery and the
refusal of the system to provide amelioration over the previous three decades.

Among the stevedores, the demand for higher wages was accompanied by
a clear exposition that the shipping companies owed workers back pay—

meaning, as they themselves explained, that they had been underpaid for many years. The employers did not deny that wages had stood still. On the contrary, they used the stagnation of the wage rate as a justification for concluding that the remuneration was perfectly acceptable. The merchants put forward *as a defense* that "as far back as 30 years ago, when sugar was fetching a higher price, the same wages were paid as are paid now when sugar is fetching a lower price."[9] One of the most recalcitrant employers was the firm of J. H. de Jonge, auctioneers, importers, and sugar brokers. In 1897, a spokesman for this firm had admitted to the Royal Commission that urban wages were down by 15 percent while rents held at the same level. But de Jonge and most shipping employers failed to take account of the high cost of living and the decreased purchasing power of wages in 1905.

Planters likewise chose to emphasize that thirty years earlier they paid the same wage when sugar fetched a higher price. They completely ignored the fact that workers never shared in the profits realized through price rises or through negotiated markets in the U.S.A. and Canada, although that surplus realization was made possible by tariff concessions that raised the cost of living for the working class consumers in British Guiana. Indeed, the two years preceding the riots were years during which the cane sugar industry was emerging out of its slump. The international Brussels Agreement had at last limited European beet sugar subsidies, and the Guianese product was establishing itself in the Canadian market (see above, chap. 2). Yet there was resistance to sharing any of these profits with the workers. An equally telling illustration of planter recalcitrance is that in responding to wage demands from factory hands, planters made no mention of reduced production costs and enhanced labor productivity in the factories resulting from technological change and the ploughing back of earlier profits into factory renovation.

Planters seemed not to recognize that productivity and the cost of living were crucial variables which should have altered the rate of wages; and it was left to the workers to take up a stance that was much closer to modern concepts of industrial relations in the capitalist world itself. Stevedores, for example, correctly noted that changes in technology and work routines intensified the rate of exploitation of dock labor. At one time, they took four or five days to load a ship with sugar. By 1905, they were loading ships of the same capacity in one and a half to two days; and because they were paid by the day with no consideration given to output, they actually suffered de facto wage reductions. On the wharves and on the sugar estates, the working class vanguard demonstrated that it had achieved a sound grasp of the historical process of labor exploitation and that it knew the situation of colonial and oppressed races to be especially backward. One inspector of police assumed the role of mediator on behalf of business interests and sought to calm the crowd at the Parade Ground. He was rebuffed by a worker who stepped forward and got straight to the point. "If you please to kindly go back and say for we that when white man work for 30 years if they don't get their money raise? We work for 30 years for the same money and now we want a raise; we want more money. . . . Is that 30 years cheap work sweeten them white man, that make so they think it hard to pay a price now?"[10]

Reports on the 1905 riots indicate a level of worker self-awareness that could only have been a leap consequent upon a long period of slow development. The stevedores of 1905 represented the highest expression of worker consciousness derived from the struggle both on and off the plantations. The clash between themselves and their employers was one between the working class and the sugar capitalists in a different guise. Most of the outward-bound cargo which the stevedores loaded was sugar. Most of the shipping firms were closely associated with the major joint-stock sugar companies such as Booker Brothers, Sandbach Parker, and H. K. Davson. Dockworkers were at a sensitive point of articulation of the colonial import-export economy. The significance of this sensitive location for the rebelliousness of dockworkers is to be seen from their history throughout the colonial world. Through contacts with seamen and through the popular press, Guianese waterfront workers would also have been aware of the struggle of dockworkers in metropolitan countries. Back in 1890, when there was an "epidemic of strikes" in Georgetown, they were led by stevedores, and they followed on the heels of the great London dock strike of the previous year. This process of class education through glimpses of international experience must have continued in the years that came after. The stevedores and the clerks of the shipping firms were among the first to hear, read, and discuss news from the outside world. In 1905, they would have had a great deal to excite their imagination. The local newspapers carried not only the evidence before the Mortality Commission at home, but also lengthy accounts of the 1905 Revolution in Czarist Russia.

Ashton Chase's *History of Trade Unionism in Guyana* lays emphasis on the organizational weakness of the Guianese working class in 1905. He attributes this weakness to the semifeudal conditions prevailing in the sugar industry, to the lack of modern large-scale industry, and to the attendant underdevelopment of proletarian consciousness.[11] The untested assumption is that organization would not have lagged far behind subjective development; but the evidence suggests precisely this. What is beyond dispute is that Guianese workers in 1905 lacked any organization equal to the conduct of uncompromising struggle. The embryonic working class organizations of the late 1880s had not survived. The People's Association had called for the formation of a trade union, but this had not materialized. The result is that grievances burst to the fore spontaneously in November 1905, and there were no structures to plan or guide the worker movement either at the place of work or in the streets. At best, ad hoc committees of workers sought audience with employers and with the colonial authorities. Alternatively, middle-class spokesmen presented themselves as negotiators.

Neither in Georgetown nor in Ruimveldt nor in West Demerara was there any leadership with anything approaching a plan to advance the interests of the working class as a whole. On 28 November, stevedores at Sandbach Parker had acted on the spur of the moment and used their practical judgment in deciding to detain a steamer which needed to be loaded to catch the tide.* During the days that followed, spontaneity was all the more evident in working-class actions. There was certainly no plan to stage violent rebellion. The corollary to this was that state agencies were largely responsible for forcing the wage protests in the direction of mass violence. As observed on the sugar estates, the edgy authoritarian response to immigrant protests often precipitated tragedy. In like manner, the destruction of life, limb, and property in December 1905 came out of the operation of the coercive state apparatus.

Whenever they were presented with an opportunity, sugar and waterfront workers ably advanced their wage demands. They went first to their employers, but the colonial state acted with remarkable speed in interposing itself between capital and labor and in taking up the defense of the employers. Georgetown stevedores wanted to negotiate directly with the principal import-export firms such as Sandbach Parker, the La Penitence Company of Curtis Campbell, Thom & Cameron, Booker Brothers, T. Garnett, Wieting & Richter, and the New Colonial Company. However, the governor issued his proclamations on 30 November, which was only the second day of the effective waterfront strike. A few members of the Chamber of Commerce were prepared to compromise, but the hard-liners easily won out because the shelter of the state coercive apparatus made stubborn refusal a practical proposition. That the governor should come out in defense of "law and order" was not surprising. But it *was* somewhat surprising that he never hid behind the formula of the colonial power being the evenhanded dispenser of justice, but instead, openly declared that his function was primarily to defend the capitalist class. Speaking to crowds at the Public Buildings on the morning of Friday, 1 December, Governor Hodgson admonished that "if you break the law in connection with your grievance, as Governor of the colony and as the person who has to protect the lives and interests—more particularly the mercantile interests—of the colony, it is my duty to see that no one breaks the law."[12] Besides, the governor's proclamation on the previous day had set the stage for the Ruimveldt tragedy, which must be in large part attributed to the refusal of the police to allow an industrial dispute to remain precisely

---

*Because of a silt bar at the Demerara estuary, ships leaving the port of Georgetown had to await the moment when (twice daily) the tides were at their highest.

that. The crowd continually told Major de Rinzy that their purpose was peaceful and that they only wanted to speak to the manager to resolve the wage question. "We ent rowing," they said. "We only come for seek for price, and we cannot go. We ent come to you [de Rinzy]; we come to the manager."[13] Major de Rinzy himself testified that the cane-cutters said, "We have not come to fight, we have come for higher wages." In spite of this, Major de Rinzy appointed himself a planting attorney, one of his orders being that the artillerymen should go into the logies and bring the laborers out to work.

After Ruimveldt, official policy deliberately excluded the possibility of any wage negotiations. Governor Hodgson's strategy was to meet each labor claim with the maximum show of force, to arrest all who could be identified as ringleaders, and to pressure the planters to take the line of a blanket denial of wage increases. The governor distinguished himself by taking command over the planter representatives in the colony. He decided what was good for capital and the colonial state in the face of popular challenge, and he whipped into compliance those managers and planting attorneys who seemed weak or vacillating. This pattern emerged clearly on the West Bank Demerara on the fourth and fifth of December. The governor personally visited Nismes, Wales, Schoonord, and Versailles—accompanied by troops of H.M.S. *Diamond* and H.M.S. *Sappho*. Some managers were prepared to make concessions. At Schoonord and Versailles, the managers had agreed to new wage rates in their deliberations with workers. But Hodgson forced them to renege on such promises. He claimed that to concede wage increases would be to encourage the spread of wage demands; he critized the manager of Versailles for panicking; and he implied that the manager of Schoonord was concerned only with getting his ripe canes cut. The governor told them plainly that they should follow his advice or he would withdraw the armed forces from their estates and leave them to the mercy of the "rioters." Endorsed in the final analysis by the entire planter class, Hodgson used coercive instruments against the workers in the belief that this was the only way to stop wage claims from spreading to estates in other parts of the country, and to discourage the vast majority of field workers from taking militant steps. The introduction of troops was also intended to be intimidatory. One Guianese in the streets suggested to a British soldier that there was no need for the latter's presence, informing him tersely and eloquently: "The people are doing nothing. It is the Government who are rioting and shooting down the people."[14]

Participation—Class and Sex Composition

What occurred in Guiana in 1905 came about mainly because large masses of people recognized the impossibility of continuing to exist as they had done up to that point and felt totally frustrated by the unavailability of channels to redress social grievances. The economic crisis spanned several social strata, and it is therefore not surprising that the riots themselves involved a large cross section of the people. Contradictions first came to the fore within the ranks of workers who sold their labor on a daily basis. Men and women of the working class voiced wage demands which gave rise to strikes and popular demonstrations; members of the middle class expressed sympathy; and much of the cutting edge of physical confrontation was provided by social elements on the fringe of the working class: namely, their unemployed compatriots and the lumpen proletariat. The crowds in the streets comprised dockworkers, bakers, artisans, clerks, housewives, hucksters, and the lumpen, who were generally referred to as "centipedes." The street demonstrators even included some respectable middle-class citizens, who were promptly denounced by the established press as "men occupying positions which should have raised them above the level to which they sank in guiding the more ignorant classes."[15]

The evidence on crowd composition does not lend itself to systematic or comprehensive reconstruction. It seems that outside of the ranks of manual laborers, several teachers and clerks went into action. These occupational groups fall into the gray area between the working class and the middle class, and probably accounted themselves the latter. The occupational group of "clerks" was itself very elastic. It seems to have been an alternative designation for those who had a modicum of primary schooling, judging from remarks by Bronkhurst (1883) and Rodway (1912). Expressing planter prejudice, Rodway wrote that "the general effect of education is a desire to become clerks, office-boys and shopmen. Field work is beneath the notice of the rising generation of black and coloured; and even the creole East Indian follows suit. The consequence is that the mercantile class is overstocked and Georgetown is pestered with a lot of idlers who have no visible means of subsistence."[16] Clerks and would-be clerks were likely to have been prominent on the streets in December 1905. Most of those in serious financial straits would have been counter clerks and salesmen in the Water Street stores, along with the most junior of the clerks in government service. The Civil List designated clerks from first class to sixth class. Creoles were not encouraged to aspire to the positions of first class clerks at a salary of $1,440 + $96 to $1,920 per annum. But even the fifth class clerk could reach a ceiling of $480 per annum, which was much more than most store clerks earned.[17]

Those members of the middle class who had substantial incomes or property distinguished themselves during the 1905 riots more for what they did not do than what they did. They did not support the colonial government. They did not rush to volunteer as special forces to restore law and order, as might have been expected of "respectable citizens." The vigilante citizens' force that patrolled the streets was composed of the handful of white residents mounted on horseback. Led by Stipendiary Magistrate William Payne, these volunteers were referred to as Payne's Cavalry. They were socially and ethnically distinct from the black and brown middle class.

The very use of vigilante groups was necessitated by the defection of the militia, a development with clear class implications. When the moment of decision came, the militia abdicated from its sworn duty to support colonial law and order. Just over one hundred men of the infantry companies failed to answer the call to arms. One sergeant of the militia named William Dathorne, a schoolteacher at the Brickdam Roman Catholic School, not only failed to turn out, but went into the crowd harassing those who did. Dathorne was not alone, judging from the harsh terms used to describe absconding militiamen, of whom it was said:

> Nor did they try to conceal their disloyalty. It appeared to give them great pleasure to proclaim their dastardly disobedience to the call of duty, by jeering at the comparatively few who had put themselves under arms for the defence of the city, while in not a few cases the deserters were even bold enough to propose to the police that they should put down their rifles and throw in their lot with the rioters.[18]

As indicated earlier, the British Guiana Militia comprised middle-class members of the community.* When formed in 1891, it included those citizens who would have received the franchise on an income qualification of $300 per annum. The list of persons who became liable for militia duty in Georgetown as of January 1905 contained 617 names, of whom 22 were qualified in terms of property and the rest in terms of income. Occupational categories were indicated for about five hundred of these (see accompanying table).[19]

Occupational Category	Number	Persons Listed
Clerical occupations	342	Clerks, clerical assistants, customs officers, civil servants, bank clerks, bookkeepers, salesmen
Artisan/Tradesman	63	Carpenters, builders, wheelwrights, coopers, tinsmiths, painters, watch makers, piano tuners, shoemakers, tailors
Petty entrepreneurs	40	Storekeepers, grocers, stationers, goldsmiths, pawnbrokers, speculators, bakers, butchers, hairdressers, dispensers, chemists
Professionals	32	Accountants, lawyers, architects
Supervisors	18	Managers, superintendents, overseers, wharfingers, agents, weighers
Journalism and printing trades	12	
Educationists	5	Headmasters, schoolmasters, school inspectors
Miscellaneous	105	

*The likelihood is that the 105 militiamen who failed to answer the call to arms were a representative sample of the lower-middle-class occupations.

A number of middle-class individuals were active behind the scenes after the disturbances had started, their purpose being to serve as mediators or negotiators on behalf of the workers. A few were self-appointed, while others were sought out to play this role. Their standing within the working community depended mainly on their record of participation in the popular-front politics which began in the late 1880s, and which was given new life with the formation of the People's Association in 1903. Several names that cropped up were identifiable as part of "the generation of 1891," who agitated for a new Constitution and benefited from the Reformed Constitution of 1891. Some of the radicals of 1891 were establishment types by 1905. For instance, D. M. Hutson, former chairman of the Reform Association, had become a member of the Executive Council and acted as solicitor general. In December 1905, Hutson accepted a brief from the police to watch over their interests during the inquest into the deaths of persons shot during the riots, having been confidentially cleared by the governor as a man who "at the present time takes a reasonable view of affairs."[20] The defection of J. Wood Davis was even more striking. Not only was he a founding member of the Reform Association, but he was also elected as a financial representative on the ticket of the People's Association. Wood Davis switched his commitments during by-elections in 1904; and he explained that he advocated a coalition of "the People and the Planters" rather than "the People *versus* the Planters."[21] Consistent with this new political line, Wood Davis and E. A. Abrahams (mayor of Georgetown) sought to reconcile workers and employers. Significantly, the paltry compromise which they negotiated was rejected by the stevedores, who preferred to return to the *status quo ante* rather than accept what amounted to insultingly inadequate recommendations.

As it turned out, the workers still had middle-class allies who remained loyal to populist ideals. Their friends included a few Portuguese businessmen. For instance, workers negotiated directly with the local Portuguese firm of J. P. Santos & Co., the only shipping employer whose premises were kept open on Water Street on the afternoon of Thursday, 30 November. The strikers went there and bargained with the two partners, Santos and Pereira, who immediately promised an increase of wages when it became necessary to employ "outside" labor. On the fateful "Black Friday," the governor tried to arrange a meeting between himself and employers of stevedores at the Public Buildings. The crowds allowed only two employers to pass: namely, Santos and the representative of Curtis Campbell & Co. At this meeting with the governor, J. P. Santos expressed the opinion that the existing rates of pay were inadequate, and that he would be willing to pay 72 cents per day for adults, 56 cents for "boys" and 16 cents per hour for periods shorter than one day. These proposals would have been considered satisfactory by workers.

A few radical middle-class leaders had won the respect of the broad masses through their roles in the People's Association. Foremost among

A. A. Thorne, educator, politician, and trade unionist (born Barbados)

these were A. A. Thorne, Dr. J. M. Rohlehr, and Patrick Dargan. Because they were well known for their militancy, the strikers sought them out; and they responded by trying to publicize worker grievances and worker versions of altercations between themselves and the employers or the police. Thorne had always been an indefatigable worker on questions of educational reform. In 1894, he had established in Georgetown a private secondary school known as the "Middle School." This drew the bond closer between himself and aspiring postprimary students who had no hope of entering Queen's College or the Catholic Grammar School. As would be expected, Dr. Rohlehr's specialty was the question of health and sanitation. After fighting the battle of his own registration, he campaigned for government medical facilities to be provided to the villages and other rural settlements. Dargan was rather less consistent. He had fallen under a cloud as far as the People's Association was concerned, because of some very strange proplanter pronouncements on immigration and on the issue of overseers who sexually exploited female indentured laborers. But in December 1905, Dargan rebuilt his popular reputation—as an advocate in court on behalf of relatives of those killed and as a member of the Court of Policy, where he asked questions which probed and embarrassed the regime. He launched a weekly newspaper, the *Creole* hammered the colonial administration over the riots and the shootings. Dargan, in his capacity as a lawyer, was also involved in one of the most sensational developments in Guiana's colonial legal history, which was the filing of actions against the inspector-general and a major of the Police Force alleging that they were criminally liable for the deaths of persons shot by the police.

It must be repeated that lawyers and other middle-class persons were not the leaders of the strikes nor of the street demonstrations. They refuted the charge that they ever incited any rioters; and they pointed to the many public instances where their voices were raised in the cause of moderation—especially when the crowds surged around the Parade Ground, Government House, and the Public Buildings on Friday, the first of December. The middle strata had a particular aversion toward the lumpen proletariat, and they saw the actual riots as the work of the lumpen. Even A. A. Thorne, who stood most firmly on the side of the wage earners, explicitly disassociated himself from the "rabble" and the "centipedes," who supposedly did the looting and the stoning.

The term "centipede" came to be associated with a small quasi-criminal segment of hustlers who were resident in Georgetown—the products of rural-urban migration and unemployment both in the countryside and in the city. Many of them worked on the waterfront when the opportunity arose, and in December 1905, they would naturally have gravitated toward the protest activity that had a direct bearing on their material existence and that was readily compatible with their volatile life-style. Even so, the insistence on a major role played by the "centipedes"—both male and female—springs partly from the stilted morality of the middle class and partly from the official need to find scapegoats.

The deteriorating social situation in Guiana at the turn of this century had led to increased crime in Georgetown, and the phenomenon of urban youth gangs had come to the fore. These gangs armed themselves with hackia sticks and paraded through the streets at night, terrorizing the inhabitants. It does not appear that the "centipedes" did much more than use abusive language, but an authoritarian response was popular among all layers of the middle class. During 1904, there were letters to the press denouncing this "vagabondage"; magistrates in Georgetown promised to deal harshly with "centipedism"; ministers of the church preached sermons on the "evil"; and the Annual Conference of the Teachers' Association passed a resolution in December 1904 calling upon the authorities to stamp out those who terrorized peaceful citizens. Against this type of background, the very use of the term "centipede" was emotive, and makes it difficult to discern from the available sources what was the precise role of lumpen-proletarian elements in the riots.

The problem of determining the specific roles of sections of the crowd is especially acute when dealing with the involvement of women. Of the 105 persons convicted in the Georgetown Magistrates' Courts as a consequence of the riots, 41 were female. Another 45 persons were charged but had the charges withdrawn or dismissed; and of these, 19 were female.[22] The implication could well be that at least one in every three "rioters" was a woman, a credible ratio given the large proportion of women in the city of Georgetown

at the time. Because of a heavy preponderance of males among the indentured immigrants, there were more males than females in the population of
British Guiana in the nineteenth century, but according to the census of
1891, the reverse was true in Georgetown.

Strong female participation in the riots would also have been understandable in terms of the depressed conditions facing women of the working class.
Over the latter part of the nineteenth century, these conditions had, from
time to time, attracted public interest. The *Reflector* of 19 October 1889
expressed forward-looking sentiments when it editorialized that "the day will
come when the advocates for Reform will have to include in their programme
the question of equal rights and privileges for women." Shortly afterward,
another newspaper drew attention to the condition of seamstresses who were
employed by the large Water Street firms in making men's pants at a rate of
pay which caused the commentator to make a parallel with the notorious
"sweating trades" of London.[23]

Between 1891 and 1905, the most important group of female Guianese
workers were the hired domestics. When stevedores marched on 30 November
and 1 December, they pulled fellow stevedores off their jobs. Meanwhile, the
women concentrated their attention on domestics, and it is a plausible
inference that many of those who took to the streets were themselves domestics, especially in view of the fact that almost one in four women in the city
was a domestic. The 1891 census placed female domestics at the high figure
of 7,432 out of a total female population of 28,355. On 2 December, women
carrying a prepared meal to policemen were attacked at the very entrance to
the police station by another group of women. In part, this can be explained
by the generalized anger directed at policemen for the shootings of the
previous day, but it is also highly probable that the attacking women were
trying to bring their own "strike-breakers" in line, because the sale of prepared food to certain categories of employed persons was one of the activities
to which working-class women turned.

There were, of course, women who were not wage earners or self-employed persons; women who lived in the tenement yards of Georgetown and
existed as best they could. Like the males in "centipede" gangs, they developed a reputation for ready resort to abuse and petty violence. Several of these
women became folk characters; even the sheriff of Demerara, Henry Kirke,
became enamored of one such character, a woman popularly known as "the
Tigress of Tiger Bay."[24] Some light is thrown on the condition of this type
of urban woman by the activities of the Salvation Army, which distinguished
itself in Guiana, as elsewhere, through its concern for impoverished and
marginal groups in the society. At the turn of the century, one of the schemes
of the Salvation Army was the construction of an Industrial Rehabilitation
Centre as a home for "fallen women" in Georgetown. The Rev. W. B. Ritchie
(Presbyterian) supported the Salvation Army in this endeavor but pointed

out that while prostitution undoubtedly existed, the predicament of prostitutes was connected with the larger problem of unemployment, which adversely affected the welfare of most women in the colony of British Guiana.[25]

As part of a policy of denying official responsibility for certain social conditions, the Georgetown *Daily Chronicle* described the demonstrations as being led by "women of the street," and blamed them for the attacks on houses of peaceful citizens and the sacking of stores. When such statements filtered through the London *Morning Post*, the English public was informed that "the rioters were largely composed of half-civilised Amazons and idle ruffians calling themselves centipedes."[26] At this point, the allegations lose all touch with reality.

Women from all levels of the working people were involved in the 1905 riots. Court records do not sustain the slur that even those arrested were all rowdies, viragos, prostitutes and the like. One encounters reference to a "badly-clad 'lady' of the centipede class" and to one "Daisy, the centipede Queen"; but in general, the absence of such appellations is striking, because the prosecution would presumably have been at pains to point out where persons charged had previous criminal records—whether they were men or women. There were a few women who participated in the East and West Bank labor struggles, and these were undoubtedly genuine wage laborers. Dorothy Rice was part of a subsequent delegation from Ruimveldt that put the case for workers on that estate. She was one of the shrinking number of Afro-Guyanese women who still remained within estate field employment, and she explained how she earned no more than six or seven shillings per week at cane-cutting, in spite of having her two daughters assist her with fetching the canes. Dorothy Rice marked out her task on Monday, started on Tuesday, and worked until 11:00 A.M. on Saturday.[27] Her counterparts in the urban settings of Georgetown would have been washerwomen, seamstresses, street vendors, and, above all, domestics in private employment.

Unemployment and underemployment redounded most viciously on female dependents. Some women were civil-law or common-law wives; many others cohabited for periods of varying length with one male or another. They sought to earn for themselves, but few survived without turning to an employed male relative, a husband, a "child-father" or some such. Little wonder then that the women were so vociferous and so active during the riots. They were backing their men, and they were also fighting for themselves and for the reproduction of their families—as they had done before in 1889 when they attacked the Portuguese retailers. Not surprisingly, the Portuguese Pawnbrokery was the first business premise to be broken into by rioters in December 1905. Women were particularly victimized by pawnbrokers, and they sacrificed many a piece of jewelry lodged as security for loans which were never repaid. They may not have engineered the break-in, but like all members of the urban working class of the period, they would certainly have sympathized with this direct reprisal against the usurious pawnbroker.

Official accounts of the 1905 occurrences paid considerable attention to the role of women. Governor Hodgson had held office in West Africa. He made a telling comparison between the women of Guiana and the women of West Africa, who had convincingly demonstrated their resistance to colonial rule; and he tried to persuade the men of Guiana that the women were the ones causing trouble and that they should be kept quiet. Whether the men were capable of carrying out such a task was itself debatable. One observer had earlier pointed out that Guianese women of the working class tended to act independently, even at the risk of rupture with their partners.[28] As it turned out, there was no contradiction between men and women. They joined together under a working-class banner—"16 cents an hour or no work."

Having denied that leadership of the 1905 riots was in the hands of the middle class or the lumpen proletariat (male or female), it still remains to pinpoint, if possible, the leadership within the ranks of the workers. Trotsky has observed that there are always such leaders, even when there is no overt organization and even when the *personae* are left nameless as far as historians are concerned.[29] Without pretending any comparison with the Russian Revolution, one might apply the insight to the modest events in Guiana in 1905. A reading of the official and newspaper reports shows that within the masses on the streets, there were individuals who stood out as bold and decisive. Little is known of the stevedores who initiated the strike action. According to one source, Hubert Nathaniel Critchlow (then himself a docker) persuaded the "boys" to strike as soon as their bargaining position was improved by the presence of about six ships in harbor. Critchlow was arrested but released without being charged, so that his name does not appear on the court records.[30] Those who did come to the attention of the authorities as leaders did not reappear subsequently as national trade unionists. The nameless spokesman at the Parade Ground who sent the police inspector to report to his capitalist bosses was a working-class leader. On the West Bank Demerara, Phillip Washington of Toevlugt was the recognized strike leader, his contribution being that he mobilized in Bagotstown and brought out the workers of Nismes, Wales, and Schoonord. Those who led the strikes also demonstrated their personal courage when confronted by the police on the streets. In one instance, the behavior of one of the "rioters" in Cummingsburg was so courageous that the inspector-general of police virtually supplied a testimonial on his behalf by stating:

A man whose courage could not be questioned ventured to within a short distance of the police while the shooting was going on. He was a dangerous fellow at close quarters and he was ordered to be shot, but notwithstanding that he was so near, shot after shot was discharged at him without harming him. Standing face to face with the police he braved the desperate situation, striking himself on the chest and inviting the police to kill him. It was only when it seemed likely that he would be charged at that he desisted and cleared out. Although I was bound to order him to be fired at, personally I felt glad that the plucky fellow managed to escape.[31]

As in any riot, several of the persons killed or wounded were innocent bystanders; but the above incident shows that the police singled out particular individuals as targets. Their own evidence on the Ruimveldt shootings make it clear that the police ordered the elimination of any demonstrator whom they had reason to consider a strike leader. The Ruimveldt scenario is worth reviewing so as to identify those workers who took the initiative. The strike at Ruimveldt started among porters attached to the factory on Wednesday, 29 November. The following day was relatively quiet, but early on the Friday morning other categories of factory workers combined to close the factory. The militant who effected this shutdown was known among his coworkers as "Long Walk." "Long Walk" lived in La Penitence; he was a building hand employed on one of the clarifiers; and it was he who went from worker to worker urging that no one should stay on without the promise of increased wages. "Long Walk" was in the forefront of the demonstration when the police arrived and was one of those seriously injured. A porter named Haynes of Meadow Bank also stood his ground when the police read the Riot Act at Ruimveldt, and he too was injured. These two were the factory workers who paid their dues to the working class on Friday, 1 December.

As an immediate sequel to industrial protest at Ruimveldt, a cane-cutter named George Henry was arrested. It was charged that "he did openly carry a dangerous weapon," the dangerous weapon being nothing other than a cutlass, the instrument of his trade. George Henry, otherwise known as George Beckles, had led cane-cutters straight from the fields on receiving word that the factory workers were on strike. The field workers downed their cutlasses when requested to do so by the police, but they objected when the police tried to gather them up. George Henry had already been pointed out as a "ringleader" by the manager, who further alleged that Henry had beaten him up. The police therefore pounced on Henry and there was a scuffle; he was subsequently sentenced to six months and lashes. Henry fared much better than another so-called ringleader, Robert Chapman. "Bobby," as he was popularly known, refused to back off when the police issued their threats. He was another marked man; Major de Rinzy admitted that he pointed to Bobby Chapman and gave the order that he be shot in the legs. A policeman fired twice and missed, and another was told to do a better job.[32] Chapman died from arterial hemorrhage shortly after being cut down.

He was the first victim and the first martyr produced by the 1905 confrontation.

All who were shot at Ruimveldt were definitely vanguard workers in a period when there was no organization for workers. Field and factory hands had legitimate wage claims and they stood their ground whenever the police read the Riot Act and prepared to open fire. A brother and sister with the surname Braithwaite were both in this category, and they were both injured. Several others who did not sacrifice life or limb were nevertheless prominent in the leadership. For instance, a deputation of some twenty-five cane-cutters marched from Ruimveldt on Monday, 4 December, to place the facts of their case before Dr. Rohlehr and before the press. They marched in pouring rain, led by James Welcome, a Berbician then living in Albouystown.[33]

The Colonial State and Colonial Authority

As was the fashion of the age, all worker leaders were deemed "ringleaders" and treated as criminals by the colonial state. Naturally enough, the courts were an integral part of the machinery for punishing the offenders and restoring normality after the riots. The attorney-general stated that those who did not disperse after a reading of the Riot Act were guilty of an indictable felony, punishable by penal servitude for life. However, the government opted to use the Summary Convictions Ordinance of 1893, which came into operation as soon as Georgetown was "proclaimed" on 30 November. No charges were brought against anyone for riotous assembly, sedition, or any such serious offenses. Instead, the courts dealt with dozens of cases under the heads of "disorderly conduct," "dangerous weapons," "throwing stones," and "assaulting police." The bail was punitive in most instances. Phillip Washington of Toevlugt was asked to pay $480 to secure bail and the court demanded surety in like amount. Under the Summary Convictions Ordinance, it was possible to apply the penalty of flogging. This the court was only too happy to do in the case of male offenders, while for women the magistrate reserved the archaic penalty of shaving the head. It required a directive from the colonial secretary to the governor before the cutting of women's hair was discontinued, the Colonial Office itself having described the punishment as "unnatural" and "medieval."[34]

In part, the government chose to try rioters summarily because the penalties of flogging and head-shaving were applicable under an amendment made to the Summary Criminal Offences Ordinance in 1904, supposedly to deal with "centipedes." But the more profound reason for not trying anyone indictably was the lack of confidence in jury trials. The captain commanding H.M.S. *Diamond* reported to the Admiralty that the British Guiana authorities were convinced that no jury would convict.[35] The jury list was normally a roster of the "respectable" citizens of the community, but this category of citizens included the militia, and the militia had deserted. Actually, the question of the efficacy of jury trial had come up before 1905 in the colonial annals of British Guiana. Whenever defendants were being tried in a socially explosive situation, the colonial state expressed reservations as to whether a jury of twelve could be found to convict those whom most persons considered victims rather than wrongdoers. As far back as 1871, the indentured immigrants who rioted at Plantation Devonshire Castle were freed by juries which did not even include Indians. By 1905, several such experiences had suggested to the government that a magistrate was "safer" than a jury chosen from among the people.

The courts punished a number of rioters, and they dismissed cases against Lushington and de Rinzy, who were charged by private citizens with being criminally culpable in the deaths of rioters. A military tribunal dealt with the militiamen who deserted. Five were dismissed and sentenced to imprisonment from 6 January 1906. But a decision was soon taken to calm inflamed passions. Imprisoned militiamen were released after one month, and the authorities halted legal action that was pending against others. Instead, Sergeant Dathorne and several others were simply dismissed.[36]

In pursuing the analysis of the response of the colonial state to a moment of crisis, one has to devote some attention to the personal role of Sir Frederick Hodgson, the governor in office. A governor was the chief executive of a colonial state based on colonial capitalism; ultimately, all governors had to defend the capitalist class when it was threatened. But different officeholders had differing conceptions of how far and how quickly they should act in alliance with the employers. Occasionally, a Governor sought to stand for an "imperial trusteeship" greater than the interests of individual capitalists. For example, Swettenham, who preceded Hodgson, had a serious altercation with the New Colonial Company and other sugar plantation companies because he insisted that they respect the legislative and administrative provisions regulating the conduct of managers and overseers vis-à-vis indentured Indian women. It was widely felt in Guiana that Swettenham's abrupt transfer to Jamaica in 1904 was a direct result of this confrontation, and that Hodgson (a former postmaster-general in British Guiana in 1882) was a replacement aimed at conciliating the big capitalist companies.[37] Just over a year after he had taken office, the 1905 riots gave Hodgson the opportunity to affirm in no uncertain terms where the chief executive stood in relation to the contending classes.

The *Daily Chronicle* could not have been described as antigovernment. During the first few days of the disturbances, it came down firmly on the side of law and order and castigated the "centipedes." However, after the governor's intervention on the West Bank Demerara, the *Daily Chronicle* referred to him as a bigoted partisan of planter interests. This newspaper balked at

Hodgson's reversal of the independent decision of some planters who responded favorably to wage demands. In fact, this action was questioned by the secretary of state for the colonies, whose doubts and censure were obliquely expressed in a letter of 13 December. The Colonial Office was concerned that the governor in Guiana was taking decisions that made it appear that he was concerned only with the interests of the planters, and that workers' claims were not being considered even when legitimate. Governor Hodgson was specifically asked for more information as to what had occurred on his visit to the West Bank factories. His reply repeated planter rationalisations that the wage rate had been peaceably accepted over the previous decade and that this was convincing proof that no genuine worker grievances existed.[38]

It was Africans who walked off the job on the estates of the East and West Banks Demerara, and Indians were absent from the demonstrations. These facts were given great weight by Governor Hodgson. His telegrams and letters on the issue were not entirely false, but they were extremely tendentious and at times conveyed the incorrect impression that the riots were attacks by Africans against Indians, or at least, initiatives by Africans from which Indians actively disassociated themselves. The apparently racial split was a reflection of the division of labor which still tended to concentrate Africans in the estate buildings or—in the fields—only as cane-cutters. Most of the dissatisfaction was first voiced by factory workers, and this explains the absence of Indians at the outset. A report of Africans at Ruimveldt forcibly keeping Indians way from the job site amounts to a description of the only labour practices available in an era before trade unionism. Such coercion occurred at Ruimveldt because Indian porters were taken to fill the places of Africans who had withdrawn their labor. However, there was no further conflict; Indians stayed in their logies at Ruimveldt on 1 December. The classic technique of using Indians to police Africans and vice versa never came into play in the December unrest. Without direct state intervention, there was even the possibility that for the first time, the various racial, occupational, and legal barriers within the plantation work force would have been transcended.

At Plantation Versailles, the wage demands by strikers resulted in management promising wage increases for *both African and Indian workers*. The governor's initial accounts of the incident entirely overlooked this aspect, and he was accused of deliberately withholding this information to buttress his case that grievances were restricted to one race group. Subsequently, the governor stated that the full facts were not at his disposal when he made his famous trip to the West Bank estates on 4 December.[39] At the very least, the governor was guilty of gross carelessness in his investigation and report; and this carelessness was a logical consequence of his determination to proceed with utmost haste so as to prevent Indians from taking up wage claims on the various estates. He conceded to the Colonial Office that "the East Indian immigrant is equally as interested as other labourers in any demand for higher wages; and probably would, if he saw that concessions were being made, have to be reckoned with."[40] Admissions of this sort were made in January 1906, a few weeks after the riots, and they conclusively show that the governor consciously sought to preempt further widespread and unified action by the working class.

In 1896, de Rinzy was a captain.* He fired on striking Indian workers at Non Pareil. By 1905, de Rinzy was promoted to major, and he seemed equally at home shooting African workers at Ruimveldt. The interpretation of the 1905 upheaval as a racial phenomenon could only have been made persuasive by completely covering up the many expressions of grievances by Indian workers—at Non Pareil in 1896, at Friends in 1903, and, on a lesser scale, on almost every sugar plantation in the years immediately preceding the 1905 riots. Stevedores, factory hands, cane-cutters, and gold miners were predominantly African in origin. The colonial regime did not want social unrest to spread geographically, but above all, they feared that rebelliousness might extend beyond the confines of urban and villagized Afro-Guyanese to embrace the many thousands of Indians who were indentured and ex-indentured residents on the estates. The official policy in 1905 was designed to prevent the spread of strike action and combination across racial lines.

Governor Hodgson and the plantation capitalists were able to achieve most of their objectives quickly. Three hundred police in Georgetown and the presence of imperial warships in port settled matters within days. In the meantime, however, the colonial state had lost certain intangibles in the way of moral authority. This is confirmed by a glance at some aspects of crowd behavior during the riots. The first notable incident was when Major de Rinzy read the Riot Act at Ruimveldt and concluded with the usual formula, "God save the King!" At this point, one man shouted, "The King don't know a dam' about us. He don't care about us and our pay."[41] With this kind of attitude growing among the crowds, it is not surprising that the king's servants were given scant respect, Magistrate Brummell was jeered at when he read the Riot Act in Georgetown, and the attorney-general and magistrates were targets for abuse and physical attacks throughout the disturbances. But it was the Governor who attracted the greatest odium, and he was a man who obviously had a highly developed sense of dignity in his representation of imperial authority. While he was governor of the Gold Coast, Hodgson had totally misapprehended the significance of the Golden Stool of Asante. To satisfy his sense of imperial prestige, he had demanded that this sacred object be brought for him to sit on! This touched off war between the British and

*This same officer again featured in the Plantation Rose Hall shootings of 1913.

the Asante in 1900.[42] Interestingly, the Guianese press had followed the Asante war carefully, and had several times alluded to the questionable judgment of Governor Hodgson.[43]

On the morning of "Black Friday," a throng of several hundreds had carried the wounded from Ruimveldt to Government House, stoning the guards in the process and successfully demanding that the governor come down to the garden to speak to them. That afternoon, the focus shifted to the Public Buildings. The governor was prepared to confer with middle-class spokesmen for the strikers, namely, Wood Davis, A. A. Thorne, Dr. Rohlehr, Dr. Wills, and Mr. S. E. Wills. About thirty other persons forced their way in before the gates were closed, and Thorne prevailed on His Excellency to let the people in to hear what was being said on their behalf. The gates were therefore reopened and several hundreds rushed into the precincts of the Public Buildings. The governor was confronted by an old man who turned out to be the father of one of the victims of police fire. "My son shot dead, dead," was all that the old man could manage to say.[44] The governor conveyed his condolences. In his public speech from the balcony, Hodgson expressed deep regret at the killings; but he himself has honestly recorded that this statement was greeted with shouts of skepticism. The middle-class liberal Wood Davis called on the working people to remove their caps as a sign of respect for the governor, but the people had gone beyond this stage and met the suggestion with loud and irreverent laughter. Not only was the governor penned in the Public Buildings for some time, but his exit proved very difficult. The carriage in which he was supposed to leave was stoned, and from the viewpoint of safe movement, put out of action. Hodgson therefore made his way to Government House on foot, accompanied by an armed phalanx of police with fixed bayonets and by a jeering, insulting crowd.

For a brief while, the substance as well as the aura of colonial power was endangered. The police were unable to keep the Public Buildings secure; they were unable to make any arrests; and they were barely able to guarantee the safety of the governor. The senior police officers were themselves evoking a violent response. De Rinzy's name was coupled with the Ruimveldt shootings. One woman caught him by the throat, and he later testified that the crowd was excited by the mere sight of him. Then there was Inspector-General Lushington, who bore the overall responsibility for the Georgetown shootings, and who (according to some reports) had had recourse to inflammatory and threatening language. The people viewed de Rinzy and Lushington as murderers in the literal sense of the word, and although the police did restore order, the colonial state deemed it imperative to bring in the reinforcements of British troops. The failure of the militia also jolted the local authorities psychologically. The militia was an auxiliary to the police force, and was expected to help in a difficult situation until imperial forces arrived. Even if its practical value was limited, it was designed as an agency of colonialist socialization. The (acting) governor in April 1891 had urged the formation of a citizens' militia because "the habits of discipline and precision encouraged by a military training are of incalculable value as an educational agency in a colonial community."[45] Up to a few months before the outbreak in 1905, the two infantry companies of the militia were reportedly in good spirit, and were sharply turned out at parades. Why the sudden turnabout? What had happened to the fourteen years of colonialist education since 1891? These were questions which must surely have perturbed the administration.

In the weeks following the riots, the colonial state apparatus moved swiftly to shore up that section of its defenses left exposed by the defection of the militia and by the ability of the rioters to dominate large parts of the city. The latter problem was defined logistically as requiring greater mobility for the police. The decision was therefore taken to start a mounted police branch for riot control, comprising initially forty mounted policemen. In place of the unreliable militia, the government sought to establish a volunteer force from among locally resident whites and senior employees of the large merchant firms. To this end, the legislature reintroduced the provisions of an earlier Volunteer Ordinance (No. 2 of 1878). Throughout the discussions on the mounted police and the volunteer force, there was a clear conception that local armed forces had as their principal function the suppression of local discontent.

The strengthening of the coercive state apparatus was implemented without delay. What the government found difficult to handle was the remarkable estrangement of the people. Their rejection of colonial authority lasted, not for days or weeks, but for months, and in some respects their resistance was better coordinated. Popular spokesmen pressed for an enquiry into the alleged use of indiscriminate and undue violence in suppressing the riots; workers demanded full-scale investigation into the impact of indentured immigration and into the conditions of labor as a whole; and the People's Association was revived to draw together the grievances of men and women, urban and rural dwellers, and laborers from the bush as well as the coast. On 29 January 1906, artisans and workers packed into the Town Hall (Georgetown) to unite a series of demands into a petition sponsored by the People's Association. The petition received just over six thousand signatures and was eventually forwarded to the Colonial Office via the Trinidadian Pan-Africanist H. Sylvester Williams.[46] In assessing the petition, the Colonial Office had before it adverse reports which stated that many injudicious speeches had been made at the meeting of 29 January and that Dr. Rohlehr had called upon the people to form a trade union. This was not the first appeal of its kind and it was not immediately implemented. There was no industrial organization representing workers, and there was no working class political party. But workers had access to the People's Association and to two newspapers, the *People* in New Amsterdam and the *Creole* in Georgetown. The

Creole in particular reflected the mood of the people in its invectives, and it carried its criticism to the point of libel against the governor.[47]

At the end of January 1906, the Executive Council advised the governor that something had to be done to appease the continued anger of the population. The governor seemed much more concerned with the fact that the people's demeanor was inconsistent with due respect for the king's representative, and it was quite some time before he could feel satisfied on this score. As late as July 1906, dispatches highlighted the presence of groups standing around Georgetown talking politics and discussing the court cases in which Inspector-General Lushington and Major de Rinzy were involved. The Guianese masses also shared the experiences of broader international struggle. Every new outbreak of fighting in Russia, every reported mutiny among the Czarist imperial troops, the African uprisings in Natal, warnings given by African domestic servants to their mistresses in Johannesburg, socialist demonstrations in London, the seizure of land by the unemployed—all of these items found a place in the local press to the exclusion of what the governor considered to be more "interesting" news and with the consequence of creating what he described as an "artificial" situation of unrest.[48] There was another small strike of Georgetown stevedores on the waterfront in September 1906; and it was not until the following month that the governor breathed with relief. He had previously been treated like an outcast by the people, and was delighted that this phase had come to an end. As he explained:

> During the long drawn out prosecutions of police officers, I had driven and walked about Georgetown without receiving a single salute. Now the usual marks of respect are everywhere shown. It is the same at popular gatherings. In the early part of the year in the principal Wesleyan Church at the annual meeting, I was received with unconcealed impatience even within the walls. Now . . . discontent and sulkiness . . . have gone.[49]

Almost one year had elapsed between the outbreak of the riots and the governor's all-clear signal in October 1906. Over the course of post-Emancipation history in Guiana, the 1905 riots marked a high point in sustained popular agitation. Small qualitative changes in the consciousness of the work force were registered, and after 1906 these changes became operational in the form of attempts at the organization of the working class for industrial and trade union struggle.

CONCLUSION

From the standpoint of imperial history, there was nothing splendid or exciting about the years 1880-1905, as far as the West Indies were concerned. True, the United States was then staking its claim to Puerto Rico and Cuba; but for Britain and France, the Caribbean had outlived its usefulness in the elaboration of the world capitalist system. This was the period when the Caribbean had become "little more than a geographical expression—the outcome of the historic decline of the sugar industry in the second half the nineteenth century."[1] Yet, new frontiers of imperialism were then being established in Africa and Asia. One alludes to this international pattern as a reminder that many of the fundamental conditions for Guyanese history were externally determined. Guyanese society as it emerged in the early part of this century was unique, in so far as any given social formation constitutes a specific entity at a given point of time. But, within the territory of Guyana, capitalism was then the dominant mode of production, realizing itself through a colonial nexus. It is legitimate to assess the Guyanese past as part of the history of underdeveloped societies and, more precisely, as part of the history of the underdeveloped plantation societies of the Caribbean.

The Royal Commission that held hearings in British Guiana in 1897 was brought into existence by widespread distress in the West Indies, and its appointment was little more than a gesture in the face of want of interest and abandonment. Joseph Chamberlain (as secretary of state for the colonies) seemed to have been saying something different in 1895, but metropolitan assistance for West Indian economic development was not a feature of colonial rule at this juncture. Persistent poverty and other negative aspects of the plantation system were very evident in British Guiana. They provide ample illustration for the now well-known theses on Caribbean underdevelopment. Nevertheless, throughout this text, the attempt has been made to identify the local changes that modified the picture of underdevelopment as sheer stagnation.[2] There were, for example, significant technological advances in the factories. This technological transformation, together with the process of estate amalgamation, ensured not only the domination of capital over labor but also the elimination of small local planters by large foreign plantation companies.

On occasions, the operative historical feature was the mere fact that the beginnings of change were discernible. The plantation structure, the restrictive policy towards crown lands and village land tenure patterns together inhibited the emergence of classes from within the ranks of the working people. But it is apposite to point out that social layers such as plantation drivers and village landowners began to accumulate and were ultimately to transform themselves. Some developments at one and the same time illustrated tendencies of change and resistance to change. The expansion of the gold-mining sector is a case in point. Objectively, gold production meant economic diversification, and this must not be overlooked. On balance, however, the social and political hegemony of plantation capital was hardly shaken. Even after the liberalization of the Constitution in 1891, planter capitalists successfully resisted infrastructural expenditure on hinterland development. They kept all classes tied to the coastal habitat—so much so that gold workers were merely coastal workers who sojourned in the bush on a short-term migratory basis. The overwhelming presence of plantation capital in British Guiana also differentiated this colony from its West Indian counterparts in certain ways. The growth of a landowning peasantry was encouraged in the West Indian islands by the promotion of new cash crops, such as bananas in Jamaica and cocoa in Grenada, while in Guiana a similar development was blocked until commercial rice farming was firmly instituted by the immigrant population at the very end of the nineteenth century. In Trinidad, there was the emergence of a vibrant French Creole community which possessed landed and commercial capital, while in British Guiana metropolitan plantation capital kept advancing remorselessly at the expense of small capital.

Throughout this study, care has been taken to avoid imparting to the various social classes greater precision than they had achieved within the evolving social formation of the nineteenth century and the early twentieth century. If classes are to be defined in their mutal opposition (as would seem logical), then the differentiation of working class, peasantry, and middle class was incomplete. The most sharply defined of the existing classes in British Guiana comprised the capitalists, who owned most of the means of production, controlled the institutions of the colonial state, and secured most of the surplus alienated through wage labor or market mechanisms. The remarkable extent of planter political power ·meant that steps were taken to keep other classes underdeveloped, and the boundaries between them were very fluid. The working class was particularly restricted because of the peripheral capitalist nature of the economy and because sociopolitical relations favored the persistence of indentureship.

It is my contention that slaves became plantation workers immediately after slavery. These rural wage earners subsequently transformed themselves into a peasantry or into an urban working class or (if they retained a base in the rural areas) into a permanent hybrid of peasant and proletarian.[3] Modern field studies have drawn attention to the phenomenon of Creole villages being all but destitute of adult males at certain times, because the men were away seeking employment on sugar estates, in the city or, most frequently, in the hinterland.[4] This trend was established in the 1880s and it was never reversed. Meanwhile, the labor force in Georgetown, and to a lesser extent New Amsterdam, had been augmented by rural-urban migration involving Creole Africans and members of other racial groups. Many remained unemployed, although it was the prospect of employment that attracted them to the city. The absence of large-scale industrial enterprises was typical of capitalism in the periphery at that stage of the rise of imperialism. The working class was heterogeneous—reflecting miscellaneous job categories in an urban center which had only administrative, commercial, port, and service facilities. The dockworkers were the only large group of urban workers who had a collective experience in the same enterprise, or at least in the identical work process.

Considering the country as a whole, sugar workers were obviously far and away the most numerous group. They had an enormous potential, but the weaknesses of the working class were most evident on the sugar estates. Firstly, there was the stagnation of wages and working conditions attendant on indentureship.[5] Secondly, there were the racial and cultural distinctions which increasingly came to coincide with job specialization and residential separation. It has been argued in this study that racial conflict was far less pronounced than might have been expected from the manner in which the two main races were thrown into economic competition; but I am not seeking to minimize a crucial aspect of the historical reality. Indentureship and racial competition held back the development of a plantation workers' movement until long after the period in question.

As always, the historian is faced with the task of having to cut a complex dialectical process at two points so as to provide a convenient beginning and end. The year 1881 was not particularly distinguished in the annals of Guyana. Working people cried out at hard times. In 1905, the cry was still at hard times—a condition that existed with varying degrees of intensity throughout the period under discussion. However, working people appeared as supplicants before the Poor Law Enquiry Commission which sat in 1881; but in 1905 strikes, riots, and mass public meetings shook the composure of the colonial state and detained a British warship for months afterward. This popular activity set the stage for advance toward trade union organization and more forceful confrontation in the political arena. It is standard practice to trace the origins of trade unionism in Guyana to the years after the First World War or, occasionally, to the period starting in 1905.[6] This in itself offers good reason for probing the hidden antecedents of the worker movement. As it is, however, the tendency has been to skim over the last decades of the nineteenth century, and thus to contribute to the impression that the eventful epoch of post-Emancipation struggles was followed by a long and unrelieved "dead season."[7] But it was in the late nineteenth century that the modern political economy of Guyana took shape. Nonindentured Indians became the largest group on the plantations, rice farming was added to coastal agriculture, gold and diamond and timber industries were promoted in the hinterland, the middle class emerged as an important entity, and the formal political arena ceased to be the exclusive concern of the planter class. Each of these developments had consequences which extended beyond the contemporary reality.

This study has sought to show some of the ways in which the Guyanese working class constituted itself through its own activities. Much more will have to be researched and written on the emergence of the culture of the working people and of the wage-earning class in particular. Only the opening up of culture history can definitively indicate what made the working people exercise particular choices at given moments: what made them long-suffering or impatient or what transformed them from apathy to combat. At the present moment, enough is known to suggest that it was through political struggle that the working people (and the middle class) clarified their identity and tested their relationship with other classes and strata. One of the interesting features of Guyanese political culture was the retention of a representative system even during the heyday of colonialism and planter power. As an unintended consequence of the defence of their own privileges, planters also defended the principle of an elective government responsible to a local electorate and having real power to make decisions and to carry them out. Theoretically, the political system remained open-ended. For instance, wealth was virtually coterminous with European origins as far as the planters were concerned, but white planters defended their political privileges in economic and cultural terms and seldom used justifications that were explicitly racial. Thus it was that wealthy mulattoes became members of the Court of Electors and the Combined Court under the pre-1891 Constitution.[8] The principal argument against the lowering of the franchise in the third quarter of the nineteenth century was "the ignorance of the masses."[9] Education of the brown and black middle class eroded this basis for the defense of political privilege.[10]

In the political sphere, the representative principle has a dynamic of its own. With regard to Europe, it has been observed that the liberalism which formed the basic ideology of the bourgeoisie had no theoretical defenses against the contingency of gradual mass participation in the political process.[11] In a colonial context, the only answer to potential mass participation was the abrupt and reactionary termination of the democratic trend and its replacement by Crown Colony government—as happened in Jamaica in 1865 and in British Guiana in 1928. So long as the elective principle was constitutionally protected, the masses exerted a sort of irredentist pressure on the political system. It is highly significant that the middle classes in British Guiana sought a populist alliance with the working people for most of the period under discussion. As would be expected, divergences appeared in the political class alliance after 1891. But the alliance was soon radically re-stated by the People's Association in its commitment to electoral politics. Middle-class leaders were ambivalent, but not as ambivalent as they could and did become when their own objective class interests later diverged more clearly from those of the working people.

The social situation of the early twentieth century was still fluid. In its analysis, one must utilize the terms "working class," "working people," and "the people" to refer (in that order) to entities within larger entities, among which the contradictions were not fundamental. The riots of 1905 had a two-fold bearing on the radical alliance of "the People vs. the Planters." On the one hand, spontaneous violence was testimony to the failure of struggle by other means. On the other hand, the vicious response of the colonial state renewed middle-class and working-class resolve to unite and gain access to a measure of state power through electoral politics. The elections of 1906 accelerated the removal of planters from the legislature. They were replaced by middle-class individuals who identified themselves as men of the people. In spite of their control over the Executive Council, the plantation com-panies and the colonial state viewed such developments with disquiet. Eventu-ally, they engineered the Constitutional Coup of 1928, justifying it on extra-ordinarily specious grounds.[12] In fact, what occurred by 1928 was the maturation of the political promise implicit in the 1891 Constitution, and it is only in this context that the reverses are fully comprehensible.

In 1905, spontaneity was much more evident than organization. The Guyanese working class had then a great deal of ground left to cover. Yet, almost imperceptibly, the basis was being laid both for internal consistency and for a degree of independence from other classes in the ideological, poli-tical, and industrial spheres. Besides, the historical importance of the period lies not only in its contribution to a line of development but even more to the fact that people applied themselves creatively within the limits of the local and international situation. Between 1880 and 1905, the working peo-ple of British Guiana recognized many of the possibilities for restructuring their society so as to realize their vision of betterment. They urged the pro-motion of "minor crops," the freeing of crown lands, the pursuit of hinter-land industries, the expansion of education, and the democratization of local and central government apparatuses. The working class played a part in the agitation for the above objectives. In addition, some efforts derived their impetus exclusively or primarily from the working class. It was the nascent proletarians of the estates and the towns who strove for an end to quasi-feudal labor relations and to oppressive indirect taxation. They demanded a living wage and the institution of collective bargaining. They set up Friendly Societies and craft associations. These initiatives were not entirely without success, judged by any standards and more so when evaluated in terms of the imperialist presence. These were years when international capitalism, though in crisis, broke free of restraints and completed its domination of the entire world. Imperialism extinguished the rights of subjugated peoples to make their own autonomous history. On the coastlands of British Guiana, there were no "traditional" modes of production that had to be subverted so as to be "modernized," but there was no lack of authoritarianism. Self-expression on the part of oppressed working people in that era therefore constitutes a definite historical achievement.

APPENDIX: TABLES

Contents

TABLE 1. Rainfall in Guiana, 1880-1905 (in inches)

	Jan	Feb	Mar	Apr	May	June	July	Aug	Sept	Oct	Nov	Dec	Totals
1880	11.19	13.68	8.75	1.57	11.88	10.55	2.81	4.76	.12	2.78	8.21	1.87	78.17
1881	7.24	1.10	2.81	6.67	16.03	9.39	4.53	6.32	6.08	.14	10.34	16.67	87.32
1882	7.52	1.44	8.90	7.37	16.82	10.34	9.57	5.81	1.71	6.16	6.26	13.00	94.90
1883	3.77	2.92	1.64	7.78	5.75	12.98	14.87	5.29	.86	1.49	.75	4.84	62.94
1884	9.25	10.80	3.11	3.73	13.33	11.87	7.64	4.19	.11	—	—	10.39	74.42
1885	3.27	2.98	.74	3.10	5.35	13.35	12.22	3.62	3.19	1.50	1.06	10.67	59.05
1886	7.90	6.24	2.12	2.63	13.01	11.80	9.81	8.38	4.41	1.35	11.04	20.96	99.55
1887	20.45	16.39	7.48	6.40	3.95	6.91	8.45	2.72	1.22	.52	1.12	7.67	84.28
1888	3.80	8.13	8.33	13.88	15.82	5.47	10.32	5.33	.30	.31	.90	10.80	83.39
1889	8.45	3.07	1.83	12.10	11.09	23.23	19.38	11.21	4.54	1.88	10.38	16.36	123.52
1890	25.11	14.56	2.38	20.11	17.91	13.17	10.90	5.71	3.18	.16	2.97	9.47	125.63
1891	19.14	10.09	8.42	3.06	12.17	5.14	9.07	5.57	.53	3.63	.46	32.38	109.66
1892	9.15	20.72	9.43	12.93	7.78	24.38	11.40	8.05	5.79	1.20	5.06	12.14	128.03
1893	11.73	12.91	17.18	4.39	14.72	13.68	15.50	7.74	4.80	1.13	8.49	22.97	135.24
1894	7.68	9.41	4.88	6.53	7.08	12.11	10.21	4.04	.91	2.63	10.85	9.02	85.35
1895	16.45	1.60	5.80	2.83	11.58	9.32	9.65	4.89	.45	2.98	9.73	7.28	82.56
1896	2.40	2.19	4.57	4.47	14.27	18.93	10.13	6.47	1.59	4.03	1.80	10.18	81.03
1897	1.75	2.40	2.51	3.96	12.61	14.60	13.69	6.35	4.21	8.29	16.16	7.99	94.52
1898	9.25	3.77	22.73	13.63	10.61	13.61	11.69	7.19	4.88	3.28	3.25	17.97	121.86
1899	12.60	3.21	4.05	1.24	2.13	7.30	15.48	1.96	2.36	.75	.27	1.35	52.70
1900	13.91	10.69	6.51	8.41	9.84	10.35	9.73	5.01	1.12	2.00	4.45	6.92	88.94
1901	.92	1.15	5.14	3.13	11.25	12.15	7.24	10.23	7.18	3.48	6.74	14.27	82.88
1902	12.53	6.62	17.67	6.95	6.76	10.44	9.58	6.00	3.71	2.29	6.65	5.16	94.36
1903	5.24	2.76	8.06	10.17	16.94	22.05	7.83	5.48	7.56	.02	4.18	14.14	104.43
1904	10.56	2.63	12.17	12.98	8.22	7.47	8.95	1.84	2.72	1.08	1.92	15.21	85.75
1905	3.81	5.34	4.03	4.07	11.12	10.58	7.84	4.25	4.31	2.14	3.92	15.49	77.70

SOURCE: Reports of the Botanic Gardens.

224

TABLE 2.   Public Sea Defense Expenditure, West Coast Demerara

	Length of Sea Dams (Roads)	Period of Expenditure	Amount Expended (G $)	Expenditure per road per annum (G $)
Best	1,090	1878-1888	14,685	1.34
Windsor Forest	1,665	1868-1888	220,420	6.05
La Jalousie	281	1876-1887	15,115	4.12
Blankenburg	412	1879-1887	16,738	5.07
Den Amstel and Fellowship	330	1882-1887	1,910	1.16
Hague	495	1873-1887	40,467	5.84
Cornelia Ida	250	1877-1887	35,964	8.08
Leonora	845	1874-1887	61,787	5.60

SOURCE: "Report of the Public Works Department," M.C.P., 18 April 1888.

TABLE 3.   Sugar Products—Prices and Earnings, 1880-1904 (in Guiana dollars)

	Sugar: Average price per ton[a]	Sugar: Earnings[b]	Byproducts		Total Earnings
			Rum	Molasses	
1880	102.03	9.996,566	886,776	357,019	11,210,361
1881	104.99	9,692,443	1,361,866	360,672	11,415,181
1882	100.77	12,505,848	1,431,950	381,322	14,319,120
1883	107.26	12,510,859	1,272,730	500,347	14,283,936
1884	69.02	8,750,251	1,202,400	231,370	10,184,021
1885	69.20	6,647,251	992,366	165,792	7,805,409
1886	62.56	6,997,152	737,261	267,662	7,734,431
1887	64.01	8,633,458	670,387	212,203	9,516,047
1888	71.77	7,760,112	446,966	353,299	8,560,377
1889	79.49	9,187,886	796,099	316,925	10,302,910
1890	65.40	6,898,642	1,060,008	378,158	8,336,808
1891	68.23	7,981,157	1,281,432	212,421	9,475,080
1892	66.76	7,535,866	971,011	147,072	8,653,949
1893	69.86	7,528,896	583,603	175,800	8,288,299
1894	58.39	5,985,091	469,349	99,115	6,553,555
1895	49.64	5,021,568	581,496	76,731	5,679,795
1896	49.24	5,272,310	657,250	100,445	6,030,005
1897	48.72	4,912,910	636,408	47,136	5,596,454
1898	51.70	4,996,714	694,613	57,442	5,748,769
1899	62.38	5,288,419	1,000,282	96,442	6,385,143
1900	57.12	5,411,794	1,437,082	59,381	6,908,251
1901	47.15	4,983,182	772,061	21,134	5,776,377
1902	41.64	5,001,710	651,216	50,381	5,703,307
1903	42.73	5,381,486	489,221	43,776	5,914,483
1904	57.83	6,170,861	301,027	71,938	6,543,826

[a]Derived by calculation from Blue Books, "Exports."
[b]Given in £ sterling until 1896.
SOURCE: Blue Books, "Exports."

TABLE 4.   Plantation Sugar Production and Exports, 1880-1905

	No. of Estates in Cultivation	Estate Acreages[a] Cultivated (canes)	Uncultivated	Export Tonnages of Sugar[b]	Exports of byproducts Rum (100 gals.)	Molasses (100 gals.)
1880	113	76,930	64,951	97,683	24,633	17,001
1881	109	77,959	62,571	92,323	23,480	15,028
1882	106	79,263	62,617	124,102	29,209	17,120
1883	104	79,038	62,159	116,636	26,470	20,214
1884	105	79,502	64,379	125,321	33,400	12,854
1885	105	75,344	70,801	96,058	28,353	10,362
1886	105	76,203	76,731	111,855	24,773	20,001
1887	97	76,570	76,832	134,874	24,829	19,066
1888	96	76,625	76,581	108,122	14,073	26,604
1889	96	78,272	77,156	115,587	18,093	22,782
1890	95	79,243	78,111	105,484	20,495	23,115
1891	96	78,308	88,149	116,969	22,101	13,989
1892	79	76,101	87,581	112,880	25,791	10,176
1893	74	69,814	89,323	107,771	19,946	12,027
1894	70	68,392	88,227	102,502	18,925	13,180
1895	65	67,921	87,307	101,159	22,618	7,379
1896	63	66,908	85,288	107,073	32,912	9,132
1897	63	66,582	84,349	100,839	31,044	4,714
1898	60	66,582	84,349	96,468	27,240	5,745
1899	57	67,144	87,359	84,783	33,344	3,857
1900	57	67,144	87,359	94,745	40,238	2,310
1901	52	71,221	85,279	105,694	41,225	1,243
1902	51	73,193	82,913	120,127	42,786	3,314
1903	51	75,105	80,300	125,949	39,499	2,915
1904	46	70,880	82,091	106,716	26,716	2,915
1905	45	72,891	79,025	116,550	– – –	– – –

[a]"Cultivated" and "Uncultivated" acreages, along with a few thousand acres of plantains, constituted the total empolder under estate control.

[b]The Blue Book figures are given in hogsheads between 1880 and 1891. They are here converted at 1 hhd = 0.9 tons.

SOURCE: Blue Books: "Agriculture," "Return of Produce."

TABLE 5.   Sugar Production, Earnings and Costs, Colonial Company, 1883-1895 (per ton, in Guiana dollars)

	Earnings	Net Cost[a]	Factory Costs[b]	Net Proceeds Byproducts
1883	86.20	77.18	47.00	12.78
1884	69.86	69.98	42.48	15.34
1885	66.14	66.78	39.28	9.52
1886	58.12	55.24	29.64	6.92
1887	71.32	63.22	33.72	8.80
1888	76.50	58.54	31.02	10.26
1889	64.88	63.52	35.50	13.04
1890	66.62	58.22	28.44	13.68
1891	67.42	54.86	24.86	10.74
1892	70.02	55.98	24.84	8.02
1893	61.02	64.12	27.96	7.38
1894	46.38	43.04	23.70	8.02
1895	52.76	42.18	22.26	6.24

[a]Production overheads on this company's estates were high. Compare the figures of Andrew Hunter given to the Commission.

[b]Factory costs per ton and the cost of cultivation were separated into their component parts for selected years 1893-1895. See table 6.

SOURCE: "Report of the West India Royal Commission," 1898, #29.

TABLE 6. Costs of Cultivation and Manufacture, Colonial Company (per ton, in Guiana dollars)

					Machinery		Sea		
Cultivation									
	Salaries	Labor	Manures	Immigration	Fuel	Hospital	Defense	Total	
1893	3.88	25.58	4.46	2.44	1.52	1.26	0.02	39.16	
1894	4.08	26.78	5.60	2.96	2.78	1.30	0.04	43.54	
1895	3.74	19.52	3.32	0.62	0.80	1.08	– –	28.36	

						Labor and	Salaries				
Manufacture											
	Fuel	Supplies	Packages	Insurance	Drogherage	Immigration	and Board	Interest	Machinery	Other	Total
1893	1.80	3.80	3.96	.30	2.08	8.08	2.62	0.58	1.02	0.58	24.82
1894	2.44	4.30	3.84	.26	2.12	9.10	2.74	.56	2.20	.40	27.96
1895	2.12	2.96	3.54	.26	1.74	6.18	2.66	.56	2.34	.34	22.70

SOURCE: "Report of the West India Royal Commission," 1898.

TABLE 7.   Main Destinations of Sugar Exports, 1880-1905 (by value in Guiana dollars)

	United Kingdom	United States	Canada
1880	7,823,818	2,655,649	254,690
1881	8,201,915	2,263,003	223,612
1882	9,031,660	4,348,039	330,353
1883	7,370,664	5,775,712	447,246
1884	8,354,747	1,339,176	162,373
1885	5,996,251	1,466,300	92,038
1886	7,872,758	2,691,255	153,031
1887	5,163,381	3,885,223	192,469
1888	4,368,057	3,689,000	137,061
1889	5,501,705	4,217,994	189,652
1890	3,218,671	4,553,439	184,405
1891	3,684,239	5,316,509	211,952
1892	3,473,448	4,680,981	51,569
1893	3,308,676	4,304,479	469,841
1894	3,435,684	2,847,213	125,617
1895	2,223,132	3,150,555	207,425
1896	2,051,245	3,726,183	93,157
1897	2,055,689	3,371,323	79,160
1898	1,538,059	4,064,290	33,786
1899	2,195,632	3,995,844	70,586
1900	2,409,520	4,243,706	158,492
1901	1,508,196	3,842,431	372,863
1902	1,319,508	3,730,675	584,142
1903	1,014,268	1,938,731	2,901,306
1904	1,288,101	2,570,848	2,567,600
1905	1,811,116	1,424,372	3,122,347

NOTE: Export to other countries never exceeded 10%. The percentage of exports to the three main markets moved as followed: United Kingdom, 64.5% in 1880-82 to 38.2% in 1904; United States, 24.1% in 1880-82 to 27.4% in 1904; and Canada, 2.6% in 1880-82 to 27.0% in 1904. (See Alan H. Adamson, *Sugar Without Slaves* [New Haven: Yale University Press, 1972], table 27, p. 217.)

SOURCE: Blue Books, "General Exports."

TABLE 8.   Demographic Characteristics of the Work Force (Sex, Age, Residence)

	1881	1891	1911
Total Population	252,186	278,328	296,041
Males	140,134	151,759	153,717
Females	112,052	126,569	142,324
Ages 15-40	123,836	130,120	132,776
Ages 15-70	180,630	186,306	195,785
Rural	196,887	216,249	229,860
Urban	55,299	62,079	66,181
Georgetown	47,175	53,176	57,577
Essequibo	45,582	53,254	54,583
Demerara	159,443	173,898	175,596
Berbice	47,161	51,176	65,862
Sugar estates	84,234	90,492	70,922
Villages[a]	112,553	125,757	158,938
Hinterland settlements	11,732	21,834	26,943

[a]Villages and settlements are combined as one category in the census enumeration. The figures above separate the hinterland settlements.

SOURCE: Decennial Census, 1881, 1891, 1911.

TABLE 9.   Indentured and Time-Expired Indian Immigrants Resident in Guiana, 1880-1905

| | Estate Residents | | | | Non-Estate | |
	Indentured Adults	Unindentured Adults	Children	Total	Residents	Total
1880	22,562	25,766	12,500[a]	60,828	25,379	86,207
1881	22,752	26,979	12,500[a]	62,231	25,757	87,988
1882	21,566	28,050	12,651	62,267	27,522	89,789
1883	16,479	32,423	12,917	61,819	29,296	91,115
1884	15,251	32,637	13,287	61,175	31,503	92,678
1885	17,257	34,938	14,935	67,130	30,516	97,646
1886	17,144	35,602	16,013	68,759	31,522	100,281
1887	17,770	36,259	16,798	70,827	31,919	102,746
1888	18,243	37,241	17,900	73,384	30,465	103,849
1889	17,283	39,106	18,643	75,032	31,204	106,236
1890	15,567	39,320	17,939	72,826	34,598	107,424
1891	16,710	38,356	17,750	72,816	35,668	108,484
1892	17,339	37,032	16,640	71,011	38,662	109,673
1893	18,181	35,064	15,709	68,954	41,092	110,046
1894[b]	– – –	– – –	– – –	– – –	– – –	– – –
1895	20,480	35,158	16,139	71,777	43,972	115,749
1896	17,847	35,935	15,692	69,474	47,296	116,770
1897	15,066	35,677	15,936	66,679	49,954	116,633
1898	12,981	34,369	15,815	63,165	53,769	116,934
1899	11,169	38,080	16,365	65,614	54,729	120,343
1900	13,067	38,476	17,246	68,789	57,086	125,875
1901	14,609	39,565	18,518	72,692	57,649	130,341
1902	15,027	39,109	18,329	72,645	58,111	130,756
1903	15,024	39,456	18,312	72,792	48,733	131,525
1904	12,539	39,855	18,333	70,927	60,642	131,569
1905	11,385	39,995	19,263	70,643	62,347	132,990

[a]Approximation.
[b]Figures not available.
SOURCE: Annual Reports of the Immigration Agent-General.

TABLE 10.   Average Rate of Daily Wages for Estate Labor, 1880-1905
(in cents)

	1880-1884	1885-1895	1896-1905
Praedial			
Canecutters	40- 80	48- 96	36-84
Shovelmen	40- 60	24- 48	24-48
Weeders	24- 32	20- 32	20-36
Suppliers	32- 60	36- 60	24-48
Puntmen	36- 60	32- 48	24-48
Porters	– – –	32- 48	32-48
Factory			
Cane throwers	32- 40	24- 32	28-40[a]
Boilermen	48- 56	36- 48	32-60[a]
Firemen	48- 80	36- 48	32-60
Sugar curers	40- 54	48- 72	40-60
Boxmen	32- 40	40- 48	36-48
Megass carriers	20- 24	28- 32	24-36
Clarifiers (headmen)	48	72- 84	48-60
Clarifiers (other than headmen)	20- 24	32- 44	24-36
Distillers	32- 48	32-100	– – –
Other building hands	24- 32	16- 36	16-36
Tradesmen			
Engineers	96-200	– – –	48-96
Carpenters	80-120	– – –	48-96
Masons	80-120	– – –	60-96
Coopers	120-152	– – –	60-96

[a]From 1902.
SOURCE: Blue Books, "Agriculture."

TABLE 11.   Summary Convictions, 1881-1905

	Against the Person	Praedial Larceny	Against Property	Masters & Servants	Total[a]
1881	4,097	271	1,244	1,196	13,065
1882	3,472	106	1,128	3,495	13,694
1883	3,849	152	1,068	3,083	12,260
1884	3,703	163	1,144	2,605	11,617
1885	2,692	626	1,562	1,914	12,430
1886	2,610	169	1,039	1,839	11,245
1887	2,441	284	935	1,933	10,389
1888	2,931	391	936	2,246	11,191
1889	2,801	276	1,132	2,079	11,273
1890	2,603	182	924	2,807	12,121
1891	2,523	383	1,157	3,373	13,231
1892	2,300	196	1,763	3,235	12,462
1893	2,083	145	826	3,227	11,500
1894	2,595	165	1,123	3,055	13,299
1895	2,035	303	1,179	3,132	12,425
1896	1,865	312	969	2,675	11,597
1897	1,644	204	1,152	2,538	11,541
1898	1,880	305	1,375	2,833	12,943
1899	2,069	405	1,141	2,376	11,001
1900	2,090	329	1,191	1,964	10,773
1901	1,822	147	1,010	1,873	9,857
1902	1,933	181	909	2,918	10,509
1903	2,164	206	846	2,909	10.012
1904	2,236	379	1,348	3,307	12,975
1905	2,141	231	1,026	2,356	12,926

[a]The total includes convictions other than those named in the table.
SOURCE: Blue Books, "Criminal Statistics."

TABLE 12.   Disposal of Cases under the Masters and Servants Act, 1881-1905

	Discharged	Dismissed	Convicted	Fined	Imprisoned
1881	1,926	382	2,981	1,196	1,780
1882	2,891	310	3,495	1,689	1,805
1883	2,520	277	3,083	1,536	1,504
1884	2,289	310	2,605	1,440	1,161
1885	1,374	228	1,914	681	1,230
1886	1,280	202	1,839	734	1,099
1887	1,457	236	1,933	673	1,243
1888	1,280	454	2,246	725	1,518
1889	1,744	248	2,079	806	1,273
1890	2,692	304	2,808	1,144	1,663
1891	2,200	281	3,373	1,091	1,280
1892	2,560	406	3,256	1,168	2,067
1893	3,040	278	3,219	981	2,242
1894	2,847	182	3,265	1,190	1,857
1895	2,105	266	3,133	595	2,526
1896	1,896	270	2,675	592	2,068
1897	2,174	206	2,578	575	1,955
1898	3,011	192	2,835	623	2,161
1899	2,155	172	2,101	635	1,722
1900	2,293	140	1,967	470	1,472
1901	2,494	103	1,913	468	1,385
1902	3,233	142	2,912	543	2,345
1903	3,472	166	2,921	499	2,356
1904	3,716	157	3,308	1,190	2,049
1905	3,107	157	2,666	622	1,641

NOTE: The majority of those charged were indentured immigrants. The Immigration Agent-General also kept records of all complaints brought against immigrants, for which see table 19.

SOURCE: Blue Books, "Criminal Statistics."

TABLE 13.   Summary Proceedings against Indentured Immigrants, 1880-1905

	Population	Complaints	Withdrawn	Struck out	Dismissed	Convicted	% information to population
1880	22,718	3,990	698	336	344	2,612	17.6
1881	22,879	4,256	963	412	337	2,544	18.6
1882	21,624	5,059	1,125	777	282	2,875	23.4
1883	16,479	4,054	936	511	247	2,360	24.6
1884	15,251	3,484	785	417	343	1,939	22.8
1885	17,257	2,620	520	294	258	1,548	15.1
1886	17,144	2,610	526	286	246	1,552	15.2
1887	17,770	2,848	588	295	298	1,667	16.0
1888	18,243	3,376	730	300	301	2,045	18.5
1889	17,283	3,055	762	324	271	1,698	17.7
1890	15,567	3,732	952	359	342	2,078	24
1891	16,710	3,911	916	337	263	2,395	23.4
1892	17,339	3,755	1,024	445	252	2,034	21.7
1893	18,181	3,975	1,095	436	205	2,239	21.9
1894	22,370	5,231	1,661	501	214	2,855	23.4
1895	20,480	4,255	1,184	223	250	2,558	20.8
1896	17,847	3,474	943	230	237	2,064	19.5
1897	15,066	3,943	1,114	149	179	3,051	26.2
1898	12,981	3,872	1,302	263	186	2,121	29.8
1899	11,169	2,727	876	211	140	1,500	24.4
1900	13,067	2,531	751	212	182	1,386	19.4
1901	14,609	3,423	1,094	221	186	1,922	23.4
1902	15,027	4,453	1,448	379	88	2,498	29.6
1903	15,024	4,666	1,774	318	76	2,498	31.1
1904	12,539	5,012	2,046	357	96	2,513	33.6
1905	11,385	3,926	1,774	269	69	1,844	34.4

SOURCE: Annual Reports of the Immigration Agent-General.

TABLE 14.   The Village Economy: Village Lands—Original Prices and Value, 1896
(Selected Villages, Demerara and Essequibo)

	Transported in	No. of original proprietors	Price paid (G$)	Appraised value 1896 (G$)	Population	
					1881	1891
Plaisance	1839	101	39,000	131,835	4,002	3,187
Buxton and Friendship	1841-42	298	130,000	229,550	5,293	5,239
Beterverwagting	1841	-	22,000	78,647	1,980	2,147
Victoria	-	-	1,000	66,094	2,644	2,897
Golden Grove and Nabaclis	1848-50	-	7,200	69,404	1,326	1,405
Ann's Grove and Two Friends	1849	-	17,800	63,015	1,306	1,409
Good Intent and Sisters	1854	109	9,400	47,019	912	1,150
Bagotville	1843	-	22,500	45,792	1,990	2,403
Stanleytown	-	-	10,000	25,850	1,032	1,168
Den Amstel and Fellowship	-	-	27,000	89,462	2,393	2,357
Queenstown	-	-	22,000	98,759	1,924	2,096
Danielstown	-	-	16,000	35,254	1,220	1,130
Craig	-	-	-	11,608	395	395
Totals			332,900	992,289	26,417	26,983

SOURCE: "Report of the West India Royal Commission," 1897, Appendix C, Part 2, "British Guiana", #164.

TABLE 15.   The Village Economy: Cultivated Areas of Villages in Essequibo, Demerara, and Berbice, 1886

	Acreages	Peasant Cane	Mixed
Essequibo	3,047	40	3,007[a]
Demerara	5,847	758	5,089
Berbice	3,939	15	3,915[b]
Total Colony	12,833	813	12,020

[a]Includes rice, plantains, cassava, and fruit.
[b]Includes arrowroot.
SOURCE: "Report of the Crown Surveyor", M.C.P., 5 May 1887.

TABLE 16.   The Village Economy: Economic Census of the Villages, 1902

County	Number of Villages Sampled	Total Acreage	Number of Proprietors	Population in 1891	Value of House Property (G$)	Land Available for Extending Villages (acres)[a]
Essequibo	52	5,236	2,540	17,918	195,772	1,630
Demerara	66	27,519	5,927	45,676	841,852	3,966
Berbice	96	44,479	5,502	23,341	269,932	15,671
Total	214	77,234	13,969	86,935	1,307,556	20,267

[a]Crown land available for second and extra depths.
SOURCE: "Digest of Economic Census taken in the Villages in 1902." See A. M. Ashmore, *Memorandum on the Subject of Village Administration* (Georgetown, 1903).

TABLE 17.   Occupations (Working Adults, 15-70), 1881-1911

		1881	1891	1911
Public service	Males	1,102	1,574	1,682
	Females	31	71	252
Clergy, learned professions,	Males	722	910	1,396
& teachers	Females	347	509	1,099
Merchants, shopkeepers,	Males	2,015	2,166	2,095
& agents	Females	231	386	400
Clerks & shop assistants	Males	1,492	2,292	2,658
	Females	29	213	503
Landed proprietors, agricul-	Males	1,854	2,322	5,343
turalists, & cattle farmers	Females	225	557	2,291
Agricultural laborers	Males	63,253	59,102	50,970
	Females	28,515	37,041	35,160
Woodcutters & other	Males	3,137	6,506	6,417
laborers; gold seekers	Females	488	27	87
Mechanics & artisans	Males	9,546	9,944	10,520
	Females	0	3,749[a]	7,219
Domestics	Males	2,736	2,747	2,673
	Females	9,643	14,958	24,723
Various (including boatmen	Males	7,274	12,930	14,040
& seamen)	Females	13,780	11,150	3,824

[a]Apparently includes seamstresses.
SOURCE: Decennial Census, 1881, 1891, 1811.

TABLE 18. The Non-Plantation Sector, 1880-1904

	Gold		Timber		Balata		Total Value of All Minor Products[a]	Total Value of Exports
	Quantity (ozs.)	Value (G$)	Quantity (cu. ft.)	Value (G$)	Quantity (cu. ft.)	Value (G$)	Value (G$)	Value (G$)
1880	— —	— —	294,496	76,565	46,606	— —	1,354,235	12,564,596
1881	— —	— —	113,313	23,794	93,578	22,028	1,051,816	12,466,997
1882	— —	— —	536,425	160,925	104,262	27,906	1,082,309	15,401,429
1883	— —	— —	206,833	65,741	78,378	19,949	941,717	15,225,653
1884	250	4,894	208,983	64,340	47,295	18,010	961,733	11,145,754
1885	939	15,596	387,889	125,084	55,521	10,138	838,537	8,643,946
1886	6,518	112,042	222,968	68,185	67,828	14,300	1,109,977	8,844,408
1887	11,906	213,252	222,217	53,751	80,942	16,791	998,794	10,514,841
1888	14,507	226,718	197,531	65,266	248,484	67,580	1,158,342	9,718,719
1889	28,282	524,325	296,151	91,095	363,480	75,807	1,558,846	11,861,756
1890	62,615	1,124,756	332,115	114,101	226,809	87,572	2,039,789	10,376,597
1891	101,298	1,801,388	312,801	96,327	116,337	75,869	2,681,180	12,156,260
1892	133,146	2,366,098	325,863	104,789	237,405	98,905	3,025,473	11,679,422
1893	137,629	2,454,538	234,870	74,343	205,195	40,105	3,034,508	11,322,807
1894	134,046	2,402,141	238,993	81,529	209,095	49,028	3,237,970	9,791,525
1895	122,057	2,135,953	175,520	63,889	159,524	55,119	2,813,806	8,493,601
1896	126,107	2,237,487	404,234	148,609	325,905	98,617	3,088,320	9,118,325
1897	124,327	2,177,866	283,634	93,173	490,443	147,898	2,965,614	8,562,068
1898	112,464	1,989,346	250,463	81,044	468,569	135,135	2,774,548	8,523,317
1899	112,823	1,990,210	170,632	53,924	237,824	58,949	2,869,066	9,254,209
1900	108,522	1,886,804	287,640	87,375	425,371	94,009	3,020,098	9,928,349
1901	101,709	1,783,172	313,571	89,689	387,576	113,535	3,025,019	8,801,396
1902	102,363	1,789,585	340,260	111,764	540,800	195,058	3,079,489	8,782,796
1903	90,207	1,572,130	273,542	93,956	531,399	216,893	2,773,700	8,688,183
1904	94,617	1,690,201	293,315	117,289	501,509	252,529	3,013,205	9,557,031

[a]This includes wallaba, shingles, charcoal, coconuts, coffee, gum, and corn.
SOURCE: Blue Books; *British Guiana Directory*, 1906.

238

TABLE 19. Registered Electors, 1881-1905

	Demerara (excluding G'town)	Georgetown	Essequibo	Berbice (excluding N.A.)	New Amsterdam	Total
1881	123	467	284	48	79	1,001
1882	124	450	281	88	98	1,041
1883	137	615	273	89	96	1,210
1884	139	634	364	85	84	1,306
1885	139	621	370	90	91	1,311
1886	144	644	263	90	92	1,233
1887	235	729	258	100	96	1,418
1888	241	725	277	106	114	1,463
1889	264	740	367	122	103	1,596
1890	643	762	330	122	116	1,973
1891	626	824	272	178	146	2,046
1892	981	830	264	170	130	2,375
1893	995	830	271	173	119	2,388
1894	999	834	301	177	168	2,479
1895	972	808	331	157	148	2,416
1896	932	1,002	326	233	263	2,756
1897	982	1,032	356	292	266	2,928
1898	970	992	335	274	244	2,815
1899	923	1,026	323	271	235	2,778
1900	778	920	277	253	199	2,427
1901	893	989	308	291	195	2,676
1902	910	1,208	351	266	173	2,908
1903	945	1,232	410	343	175	3,105
1904	954	1,231	391	331	160	3,067
1905	1,017	1,241	408	342	177	3,185

SOURCE: Blue Books, "Political Franchise."

TABLE 20.   Ethnic Composition of the Population

| | | 1881 | | |
	Immigrants	Locally born	Total in each race group	% of total
Amerindians	– –	7,708	7,708	3.06
Europeans	1,617	– –	1,617	0.64
Portuguese	6,879	5,047	11,926	4.73
Africans	5,077	– –	5,077	2.01
Blacks[a]	– –	– –	– –	– –
Indians	65,161	14,768	79,929	31.69
Chinese	4,393	841	5,234	2.08
Mixed Races[d]	– –	– –	– –	– –
West Indian Born	18,318	– –	18,318	7.26
Others	1,102	– –	1,102	0.44
Total	102,547	149,639	252,186	

| | | 1891 | | |
	Immigrants	Locally born	Total in each race group	% of total
Amerindians	– –	7,463	7,463	2.68
Europeans	2,533	2,025	4,558	1.64
Portuguese	5,378	6,788	12,166	4.37
Africans	3,433	– –	3,433	1.23
Blacks[a]	– –	96,182[b]	96,182	34.55
Indians	73,031	32,432	105,463	37.89
Chinese	2,475	1,239	3,714	1.33
Mixed Races[d]	5,052	23,977	29,376	10.55
West Indian Born	15,973	– –	15,973	5.74
Others	– –	– –	– –	– –
Total	108,222	170,106	278,328	

| | | 1911 | | |
	Immigrants	Locally born	Total in each race group	% of total
Amerindians	– –	6,901	6,901	2.33
Europeans	1,730	2,207	3,937	1.33
Portuguese	1,908	8,176	10,084	3.4
Africans	1,114	– –	1,114	.38
Blacks[a]	– –	102,104[c]	102,104	34.47
Indians	59,849	66,668	126,517	42.74
Chinese	634	1,988	2,622	.89
Mixed Races[d]	– –	30,494	30,494	10.3
West Indian Born	12,268	– –	12,268	4.14
Others	– –	– –	– –	– –
Total	77,503	218,538	296,041	

[a]Blacks and Mixed Races together number 121,275 in 1881.

[b]The number of "Blacks" is given as 112,155 in 1891 but for locally born "Africans" the figure is 96,182.

[c]In 1911, the confusion in nomenclature obscures difference between locally born blacks and West Indian arrivals.

[d]"Mixed Races" includes those whose race was not stated.

SOURCE: Decennial Census, 1881, 1891, 1911.

TABLE 21.   Post-Emancipation Immigration to 1880

	Indians	Portuguese	West Indians	Africans	Chinese	Others	Total
1835-1840	396[a]	429[b]	8,092	91	– –	278	9,286
1841-1850	11,841	16,908	4,806	10,528	– –	– –	44,083
1851-1860	22,381	10,406	– –	1,965	6,665	21	42,438
1861-1870	38,717	1,533	10,180	1,476[c]	5,975	– –	57,881
1871-1880	53,327	2,170	12,887	– –	903	– –	69,281
1835-1880	127,662	61,157	35,865	14,060	13,543	299	222,969

[a]Single shipment in 1838. Resumed in 1845.
[b]Single Shipment in 1835. Resumed in 1841.
[c]Last shipment in 1867.
SOURCES: G.W. Roberts and M.A. Johnson, "Factors involved in immigration and movements in the working force of British Guiana in the 19th Century," *Social and Economic Studies*, Vol. 23, No. 1 (March 1974), 69-83.
G.W. Roberts, "Immigration of Africans into the British Caribbean," *Population* Studies, Vol. 7, No. 3 (1954), 235-62.
Dwarka Nath, *A History of Indians in British Guiana* (London, 1950).

TABLE 22.   Repatriation, 1838-1880

	Indians	Africans
1838-1840	– –	– –
1841-1850	482	⎰ 4,998
1851-1860	3,883	⎱
1861-1870	2,581	1,794
1871-1880	8,889	– –

SOURCES: G. W. Roberts, "Immigration of Africans into the British Caribbean," *Population Studies*, Vol. 7, No. 3 (1954): 235-62.
G.W. Roberts and J. Byrne, "Summary Statistics on Indenture and Associated Migration Affecting the West Indies," *Population Studies* 20, no. 1 (1966).

NOTES

———

Abbreviations

C.O.	Colonial Office
GD	Governors' Despatches (also Guyana Despatches)
G.N.A.	Guyana National Archives
L.M.S.	London Missionary Society
M.C.C.	Minutes of the Combined Court
M.C.P.	Minutes of the Court of Policy
M.M.S.	Methodist Missionary Society
P.R.O.	Public Record Office
Pln(s)	Plantation(s)
U.S.P.G.	United Society for the Propagation of the Gospel

Chapter 1

1. See remarks of the registrar-general accompanying "Results of the Decennial Census of the Population of British Guiana, taken on the 3rd April, 1881."

2. James Rodway, *History of British Guiana* (Georgetown, 1891), 1:1.

3. For a summary of present understanding among geographers, see S. Naraine, "Some Aspects of Coastal Development in Guyana," mimeographed, University of Guyana and Guyana National Archives, 1972; and Michael T. Wagner, "Structural Pluralism and the Portuguese in Nineteenth Century British Guiana: A Study in Historical Georgraphy" (Ph.D., diss., McGill University, 1975).

4. See, e.g., Beryl Richardson, *Sugar in Guyana* (London, 1969), p. 7.

5. *Report of Commission of Enquiry into the Sugar Industry of British Guiana*, London, 1949.

6. Henry Dalton, *History of British Guiana* (London, 1855), 1:484.

7. The *Argosy*, 5 December 1885.

8. For comments forwarded to the Colonial Office, see G.N.A., GD 244, 28 August 1899 (C.O. 111/513); and C.O. 111/528, letter from H. Davson, 13 March 1900.

9. L.M.S. Archives, British Guiana–Berbice, incoming letters, S. M. France from New Amsterdam, 2 March 1887.

10. M.C.C., 18 April 1879. As was often the case, planters calculated their costs in pounds sterling. The conversion rate was $4.80 to £1.00.

11. Walter Rodney, ed., *Guyanese Sugar Plantations in the Late Nineteenth Century: A Contemporary Description from the "Argosy"* (Georgetown, 1979), p. 52; and the *Chronicle*, 3 January 1883. (Hogsheads varied in size, but for freight purposes, a hogshead was equivalent to 9/10th of an English long ton of 2,240 lbs.)

12. G.N.A., GD 210, 9 July 1909 (C.O. 11/565).

13. William Russell, "Land Titles," *Timehri* 5 (1866).

14. The *Argosy*, 2 November 1884.

15. The *Chronicle*, 5 January 1902.

16. M.C.P., 27 October 1882.

17. Some of the letters and reports of Baron Siccama are to be found in G.N.A., "Drainage and Irrigation Boxes."

18. See, e.g., Gerald Case, "Report on the West Coast Demerara," Combined Court Paper no. 871 of 1916.

19. "Report of the Inspector of Villages," 1886; and G.N.A., GD 366, 25 September 1901 (C.P. 111/528). Oral informants also consistently affirmed this.

20. M.C.P., January-March 1880, 27 October 1882, 10 April 1883, and January-March 1887. See also the *Chronicle*, 7 April 1883.

21. G.N.A., GD 88, 5 April 1893 (C.O. 111/467).

22. C.O. 111/598, letter of 5 December 1914.

23. See, e.g., C.O. 111/466, West India Association of Liverpool, 24 May 1892.

24. G.N.A., GD 273, 17 August 1895 (C.O. 111/479), and GD 316, 27 September 1898 (C.). 111/505).

25. G.N.A., GD 285, 30 October 1882 (C.O. 111/425).

26. One of the major economic proposals of the late 1870s was the project for continuing the Demerara railway from Mahaica to Rosignol. Villagers of West Berbice clamored for this service. A planter resolution of 1879 opposed this extension and gratuitously reproached the villagers for their "slothfulness," See M.C.C., 18 April 1879.

27. The *Chronicle*, 21 March 1883.

28. M.C.P., 18 March 1884.

29. M.C.C., 18 April 1879.

30. The *Creole*, 3 March 1882.

31. M.C.P., 22 March 1887, report by William Russell and Arthur Braud.

32. M.C.P., 19 June 1882.

33. Frederick Engels, *Socialism, Utopian and Scientific* (New York: International Publishers, 1972), pp. 63, 64.

34. For a succinct account of international trade during the period, see Samuel D. Saul, *Studies in British Overseas Trade, 1870-1914* (Liverpool, 1960).

35. K. Wicksell, *Interest and Prices*, translated (New York, 1965).

36. M.C.C., 18 April 1879.

37. For a comprehensive treatment, see R. W. Beachey, *The British West Indian Sugar Industry in the Late Nineteeth Century* (Oxford, 1957).

38. Booker Brothers, McConnell & Co., Ltd., *Bookers Sugar* (London, 1954), p. 8.

39. A. Caldecott, "The Causes of the Commercial Depression," *West Indian Quarterly* 3 (1887).

40. John Burnett, *A History of the Cost of Living* (London, 1969), pp. 204, 214.

41. J. A. Watson, *A Hundred Years of Sugar Refining: The Story of Love Lane Refinery, 1872-1972* (Liverpool: Tate & Lyle, 1973), p. 78.

42. For this, the accepted view within the Colonial Office, see C.O. 111/480, no. 19191 and GD 341, 14 October 1895. See also Noel Deerr, *The History of Sugar*, 2 vols. (London, 1951) 2: 507.

43. The *International Sugar Journal* 2, no. 19 (1900): 440. (Earlier correspondence to this effect is found in P.R.O., C.O. 884, vol. 5, West Indies no. 82, Clarke, Nicholls & Coombs, 31 March 1898.)

44. See the annual Blue Books for this period; and Beachey, *British West Indian Sugar Industry*, pp. 41-44.

45. N. Lubbock, "Diffusion Compared with Double Crushing," *Timehri*, n.s. 4 (1890).

46. Sandbach Parker Papers, G. R. Sandbach, 24 January 1885.

47. During the seven years from April 1892 to March 1899, the average annual value of machinery imported was $217,985. This rose during the next seven years to $300,847. See C.O. 111/555, GD 90, 27 March 1907. For machinery imports between January 1883 and March 1899, see the *International Sugar Journal* 2, no. 19 (1900).

48. West Indian Royal Commission, 1897; evidence of William Douglas, Engineer of Pln. Diamond.

49. Rodney, *Guyanese Sugar Plantations.*

50. G.N.A., GD 30, 24 January 1895 (C.O. 111/476).

51. See, e.g., C.O. 111/525, letters of Duncan (12 October 1898) and Campbell (9 March 1900).

52. The *Argosy*, 26 June 1886.

53. Ethel M. Hogg, *Quintin Hogg: A Biography* (London, 1904), p. 335.

54. On the decline of the West Indian share of world production and trade, see W. Arthur Lewis, *Aspects of Tropical Trade, 1883-1965* (Stockholm, 1969).

55. See, e.g., C.O. 111/539, nos. 40252, 28770, and 29434 (Board of Trade correspondence, 1904). Two relevant enclosures are (1) "Demerara Sugar: Report of a Case under the Food and Drugs Act, Tunstall, 8 November 1894"; and (2) "Report of a Prosecution at Tredegar under the Sale of Food and Drugs Act for selling dyed sugar as 'Demerara,'" 15 January 1901.

56. Of the numerous references to this subject, see especially M.C.P., 29 April 1880, 1 November 1880. An important American court case was reviewed in the *Baltimore Sun*, 17 July 1880 (and extracted in the M.C.P., August 1880). An English case on the "Dark Sugars Question" was resolved by the House of Lords on appeal—for which, see the *Chronicle*, 4 Janaury 1883.

57. G.N.A., GD 16, 14 January 1891 (C.O. 111/459); and GD 426, 427, 30 December 1891 (C.O. 111/461).

58. C.O. 884, vol. 8, West Indies no. 137, "West Indian Commercial Relations with Canada and the United States" (1904).

59. C.O. 884, vol. 10, West Indies no. 168, "Canada-West Indies Trade Relations" (January 1910).

60. C.O. 11/555, GD 90, 27 March 1907.

Chapter 2

1. This aspect of the ending of slavery is not fully developed in Guyanese and Caribbean historiography. For a general reference, see Eric Williams, *Capitalism and Slavery* (London, 1964), pp. 201-8. With regard to Guyana, see F. R. Augier and F. C. Gordon, *Sources of West Indian History* (london, 1962), p. 184—"A Protector of Slaves declares the need for emancipation to avert further rebellion."

2. Karl Marx, *Capital* (New York: International Publishers, 1967), vol. 1, pt. 2, p. 169.

3. Considerable discussion has centered around the essential characteristics and the preferred nomenclature for the mode of production in which slavery, capitalism, and colonialism were juxtaposed. For an anlysis of direct relevance to Guyana, see Clive Y. Thomas, *Plantations, Peasants and State: A Study of the Modes of Sugar Production in Guyana* (Georgetown: Institute of Development Studies, University of Guyana; Geneva: International Labour Office, 1979).

4. Dwarka Nath, *A History of Indians in British Guiana* (London, 1950), p. 16.

5. Allan Young, *The Approaches to Local Self-Government in British Guiana* (London, 1958), p. 16. See also P. McLewin, *Power and Economic Change: The Res-*

ponse to Emancipation in Jamaica and British Guiana, Ph.D. diss., Cornell University, 1971 (Ann Arbor, Mich.: University Microfilms, 1977).

6. "Report from the Select Committee on Ceylon and British Guiana," *Parliamentary Papers*, vol. II, 1849.

7. Dwarka Nath, *Indians in British Guiana*, table 1. See also G. W. Roberts and J. Byrne, "Summary Statistics on Indenture and Associated Migration Affecting the West Indies, 1834-1918," *Population Studies* 20, no. 1 (1966), table 2.

8. Blue Book, 1880, "Agriculture."

9. "Report of the Immigration Agent-General," 1882 (table on "Average Earnings of Male Immigrants on Ten Estates for One Week in March 1882").

10. G.N.A., GD 102, 17 March 1887 (C.O. 111/438). This was also the position of Governor Wodehouse in 1854. See Hugh Tinker, *A New System of Slavery: The Export of Indian Labour Overseas, 1830-1920* (London, 1974), p. 183.

11. Report of the Immigration Agent-General, 1884.

12. G.N.A., GD 102, 17 March 1887 (C.O. 111/438).

13. G.N.A., GD 4, 2 January 1889 (C.O. 111/452).

14. C.O. 111/488, GD 353, 11 November 1896.

15. G.N.A., GD 281, 14 October 1886 (C.O. 111/436).

16. See, e.g., G.N.A., GD 133, 12 April 1887 (C.O. 111/438).

17. G.N.A., GD 98, 16 March 1888 (C.O. 111/444).

18. West Indian Royal Commission, 1897, evidence of Cavendish Boyle (government secretary).

19. Sandbach Parker Papers, G. R. Sandbach, 30 October 1886.

20. The *Argosy*, 18 April 1891.

21. Bascom of Cove & John in ibid., 3 June 1903. See also C.O. 111/537, GD 272, 14 July 1903.

22. The Sanderson Commission, *Parliamentary Papers*, 27 of 1910, evidence of Edward R. Davson.

23. Peter Ruhomon, *Centenary History of the East Indians in British Guiana, 1838-1938* (Georgetown, 1947), p. 118.

24. Blue Book, 1882, "Criminal Statistics."

25. D. W. Comins, *Note on Emigration from India to British Guiana* (Calcutta, 1893).

26. The Sanderson Commission, p. 13.

27. William des Voeux is the best-known example. Chief Justice Beaumont, dismissed in 1868, also falls into this category.

28. M.C.P., Petition 4954, October-November 1881.

29. M.C.P., letter of 8 November 1881.

30. Ordinance no. 4 of 1876 provided that employers could foward to the immigration agent a report of all absences from work. On verification, the indentures of the immigrants concerned were to be prolonged. Owing to the bother of completing the reports, employers did not take advantage of this section. It lapsed and was omitted from the immigration laws of 1891. Planters of the West India Committee demanded its reintroduction in 1895. See G.N.A., GD 5, 9 January 1895 (C.O. 111/476).

31. *The Overseer's Manual* (Georgetown, 1882).

32. Robert J. Moore, "East Indians and Negroes in British Guiana, 1838-1880" (Ph.D. diss., University of Sussex, 1970). He states (p. 142): "These gangs covered large distances in search of estates where the rate of wages had not been reduced or the task had not been lengthened. The chief characteristics of the task gang were its independence, its hard bargaining and its specialising in the most necessary and arduous work on the estates."

33. "Report of the Inspector of Villages," 1878.

34. M.C.P., November-December 1880.

35. Young, *Approaches to Local Self-Government*, table on p. 221.

36. H.V.P. Bronkhurst, *The Colony of British Guyana and its Labouring Population* (London, 1883), p. 95.

37. See, e.g., *Timehri*, n.s. 3 (1889): 190.

38. Ibid.

39. A. R. Gilzean, "Contracts with Cane Cutters," *Timehri*, n.s. 4 (1890).

40. *Royal Gazette*, 21 May 1889–article on La Grange estate refers to the Creole expression, "Rabah Rabah" or "bad wo'k." The *Colonist*, 30 October 1880, deals with the question of burning before cutting in its "Planters' column."

41. West India Royal Commission, 1897, evidence of Walter Alleyne Ireland.

42. See tables in Dwarka Nath, *Indians in British Guiana*; and G. W. Roberts and J. Byrne, "Summary Statistics on Indenture and Associated Migration Affecting the West Indies," *Population Studies* 20, no. 1 (1966).

43. By the time of the 1897 Commission, there was only one surviving muscovado estate in British Guiana.

44. "Report of the Inspector of Villages," 1882.

45. A. R. Gilzean, "Contracts with Cane Cutter."

46. In the largest and most efficient factories of the 1890s, estimates of eight to ten tons were given, but poor extraction and adverse weather could send this up to as many as twenty tons. See, e.g., West India Royal Commission, 1897, evidence of J. E. Tinne.

47. The *Argosy*, 22 October 1887.

48. Ibid., 13 November 1866.

49. G.N.A., GD 353, 11 November 1896 (C.O. 111/488).

50. "Report of the Immigration Agent-General," 1896.

51. Planter control over estate tenants in the post-Emancipation period is discussed in W. Carroll, *The End of Slavery: Imperial Policy and Colonial Reaction in British Guiana*, Ph.D. diss., University of Michigan, 1970 (Ann Arbor, Mich.: University Microfilms, 1970). The control of landlord over tenant was extended to indentured immigrants in a manner reminiscent of feudal "cottars" as well as the "tied cottagers" who survived into the early nineteenth century in England.

52. "Report of the Immigration Agent-General," 1874-75.

53. "Report of the Immigration Agent-General," 1875. For a denial of this charge, see G.N.A., GD 185, 29 July 1879.

54. D. W. Comins, *Note on the Abolition of Return Passages to East Indian Immigrants from the Colonies of Trinidad and British Guiana* (Georgetown, 1834), p. 5.

55. "Report of the Immigration Agent-General," 1879.

56. Comins, *Note on the Abolition of Return Passages*, p. 5.

57. West India Royal Commission, evidence of Joseph Monkhouse.

58. Comins, *Note on Emigration*; see section 19 of his Diary.

59. G.N.A., GD 206, 23 June 1898 (C.O. 111/504).

60. Excerpts were also published in the *International Sugar Journal*. See Walter Rodney, ed., *Guyanese Sugar Plantations in the Late Nineteenth Century* (Georgetown, 1979), introduction, pp. ix-xv.

61. The policy of selling half-acre lots of front lands is said to have started at Den Amstel (West Coast Demerara) in 1840. See Rawle Farley, "Aspects of the Economic History of British Guiana, 1781-1852" (Ph.D. diss., University of London, 1956).

62. Rodney, *Guyanese Sugar Plantations*, p. 81.

63. The *Argosy*, 26 May 1883. The Ewings were still holding this position many years later. See G.NA., GD 198, 17 June 1891 (C.O. 111/460).

64. G.N.A., GD 192, 30 June 1882 (C.O. 111/424). Some Trinidad planters also faced the same accusation—as indicated in the report of the Sanderson Commission.

65. C.O. 111/525, H. K. Davson to the Colonial Office, 13 March 1900.

66. See Michael Moohr, "Patterns of Change in an Export Economy: British Guiana, 1830-1914" (Ph.D. diss., Cambridge University, 1971).

67. West India Royal Commission, 1897, evidence of the Planters' Association and report of the Commission. It would also have been difficult to further increase the size of tasks which were already so fixed that they could not be completed in less than two days. (See Bisnauth, "East Indian Immigrant Society.")

68. Moohr, "Patterns of Change."

69. *Argosy*, 24 January, 31 January, and 7 February 1891.

70. L.M.S. Archives, Berbice, Box 11, Allen Thompson, 21 August 1879.

71. C.C. 111/510, Norman Lubbock citing letter of Duncan, 18 April 1898.

72. Ibid. See also West India Royal Commission, 1897, evidence of Joseph Monkhouse (manager of Pln. Providence); and C.O. 111/537, GD 272, 14 July 1903, enclosed copy of anti-Immigration petition.

73. Oral interviews with former sugar workers. This "stopping" of pay was one of the main grievances, as early as the Commission of 1871—for which, see Tinker, *New System of Slavery*, p. 187.

74. Even in England, the availability of cheap labor was one of the reasons why the advent of machinery was delayed to the latter part of the nineteenth century. See, e.g., Raphael Samuel, ed., *Village Life and Labour* (London, 1975), pp. 17, 18. The plantation clearly contributed to technological backwardness in British Guiana. See especially Jay R. Mandle, *The Plantation Economy: Population and Economic Change in Guyana, 1838-1960* (Philadelphia, 1973).

Chapter 3

1. This tendency was initiated by the first major scholarly work on the subject, that of Rawle Farley ("Aspects of the Economic History of British Guiana"). Farley himself was conscious of the imprecision but did nothing to clarify it. See, e.g., his note (on p. 229) to the effect that a peasant can be defined as a man who devotes the major part of his time to cultivating land on his own account and that the holders of plots of land in Guiana were more wage earners than peasants.

2. Allan Young, *The Approaches to Local Self-Government in British Guiana* (London, 1958), p. 16.

3. Conventionally, interpretations have stressed that Africans moved from estate employment as a matter of choice immediately after Emancipation. A more accurate presentation of the sequence is to be found in Robert Moore, "East Indians and Negroes in British Guiana, 1838-1880" (Ph.D. diss., University of Sussex, 1970). The scholarship on the period has tended to utilize official and planter sources and has failed to give attention to records of the L.M.S., which was close to the ex-slaves. Mrs. M. A. Henderson, missionary to Guiana from 1843, stated forthrightly that "the tyranny of the planters drove many of the people to the purchasing of land." See Thomas Henderson, *The Missionary's Wife: A Memoir of Mrs. M. A. Henderson of Demerara* (London, 1855), p. 55.

4. Young, *Approaches to Local Self-Government*, p. 23.

5. Alan Adamson, *Sugar Without Slaves* (New Haven: Yale University Press, 1972), p. 57.

6. "Report of the Inspector of Villages," 1881.

7. L.M.S. Archives, Demerara Box 10, Rev. Foreman, 3 January 1879; and Berbice Box 11, Rev. France, 2 March 1887.

8. Raymond Smith found it necessary to make a similar point in evaluating typical Afro-Guyanese villages in a more recent period. See, Raymond T. Smith, *The Negro Family in British Guiana* (London, 1956), p. 22.

9. The West India Royal Commission, 1897; evidence of Darnell Davis, Rev. F. C. Glasgow and Z. A. Lewis.

10. Richard Schomburgk, *Travels in British Guiana, 1840-1844*, ed. W. Roth (Georgetown, 1922), 1:66.

11. See especially, C. W. Wardlaw, *Banana Diseases, Including Plantains and Abaca* (London, 1972), pp. 146-75.

12. E. B. Martyn, "A Note on Plantain and Banana Disease in British Guiana, with Special Reference to Wilt," *Agricultural Journal of British Guiana*, no. 5 (1934).

13. The *Working Man*, 19 June 1872; Report of the Insepector of Villages, 1860; the *Colonist*, 27 January 1881; and H. V. Bronkhurst, *The Colony of British Guyana and Its Laboring Population* (London, 1883), p. 190.

14. See, e.g., the *Argosy*, 27 November 1880; Report of the Inspector of Villages, 1880; and Walter Rodney, ed., *Guyanese Sugar Plantations in the Late Nineteenth Century* (Georgetown, 1979), p. 31.

15. R. R. Stover, *Banana, Plantain and Abaca Diseases* (London, 1972), p. 189.

16. G.N.A., "Establishment of Coolie Settlement at Palmyra, Wakenaam, 1882-84," Chief Secretary 2144 (Miscellaneous Papers).

17. M.C.C., 28 May 1883.

18. M.C.P., Petition 940, 24 July 1880.

19. Report of the Inspector of Villages, 1879.

20. Ibid.; and M.C.P., 6 February 1880.

21. Richard W. Whitfield, *Hints on Villages, Villagers; on Drainage, Cultivation, Roads, Taxation* (Georgetown, 1873).

22. W. S. Turner, "The Condition of Our People," *West Indian Quarterly* (1885): 340.

23. Fenton H. Ramsahoye, *The Development of Land Law in British Guiana* (New York, 1966), pp. 240, 241.

24. G.N.A., GD 74, 23 May 1890 (C.O. 111/456). For earlier attempted solutions of the problem, see Ordinance no. 15 of 1880; GD 197, 3 September 1880 (C.O. 111/417); GD 55, 24 February 1883 (C.O. 111/427); and GD 176, 28 June 1883 (C.O. 111/428).

25. G.N.A., GD 74, 23 May 1890 (C.O. 111/456).

26. G.N.A., GD 94, 19 March 1898 (C.O. 111/502); and GD 400, 7 December 1898 (C.O. 111/506).

27. The *Echo*, 9 July 1887.

28. Ramsahoye, *Development of Land Law*, p. 241.

29. "Report of the Inspector of Villages," 1878.

30. "Report of the Inspector of Villages," 1889 and 1892-93.

31. "Report of the Inspector of Villages," 1885, 1889, and 1894-95.

32. C.O. 111/442, petition of Mocha residents forwarded by the British and Foreign Anti-Slavery Society, 4 November 1887.

33. L.M.S. Archives, Committee Minutes, West Indies, Box 3, Bk. 6, Enterprise villagers to the L.M.S., 18 July 1893.

34. "Report of the Director of Prisons," 1885.

35. G.N.A., GD 270, 29 December 1880 (C.O. 111/417).

36. Ibid.

37. G.N.A., GD 312, 27 September 1898 (C.O. 111/505).

38. Adamson, *Sugar Without Slaves*, p. 57.

39. Ramsahoye, *Development of Land Law*, pp. 132, 133.

40. Rodney, *Guyanese Sugar Plantations*, p. 59.

41. West India Royal Commission, 1897; evidence of F. C. Glasgow. (See Appendix C, pt. 2, British Guiana, section 164—Statement showing prices paid for village lands and present value and population.)

42. For details of leases and rents, see Court of Review: William Taylor vs. Matthew Cameron, April 1882.

43. Whitfield, *Hints on Villages*.

44. Ramsahoye, *Development of Land Law*, p. 69.

45. Court of Review, judgments of 1889.

46. West Indian Royal Commission, 1897; evidence of F. C. Glasgow.

47. M.C.C., 26 May 1887.

48. Robert Moore, "East Indians and Negroes in British Guiana, 1838-1880" (Ph.D. diss., University of Sussex, 1970), p. 160.

49. The *Creole*, 25 August 1882; the *Chronicle*, 5 January 1883.

50. G.N.A., GD 74, 18 March 1886 (C.O. 111/434); GD 245, 17 September 1886 (C.O. 111/436); GD 321, 9 December 1889; GD 200, 26 June 1893 (C.O. 111/468). See also Administration Report," 1903-4.

51. The *Argosy*, 2 March 1889.

52. Ibid., 28 June 1890.

53. During the latter part of the century, the rate from Plantation Enmore to Georgetown was $1.32 per ton, while from La Bonne Intention to Georgetown, the cost was $1.04 per ton. The sugar plantation companies considered these figures to be high, and the issue was debated at length until more recent times. See Enmore Estates, Minute Book, 20 June 1930, in Booker McConnell Papers (courtesy of the Guyana Sugar Corporation, Georgetown).

54. Blue Book, 1880.

55. U.S.P.G. Archives, Letters Received, Lichfield, 19 January 1897.

56. Thomas Henderson, *Missionary's Wife*, p. 55 (refers to the post-Emancipation huckster tax ordinance, requiring a license costing $10). When the ordinance was slightly amended in 1880, it drew renewed protests. See, e.g., M.C.P., 7 July 1880—petition 2675 by Creole laborers of Farm, West Coat Demerara, 28 June 1880.

57. M.C.C., 26 May 1887—petition by Joseph Phillips of Soesdyke, 30 April 1887. See also the petition and signatories, 16 May 1887.

58. The *Colonist*, 6 July 1881.

59. M.C.P., 5 May 1887.

60. Bernice E. Ellis, "The History of Queenstown Village," mimeographed (Georgetown, 1960).

61. Rodney, *Guyanese Sugar Plantations*, p. 31.

62. M.C.P. 11 November 1890; G.N.A., Immigration Box, no. 6414, Im Thurn to the Government Secretary, 23 September 1890; and West India Royal Commission, evidence of Z. A. Lewis.

63. Rodney, *Guyanese Sugar Plantations*, p. 49.

64. West India Royal Commission, Appendix C, pt. 1, document supplied by N. Lubbock.

65. L.M.S. Archives, Berbice, Box 10, report from Fyrish, 22 February 1868.

66. "Report of the Director of Lands," 1903-4.

67. The *Working Man*, 22 June 1872.

68. Reports of the Inspector of Villages, 1879, 1880, 1881.

69. Rodney, *Guyanese Sugar Plantations*.

70. M.C.P., 5 May 1887–Crown Surveyor's report on cultivated land in villages.

71. Blue Book, 1879, "Agriculture."

72. W. Russell, "Cane Mills and Megass as Fuel," *Timehri* 3 (1884). (The fibrous residue after crushing was then known as "megass." "Bagasse" is the term in current use.)

73. "Report of the Inspector of Villages," 1881.

74. The *Argosy*, 18 June 1881, 15 March 1884, and 29 March 1884.

75. The *Chronicle*, 13 January 1883.

76. See, e.g., M.C.P., 15 May 1880 and 27 November 1882; and the *Chronicle*, 12 January 1883 and 17 January 1883.

77. M.C.P., 4 April 1884; and Blue Book, 1884, "Report of the Public Works Department."

78. "Report of the Inspector of Villages," 1886.

79. The *Argosy*, 13 November 1880.

80. C.O. 111/531, G.D. 37, 5 February 1902–enclosed letter dated 31 January 1902.

81. The *Argosy*, 5 May 1888 and 25 April 1891; and the *Nugget*, 8 December 1883.

82. "Report on Agriculture," 1896-97; and "report of the Inspector of Villages," 1898-99.

83. The annual Blue Books presented data on acreages of plantains grown on estates. This category increased from 2,400 acres in 1881 to 5,200 acres in 1886. For public comment on plantain exports, see the *Royal Gazette*, 11 January 1887 and the *Chronicle*, 1 January 1902.

84. U.S.P.G. Archives, Letters Received, British Guiana–Bishop's report, 5 February 1896.

85. Most Africans in Guiana came from the "yam belt" of West Africa (extending from the Ivory Coast to eastern Nigeria). It is significant that the "Timinis" were cited as the rice growers of the early nineteenth century in Berbice, because the Temne (of Sierra Leone and Libera) were one of the principal ethnic groups in the "rice belt" of West Africa. See Walter Rodney, *A History of the Upper Guinea Coast* (London, 1970).

86. W. Russell, "Rice," *Timehri* 5 (1886).

87. A. R. Gilzean, "Rice Cultivation in British Guiana," *Timehri*, n.s. 1 (1887).

88. The *Colonist*, 14 April 1881.

89. Gilzean, "Rice Cultivation".

90. Lesley Potter, "The Paddy Proletariat and the Dependent Peasantry: East Indian Rice-growers in British Guiana, 1895-1902," Ninth Conference of Caribbean Historians, Barbados, 1977.

91. M.C.C., 18 May 1880. See also West Indian Association, Glasgow–Minute Bk. 5, Report of the Directors for 1881.

92. G.N.A., GD 238, 24 July 1882 (C.O. 111/424).

93. "Report of the Crown Surveyor," 1880; and GD 235, 4 November 1880.

94. The *Chronicle*, 12 January 1883.

95. See, e.g., C.O. 111/500, Confidential 24682, Henry K. Davson, 11 November 1897.

96. The *Colonist*, 14 April 1881.

97. Potter, "The Paddy Proletariat and the Dependent Peasantry."

98. See Michael Moohr, "Patterns of Change in an Export Economy" (Ph.D. diss., Cambridge University, 1971).

99. See, e.g., Reports of the Surgeon-General, 1880, 1881, and (especially) 1884.

100. "Report on General Mortality and Infant Mortality," M.C.C., Special Session 1906.

101. Moohr, "Patterns of Change in an Export Economy."

Chapter 4

1. West India Royal Commission, 1897, report of the Commissioners.
2. See, e.g., the *Working Man*, 17 April 1872; and the *Argosy*, 1 October 1887.
3. The *Argosy*, 9 March 1889; and "Report of the Comptroller of Customs," 1889.
4. Sandbach Parker Papers, G. R. Sandbach, 15 August 1889; and West India Royal Commission, 1897, evidence of Michael McTurk.
5. Report on the Balata Industry by C. B. Jenman, presented to the Combined Court in 1884. (Published in *Timehri* [1885].)
6. Blue Books, 1880-1905, "Exports."
7. Ibid.; and especially the Report of the Comptroller of Customs, 1880.
8. Ignatius Scoles, *Sketches of African and Indian Life in British Guiana* (Georgetown, 1885), p. 10. (The Rev. Father Scoles, S.J., was the designer of the Municipal Buildings, Georgetown. They were built mainly of pitch pine, with only a little greenheart and crabwood.)
9. U.S.P.G. Archives, Missionary Reports (MS), British Guiana–Cabacuri, 31 December 1872, and Skeldon, 31 March 1884.
10. Minutes of the Building Committee, St. George's Cathedral. (This reference was kindly supplied by Mr. William McDowell from work in progress on the history of Georgetown.)
11. G.N.A., GD 310, 12 August 1902 (C.O. 111/535).
12. The *Argosy*, 1 October 1887. The firm in question advertised as makers of furniture from "Colony woods," and secured the Philharmonic Hall as a display center. See the *Reflector*, 6 July 1889.
13. Report of the Government Land Department, 1894-95. For a reference to Smith Bros., see the *Nugget*, 17 November 1888.
14. Sandbach Parker Papers. This collection contains many references to Bugle. See espeically letters from Georgetown dated 23 May 1889, 28 March 1890, and 21 September 1904.
15. Blue Books, 1905-6, "Administration Reports."
16. See, e.g., the *Colonist*, 29 December 1880.
17. R. Tenant, *British Guiana and its Resources* (London, 1895), pp. 56-58.
18. West India Royal Commission, 1897, evidence of Michael McTurk.
19. C.O. 111/485, Confidential 606860 of 1896.
20. G.N.A., GD 356, 9 October 1901. Given the census data of 1911, the estimate appears on the high side. (See Table 17).
21. G.N.A., GD 33, 27 February 1880 (C.O. 111/416). For the early history of the gold industry, see also Evarard Im Thurn, "Notes on British Guiana," *Proceedings of the Royal Colonial Institute* 24 (1892).
22. The *Argosy*, 26 September 1891; and R. Perkins and J. Hosken, *Gold Fields on the Barima* (Georgetown: Government Printer, 1895).
23. Vincent Roth, *Pathfinding on the Mazaruni, 1922-24* (Georgetown, 1949), p. 7. For discussions of Bartica, see Report of the Department of Mines, 1896-97; and West India Royal Commission, evidence of S.E.R. Forbes.
24. G.N.A., GD 247, 10 June 1887 (C.O. 111/439).
25. West India Royal Commission, 1897, evidence of Monkhouse and Tinne. They suggest departures either in August-September or in January. Absence during Christmas was not popular for any category of workers in the bush. See, e.g., Sandbach Parker Papers, G. R. Sandbach, 7 November 1889.
26. The *Argosy*, 24 May and 28 June 1890.

27. G.N.A., GD 88, 28 March 1890; and *Timehri*, n.s. 4 (1890).

28. The *Argosy*, 31 September 1891.

29. Tenant, *British Guiana*, pp. 44-47.

30. West India Royal Commission, 1897, evidence of R. Perkins.

31. Administration Reports, 1903-6.

32. See, e.g., the *Chronicle*, 1 January 1902.

33. This was noticeable in random interviews with Afro-Guyanese whose working lives were in the 1930s and 1940s. The pattern had been established several decades earlier.

34. See, e.g., Jay Mandle, *The Plantation Economy* (Philadelphia, 1973).

35. G.N.A., GD 258, 27 November 1879.

36. C.Q. 111/550, Confidential no. 15246, 6 April 1906 (section on West Demerara); and GD 107, 23 April 1906. For an intervening year, see G.N.A., GD 147, 27 April 1895 (C.O. 111/477).

37. The *Colonist*, 4 June 1881.

38. M.M.S. Archives, Guiana, incoming letters, local preachers and class teachers of Trinity and Bedford, 4 April 1881.

39. See, e.g., E. P. Thompson, *The Making of the English Working Class* (London, 1968), pt. 2, sec. 8.

40. *The Koh-I-Noor Jubilee Gazette*, 22 June 1897, in C.O. 111/494.

41. Report of the Venn Sugar Commission, 1948.

42. The *Argosy*, 2 February 1889. (There was at the time a campaign to plant more flowers.)

43. Ibid., 4 December 1880.

44. These names occur in a number of sources, notably in petitions to the Court of Policy and to the Combined Court and in the contemporary newspapers. See also, H. V. Bronkhurst, *The Colony of British Guyana and Its Labouring Population* (London, 1883), p. 103.

45. Alan Adamson, *Sugar Without Slaves* (New Haven, 1972), pp. 83, 84.

46. Enquiries among living informants have produced only vague recollections of the name outside of the context of the empolder.

47. M.C.P., 23 November 1886, See also the *Echo*, 25 September 1889.

48. The *Argosy*, 8 June 1889, 17 January 1891, 19 December 1891.

49. Ibid., 20 July 1890.

50. Court of Review, 1897—Kryenhoff vs. Glasgow.

51. C.O. 111/550, Confidential no. 15246, 6 April 1906.

52. Brian Moore, "The Social Impact of Portuguese Immigration into British Guiana after Emancipation," *Boletin de Estudios Latino Americanos y del Caribe*, ser. 19 (december 1975).

53. The rise of the Portuguese community in British Guiana is well documented. Discrimination in favor of Portuguese businessmen has been alluded to by several writers, starting with James Rodway. The point is fully researched by Michael Wagner, "Structural Pluralism and the Portuguese in Nineteenth Century British Guiana" (Ph.D. diss., McGill University, 1975).

54. J. Rodway, *Stark's Guide Book and History of British Guiana, 1892* (Georgetown [1893?]), p. 34; and M.C.P., 15 March 1887, petition of Manoel Fernandes.

55. The *Argosy*, 19 November 1881, reporting Rev. Ketley's talks with villagers of Strick-en-heuvel, West Bank Demerara.

56. West India Royal Commission, 1897, evidence of Michael McTurk.

57. Lesley Potter, "Internal Migration and Resettlement of East Indians in Guyana, 1870-1920" (Ph.D. diss., McGill University, 1975).

58. Cecil Clementi, *The Chinese in British Guiana* (Georgetown, 1915).

59. G.N.A., GD 193, 15 August 1879.

60. Bronkhurst, *The Colony of British Guyana*, p. 208.

61. U.S.P.G. Archives, Missionary Reports (MS), 1883, report from Bladen Hall, East Coast Demerara.

62. G.N.A., GD 275, 1 August 1900.

63. Potter, "Internal Migration and Resettlement."

64. Reports of the Immigration Agent-General in the 1880s.

65. D. W. Comins, *Note on Emigration from India to British Guiana* (Calcutta, 1893), Diary, pp. 20-35.

66. Potter, "Internal Migration and Resettlement."

67. Dale A. Bisnauth, "The East Indian Immigrant Society in British Guiana, 1891-1930" (Ph.D. diss., University of the West Indies, 1977).

68. Hugh Tinker, *A New System of Slavery* (Oxford, 1974), p. 178.

69. Bronkhurst, *The Colony of British Guyana*, p. 320.

70. For a list of compounders on return ships, see Dwarka Nath, *A History of Indians in British Guiana* (London, 1950), table 10.

71. Bronkhurst, *The Colony of British Guyana*, p. 72.

72. H. V. Bronkhurst, *Among the Hindus and Creoles of British Guyana* (London, 1888), p. 199.

73. G.N.A., GD 173, 3 September 1881; and various to GD 270, 25 November 1881.

74. G.N.A., GD 229, 21 July 1882 (C.O. 111/419.

75. G.N.A., GD 76, 19 February 1887 (C.O. 111/438).

76. C.O. 111/478, No. 10260 and GD 253, 22 July 1895.

77. L.M.S. Archives, Berbice, Box 10—New Amsterdam, 22 February 1868, and Committee Minutes, West Indies, Box 3, Bk. 6, 26 July 1880.

78. L.M.S. Archives, Berbice, Box 10—Brunswick, 20 February 1868.

79. Paul B. Beatty, Jr., *A History of the Lutheran Church in Guyana* (Georgetown, 1970).

80. L.M.S. Archives, Demerara, Box 10, folder 4—Guiana District Council, 2 March 1881.

81. M.M.S. Archives, Campbell, 5 July 1881.

82. Ibid., Claxton, 23 February 1883.

83. Ibid., G. H. Jones, 24 March 1881.

84. W. W. Evans, *Biographical Portraits* (Georgetown, n.d.). The sketch of J. R. Moore first appeared in the *Echo*, 1 June 1905.

85. Ibid.; and N. E. Cameron, *150 Years of Education in British Guiana, 1808-1957* (Georgetown, 1968), p. 45. Thomas Trenton (1828-1907) received teacher training in England. He taught C. B. Carto, who acquired the then unusual qualification of B.Sc. and returned to become headmaster of "Mission School" from 1865 to 1890.

86. N. E. Cameron, *150 Years of Education*, pp. 23-40; and idem, *A History of Queen's College of British Guiana* (Georgetown, 1951).

87. M. Shahabudden, *Constitutional Development in Guyana, 1621-1978* (Georgetown 1979), p. 416.

88. *Annual Report of the Congregational Union* (Georgetown, 1895).

89. Henry Kirke, *Twenty-Five Years in British Guiana* (London, 1898), p. 37. For Lynch, see also Evans, *Biographical Portraits*.

90. The *Argosy*, 17 June 1882.

91. G.N.A., GD 127, 19 April 1898 (C.O. 111/503).

92. R. Tenant, *British Guiana*, pp. 82, 83. The two clubs were the (elite) Georgetown Club and the British Guiana Club.

93. G.N.A., GD 148, 1 June 1886.

94. M.C.P., 17 April 1888, petition of John M. Rohlehr, 17 February 1888.

95. M.M.S. Archives, group letter of 4 April 1881.

96. The *Echo*, 11 November 1887.

97. G.N.A., GD119, 2 April 1902 (C.O. 111/536).

98. The *Chronicle*, 28 July 1900.

Chapter 5

1. For presentation of this point, see Harold Lutchman, "Middle-Class Colonial Politics: A Study of Guyana with Special Reference to the Period 1920-31" (Ph.D. diss., University of Manchester, 1970). The details of the process are provided by M. Shahabuddeen, *Constitutional Development in Guyana, 1621-1978* (Georgetown, 1979).

2. Cecil Clementi, *A Constitutional History of British Guiana* (London, 1937), pp. 109, 122, 126, 257, 261.

3. R. H. Whitfield, *The Present and Future Prospects of British Guiana* (London, 1872)—as cited by Harold Lutchman, "Middle Class Colonial Politics" (Ph.D. diss., Manchester University, 1970).

4. West India Association, Glasgow, Minute Bk. 5, Report of Meeting of Sugar Bounties Committee, 1 April 1880.

5. See, e.g., Morley Ayearst, *The British West Indies: The Search for Self-Government* (London, 1960), pp. 108-10.

6. Shahabuddeen, *Constitutional Development in Guyana*, pp. 298, 299.

7. These names are listed in the Minutes of the Court of Policy and in the Blue Books.

8. Sandbach Parker Papers, W. H. Sherlock, 29 August 1889.

9. See, e.g., West India Royal Commission, 1897, evidence of J. E. Tinne.

10. F. V. McConnell, *The Birds of British Guiana* (London, 1916-21).

11. Sandbach Parker Papers, G. R. Sandbach, 24 June 1885.

12. Ibid., G. R. Sandbach, 16 October 1885.

13. Ibid., G. R. Sandbach, 14 March 1887.

14. Walter Rodney, *Guyanese Sugar Plantations in the Late Nineteenth Century* (Georgetown, 1979), pp. 18, 23. Much the same sentiments were expressed by Sheriff Henry Kirke. See his *Twenty-five Years in British Guiana* (London, 1898), p. 29.

15. P. McLewin, "Power and Economic Change: The Response to Emancipation in Jamaica and British Guiana" (Ph.D. diss., Cornell University, 1971).

16. Allan Young, *The Approaches to Local Self-Government in British Guiana*, (London, 1958), pp. 35-38 and Appendix 8.

17. N. E. Cameron, *The Evolution of the Negro*, 2 vols. (Georgetown 1929-34), 2:12.

18. Young, *Approaches to Local Self-Government*, pp. 57-59, 93-95.

19. L.M.S. Archives, Berbice, Box 10, letter from Rodborough, West Coast Berbice, 8 May 1867.

20. Alan Adamson, *Sugar without Slaves* (New Haven, 1972), p. 88.

21. G.N.A., GD 285, 3 October 1882 (C.O. 111/425).

22. Ibid.

23. G.N.A., GD 4, 4 January 1883 (C.O. 111/427).

24. G.N.A., GD 407, 22 October 1887.

25. G.N.A., GD 57, 9 February 1886 (C.O. 111/438).

26. See, e.g., Cameron, *Evolution of the Negro*, 2: 19; Adamson, *Sugar without Slaves*, pp. 90, 91; and (for a slightly different view) Shahabuddeen, *Constitutional Development in Guyana*, p. 383. Governor Henry Irving was also unpopular with the

Creoles of Trinidad, where he served prior to his tenure in Guiana. See J. J. Thomas, *Froudacity: West Indian Fables Explained*, new ed. (London, 1969).

27. Report of the Inspector of Villages, 1890.

28. The *Reflector*, 6 July 1889.

29. The *Echo*, 12 April 1890.

30. G.N.A., Government Secretary No. 2970, petition from Ann's Grove and Two Friends, April 1891.

31. The *Echo*, 6 October 1887.

32. Ibid., 10 March 1888 and 23 June 1888.

33. These events were covered in the *Liberal* and the *Reflector* between May and August 1891.

34. Young, *Approaches to Local Self-Government*, p. 111.

35. Cameron, *Evolution of the Negro*, 2: 20.

36. The *Echo*, 22 October 1890.

37. H. L. Palmer, *Village Economics and Polity: A Study of the Parochial Administration of British Guiana* (Georgetown, n.d. [ca. 1924]), pp. 5, 6.

38. Cameron, *Evolution of the Negro*, 2: 24; and L. Crookall, ed., *Manual of the Congregational Union of British Guiana for 1894* (New Amsterdam, 1894), p. 20.

39. Adamson, *Sugar without Slaves*, pp. 78, 79.

40. G.N.A., GD 407, 22 October 1887 (C.O. 111/440).

41. C.O. 111/44[?]. Confidential, 5 July 1888.

42. Clementi, *Constitutional History*, p. 311.

43. G.N.A., GD 125, 12 May 1886 (C.O. 111/438).

44. C.O. 111/455, Confidential, 3 January 1890.

45. C.O. 111/455, GD 4, 3 January 1890.

46. C.O. 111/453, Confidential, 13 September 1889.

47. Adamson, *Sugar without Slaves*, p. 152; and J. W. Harper-Smith, "The Political Development of British Guiana since 1891" (B.Litt. thesis, Oxford, University, 1964).

48. Sandbach Parker Papers, W. H. Sherlock, 15 August 1889.

49. C.O. 111/456, Confidential, 20 May 1890, and Confidential, 23 May 1890; and C.O. 111/457, Confidential, 5 November 1890.

50. The *Reflector*, 25 July 1891.

51. Clementi, *Constitutional History*, pp. 313, 314. For later developments, see Harold Lutchman, *The 1891 Constitutional Change and Representation in the Former British Guiana*, (Georgetown, n.d. [ca. 1973] – and M. Shahabuddeen, *Constitutional Development*, ch. 19.

52. W. W. Evans, *Biographical Portraits* (Georgetown, n.d. [ca. 1909]).

53. H. K. Davson, "British Guiana and its Development," *Proceedings of the Royal Colonial Institute* 29 (1908).

54. For a review of the early history of the Reform Club, see the *Liberal*, 4 July

55. Namely, the editors of the *Royal Gazette* and the *Echo*. They managed to secure support from English journalists, for which see C.O. 111/450, National Association of Journalists, 2 October 1889.

56. The *Echo*, 19 November 1887 and 3 December 1887.

57. Evans, *Biographical Portraits*.

58. For public comments on Drysdale, see the *Royal Gazette*, 21 April 1889, 20 June 1889; and the *Echo*, 2 July 1887 and 5 November 1887. His demise as a sugar planter is mentioned in Sandbach Parker Papers, G. R. Sandbach, 14 April 1887.

59. The *Royal Gazette*, 14 September 1889.

60. The clash between planters and the Portuguese was a relatively new development. See the *Royal Gazette*, correspondence of 29 March 1889.

61. *O Portuguez*, no. 482, 30 March 1889.

62. Ibid., no. 420, 14 January 1888; no. 453, 8 September 1888.

63. See, e.g., Edith Brown, *The Life Story of Andrew Benjamin Brown* (Georgetown, n.d.), p. 13.

64. The banana question was dealt with in M.C.P., 1889 and 1890. Public comments are found in the *Reflector*, 25 May 1889, 24 August 1889, and 30 November 1889; in the *Echo*, April-May 1890 and 4 July 1891; and in the *Nugget*, February-May 1889.

65. See Reform Petition published in the Royal Gazette, 31 March 1889. On 2 August 1889, a correspondent of the *Echo* referred explicitly to "that class which has grown up between capital and labour."

66. The *Reflector*, 17 August 1889.

67. The *Echo*, 11 January 1890.

68. L.M.S. Archives, Berbice, Box 11, report of 29 October 1889.

69. The *Echo*, 1 October 1890.

70. Ibid., 15 October 1890.

71. C.O. 111/456, Confidential, 20 May 1890 (figures supplied by Plns. Uitvlugt, Peter's Hall, Windsor Forest, Reliance, Bel Air).

72. The *Official Gazette*, 20 October 1890 and 29 January 1891.

73. The *Echo*, 26 October 1889.

74. Ibid., 14 July and 21 July 1888.

75. M.C.P., 27 August 1889, petition from New Amsterdam; and M.C.P., 17 July 1900, first reading of a bill "to enable Dr. John Monteith Rohlehr to be registered as a Medical Practitioner in this Colony."

76. The *Echo*, 15 June 1889.

Chapter 6

1. In the historiography on slavery, it has also been necessary to emphasize that it is pointless to divide slaves simply into docile and rebellious types. See, e.g., the perceptive study of John Blassingame, *The Slave Community* (New York, 1972).

2. Dwarka Nath, *A History of Guyana*, vol. 2 (London, 1975); see ch. 4.

3. Peter Ruhomon, *Centenary History of the East Indians in British Guiana, 1838-1938* (Georgetown, 1947), p. 118.

4. W. Alleyne Ireland, *Demerariana* (Georgetown, 1897).

5. Court of Review, 1882.

6. H. V. Bronkhurst, *The Colony of British Guyana and Its Laboring Population* (London, 1883), p. 152. This practice continued throughout the period under discussion. See, e.g., Chandra Jayawardena, *Conflict and Solidarity on a Guyanese Plantation* (London, 1963), p. 59 (citing evidence from 1924).

7. *Parliamentary Papers*, no. 49 of 1873.

8. G.N.A., GD 200, 7 September 1880.

9. M.C.P., 31 March 1882, returns forwarded for January-December 1881; and Blue Book, 1883.

10. D. W. Comins, *Note on Emigration from India to British Guiana* (Calcutta, 1893), p. 96.

11. W. A. Orrett, *The History of the British Guiana Police*, (Georgetown, 1951), pp. 27, 32. See also annual reports of the Immigration Agent-General.

12. West India Royal Commission, 1897, evidence of the Planters' Association.

13. J. G. Pearson. *New Overseer's Manual; Or, The Reason Why of Julius Juggler* (Georgetown, 1890), p. 57.

14. West India Royal Commission, 1897, evidence of Bechu.

15. G.N.A., GD 83, 19 March 1895 and GD 200, 10 June 1895 (C.O. 111/477). The stated occupations of the defendants included "driver" and "shopkeeper," attesting to the length of time they had been in Guiana.

16. West India Royal Commission, 1897, evidence and statement of Bechu.

17. C.O. 111/516, No. 14444, India Office to Whitehall, 7 June 1899.

18. *Parliamentary Papers*, no. 49 of 1873. See also Dale Bisnauth, "The East Indian Immigrant Society in British Guiana, 1891-1930" (Ph.D. diss., University of the West Indies, 1977).

19. W. Alleyne Ireland, *Demerariana* (Georgetown, 1897), p. 56; and G.N.A., GD 68, 14 March 1890.

20. E.g., in 1895, one of the convicted "ringleaders" at Pln. Success was described as high-caste. (See G.N.A., GD 200, 10 June 1895–C.O. 111/477).

21. See, e.g., G.N.A., GD 305, 9 September 1891, and GD 160, 11 May 1895 (C.O. 111/477).

22. G.N.A., GD 190, 20 May 1903 (C.O. 111/538).

23. *Overseer's Manual* (Georgetown, 1882)–section on "the duties of overseers"; and G.N.A., GD 4, 2 January 1889.

24. Immigrant transfers were sometimes queried by the Colonial Office. (See, e.g., G.N.A., GD 77, 14 March 1898.)

25. G.N.A., GD 353, 11 November 1896 (C.O. 111/488); GD 389, 8 December 1896 (C.O. 111/489).

26. G.N.A., GD 190, 20 May 1903 (C.O. 111/537); and GD 242, 24 June 1903.

27. G.N.A., GD 348, 25 August 1903 (C.O. 111/538).

28. The *Royal Gazette*, 21 May 1889 (reference to La Grange, West Bank Demerara).

29. *Overseer's Manual.*

30. Court of Review, 1880.

31. *Overseer's Manual.*

32. Ibid.

33. Pearson, *New Overseer's Manual*, p. 27.

34. The *Argosy*, 4 July 1903; and G.N.A., GD 272, 14 July 1903 (C.O. 111/537).

35. H. V. Bronkhurst, *Among the Hindus and Creoles of British Guyana* (London, 1888), p. 301.

36. N. E. Cameron, *The Evolution of the Negro*, 2 vols. (Georgetown, 1929-34), 2:18.

37. The *Echo*, 11 February 1888, 17 March 1888; and the *Royal Gazette*, 10 March 1889.

38. The *Echo*, 4 June 1890.

39. Ibid., 23 March 1889.

40. The chief justice did not advise commutation, and he was critical of the governor's decision.

41. The *Echo*, 6 August 1890.

42. Ibid., 27 August 1890.

43. Ibid., 23 August 1890.

44. The *Argosy*, 23 August 1890; the *Echo*, 27 August 1890.

45. The *Royal Gazette*, 20 September 1889.

46. The *Working Man*, 9 March 1872.

47. Cameron, *Evolution of the Negro*, 2: 51.

48. G.N.A., GD 284, 26 August 1895 (C.O. 111/479).

49. Cameron, *Evolution of the Negro*, 2: 24, 25.

50. W. W. Evans, *Biographical Portraits* (Georgetown, n.d. [ca. 1909]).

51. Allan Young, *The Approaches to Local Self-Government in British Guiana*

(London, 1958), pp. 121, 122; and A. M. Ashmore, *Memorandum on the Subject of Village Administration* (Georgetown, 1903). (See tables.)

52. Ashmore, *Village Administration*, p. 14.

53. H. L. Palmer, *Village Economics and Polity: A Study of the Parochial Administration of British Guiana* (Georgetown, n.d. [ca. 1924], p. 18.

54. The *Liberal*, 19 Janaury 1892.

55.Ibid., 8 October 1891.

56. Ibid., 16 February 1892.

57. G.N.A., GD 309, 13 October 1894 (C.O. 111/473).

58. The Colonial Office disapproved of the reimposition of customs duties on basic food imports; but the governor misread his instructions and acted to the contrary. The Colonial Office then accepted the fait accompli. See G.N.A., telegraphed dispatch, 5 September 1894, and GD 279, 15 September 1894 (C.O. 111/473–telegram numbered 15785). See also, Alan Adamson, *Sugar Without Slaves* (New Haven, Yale University Press, 1972), p. 251.

59. G.N.A., GD 103, 8 April 1891 (C.O. 111/459).

60. C.O. 111/477, Confidential 5917, 18 March 1895.

61. West India Royal Commission, 1897, evidence of James Thompson.

62. G.N.A., GD 198, 11 June 1896 (C.O. 111/486).

63. The *Chronicle*, 12 September 1900.

64. There was probably sound basis for this rumor. The governor found it necessary to write a confidential report on Shirley in November. See C.O. 111/522, Confidential 39787, 16 November 1900.

65. The *Chronicle*, 16 December 1900.

66. For the formation of the *People*, see the *Chronicle*, 24 March, 23 April, and 3 October 1901.

67. The *Chronicle*, 24 October 1901.

68. Ibid., 15 July and 27 August 1903.

69. The People's Association published a substantial manifesto in February 1906, a copy of which is in C.O. 111/553, enclosed with GD 400, 7 December 1906.

Chapter 7

1. M.C.P., November 1880, petition of A. S. Moore.

2. Ibid.

3. Ibid.

4. C.O. 111/537, GD 272, 14 July 1903.

5. Ibid.

6. C.O. 111/550, GD 107, 23 April 1906, petition of the People's Association.

7. C.O. 111/473, no. 19449, 3 November 1894.

8. C.O. 111/473, GD 318, 18 October 1894.

9. Sanderson Commission, evidence of Thomas Summerbell.

10. H. V. Bronkhurst, *Among the Hindus and Creoles of British Guyana* (London, 1888), p. 26.

11. C.O. 111/543, no. 10747, encloses copy of *Daily News*, 24 March 1904.

12. C.O. 111/571, Secret, 10 June 1910. See also Peter Ruhomon, *Centenary History of the East Indians in British Guiana, 1838-1938*, (Georgetown, 1947).

13. The *Chronicle*, 9 November 1900 and 29 December 1900.

14. Lesley Potter, "Internal Migration and Resettlement of East Indians in Guyana, 1870-1920" (Ph.D. diss., McGill University, 1975); and D. A. Bisnauth, "The East

Indian Immigrant Society in British Guiana, 1891-1930" (Ph.D. diss., University of the West Indies, 1977).

15. I. D. Sukdeo, "Racial Integration with Special Reference to Guyana" (Ph.D. diss., University of Sussex, 1969).

16. See, e.g., Cheddi Jagan, *The West on Trial: The Fight for Guyana's Freedom* (London, 1966; Berlin, 1971).

17. Cited by P. Skinner, "Group Dynamics in British Guiana," *Annals of the New York Academy of Sciences* 83 [19??].

18. For an important contribution to this discussion, see Bisnauth, "The East Indian Immigrant Society."

19. The *Argosy*, 28 March 1891.

20. H. V. Bronkhurst, *The Colony of British Guyana and Its Labouring Population* (London 1883), pp. 359-365; idem, *Among the Hindus and Creoles*, p. 26. See also D.W. Comins, *Note on Emigration from India to British Guiana* (Calcutta, 1893), p. 80; and the *Argosy*, 11 December 1880.

21. Cultural differences are assigned great weight by Philip Singer, "Hinduization and Creolization in Guyana," *Social and Economic Studies* 16, no. 3 (1967); Paul Singh, *Guyana: Socialism in a Plural Society* (Fabiam Society), London, 1972; and Malcolm Cross, *The East Indians of Guyana and Trinidad* (Minority Rights Group), London, 1972.

22. Robert Moore, "East Indians and Negroes in British Guiana 1838-1880" (Ph.D. diss., University of Sussex, 1970).

23. The *Working Man*, 8 June and 19 June 1872.

24. Bronkhurst, *The Colony of British Guyana*, p. 212.

25. Robert Moore, "East Indians and Negroes in British Guiana."

26. For a discussion of the Quashie stereotype, see Orlando Patterson, *The Sociology of Slavery* (London, 1967).

27. Bronkhurst, *Among the Hindus and Creoles*, p. 186.

28. Rollo Ahmed, *I Rise: The Life Story of a Negro* (London, 1937), p. 39. (This is the autobiography of one Caleb Buller, a Guianese.)

29. See Bisnauth, "The East Indian Immigrant Society."

30. The *Chronicle*, 18 January 1883.

31. M.C.C., 4 May 1886. (The petition was presented by a sympathetic financial representative, T. W. Phillips.)

32. Potter, "Internal Migration and Resettlement of East Indians in Guyana."

33. See M.C.P., 5 May 1887, correspondence from Murray to Russell.

34. Reports of the Inspector of Villages, 1893, 1894.

35. M.C.P., 1 November 1880, petition of Tooral Singh (Leguan), 30 September 1880; and G.N.A., Government Secretary no. 761, 5 February 1894.

36. Dwarka Nath, *A History of Indians in British Guiana* (London, 1950), p. 94.

37. C.O. 111/512, GD 68, 29 March 1899.

38. Lesley Potter, "East Indians and the Afro-Guyanese Village Settlement Patterns and Inter-group Relationships, 1871-1921," Fourth Conference of Caribbean Historians, Mona, Jamaica, 1972. (The element of racial antagonism in the Huis t'Dieren scheme is touched on here.)

39. The *Chronicle*, 10 July 1880.

40. M.C.P., March 1881, letters from Veeraswamy, January and February 1881.

41. M.C.P., March 1881.

42. G.N.A., Government Secretary No. 2144, Establishment of Coolie Settlement at Palmyra, Wakenaam, 1882-84.

43. Essex Record Office, D/DVv 74, Henry Bullock, 11 March 1900.

44. The *Echo*, 11 March 1890.

45. The *Colonist*, 20 July 1881.

46. Raphael Samuel, ed., *Village Life and Labour* (London, 1975), pp. 37. 38.

47. See Alan Adamson, *Sugar without Slaves* (New Haven, 1972), p. 82.

48. Bronkhurst, *Among the Hindus and Creoles*, p. 18.

49. The *Colonist*, 26 and 27 April 1881.

50. Blue Book, 1901.

51. J. Van Sertima, *Among the Common People of British Guiana* (Georgetown, 1897), p. 55.

52. Ibid.

53. Bronkhurst, *Among the Hindus and Creoles*, p. 210. See also M.M.S. Archives, incoming letters, Bronkhurst, 21 September 1887.

54. Oral informants frequently used this phrase. A missionary report of 1904 must also have been citing Creole informants when it stated that indentured immigration was "taking the bread out of their mouths." See U.S.P.G. Archives, Bishop's report, 23 February 1904.

55. I. D. Sukdeo, "Racial Integration with Special Reference to Guyana." See also Walter Rodney, "Barbadian Immigration into British Guiana," Ninth Conference of West Indian Historians, Cave Hill, Barbados, 1977.

56. C.H.G. Legge, "Mutual Benefit Associations–The Friendly Societies Ordinance (British Guiana) 1883," *West India Quarterly* 1 (1885).

57. See, e.g., *Parliamentary Papers*, 1848, Report on British Guiana and Mauritius.

58. For incidents of racial policing, see W. A. Orrett, *The History of the British Guiana Police* (Georgetown, 1951).

59. Brian Moore, "The Social Impact of Portuguese Immigration into British Guiana after Emancipation," *Boletin de Estudios Latino Americanos y del Caribe*, ser. 19 (December 1975).

60. Roy Glasgow, *Guyana: Race and Politics among Africans and East Indians* (The Hague, 1970), p. 75.

61. Bisnauth, "The East Indian Immigrant Society."

62. H.J.M. Hubbard, *Race and Guyana: The Anatomy of a Colonial Enterprise* (Georgetown, 1969), p. 27.

Chapter 8

1. See, e.g., Frank Cundall, *Political and Social Disturbances in the West Indies: A Brief Account and Bibliography* (Kingston, 1906).

2. The *Chronicle*, 30 November 1905. The *Chronicle* gave comprehensive coverage to these events and subsequently published a compilation entitled *The Riots of 1905: Details of the Outbreak, Its Causes and the Measures Taken for Its Suppression; Inquest on the Victims and Punishment of the Rioters* (Georgetown, 1906). (To be cited subsequently as *The Riots of 1905*.)

3. For the Proclamation, see M.C.P., 28 December 1905.

4. The *Chronicle*, 2 December 1905.

5. C.O. 111/547, GD 364, 28 December 1905. This dispatch, along with all other telegrams and letters on the Riots, was presented to Parliament as *Correspondence Relating to Disturbances in British Guiana*. This document is available in the G.N.A. and in the P.R.O., C.O. 884, vol. 9, West Indies no. 151 (1906).

6. M.C.C., Special Session 1906, "Report on General Mortality and Infant Mortality."

7. Henry Kirke, *Twenty-five Years in British Guiana* (London, 1898), p. 308.

8. The *Chronicle*, 21 January 1902.

9. Ibid., 30 November 1905.

10. *The Riots of 1905*, p. 6.

11. Ashton Chase, *A History of Trade Unionism in Guyana, 1900-1961* (Georgetown, 1964), p. 27.

12. *Correspondence Relating to Disturbances*, p. 14.

13. The *Chronicle*, 5 December 1905.

14. Ibid., 6 December 1905.

15. *The Riots of 1905*.

16. James Rodway, *Guiana: British, Dutch and French* (London, 1912), pp. 158, 159.

17. When Sandbach Parker employed an experienced Chinese clerk in their George-town store in 1902, they paid him $600 per annum. See Sandbach Parker Papers, letter of 23 June 1902.

18. The *Chronicle*, 6 December 1905.

19. The *Official Gazette*, 29 January 1906.

20. C.O. 111/546, Confidential, no. 35307, 18 September 1905.

21. The *Chronicle*, 16 and 19 August 1904.

22. M.C.P., 28 December 1905.

23. The *Argosy*, 23 August 1890.

24. Kirke, *Twenty-five Years*, pp. 48, 261.

25. The *Chronicle*, 24 October 1903.

26. C.O. 111/547, no. 45392, 23 December 1905.

27. *The Riots of 1905*; the *Chronicle*, 5 December 1905.

28. Kirke, *Twenty-five Years*, p. 48.

29. Leon Trotsky, *The History of the Russian Revolution*, 3 vols. (New York, 1936), 1: 140-45.

30. C. V. Alert, *Life and Work of Hubert Nathaniel Critchlow* (Georgetown, 1949), p. 9.

31. The *Chronicle*, 5 December 1905.

32. Ibid. and C.O. 111/547, no. 43766, 10 December 1905.

33. *Ibid.*

34. C.O. 111/551, GD 162, 1 June 1906; and *Correspondence Relating to Distur-bances* (Secretary of State to the Governor, 8 February 1906).

35. *Correspondence Relating to Disturbances* (Captain of the *Diamond*, 20 December 1905).

36. C.O. 111/549, no. 2822, Confidential, 9 January 1906.

37. See, e.g., the *Chronicle*, 9, 10, and 16 July 1905.

38. The flow of correspondence was somewhat confused partly because Elgin took over duties from Lyttelton as colonial secretary early in January 1906 and partly be-cause there was a crisscrossing of telegraphic correspondence and regular mail. The issue of the West Bank estates can be followed in *Correspondence Relating to Disturbances*.

39. C.O. 111/549, No. 4067, Confidential, 16 January 1906.

40. C.O. 111/549, No. 2822, Confidential, 9 January 1906.

41. The *Chronicle*, 6 December 1905.

42. R. S. Rattray, *Ashanti* (London, 1923).

43. See, e.g., the *Chronicle*, 1 November 1900, 20 September 1901.

44. Ibid., 2 December 1905.

45. G.N.A., GD 103, 8 April 1891 (C.O. 111/549).

46. C.O. 111/550, GD 107, 23 April 1906 (Colonial Office Minute of 7 June 1906).

47. C.O. 111/550, 21 April 1906. (Encloses copy of the *Creole*, vol. 1, no. 15, 7 April 1906).

48. C.O. 111/551, Confidential, 26 July 1906.
49. C.O. 111/552, Confidential, 12 October 1906.

Conclusion

1. Gordon K. Lewis, *Puerto Rico: Freedom and Power in the Caribbean* (New York, 1963), pp. 23, 40.

2. Jay Mandle's application of the underdevelopment thesis to Guyana is open to criticism on the score of exaggerating the stagnation. See his *The Plantation Economy* (Philadelphia, 1973).

3. Similar patterns of class formation have been discerned in other Caribbean societies. See especially Richard Frucht, "A Caribbean Social Type: Neither 'Peasant' nor 'Proletarian,'" *Social and Economic Studies* 13, no. 3 (1967). (Reprinted in Michael Horowitz, ed., *Peoples and Cultures of the Caribbean* [New York, 1971].)

4. See, e.g., Raymond Smith, *The Negro Family in British Guiana* (London, 1956).

5. One gets the impression of suspended time when comparing reports concerning the social and legal conditions of immigrants between 1871 and 1920.

6. Ashton Chase, *A History of Trade Unionism in Guyana, 1900-1961* (Georgetown, 1964). See also W. Arthur Lewis, *Labour in the West Indies* (London, 1939); and Zin Henry, *Labour Relations and Industrial Conflict in Commonwealth Caribbean Countries* (Port of Spain, 1972).

7. Inattention to the late nineteenth century is strikingly illustrated in a popular history, that of Vere T. Daly, *A Short History of the Guyanese People* (Georgetown, 1966).

8. Cecil Clementi, *A Constitutional History of British Guiana* (London, 1937), p. 542 (Appendix Q).

9. M. Shahabuddeen, *Constitutional Development in Guyana, 1621-1978* (Georgetown, 1979), p. 379.

10. It was partly as a consequence of this change that justifications became more overtly racist, as in the case of H. K. Davson, cited in chapter 6. The climate of imperialist expansion in Africa also seemed to revive the racist ideology which had its origins in slavery.

11. E. J. Hobsbaum, *The Age of Capital, 1848-1875* (London, 1975), pp. 98, 99.

12. Colonial Office rationalizations in 1928 are partly exposed by J. W. Harper-Smith, "The Colonial Stock Acts and the British Guiana Constitution of 1891," *Social and Economic Studies* 14, no. 3 (1965).

BIBLIOGRAPHY

Guyana National Archives and Public Record Office

The two principal archives consulted were the Guyana National Archives (Georgetown) and the Public Record Office (London). The two complement each other to some extent, and it is useful to consider the holdings of the Guyana National Archives (G.N.A.) in relation to the well-known Public Record Office (P.R.O.). The G.N.A. has conserved bound volumes of copies of all "Governor's Despatches," that is to say, handwritten or typed duplicates of the official communications forwarded by each governor to the respective secretary of state for the colonies. The majority (but not all) of these Governor's Despatches are to be found in the Colonial Office series (C.O. 111/. . .) of the Public Record Office, where they were, of course, received as incoming correspondence.

The C.O. 111/. . . files have distinct advantages over the extant documentation of the G.N.A. Firstly, the *enclosures* to the Governor's Despatches are available, in contrast to the Guyana holdings where the Despatches sometimes amount to no more than covering letters which allude to enclosures which were not copied. Secondly, the C.O. 111/. . . series includes the minuted comments of Colonial Office functionaries and the final draft instructions sanctioned in the name of the secretary of state for the colonies. Thirdly, the C.O. 111/. . . series preserves "confidential" and "secret" correspondence as well as correspondence originating in the United Kingdom and directed to the Colonial Office.

The P.R.O. has been extensively and intensively utilized by researches into Guyanese history. This applies, for example, to the recent work of Alan H. Adamson and to several doctoral dissertations that are unpublished. The same cannot be said for the G.N.A. The work of M.N. Menezes deals with the otherwise neglected Amerindian history, and it is also unusual in so far as it draws upon the G.N.A. Research for the present study began in the G.N.A., and the P.R.O. was consulted to fill the many gaps that were revealed. The reference procedure adopted is intended to facilitate the researcher who has access to *either or both* of the two repositories. In this respect, the most important item of identification is the number of the Governor's Despatch, which appears in the Despatches of the G.N.A. as well as in the P.R.O. When the Colonial Office received "confidential" or "secret" letters from governors, this correspondence was given a different set of numbers. The authors of letters are identified in the reference notes only when they wrote independently of the governor. The procedure has dispensed with the naming of governors and respective colonial secretaries, since the principal justification of that notation lies in the identification of the relevant officials as part of a

265

discussion of their respective policies. The latter aspect lies outside the concerns of the present study.

The following examples of citations will clarify how location is indicated for the two repositories:

1. G.N.A., GD 4, 3 January 1890 (C.O. 111/455). This enables the researcher in Guyana to locate the document in the volume containing Governor's Despatches for 1890. At the P.R.O., it would be equally straightforward to pinpoint GD 4 (and enclosures) within volume 455 of the C.O. 111/... series. The volume in question covers the period January-March 1890, and the letter would usually be cited as "Gormanston to Knutford, no. 4, 3 January 1890."

2. C.O. 111/553, GD 400, 7 December 1906. This form of citation means that the relevant material is found in the enclosures or the Colonial Office minutes, and that the outgoing Despatch held in the G.N.A. is of no assistance whatever. Where there is no reference to the G.N.A., it may also mean that a) the governor's communication was 'secret' or "confidential," or b) the correspondence originated in the United Kingdom. See, e.g., C.O. 111/460, no. 16439, Confidential, 29 July 1891; and C.O. 111/ 426, no. 1252, West India Association of Liverpool, 20 January 1882.

3. G.N.A., GD 258, 25 August 1884. Here (conversely) the omission of a reference to the P.R.O. indicates that the material was not encountered there.

The G.N.A. also contains a number of miscellaneous papers. These are sometimes "boxed," and are referred to as such: for example, "G.N.A. Drainage and Irrigation Box." Most of the unbound papers are not yet regularized to permit location, citation, and subsequent access. However, the series of bound volumes do allow for scholarly reference. These include Blue Books, Official Gazettes and copies of each decennial census. The bound official documents of the G.N.A. are usually more complete than those preserved in the P.R.O., notably in the case of Minutes of the Court of Policy and Minutes of the Combined Court, early copies of which are held in the G.N.A. series. In the early 1880s, several reports of government departments were preserved in the Minutes of the Court of Policy or the Minutes of the Combined Court after having been presented to the legislature. The reports of the Inspector of Villages and the Immigration Agent-General are particularly useful. Unfortunately, some bound administration reports have deteriorated considerably.

Other Archives (U.K.)

Most of the archives in the United Kingdom which contain material on Guyanese history are listed in Peter Walne, *A Guide to Manuscript Sources for the History of Latin America and the Caribbean in the British Isles*

(London, 1973). The minor repositories named therein have generally been underutilized by scholars researching in Britain. This applies in particular to the church and missionary archives, which have constituted one of the mainstays of historical reconstruction in other colonial contexts. The three church archives which yielded material were those of:

a. the London Missionary Society (now housed as part of the Archives of the Council for World Mission at the School of Oriental and African Studies);
b. the Methodist Missionary Society (consulted at the London headquarters of the society but slated to be transferred to the School of Oriental and African Studies);
c. the (United) Society for the Propagation of the Gospel (housed by this Anglican Society in London).

Outside of the Colonial Office and the churches, further documentation on British Guiana was mainly generated by business contacts. The direct link through metropolitan plantation owners is illustrated by the Minute Books of the West India Association, Glasgow. These are held at the Mitchell Library, Glasgow (and not at the Glasgow City Archives, as indicated by Peter Walne, *A Guide to Manuscript Sources for the History of Latin America and the Caribbean in the British Isles* [London, 1973], p. 381). The Liverpool connection was not easily documented. The Liverpool Record Office has a large collection of "Parker Papers," which make occasional reference to British Guiana but do not demonstrate the close and unbroken connection between Guiana and Liverpool in the period. Sandbach Parker & Company were registered as a Demerara company. Their principals were Sandbach Tinne & ·Company of Liverpool, owning plantations as well as ships, which contracted to carry Indian immigrants to Guiana. Sandbach Parker & Company served as "town agents" for the Sandbach estates as well as for other plantations, and the firm entered into regular business correspondence with Sandbach Tinne of Liverpool. This commercial correspondence was presumed to have been destroyed. However, with the assistance of Dr. Colin Clarke of the University of Liverpool, the author tracked a significan⁺ body of this material to the basement of a firm of accountants in London. I have referred to this material as "The Sandbach Parker Papers." The letters all originate in Guiana and were usually signed by the head of the local firm. The citation of author and date should be sufficient to identify the documents when they are permanently housed—probably at the Library of the University of Guyana.

Occasionally, the U.K. archives contain material generated by the personal contact of Britishers with life in Guiana. This is true of the papers of David Chalmers at the Library of the University of Edinburgh and those of Henry Bullock at the Essex Record Office, Chelmsford. The two individuals were, respectively, Chief Justice of British Guiana (1879-94) and overseer-manager on Berbice plantations (1861-93). Their papers were of marginal value but Chalmers's were accompanied by rare copies of the first printed judgments of the Court of Review.

Newspapers

Newspapers constitute a secondary source in so far as they reported official events such as proceedings of the Court of Policy or carried statistics which originated in Blue Book compilations. However, newspapers were also a primary source for certain data. The "facts" adduced by newspapers are of course subject to verification like any other set of reputed "facts," but the opinions expressed are useful in their own right. The newspapers of British Guiana were consulted principally at the G.N.A. The *Argosy* and the *Chronicle* are also available at the British Newspaper Library (Colindale), while copies of the *Royal Gazette* are preserved in the P.R.O. But the smaller newspapers, which were very close to the working people and the middle class, are to be found only in the G.N.A.: notably the *Echo*, the *Reflector*, the *Colonist*, the *People*, the *Nugget*, the *Working Man*, *O Portuguez*, and the *Liberal*. The condition of these publications in the G.N.A. leaves much to be desired, and their perusal was complicated by the problem of fragility and deterioration.

Printed Primary Sources

Historical underdevelopment is also reflected in the material base for historical reconstruction. Printed series of official documents are not available, except for the Annual Blue Books, the Administration Reports, and the *Official Gazette*, copies of which were compiled into semiannual editions. From the metropolitan end, the well-known *Parliamentary Papers* were accessible, the most relevant being the "Report of the West India Royal Commission," 1898 (P.O. No. 50, 1898).

Secondary Sources

Because of a poorly developed historiography, even those books which could serve as secondary sources are still relatively inaccessible. Yet a larger number of authors observed and recorded contemporary events than might initially be expected. In the absence of local publishing houses, the newspapers occasionally fulfilled this function, although most monographs on British Guiana in the nineteenth century were understandably published in England. The contemporary works that are decisive for an understanding of the period (and that have been referred to frequently in this study) are listed below as part of the general bibliography of monographs and articles, attention being drawn to their importance by way of an asterisk.

It is also to be noted that the journal *Timehri* constituted a cultural feature of special significance. With the exception of short breaks due to financial crisis, this journal was in operation for the greater part of the period under discussion, providing an intellectual outlet for planters, officials, and professionals with a literary and scientific bent. A great deal of valuable historical materials is preserved in the pages of *Timehri*.

Oral Sources

Finally, mention must be made of the attempt to tap oral sources. Dozens of workers and retired workers were interviewed at random in the coastal area between 1975 and 1977. As expected, no structure exists for the retention and handing down of experiences through oral means. Rather, one is faced with an impressionistic recollection of events at both first and second hand. At no point in this study has oral information been used as the factual basis for interpretations. Its function was corroborative, and it also provided general orientation with respect to the attitudes of workers. Even more than the popular newspapers, the oral information assisted the author in arriving at a position of empathy with the working people. In precisely the same situation, Moreno Fraginals used the memorable words, "I had a personal interview with the past."*

Books and Articles

Adamson, Alan H. *Sugar without Slaves: The Political Economy of British Guiana, 1838-1904*. New Haven: Yale University Press, 1972.

Ahmed, Rollo. *I Rise: The Life Story of a Negro*. London, 1937.

Alert, C. V. *Life and Work of Hubert Nathaniel Critchlow*. Georgetown, 1949.

Ashmore, A. M. *Memorandum on the subject of Village Administration . . . from 1838-1902*. Georgetown, 1903.

Ashworth, William. *A Short History of the International Economy since 1850*. London, 1964.

Augier, F. R.; Gordon, S. C.; Hall, D. G.; and Rickford, M. *The Making of the West Indies*. London, 1960.

Augier, F. R., and Gordon, C., eds. *Sources of West Indian History*. London, 1962.

Beachey, R. W. *The British West Indian Sugar Industry in the Late Nineteenth Century*. Oxford, 1957.

Beatty, Paul B., jr. *A History of the Lutheran Church in Guyana*. Georgetown, 1970.

Beckford, George L. *Persistent Poverty: Underdevelopment in Plantation Economies of the Third World*. Oxford, 1972.

Bennett, George W. *A History of British Guiana*. Georgetown, 1875.

Best Lloyd. "Outlines of a model of pure Plantation Economy." *Social and Economic Studies* 17, no. 3 (1968).

*Manuel Moreno Fraginals, *The Sugar Mill: The Socio-Economic Complex of Sugar in Cuba* (New York, 1976).

Bisnauth, Dale Arlington. "*The East Indian Immigrant Society in British Guiana, 1891-1930.*" Ph.D. dissertation, University of the West Indies, 1977.

Bookers Sugar. London, 1954. (Supplement to the Accounts of Booker Brothers, Mc Connell and Co., Limited, 1954)

*Bronkhurst, H.V.P. *The Colony of British Guyana and Its Labouring Population.* London, 1883.

*_____. *Among the Hindus and Creoles of British Guyana.* London, 1888.

*_____. *A Descriptive and Historical Geography of British Guyana and the West India Islands.* London, 1886.

Brown, Edith. *The Life Story of Andrew Benjamin Brown.* Georgetown, n.d. (ca. 1924).

Burnett, John. *A History of the Cost of Living.* London, 1969.

Cameron, Norman Eustace. *The Evolution of the Negro.* 2 vols. Georgetown, 1929-34.

_____. *A History of the Queen's College of British Guiana.* Georgetown, 1951.

_____. *150 Years of Education in British Guiana, 1808-1957.* Georgetown, 1968.

_____, ed. *Guianese Poetry: Covering the Hundred Years' Period 1831-1931.* Georgetown, 1931 (Kraus reprint, 1970).

Carroll, W. "*The End of Slavery: Imperial Policy and Colonial Reaction in British Guiana.*" Ph.D. dissertation, University of Michigan, 1970. Ann Arbor, Mich.: University Microfilms, 197

Carter, Martin. *Poems of Resistance.* London, 1954; *Poems of Succession.* London, 1977.

Chase, Ashton. *A History of Trade Unionism in Guyana, 1900-1961.* Georgetown, 1964.

Clementi, Cecil. *The Chinese in British Guiana.* Georgetown, 1915.

_____. *A Constitutional History of British Guiana.* London, 1937.

Combined Court Sketches. Georgetown, 1883 (reprinted from the *Demerara Daily Chronicle*).

*Comins, D.W.D. *Note on Emigration from India to British Guiana.* Calcutta, 1893.

_____. *Note on the Abolition of Return Passages to East Indian Immigrants from the Colonies of Trinidad and British Guiana.* Georgetown, 1894.

Crookall, L. *British Guiana; or, Work and Wandering among the Creoles and Coolies, the Africans and Indians of the Wild Country.* London, 1898.

_____, ed. *Manual of the Congregational Union of British Guiana for 1894.* New Amsterdam, 1894.

Cross, Malcolm. *The East Indians of Guyana and Trinidad.* London: Minority Rights Group, 1972.

Cruickshank, J. G. *Pages from the History of the Scottish Kirk in British Guiana.* Georgetown, 1930.

Cundall, Frank. *Political and Social Disturbances in the West Indies: A Brief Account and Bibliography.* Kingston, 1906.

Dalton, Henry G. *History of British Guiana*. 2 vols. London & Georgetown, 1855.

Daly, P. H. *Story of the Heroes*. Georgetown, 1949.

Daly, Vere T. *A Short History of the Guyanese People*. Georgetown, 1966. (Revised ed., London, 1975.)

Davson, H. K. "British Guiana and its Development." *Proceedings of the Royal Colonial Institute* 29 (1908).

Deerr, Noel. *The History of Sugar*. 2 vols. London, 1949-50.

Depres, Leo A. *Cultural Pluralism and National Politics in British Guiana*. Chicago, 1967.

Des Voeux, G. W. *Experiences of a Demerara Magistrate, 1863-69*. Edited by Vincent Roth. (Vol. 1 of *My Colonial Service*.) Georgetown, 1948.

_____. *My Colonial Service*. 2 vols. London, 1903.

*Evans, W. W. *Biographical Portraits*. Georgetown, n.d. (ca. 1909).

Fairrie, Geoffrey. *The Sugar Refining Families of Great Britain*. London: Tate & Lyle, 1951.

Farley, R.E.G. "Aspects of the Economic History of British Guiana, 1781-1852: A Study of Economic and Social Change on the Southern Caribbean Frontier." Ph.D. dissertation, University of London, 1956.

_____. "The Rise of the Peasantry in British Guiana." *Social and Economic Studies* 2, no. 1 (1954).

_____. "The Rise of Village Settlements in British Guiana." *Caribbean Quarterly* 2, no. 1 (1964).

Farrar, Thomas. *Notes on the History of the Church in Guiana*. Georgetown, 1892.

Frucht, Richard. "A Caribbean Social Type: Neither 'Peasant' nor 'Proletarian.'" *Social and Economic Studies* 13, no. 3 (1967).

Gilzean, A. R. "Contracts with Cane Cutters." *Timehri*, new series 4 (1890).

_____. "Rice Cultivation in British Guiana." *Timehri*, new series 1 (1887).

Harper-Smith, Jones W. "The Colonial Stock Acts and the British Guiana Constitution of 1891." *Social and Economic Studies* 14, no. 3 (1965).

Henderson, Thomas. *The Missionary's Wife: A Memoir of Mrs. M. A. Henderson of Demerara by Her Husband*. London, 1855.

Henry, Zin. *Labour Relations and Industrial Conflict in Commonwealth Caribbean Countries*. Port of Spain, 1972.

Hogg, Ethel M. *Quintin Hogg: A Biography*. London, 1904.

Horowitz, Michael M., ed. *Peoples and Cultures of the Caribbean*. New York, 1971.

Im Thurn, Everard. "Notes on British Guiana." *Proceedings of the Royal Colonial Institute* 24 (1892).

International Sugar Journal, The 1 (1899)-8 (1906).

*Ireland, W. Alleyne [Langton]. *Demerariana*. Georgetown, 1897.

Jayawardena, Chandra. *Conflict and Solidarity on a Guyanese Plantation*. London, 1963.

Jenkins, Edward. *The Coolie: His Rights and Wrongs*. London, 1871.

*Kirke, Henry. *Twenty-Five Years in British Guiana*. London, 1898.

Laurence, K. O. *Immigration into the West Indies in the 19th Century.* Kingston, 1971.

_____. "The Establishment of the Portuguese Community in British Guiana." *Jamaican Historical Review* 5 (1965).

Lewis, Gordon K. *The Growth of the Modern West Indies.* New York, 1968.

Lewis, W. A. *Labour in the West Indies.* London, 1939.

_____. *The Evolution of the Peasantry in the British West Indies.* London, 1936.

_____. *Aspects of Tropical Trade, 1883-1965.* Stockholm, 1969.

Lobdell, Richard. "Patterns of Investment and Sources of Credit in the British West Indian Sugar Industry, 1838-97." *Journal of Caribbean History*, no. 4 (1972).

Lutchman, Harold. "Middle Class Colonial Politics: A study of Guyana with Special Reference to the Period 1920-31." Ph.D. dissertation, Manchester University, 1970.

_____. *The 1891 Constitutional Change and Representation in the Former British Guiana.* Georgetown, n.d. (ca. 1973).

McLewin, P. *Power and Economic Change: The Response to Emancipation in Jamaica and British Guiana.* Ph.D. dissertation, Cornell University, 1971. Ann Arbor, Mich.: University Microfilms, 1977.

MacMillan, Allister. *The Red Book of the West Indies.* London, 1909.

_____. *The West Indies, Past and Present, with British Guiana and Bermuda.* London, n.d. (Revision and extension of the above *Red Book.*)

Mandle, Jay R. *The Plantation Economy: Population and Economic Change in Guyana, 1838-1960.* Philadelphia, 1973.

Marshall, W. "Notes on Peasant Development in the West Indies since 1938." *Social and Economic Studies* 17, no. 3 (1967).

Menezes, Mary Noel. *British Policy Towards the Amerindians in British Guiana.* Oxford, 1977.

Milliroux, Felix. *Demerara: The Transition from Slavery to Liberty.* Translated. London, 1877.

Moohr, Michael. "Patterns of Change in an Export Economy: British Guiana, 1830-1914." Ph.D. dissertation, Cambridge University, 1971.

Moore, Brian L. "The Social Impact of Portuguese Immigration into British Guiana after Emancipation." *Boletin de Estudios Latino Americanos y del Caribe,* ser. 19 (December 1975).

Moore, Robert James. "East Indians and Negroes in British Guiana, 1838-1880." Ph.D. dissertation, University of Sussex, 1970.

Morris, D. "Planting Enterprise in the West Indies." *Proceedings of the Royal Colonial Institute* 14 (1882-83).

Nath, Dwarka. *A History of Indians in British Guiana.* London, 1950.

Netscher, P. M. *History of the Colonies Essequebo, Demerary and Berbice.* Translated. The Hague, 1888.

Newman, Peter. *British Guiana: Problems of Cohesion in an Immigrant Society.* London, 1964.

Orrett, W. A. *The History of the British Guiana Police.* Georgetown, 1951.

*Overseer's Manual, The. Edited by E. C. Luard and F. C. Thorne. George-
town, 1882.

Owen, Roger, and Sutcliffe, Bob, eds. Studies in the Theory of Imperialism.
London, 1972.

Palmer, H. L. Village Economics and Polity: A study of the Parochial Administration of British Guiana. Georgetown, n.d. (ca. 1924).

Pascoe, C. F. Two Hundred Years of the S.P.G. Vol. 1. London, 1901.

Pearson, J. G. New Overseer's Manual; or, The Reason Why of Julius Juggler.
Georgetown, 1890.

Perkins, R., and Hosken, J. Gold Fields on the Barima. Georgetown: Government Printer, 1895.

Potter, Lesley M. "East Indians and Afro-Guyanese Village Settlement
Patterns and Inter-group Relationships, 1871-1921." Fourth Conference
of Caribbean Historians, Mona, Jamaica, 1972. Mimeographed.

_____. "Internal Migration and Resettlement of East Indians in Guyana,
1870-1920." Ph.D. dissertation, McGill University, 1975.

Premium, Barton. Eight Years in British Guiana: Being the Journal of a
Resident in the Province of British Guiana from 1840-1848. London,
1850.

Ramsahoye, Fenton H. The Development of Land Law in British Guiana.
New York, 1966.

Rauf, Mohammad A. Indian Village in Guyana. Leiden, 1974.

Roberts, G. W. "Some Observations on the Population of British Guiana."
Population Studies 2, no. 1 (1948).

_____, and Byrne, J. "Summary Statistics on Indenture and Associated
Migration Affecting the West Indies." Population Studies 20, no. 1 (1966).

*Rodney, Walter, ed. Guyanese Sugar Plantations in the Late Nineteenth
Century: A Contemporary Description from the "Argosy." Georgetown,
1979.

Rodway, James. History of British Guiana from the year 1668. 3 vols. Georgetown, 1891-94.

_____. The Story of Georgetown. Georgetown, 1920.

_____. Guiana: British, Dutch and French. London, 1912.

_____. Stark's Guide Book and History of British Guiana, 1892. George-
town [1893?].

Roth, Vincent. Pathfinding on the Mazaruni, 1922-1924. Georgetown, 1949.

Ruhomon, Peter. Centenary History of the East Indians in British Guiana,
1838-1938. Georgetown, 1947.

Russell, William. "Cane Mills and Megass as Fuel." Timehri 3 (1884).

_____. "Rice." Timehri 5 (1886).

Samuel, Raphael, ed. Village Life and Labour. London, 1975.

Saul, Samuel B. Studies in British Overseas Trade, 1870-1914. Liverpool,
1960.

Schomburgk, Richard, Richard Schomburgk's Travels in British Guiana,
1840-1844. Edited by W. Roth. Georgetown, 1922-23.

Scoles, Ignatius, *Sketches of African and Indian Life in British Guiana.* Georgetown, 1885.

Shahabuddeen, M. *Constitutional Development in Guyana, 1621-1978.* Georgetown, 1979.

Singer, Philip. "Hinduization and Creolization in Guyana." *Social and Economic Studies* 16, no. 3 (1967).

Skinner, P. "Group Dynamics in British Guiana." *Annals of the New York Academy of Sciences* 83 (   ).

Smith, M. G. *The Plural Society in the British West Indies.* Los Angeles, 1965.

Smith, Raymond T. *The Negro Family in British Guiana.* London, 1956.

_____. "Social Characteristics of Indian Immigrants to British Guiana." *Population Studies* 4, no. 1 (1948).

_____. *British Guiana.* London, 1962.

Stoby, E. S. *British Guiana Centenary Year Book, 1831-1931.* Georgetown, 1931.

Sukdeo, Iris Devika. "Racial Integration, with Special Reference to Guyana." Ph.D. dissertation, University of Sussex, 1969.

Tenant, R. *British Guiana and its Resources.* London, 1895.

Thomas, Clive Y. *Plantations, Peasants and State: A Study of the Modes of Sugar Production in Guyana.* Georgetown: University of Guyana; Geneva, International Labour Office, 1978.

Tinker, Hugh. *A New System of Slavery: The Export of Indian Labour Overseas, 1830-1920.* Oxford, 1974.

Van Sertima, J. *Among the Common People of British Guiana.* Georgetown, 1897.

_____. *Scenes and Sketches.* Georgetown, 1899.

_____. *The Creole Tongue.* New Amsterdam, 1905.

Wagner, Michael J. "Structural Pluralism and the Portuguese in Nineteenth Century British Guiana: A Study in Historical Geography." Ph.D. dissertation, McGill University, 1975.

Walne, Peter. *A Guide to Manuscript Sources for the History of Latin America and the Caribbean in the British Isles.* London, 1973.

Watson, J. A. *A Hundred Years of Sugar Refining: The story of Love Lane Refinery, 1872-1972.* Liverpool: Tate & Lyle, 1973.

Webber, A.R.F. *Centenary History and Handbook of British Guiana.* Georgetown, 1931.

Whitfield, Richard W. *Hints on Villages, Villagers; on Drainage, Cultivation, Roads, Taxation.* Georgetown, 1873 (reprinted from the *Creole* newspaper).

Wight, Martin. *The Development of the Legislative Council, 1606-1945.* London, 1946.

Young, Allan. *The Approaches to Local Self-Government in British Guiana.* London, 1958.

INDEX

___

Abrahams, E. A., 203

Adamson, Alan, 70

Affiance plantation, indentured immigrants on, 55

African Creoles: as farmers, 77, 80; frustrations of, 180; giving up plantains, 83; the law and, 150-61; outmigration of, 74; as peasants, 70; response of, to parate, 68

African immigrants, 33

African Methodist Episcopal Church, 106

Africans: building canals, 3-4; common grounds with Indians, 179; conflicts with Indians, 184-85; as Dutch slaves, 2; in gold and balata, 102; in goldfields, 98; leaving plantations, 57-58; moving away from estates, 53; opposing Indians, 174-75; as peasants, 60-62; on plantations, 57; rice growing by, 84; in riots, 212; stereotypes of, 180

African villagers, 44-45

Agricultural Improvement Societies, 167

Albion plantation, labor force of, 55

Allan, R., 146, 147

Allick, John, 105

Amalgamation of sugar estates, 25

Ameo, Abel, 81

American Civil War, impact of, 78

Amerindians, 1; excluded from balata industry, 96-97; location of settlements of, 2

Anglican Church, native pastors of, 115

Anna Catherina village, 55

Annandale plantation, new canal for, 4

Anna Regina plantation: and composition of labor force, 54; growing rice at, 84, 85; on labor shortage, 100; wage rates at, 49; women vendors at, 77

Ann's Grove village: growing canes, 79, 80-81; petitioning legislature on blocking of drainage channels, 132; support of Irving by, 131

Aqueduct, 81

Argosy: on Canals Polder Scheme, 74; on composition of plantation labor force, 54-55; on drought of 1884, 5; on labor shortage, 1891, 100; on peasants, 83;

on small estates, 127; support of planters by, 140; on village contracts, 50

Arnold and sugar industry, 25-26

Artisans: decline of, 104; wages of, 103

Aurora plantation, 100

Bagotville village, 55; growing canes, 79; taxes of, 66

Balata, output of, 92

Banana industry, 144, 149

Barbadians, as canecutters, 58

Barbados: Creoles from, develop solidarity with Guianese, 187; indentured laborers from, 48-50

Barbour-James, J. A., on Bishop's College, 116

Barr, Alexander, contests election, 168

Bascom, C. L.: on cane farming, 81; and Court of Policy, 124; on Quintin Hogg, 127

Bath plantation: employment at, 75; hiring Africans, 57

Bechu: on conditions of immigrants, 155, 156; on indentureship, 177-78; before West India Commission, 159

Beckles, George, 209

Beet sugar: bounties, 20-23; subsidies, 197; surcharge on, 28-29

Bel Air plantation: abandonment of, 5; amalgamation of, 25; immigrants on, 35

Berbice Cotton Grower's Association, 78

Betervernagting village: cane production by, 79-80; support of Irving by, 131

Better Hope plantation: amalgamation of, 25; immigrants on, 56; laborers on, 55

Bishop's College, 116

Blairmont plantation, hiring of Africans by, 57

Blankenburg plantation, 55

Board of Trade, on sugar bounties, 22

Boerasirie, plantain supplies at, 77

Boerasirie Conservancy, 15, 74

Booker Brothers: on beet sugar bounty, 20; exports by, 96; on prices and production, 29; shipping, 198, 199; survival of, 26

275

This book was set in IBM Selectric Press Roman text and display by Culpeper Publishers from a design by Alan Carter. It was printed on 50-lb. Eggshell Offset Cream and bound by the Maple Press Company.